Passionate Marriage

Also by David Schnarch

Constructing the Sexual Crucible:
An Integration of Sexual and Marital Therapy

Passionate Marriage

*Love, Sex, and Intimacy in Emotionally
Committed Relationships*

David Schnarch, Ph.D.

W. W. Norton & Company

New York London

All personal vignettes and stories from workshops and presentations are true. Full length case vignettes are composites from actual cases. Vignette of the Couples Retreat in Chapter 14 is a composite from several retreats (identifying information has been altered); the composite scene accurately represents common occurrence.

Passionate Marriage™, Passionate Couples™, Sexual Crucible™, Crucible™, Sexual Crucible Approach™, and Crucible Approach™ are trademarks owned by David Schnarch. Website http://www.passionatemarriage.com

Composition by ComCom.
Manufacturing by Haddon Craftsmen, Inc.

Library of Congress Cataloging-in-Publication Data
Schnarch, David Morris, 1946-
    Passionate marriage: love, sex, and intimacy in emotionally
committed relationships / David Schnarch.
        p.   cm.
    Includes index.
    ISBN 0-393-04021-6
    1. Sex in marriage.   2. Sex therapy.   3. Marital psychotherapy.   I. Title.
RC557.S312   1997
616.89'156—dc21   96-40893   CIP

W. W. Norton & Company, Inc.
500 Fifth Avenue, New York, N.Y. 10110
www.wwnorton.com

W. W. Norton & Company Ltd.
Castle House, 75/76 Wells Street, London W1T 3QT

0 9 8 7 6 5 4 3 2

To my wife,

RUTH MOREHOUSE
who has helped me learn more about love and marriage
than I ever hoped I'd know

In memory of

ESTELLE SCHNARCH
My beloved grandmother

THEODORE URBAN
My friend for twenty-seven years

Acknowledgments

A book about emotionally committed relationships is a testimony to the enormity of people sharing their lives. In the final analysis, this is all we have to offer each other. That "all," however, has been a bounty in my own life. If there is any richness and depth to this book, it is the accumulated wealth of experience with many wonderful human beings. The people who populate my life are treasures, and having lost a few to illness and aging I now cherish and appreciate them all the more.

I am indebted to the courageous couples who let me witness their struggles: my psychotherapy clients and participants at the Couples Retreats. The same is true of people at my workshops and lectures who shared personal anecdotes and created memorable events. Through them I've been granted the opportunity to see beyond the limits of my own experience. Without that, I'd never have recognized the intricacies and wonder of marriage as a system for personal growth. In sharing their lives they have honored and enriched me and often moved me to tears. Their struggles and triumphs document the heroism in everyday acts of differentiation and fuel my spirituality. I hope telling their stories with reverence and respect will honor them.

William Masters and Virginia Johnson have made an indelible and unmatched contribution to sexual science and health care. I am particularly grateful to Dr. Masters for how he has touched my life with his

7

work, his graciousness, and his integrity. Murray Bowen has also indelibly marked my life through his magnificent development of differentiation theory. We never met before he died in 1990, but I wish we had. In different ways, these people's lives paved the way for what you will read here. It is easy to see new horizons when you stand on the shoulders of giants.

I have been blessed with good friends who are outstanding professionals in their own right. Their friendship and encouragement over the years have sustained me; I've relied on their expertise and suggestions in writing this book: Joshua and Peggy Golden gave comments and suggestions on an early draft. Marty Klein introduced me to author/teacher Hal Bennet, who showed me how to write a book proposal and sharpen my writing style. Sally Maison and Walker Meade reviewed semi-final drafts of the manuscript and helped keep the tone on track; Bernie Zilbergeld offered important suggestions that substantively improved it.

Since graduate school, Barry Lester has been a close friend, colleague, jokester, and provocateur. Barry showed me the link between new ways of seeing adult relationships and new ways of understanding infants and human development. He, like James Maddock and Noel Larson, reviewed the manuscript and provided invaluable comments and suggestions. Jim and Noel shared generously of their sharp dialectical thinking. Yvonne Dolan and Charlie Johnson offered ideas, encouragement, and their home: they were instrumental in our move to Colorado. Of people I treasure, these are some of the gems.

This is the second book I've done with Susan Munro, my editor at Norton. I am indebted to her and Margaret Ryan, who also did editing on the current project. This final version has improved markedly from their input; their commentaries have expunged any remaining fragility I might have had as a writer. Thanks to Christi Albouy for retyping the manuscript. I am also grateful to my agent, Owen Laster, Vice President of William Morris Agency, who handled negotiations for this book.

I have saved my greatest appreciations for those closest and dearest to me. I could easily say that without my mother and father, Rose and Stan Schnarch, this book would not be possible. But I mean this in more than the obvious way. Far beyond giving me life, their goodness and kindness have shown me what is meaningful in life. Their love for each other, and for me and my brother, Steve, has both inspired and fueled my own growth. I am grateful they have let me tell you about them later in this book.

My wife, Ruth, and my daughter, Sarah, have given up a lot so this book could come to fruition. They put up with my nose glued to a computer screen, my brain buried in reams of paper, and my free time shot to hell. They have been patient, understanding, and cooperative beyond measure. Writing this book in the midst of relocating our family to Evergreen has been an enormous challenge. Ruth took over much of the household responsibilities, and Sarah tolerated the frustration of having me home (writing) but unavailable. With pride and gratitude I'll introduce you to them in this book. Without Ruth and Sarah, my life would be a pale shadow of what it is now. Of all those who have touched me, their fingerprints are the most evident on my heart.

Contents

Introduction

I do not hold that practical truths can be made plain in the market place.

—Denis DeRougemont
LOVE IN THE WESTERN WORLD

Let me welcome you by sharing a personal vignette:

When I was a young graduate student at Michigan State University, I chose a charismatic professor to be chairman of my research thesis for my master's degree. Unfortunately for me, the results at best failed to confirm—and possibly negated—my mentor's clinical approach. Fortunately, the statistics expert on my thesis committee was Jack Hunter, a gifted mathematician, who taught me a lot more than the meaning of numbers.

My professor pressured me to write my thesis as if the results were equivocal; Jack showed me how the data suggested otherwise. After I spent a year writing my thesis from both viewpoints, my mentor decreed this second analysis would be reduced to a footnote (literally). Shocked and frightened, I appealed to the other faculty members on my thesis committee. They told me to "work it out" with my mentor. One said privately, "Look Dave, we have to live with him a lot longer than we have to live with you. Give him what he wants."

That person was not Jack Hunter. Jack said to me, "Dave, once you sign your name to that thesis, it's on there forever. You can always do another master's thesis. Do what you think you should do."

"I'd be throwing away years of work!"

"Then do what you think you should do."

There were times I was angry at Jack—and at myself—because he encouraged me to do what I thought was right. But now I count this among the truly great things in my life (that I don't want to do again). My next two years were devoted to an entirely new thesis (with a new chairman). In the acknowledgments section of my master's thesis lies an unknowing statement of differentiation:

> I have learned something about quality research, and also that the emotional prices involved in making "expedient" and "pragmatic" concessions often far exceed the effort needed to stand behind my own convictions. There are considerable emotional costs in receiving one master's degree for the price of two master's theses, and I have been fortunate to have friends who were willing to bear with me while I was paying them.

I tell you this story for several reasons: for one, it illustrates *differentiation,* a cornerstone of a passionate marriage—and of this book. By differentiation, I'm referring to standing up for what you believe. Calming yourself down, not letting your anxiety run away with you, and not getting overreactive. Not caving in to pressure to conform from a "partner" who has tremendous emotional significance in your life (in this case, my professor/chairman). Great abilities to have when you're married.

This is how I learned about differentiation in graduate school. Not as theory in a classroom, but as a life-shaping incident that helped bring me to the point I can write what you're reading. (I encountered differentiation as a concept in my professional work a decade later.) At the time, I had no idea what good preparation I was receiving for marriage, and for developing what you'll learn in this book.

The second reason I've shared my experience is because *your* differentiation is important in two ways: you'll probably have to differentiate from much of what you've learned—and society still believes—about how to achieve hot sex and deep intimacy, if you're interested in having either. It doesn't involve "communication" or giving in to your partner—it involves "holding onto yourself." That's the second way your differentiation is important: you'll probably have to increase your differentiation if you want to explore your sexual potential with your spouse.

In my evolution as a therapist and teacher (and a husband), I've had to increase my own differentiation. I found anomalies in contemporary sexual and marital therapy—and common views of sex and intimacy—

that rocked me to my core. Sex therapy had almost no consideration for marriage as a system, and nothing to do with passion and eroticism—wet sex. (For example, ask yourself: what lies *beyond* orgasm? This book answers that question.) Likewise, most marital therapies didn't work when applied to sex. This didn't bother lots of therapists because sex therapy and marital therapy were—and still are—primarily separate disciplines. But these shortcomings directly affect how you approach sex. And they affect everyone in society.

Once I recognized all this, it was like I was back with Jack Hunter; my differentiation was again tested. Could I leave the "tried and true" methods of contemporary martial therapy and sex therapy? The end result of my five-year crucible was publication of *Constructing the Sexual Crucible: An Integration of Sexual and Marital Therapy*. Many ideas you'll encounter here are fully documented there through research reviews, detailed discussions, and extensive references. In it I wrote: "Psychotherapy is an aberration of the last hundred years. Sexual-marital therapy, in particular, is like the first bud off an immature fruit tree: a fruit in name, but unsweet and perhaps better eaten gingerly in lieu of the second crop. It is also inherently a product of its own time: its 'solutions' reflect our own view of problems and their solutions, rather than some profound knowledge of the nature of marriage per se."

Constructing the Sexual Crucible is difficult reading but many plowed through it and survived. Although primarily intended for therapists, "civilians" from around the world started writing to describe its personal impact on them. They encouraged me to write a new book, one more practical and accessible for the general public. Therapists also asked for a book they could use with their clients. *Passionate Marriage* is the result. Much of the material included here does not appear in my previous book.

The first five chapters of *Passionate Marriage* build a new framework that gives your existing sexual relationship new meaning, utility, and options. The next five give explicit details of ways to improve sex and intimacy. The last four chapters cover how sex and intimacy really operate in marriage (like a complex system). In each section you will find material the likes of which you have not encountered before.

Romantic love is a relatively new development of which we know little, especially within marriage. In *Love in the Western World*, Denis DeRougemont notes that Western culture has no history of *happy* romantic love within marriage; the notion of romantic love didn't even exist until the twelfth century. Our literature holds stories of spouses finding love *outside* of marriage, but even then it is tragic. DeRougemont says we view passionate love as an irresistible impulse that sears and annihilates us in its triumph. We approach romance like a privileged form of suffering that makes us feel more alive—living dangerously, magnificently, and tragically.

We know relatively little about joyous sex and lasting intimacy within long-term marriage. For longer than not, marriages were arranged for social, economic, and political reasons. Yet, at no time in history have people expected as much gratification and fulfillment from their relationship. The high divorce rate reflects our exalted expectations—and our inability to meet them. While modern society implies all personal problems (intimacy, sex, and otherwise) can be solved by applying an existing psychological technology, that expertise hasn't materialized. And in our ignorance, we've developed approaches that actually interfere with what we think we seek.

More people are living longer and remaining physically and mentally fit, but what's the point when you're living in a "dead" relationship? Who's interested in passionate marriage? Couples hoping to avoid the endless string of disposable marriages. Partners who want to do more than coexistence. AIDS makes hot monogamy increasingly attractive. More couples are hoping (against hope) that sexual sparks will last "till death do us part"—and that they needn't flirt with AIDS to get it.

Maybe you're someone who knows about eroticism but you're married to someone who's clueless. Maybe you're starting out on your sexual career and want to know the difference. Maybe you're asking yourself, "Is this all there is to my love (sex) life?" Take heart: marriage is more elegant than we dare believe. It can bring you bliss, but it's harder than many people recognize.

Going forward will cost you. Progress and personal growth always do. It may cost cherished beliefs you thought could protect you or show you a way out. It will cost you the "self" you've been to become who you want to be. You may already be facing similar choices—not because your marriage is flawed, but because it's part of marriage's natural processes.

I intend this book to be personal. Writing this has been a profoundly intimate experience—I hope it's also one to read it. You'll be looking into the heart of my personal reality, and my life's work. I've tried to be respectful the same way I am with my clients: I've said things as straight and honestly as I can. What you're about to read is important to me. I hope it will be the same to you.

My goal is to touch you, to move you to "hold onto yourself" and embrace your partner. I hope that you will be patient with yourself—because we grow exceedingly slowly—and not waste another moment moving forward with your life.

I intend to appeal to your heart *and* your head, so you can shape your life by channeling your emotions *and* judgment (rather than burying one or the other). Both are important in your differentiation. Growing the "feminine" *and* "masculine" in all of us is part of differentiation, and part of what's so badly needed in our psychology and our society.

Let me also clarify a few possible misinterpretations.

Although this book focuses on marriage, it applies to unmarried couples. I use the term "marriage" as shorthand for any emotionally committed relationship. I'm not referring to marriage as a legal entity for three reasons: (a) many legally married couples have yet to get married emotionally; (b) marriage is not a one-time commitment—I talk of people becoming *more* married; and (c) there are many places around the world where gays and lesbians are not permitted to legally sanction their relationship.

What's written here also works for people who are single. (I use the same approach when seeing clients individually.) While differentiation always occurs in relationship, it doesn't need to be a "committed" one; my master's thesis story illustrates this perfectly. Singles go through the differentiation process like anyone else; they do it with their parents, friends, lovers, and coworkers. Married people just have an "advantage": things heat up when you feel the "knot" is tied and the door is sealed.

I've given up trying to avoid the inherent sexism in our language. Sometimes I refer to a partner as "she" or "he" without mentioning the opposite gender (although it applies). My intent is to slight no one, nor to give any suggestion by omission. My main focus is to make complex ideas easier to comprehend.

Instead of assuming that my suggestions are "one size fits all," please realize that different couples will experience varying benefits from this book. *Passionate Marriage*'s backbone theory (*differentiation*) says that well-differentiated adults don't need much prodding to change in needed ways. The less differentiated you are, the more likely (and severely) your marriage will bog down and require a crisis—or a therapist—to blast through emotional log-jams. This is neither a shortcoming of this approach nor an apology. It's just the way it is.

Lots of people have taken *Passionate Marriage*'s ideas and suggestions to heart and harnessed the "people-growing processes" of their marriage. These processes are inherent to marriage and don't need a therapist to start (or stop) them. It's remarkable what determined people can do on their own; it's also remarkable how much a good therapist can help. Whether you are "going it alone" or seeking assistance, your experiences with *Passionate Marriage* should serve you well.

If you're like me, you're suspicious of "experts" who promise intimacy and eros in ten easy steps. It's bound to be hokum—if it's so easy, why aren't more people doing it? The point is, the process of marriage isn't easy and neither is what follows. If you're like my clients, however, you don't need it easy; you just need it to work.

The issue of "trust" is one huge boondoggle in marriage, and in marital and sex therapy, too. That's why I take a different stance: there's no reason to believe in an approach until *after* it works. If it doesn't, there's no reason to believe in it at all. If it works, then believe it but recognize it's not your belief that makes it work. It's the other way around. I don't ask you to take what I'm saying on blind faith. Trust your own experience.

So, contrary to books that encourage you to look upon the author as your trusted guide, don't trust me. You have no reason to, and it's not helpful to your differentiation. Trusting me isn't going to change you; trusting (and mobilizing) yourself will. The endpoint of differentiation is being willing and able to trust *yourself.* If *Passionate Marriage* makes sense to you, use your own judgment about what you do with it.

I believe what's relevant is what works for *you,* not what works for other people. Our lives are the only meaningful measure, and you can use this book as a yardstick: as you read, draw a line beside passages that speak to you. (I use two lines for things that really speak to me.) Reread this book at some point in the future and repeat the process. If the lines haven't moved, you're either onto a deep truth or you're not growing.

If you try this, I don't recommend sharing your book with your spouse. Books become highly personal. I suggest everyone gets his or her own book (that's the differentiated way). If you're going to learn to hold your own hand, you might as well have your own book too.

By the way, don't bother underlining passages for your spouse to read, or leaving this book open where he or she is likely to find it. If you're not ready to speak for yourself, then you're probably not ready to hold onto yourself through the ensuing discussion.

It's impossible to grasp this book—or the reality of marriage—solely through your intellect. Like marriage, you only know it by experiencing it. This book won't make you an expert on sex and intimacy; that job remains for marriage. As you'll read in Chapter 1, marriage is an exquisite teacher. This book helps decipher the lessons. I hope you'll become engrossed in *Passionate Marriage* and in your own reactions. I also hope you'll approach this with an open heart, honesty, and charity.

I have been truly blessed. After my two greatest blessings, my wife, Ruth, and my daughter, Sarah, I count being the person who writes this book. That I finish writing it today, on my fiftieth birthday, seems to be part of my bounty. Today the aspens are golden, the mountains are white-capped from last night's snow, the sun is dazzling, and the deep blue sky is laced with clouds. As you read on, you'll appreciate this is more than just a weather report. This is the best birthday of my life.

David Schnarch
September 18, 1996
Evergreen, Colorado

When love beckons to you, follow him
Though his ways are hard and steep.
And when his wings enfold you yield to him,
Though the sword hidden among his pinions may wound you.
And when he speaks to you believe in him,
Though his voice may shatter your dreams as the north wind
    lays waste the garden.
For even as love crowns you so shall he crucify you. Even as he
    is for your growth so he is for your pruning.
Even as he ascends to your height and caresses your tenderest
    branches that quiver in the sun,
So shall he descend to your roots and shake them in their
    clinging to the earth.

From *The Prophet* by Kahil Gibran

The Basics

Chapter 1

Nobody's Ready for Marriage—Marriage Makes You Ready for Marriage

Marry and with luck
it may go well.
But when a marriage fails
those who marry live at home in hell.

—Euripides, 408 B.C.

"We came here because we had a sexual problem, but you've helped us recognize it's something much larger." Karen and her husband are leaving my office after our final session. Her smile and gratitude make clear her intent. She speaks like a person who has stumbled upon new possibilities, not like someone who has learned she is more damaged than she thought.

Karen and her husband have flown in to see me for three-hour therapy sessions on three consecutive days. We've come a long way from where Ken, age fifty-seven, opened our initial meeting with his characteristic wit. "Our relationship is good and we want to make it better. Karen asked for time to work on our sexual difficulties, and I gave her twenty-four years! That's my contribution to our lack of sexual progress."

Karen, age fifty-three, showed the courage that would surface in our subsequent encounters. "Initiation became my responsibility. Five years into our relationship I was unhappy sexually—so unhappy that I researched the leaders in sex therapy at the time, and Ken and I went to one of them. We did sensate focus exercises . . . and it totally glossed over my problem. My therapist thought we were a model couple in treatment—we always look better than we feel." Ken nods from the sidelines, giving Karen center stage.

"Sex is routine when we have it," Ken adds. "I know I should be more aggressive, but I'm not and for that I feel guilty towards Karen. My motivation for sex used to be more physiological. I've lost some of my sex drive in recent years."

"My lack of sexual desire has always been a problem, too." Karen sounds like she wants everything out in the open once and for all. "I never want sex until we're actually doing it. I like the physical pleasure of touching and orgasm, but it's always a struggle for me. I went on estrogen last year, which helped my lubrication, but it did nothing for my desire. I even tried testosterone for six months but nothing happened so I stopped."

Karen is a tall, comfortable-looking woman who dresses well. Her easy laughter and eagerness to please are likely to put men at ease and signal other women that she'll be no threat. When she's nervous, she echoes the last words of your sentence to show she's following you. Her sincerity and caring, however, don't come from insecurity. Underneath there is a solidity about her.

Ken is taller and thinner, and his tousled white hair and graying beard make him look like the stereotype of an eccentric professor. His appearance is clean but his clothes are rumpled. Few people can match his intelligence, and his esoteric work in theoretical mathematics makes shop talk in social gatherings impossible. Although warm and friendly, he is awkward sharing his feelings with others. He's quiet, apparently used to keeping his thoughts to himself.

As if suddenly self-conscious about their disclosures, they lapse into silence. After several quiet moments, I ask, "What else should I know?"

"Well," says Karen slowly, "I have another problem that's hard to talk about. I've always been upset by my sexual fantasies. Ken knows some of this because I get lost in my fantasies while we're having sex. He can tell sometimes I'm off somewhere. When we have sex and I'm not aroused, I turn myself on with these fantasies—even though I feel bad about them."

"How often are you off in your fantasies during sex with Ken?"

"I've been less fantasy-dependent since we attended your Couples Retreat. I still go in and out of fantasy to get fully aroused and reach orgasm. But now I want to be with Ken."

"Yes, that's our big progress," Ken quips, "now I have her *some* of the time. She used to be gone about half the time. Now it's maybe 25 percent."

"It's gone from 95 percent to about 50," Karen says gently. She monitors his response, trying to avoid hurting him. "I envy how easily Ken gets aroused. He's a great lover. He's patient and he stays with me. If I get more erotic, he gets more aroused. I want to be aroused sooner, even before Ken actually touches me."

I can see Karen is trying to share the spotlight with Ken, who prefers not to speak unless he thinks he's got something worthy to add. She's walking the marital tightrope of trying to reassure him everything is good while also pushing for change. As they sit near each other on the couch, neither pulls away when they touch by chance. She reaches for him often, reassuring both of them. "What else is happening?" I ask.

"Two months ago I told Ken that I don't find the way he dresses to be very sexy—he rarely buys clothes. I said, 'I get attracted to sexy men, and I want to have those feelings toward you.' " Anxiety in the room shoots up a notch.

"I don't feel like a sexy man," Ken says defensively when he thinks it's his turn. "And I don't like pretending to be one."

"I'm on the other side pretending *not* to be sexy. I usually don't dare let on what's inside me," Karen adds emphatically.

"Oh, this is great!" Ken is doing his best to appreciate the irony. "You have no desire and you're hiding your sexiness. My desire is diminishing, and I wish I had something to hide." Karen reaches out to reassure him. She looks hurt and withdraws her hand when he continues to look dejected. I try to keep the session moving forward.

"It sounds like you folks are playing hide-and-seek with your eroticism. How often do you actually have sex?"

"For the last five or ten years it's been once a week." Ken speaks with the assurance of someone comfortable collecting data, but his tone hints that he's feeling inadequate. "When I was hornier, I thought about initiating every night."

Karen communicates on two levels simultaneously, partly stating her preference, partly reassuring Ken. "Frequency is less important to me than feeling freed up during sex. I want more quality to it. Now it mostly occurs on Saturday mornings."

"Because that's a time you're relaxed and refreshed, or because you're both already there and no one has to do much to initiate?"

Karen's response is instantaneous. "Because it doesn't take much initiative or creativity." I notice Karen doesn't always have to support Ken—or defend herself. She can say it straight. Ken nods wistfully in agreement. "When sex is good, we usually don't try again soon. I worry that it won't be as good the next time," he confesses.

"For me it's just the opposite," Karen says. "When it's good I'm more hopeful, but then I don't act on it."

"Why don't you?" I ask, adding, "Not that you're supposed to."

"I don't know. Sometimes I think about it before Ken gets home, but I lose it when he's here."

"Wait a minute," I cut in. "It's sounds like you have sexual imagery and get aroused sometimes before you have sex. That's different from what I thought you said before."

"That's right. That's also changed since the Couples Retreat. Sometimes now I get aroused before we start, but it doesn't last."

Do you find it curious that someone who complains about not having sexual desire gets lost in richly detailed fantasies during sex? I do. If anything, it sounds to me like Karen has a robust sexual fantasy life. When people examine the apparent contradictions in their sexuality, it becomes their window into new ways of living. To Karen, her lack of sexual desire and uncomfortable intrusive fantasies are two separate problems. I begin to wonder how they might be connected.

Later in the session Karen tells me she reaches orgasm one way or another in almost all their sexual encounters. Ken's orgasm is never in question, although in the early years of their marriage she rarely touched his penis. He, on the other hand, usually fondled her breasts and genitals trying to arouse her. Ken always made sure Karen had her orgasm before he ejaculated. "He never has a problem getting an erection," she says, half envious and half complaining.

Karen also tells me she's been getting more active and experimenting sexually in recent years. She often strokes his penis and occasionally mounts him for intercourse. "I've experimented letting Ken come in my mouth twice this year—something I'd never do before."

"She's still not really keen on it," Ken adds.

"I don't feel adequate doing it yet," Karen says with a trace of defensiveness. "I'm particularly uncomfortable with it if he's been inside me."

"Why is that?"

"I'm uncomfortable tasting my vagina. I've read all the women's lib books, but I guess I still think it's unclean."

Another emotional window suddenly appears. "Tasting your husband's penis doesn't bother you?"

"Not anymore."

"That's an interesting form of self-rejection. You think your partner's genitals are cleaner than yours."

Karen eyes widen in sudden recognition. Something she already knew about herself has surfaced where she never expected—oral sex.

"I've always rejected myself," she says unhappily. "I don't like that about myself."

Her quiet decisiveness suggests that Karen has reached a turning point. I decide not to push her to say more about it. If and when she's ready to do something about it, I want it clear that she's acting on her own.

I start to wind up the session, thinking we've already witnessed the main event. Almost as an afterthought, I ask, "You've told me a tremendous amount in a very short period of time. Anything else I should know now?"

Karen and Ken eye each other for a long moment. She finally turns towards me. "I'm troubled by the content of some of my fantasies."

"Which fantasies?" I sense we're about to enter a whole new level.

"One or more men forcing me to have sex in painful or degrading ways—S and M fantasies that embarrass me because they turn me on. They've gotten better, but they still bother me."

Karen obviously thinks what she's saying is embarrassing—only she doesn't seem to be *feeling* embarrassed. She seems to be gaining strength as she talks. Ken is staring at her. He's gone from feeling protective, to being proud, to being in awe of her. He's heard some of this before, but he's never seen her so unashamed. I sense a demonstration of an important link between fantasy and actual sexual encounters is about to unfold.

"In what way have the fantasies gotten better?"

"There's still an authoritarian man or men telling me what to do—but it's things that arouse me. Sometimes I'm asking them to teach me about sex. The fantasies seem more consensual. I still feel guilty about them, especially when I'm having sex with Ken."

"Did you know that your arousal pattern and imagery are common?"

"I'm not the only one?! What's causes them?"

"I'll gladly discuss that later, but I don't want to talk theory. For now, let's stick with your experience. If the theory is useful, we'll arrive at the same place by following what's true for you."

"I don't have any more to say about it." Karen looks disappointed and waits a few moments to see if I'll tell her what she wants to hear. I don't, and she changes the topic.

"What's true for me is I don't initiate now because I'm afraid of looking pathetic and fraudulent. Body-image—being fat—has always been a problem." Karen realizes I'm looking at her. "I'm not that heavy now,

but it really was a problem when I was younger. Occasionally I fantasize taking off all my clothes and coming to bed wearing just a necklace, but I don't have the nerve."

I don't say anything for a few moments. "Nerve . . . or integrity?" I
ask quietly.

"Integrity?"

"Look at yourself through the lens of your sexuality. When you look
at the issue of wearing only your necklace and a smile, what do you see?"

Karen's insight from the oral sex discussion is still fresh. This time it
only takes her a moment. "I'm putting myself down, telling myself I'm
not attractive, that only beautiful women should do that." She's proud
and upset in the same instant.

"So the issue isn't just lacking the courage of your beliefs. It's not just
that you feel bad and then don't follow through. When you back down,
you denigrate yourself."

Karen is taking it all in. "But what does this have to do with integrity?"

"*Integrity* and *integration* are one and the same. You're describing a
lack of integration between who you think you are and who you aspire
to be. In fact, if I've read you right, when you said 'I don't like that about
myself' during our discussion of oral sex, you were coming upon it as
an integrity issue—not as a genital issue." Karen's eyes widen.

"Absolutely! All my life I've never felt good enough."

"Good enough for whom and what?"

"I used to think, good enough for Ken—or anyone else! Good
enough to act the way I think a *real* woman would!"

"Is that an integrity issue?"

"I guess it is."

"Is the issue of tasting your own vagina the same thing?"

"What?"

"You act as if Ken's penis is clean enough to taste but your vagina is
too dirty. Are you putting yourself down while you're having sex? Does
it ever bother you that Ken gets more pleasure from your body than you
do?"

"You're not just talking about sexuality! This is the story of my life.
Everyone gets more pleasure from me than I do. That's starting to
make me angry. I belong more to everyone else than to myself!" Karen
pauses to glance at Ken. "It's staring me in the face! I'm amazed I could
avoid this for so long."

"Sexuality is a powerful window into who we are."

Karen's personal development is starting to take off. Ken decides it's time to speak up. "Can you do that with me—see *me* through our sex practices?"

"Sure. This may sound strange, but it's like sex hasn't really been personal for either one of you. Karen is lost in her fantasies, and you've had sexual desire out of hormonal drive. You've wanted to reduce your sexual tensions, but not necessarily because you crave *her*. You think the problem is that you're getting older, that the hormones are tapering off. But if you want to keep your sex alive, you have to grow up—we all do. The solution involves shifting from desire out of horniness to desire for *Karen*—wanting to share something with her. It's the shift from impersonal sex, like boys have, to having sex like a man."

Ken doesn't say much, but he's ready to hear more. "We can also understand your sexual pattern in another way. If you accept Karen's report at face value—which I'm not telling you to do—the fact that you can't tell when she's 'gone' during sex means either that she is a fantastic actress or you don't have much experience being close to the people you love. Like in your childhood family."

Ken stifles his surprise. "We loved each other," he says, not totally believing it, "but my family was sort of distant. We traded ideas, not hugs, and we didn't talk about feelings. I spent most of my time reading in my room." He pauses several seconds, silently redigesting his youth. When he returns from his solitary review, it's as if he's on a different track. "Karen wants to 'dress up' for sex—even if it's just a necklace. She wants me to dress better, too. I've always been afraid to draw attention to myself, in bed or out. It's just not me. Do I have to?"

Suddenly it's clear I have more traction with Ken by staying in the present than talking about the past. "I can't answer that for you. It sounds like you want to maintain a low profile the same way you did growing up, even though you don't want to live now in that kind of house. You decide if you want to continue living that way."

"I'm not as good at dealing with this as Karen."

"You may not be as good at it, but you seem to have the same problem: you're tugging against the limits of your self-image 'leash'—being a 'sex object' and wearing nice clothes. As long as you dress down, you don't bump into your low self-esteem."

Ken nods, more to keep me talking than because he fully agrees. He's used to keeping his own counsel and he needs time to think about this. There's no point pushing him. I turn to address both of them.

"You can get in bed as the person you know yourself to be or as who you'd like to be. That doesn't necessarily mean you're not being yourself. The process of *becoming* can lead you to act in ways that still exceed the limits of your self-image. In doing what we aspire to be, we become that person. But you decide."

I nod towards Ken. "Is refusing to wear nice clothing your way of defending yourself against pressure from Karen—or a response to your anxieties and insecurities? If the clothes really feel phony to you, I hope you don't buy them. I never encourage anyone to sell themselves out." Ken seems to be wondering if I'm on his side or not.

Karen jokes, "His idea of dress-up is L. L. Bean." Ken shrugs sheepishly. "Whatever it is," I reply, "it's his body. If *you* are interested in dressing up, why not check out what's new in necklaces? Another client I worked with once said to me, 'Doc, I finally got it. You don't *think* your way to a new way of living. You *live* your way to a new way of thinking.'"

Karen and Ken give each other another long look. They leave my office quiet and hopeful, holding hands, lost in their own thoughts.

Karen and Ken enter our second day's session all smiles. They sit closer on the couch than they had the day before. "Sex was different last night!" they both volunteer. Karen says with pride, "I walked into the bedroom wearing only my necklace! Ken's eyes were bulging out in disbelief. Once we started, every thought that came to mind I said. That's *very* unusual for me—no screening." Ken smiles in agreement.

"You had a taste of *self*-validated intimacy. It's the key to intense sex and intimacy."

Karen looks puzzled for a moment and then brightens. "I remember you discussing self-validated intimacy at the Couples Retreat. That's when you don't expect your partner to validate or accept what you disclose. *You* validate yourself as you show your partner who you really are. But how does that apply to what we did?"

"Weren't you doing exactly that when you wore just the necklace? Isn't sharing your thoughts without screening—without focusing on your partner's possible response—an even better example?"

"Now I get it!" Karen beams in recognition.

"I guess I'm a little slower than Karen," Ken says apologetically. "I really screwed things up. I made my usual move: I asked Karen what she wanted me to do for her sexually, instead of revealing what I wanted to do. I played it safe and tried to get her to stick her neck out. As soon as I realized what I was doing, I backed up. Karen realized what I was doing and laughed."

"I saw Ken slip back into his old style, but he was really trying." Her eyes are smiling along with her lips.

What stands out as I listen to last night's happenings is the difference in *tone*—there are nuances of meaning that make all the difference in the world. In this case, the tone was lighter. The message between them was "this is going to be different." Karen had opened with a high ante in her bid to jazz up their sex. Ken made a counter-offer to lower the self-disclosure, but didn't fold when Karen called him on it.

"If you look at what happened, you can see that the level of intimacy and eroticism between you is negotiated early in the encounter. It's that way for many people, although we rarely recognize it. No wonder your former strategy of 'let's keep going and maybe it will get better' doesn't work."

Karen's eyes twinkle as she holds Ken's hand. "I think we had another example of self-validated intimacy. I took Ken inside my head while we had sex. I told him about a fantasy I was having as it unfolded. I imagined I was going to a sex club where men take care of women and give them peak sexual experiences. Ken listened for several minutes, and then I said, 'I have an idea, why don't you leave the room and come back in and let's see what happens.' He did, we did, and it triggered more pictures in my head. I told him and we did them. It was amazing."

"I have no doubt!" I said, "Behavior needs to follow the internal connection, not the other way around."

Ken suddenly stops making moon eyes with Karen and turns towards me. "Say that again—I've never heard that before."

"You let the sense of connection between you determine your behavior. By sharing the fantasy you followed your connection and did what came out of that. You didn't touch each other hoping to produce emotional connection. You used to touch the way you thought would make you feel connected—such as stroking each other's genitals. When it didn't work, you thought there was some problem in your technical skill. Maybe now you can see you were barking up the wrong tree."

Ken is processing this and hits a snag. "Wait. Aren't you contradicting what you said last session about behavior leading self-esteem? We were talking about me wearing nice clothes and Karen wearing just her necklace to bed. You said we could stretch our self-esteem by doing things that seemed beyond who we saw ourselves to be."

"I'm glad you're thinking this through for yourself. I don't think I'm contradicting myself, but don't take my word for it. Check this out from your own experience: if you want to expand sex and intimacy between you, you have to do things that seem beyond the person you've always been. But in the same moment, you have to establish a basic sense of connection with your partner to start with, and then let it dictate the sexual things you do together. This comes together if you think of it this way: what part of you do you use to touch—meaning make contact with—your partner? Do you touch your partner from the best in you? Or do you reach out from the part that feels inadequate or wants to hide? If you do it from that part, you'll drop the emotional connection and resort to touching each other's genitals to try to get something going."

Karen looks meaningfully at Ken. "I'm realizing I don't have sex *with you* when we're together. I shut you out, and shut myself out of what we can have."

"You're not the only one!"

"That's quite a revelation!" I want to underscore what's happening between them.

"Well, that's not all," Karen says proudly. "I woke Ken up at five this morning to have sex. That's another first—I never do that. I was lying in bed having a sexual fantasy, and I told it to him. Ken picks me up at a bar. Literally. I go there first and wait for him."

"This sounds like it isn't just a fantasy. Do you want to play this out for real?"

"Absolutely! But in the fantasy I had this morning, another man sits down next to me and tries to pick me up. I tell him I'm waiting for my husband to pick me up. He says, 'Oh, your husband is meeting you here?' I say, 'No, he's going to *pick me up,* just like you're trying to do.' He's jealous. I tell him he can watch, but he has to stand to the side, out of the way. The idea of him watching turns me on. Ken shows up in a sexy silk shirt, and after we kiss a little we leave to have sex."

Ken finds his voice. "As we were having sex last night, Karen told me how to tease her. The way she was talking turned me on just as if she was stroking me."

"If I understand right, you're not just talking about teasing as a style of touch. You're talking about an *attitude.* Teasing someone is a mind-set. It's not effective if it's done without the emotional engagement."

"Correct! We didn't just 'go at it.' I felt less responsibility for making everything right," Ken affirms.

"That's not all!" Karen adds with a flourish. "I tasted myself! It was part of our fantasy. When I talked about it with you last session, I imagined an awkward experience—like giving myself a medical exam. Instead I told Ken, 'I want to suck your penis, but I want you to enter me first. I think it would be nice to taste both of us instead of just you.' It was entirely different from what I had anticipated. I had no fear or revulsion."

"At the end of the evening Karen burst into tears." Ken doesn't seem totally sure this is good.

"I felt so much love for him. It hurt—bittersweet. I was aware we wouldn't always be together. My fantasies didn't tune him out. The way we used them this time brought us together. Suddenly fantasy and reality came together so intensely. I cried a long time."

"That sure doesn't sound like autistic sex! You challenged yourselves and it resulted in an intense connection."

Ken nodded. "While all this is going on I'm wondering, *Is she playing a role or is this a side of Karen I've never seen before?* It's like I'm with a new woman. I'm fifty-seven, she's fifty-three, we've been together twenty-six years, and I can hardly believe we're doing this."

"Correct me if I'm mistaken, but the belief you're referring to is believing in yourselves."

"Yup!" said Karen. "That's it! It's getting the inside outside. It feels great! I have a totally different experience of my fantasies—now they're a resource in our lovemaking. Finally, it's literally like *making* love. I can feel the difference!"

"So when you look at yourself through your sexuality now, what do you see?"

Karen pauses to take stock. "A *woman*. I'm no longer embarrassed by my fantasies . . . actually, I'm rather proud of myself."

"I'm not sure I can keep up with this new woman." Ken is praising Karen and telling me his fear at the same time.

"You can't if you approach her with that tone of self-defeatism."

"*I* think he can! I loved seeing the little-boy excitement and playfulness in him—particularly since this had nothing to do with being a little boy. The *man* in him stepped out to meet me. In fact, Ken played out different men in my fantasy. He changed his voice and mannerisms as he took on different roles. He *never* lets himself play like that!"

Ken isn't totally comfortable being so complimented or exposed. He shifts the topic slightly by telling me something else of importance: "Now that I'm older, I last longer during intercourse. I used to think it allowed us to experiment with more positions. Now I see it another way. What you call our 'tone' is different. We can relax. I don't have to tune her out to delay orgasm like I once did." Ken turns to look at Karen for a long time. "I'm realizing how orgasm-focused we've been. *I've* been! If you'd have asked me a week ago, I would have denied it. I just couldn't see it. I'm realizing I bring Karen to orgasm first all the time because I'm afraid I won't have an erection after I climax. That's just another version of being orgasm-focused, isn't it?"

Suddenly, we've got meaning everywhere! Ken's insight is so accurate and important it would be easy to agree. But I'm also clear Ken isn't really asking me a question—he's already pretty sure of the answer and anticipates praise for his insight. He's making a bid for me to validate him. Out of respect and belief in him, I'm not going to take the one-up position he's offering. But how far can I go before Ken feels like he's back with his uncommunicative family?

My clients pay me to help them, not to nurse them, but sometimes it's not easy doing what needs to be done. Trading on everything we've developed, I look Ken in the eye and invite him to join me as a competent man. "If you're becoming more of a man—especially, your *own* man—why not answer your question for yourself?"

Ken clearly isn't expecting my response. We talk a few minutes more. He walks out a little shaken. Karen looks a little worried.

Ken opens our third and final session with unusual vigor. "We're having a wonderful time, but we're not getting to see much of your beautiful town. We're spending lots of time having sex."

"I had this idea to switch roles," Karen says, not missing a beat. "I showed him how I want to be seduced."

"We've never done anything like this before," Ken adds. "I'm getting used to this new woman. And to make a bad pun, we're putting our issues to bed."

Karen and Ken explain his comment. The previous evening they successfully discussed a bad experience that had hung over their marriage for fifteen years. Their tradition was to take turns surprising the other with dinner at a restaurant on their anniversary. Fifteen years ago Karen surprised Ken by bringing him to a resort where they could have sex in a private hot tub. Ken felt threatened and couldn't get an erection—a rare experience for him. His response was to shame Karen into backing off. Karen was confused and hurt by his response and began to doubt herself. She withdrew sexually for many years thereafter.

"Last night we talked about it," Karen says. "And then we did something about it. I *did* him! I tied his hands to the bed to make the point. Ken had the courage to let me take him."

Ken starts to blush. "I felt selfish just taking from Karen," he confesses.

"Do you enjoy going out to dinner with someone who always insists on paying the check?" I ask.

"No, I don't." Then Ken realizes the question applies to him. "You mean my giving to Karen can be *selfish?*"

"You decide. It sounds like letting her give you sexual pleasure challenges your identity and self-worth. Good for you! You—"

"Thanks a lot!" Ken cuts in with mock anger. He's grinning from ear to ear. "Go ahead, I know what you mean!" We're all laughing now.

"You like sending your wife 'into orbit' and hearing her moan. Why shouldn't she have the pleasure of feeling her own sexual abilities and listening to *you* scream? And if you're feeling generous, why shouldn't you be the one to give it to her?"

"I wish we'd done this earlier," Ken says wistfully.

"What makes you think you could have? It's taken every bit of development you've got to do what you did last night. The sex you're starting to have is not for kids—or for immature adults. You can't go forward berating and rejecting yourself. Do you want to turn your most recent accomplishment into inadequacy retrospectively?"

"No, I just wish we could have shared this sooner."

"It takes a long time for a human being to mature sexually."

"Well, at least we're on the road. This is what I thought our honeymoon was supposed to be. We did something else last night that has been a long time in coming. When Karen untied me, I *did* her!"

"Yes indeed he did!" Karen smiles like the Cheshire Cat. "But what I'm seeing is that it's really not about sex in the usual sense. *This is about who we've been, where we've come from, and becoming who we can be.*"

I couldn't have said it better.

A New Picture of Sex and Intimacy

Does Ken and Karen's process seem remarkable? It's the kind of thing I've learned is possible from watching my clients do it. But it still amazes me every time it happens. And it happens frequently.

This wonderful couple revolutionized their sex and intimacy in part because they received a therapy that's a revolution in integrating sexual and marital counseling. You may have been surprised at different points by the frankness of our dialogue, or by how they found personal meaning in their sexual behavior, or by the ways in which they were challenged to grow. These are just some of the ways in which this approach differs from conventional sexual or marital therapy. The fundamental

changes go much further—right to the ways we understand sex and intimacy and how best to handle marriage.

It will take this whole book to explain these new ways to understand
emotionally committed relationships. Along the way we'll challenge
ideas so widely accepted as truths that at first you might wonder why
we're bothering to consider them at all. Some are such sacred cows that
it seems like hubris to suggest they are wrong. But by the book's end
you'll probably shed many popular beliefs, if your experience is anything
like Karen and Ken's. You'll see yourself, your partner, and your marriage in an entirely new light. And more importantly, you'll have new
ways of using physical contact and intimate connection to bring yourself and your relationship alive and keep it that way.

I believe married couples suffer under the burden of several misun-
derstandings that have been so widely accepted that we don't even suspect this possibility. These distortions, which concern how we
understand intimacy, "good communication," and sexuality, all involve
a similar kind of error. In each case we've seen only a portion of the
process and convinced ourselves that our truncated view defines the
whole thing. In other words, the way we commonly think about how
intimacy and sex work in marriage is only part of the picture. As a result, many couples establish false expectations through which they conduct and evaluate their relationship.

For example, we've taken one kind of intimacy—the type in which
our partner accepts and validates us—and convinced ourselves this is
what intimacy is per se. Thus, we assume that intimacy hinges on acceptance and validation from our partner. Likewise we've confused
"good communication" with being understood the way we want and
getting the response we expect. We never consider the kind of intimacy
where we validate our own disclosures when our partner doesn't. This
is *self-validated* intimacy—the kind of intimacy that made Karen and
Ken's marriage more intimate and expanded their sexual repertoire.
(Chapter 4 is devoted to discussing self-validated intimacy.)

If you're asking yourself, "You mean intimacy doesn't involve acceptance and validation from my partner or feeling secure enough to
disclose?" you're having the same reaction I did when my understanding of intimacy fell apart—and coalesced into something more meaningful and useful. As you'll learn in later chapters, intimacy is nature's
latest "experiment" (because it uses the part of our brain that evolved
last), and we're still trying to understand what it is and how it works in
long-term relationships.

A sociologist once observed that the prevalence of intimacy themes in mass media, pop psychology, and "alternative lifestyles" suggests that we're driven by hunger for intimate union. It may look like this on the surface, but my clinical work helped me realize that there's actually something else going on. We're driven by something that makes us look like we crave intimacy, but in fact we're after something else: we want someone else to make us feel acceptable and worthwhile. We've assigned the label "intimacy" to what we want (validation and reciprocal disclosure) and developed pop psychologies that give it to us—while keeping true intimacy away. We've distorted what intimacy is, how it feels, how much we really want it, and how best to get it. Once we realize that intimacy is not always soothing and often makes us feel insecure, it is clear why we back away from it.

The same "mistaking the part for the whole" distortion has occurred with sexual desire. In 1929, humorists James Thurber and E. B. White published *Is Sex Necessary?* In it they wrote:

> Sex is less than 50 years old. The sublimation of sex, called Love, is much older—although purists question the existence of Love prior to 1885, on grounds there can be no sublimation of a non-existent feeling.
>
> Quite regardless of whether the urge for food or sex came first, the sex "urge" creates a much greater stir. . . . Sex urge has upset the whole Western World because, while the urge to eat is a personal matter concerning only the hungry person, the sex urge involves (for its true expression) another individual. It is this "other person" that causes all the trouble.

What may escape attention on first reading is that Thurber and White considered sexual desire to be a drive to satisfy a biological hunger, much like our need for food. That's because the "biological hunger" view of sex is deeply rooted in society. So deep, in fact, that it permeates the way many therapists approach problems of low sexual desire. Using the same rationale as humorists Thurber and White, they refer to it as "sexual *anorexia*"—a sexual "eating disorder." The notion behind this is that since desire for sex is supposedly like desire for food—a basic biological drive—you have to be pretty screwed up not to want either one.

Superficially, the common idea that sex is a natural biological drive seems reasonable. After all, isn't sex drive a function of hormones? Isn't sex encoded in all animals? If sex drive weren't "normal," wouldn't our species die out?

While there's some truth to these notions, they limit our perspective on *human* sexuality and interfere with sexual satisfaction. We don't realize that seeing sex as a "drive" makes us focus on relieving sexual tensions rather than wanting our partner. It may be true that the more tension ("horny") people feel, the more they tend to seek relief—but if that's the only reason you think your partner wants to be with you it tends to kill sex and intimacy in marriage. It's hard for couples to approach this any other way: even the diagnostic manuals used by physicians and therapists conceptualize sexual desire as eagerness for sexual behavior rather than desire for your partner. Focusing on desire as motivation *for* sex overlooks the many couples who struggle to increase desire (passion) *during* sex. (Chapter 5 focuses on an intimacy-based view of sexual desire that corrects this.)

Seeing sexual desire as a biological drive sets us up to believe we're automatically supposed to know how to have sex—although humans take longer to reach full sexual maturity than any species on earth. It also makes us think we should want sex all the time—although human sexual desire is more affected by circumstance and meaning than in lower species. But you can't make sex more intimate or ever feel wanted *(chosen)* using this approach because hormones, hunger, and sex "drive" don't choose. It doesn't help couples like Karen and Ken keep sex alive as their hormonal urges taper off with age.

What I said earlier to Karen and Ken holds true for the rest of us: examining the contradictions in our sexuality can become our window into new ways of living. Espousing "be with your partner!" and "communicate!" doesn't shield us from approaches that jump-start arousal *but destroy intimacy in the process.* For example, common but misguided encouragement to "focus on your sensations" takes you away from your partner and causes some people to feel pressured to have an orgasm. It promotes a mechanical approach to sex that often leaves partners feeling ignored and "used."

Consider the fact that techniques used to treat low sexual desire often *create* low sexual desire when couples do the same thing spontaneously. For instance, some therapists encourage embittered couples with low sexual desire to "bypass" (ignore) their partner and fantasize about someone else. Although sometimes it "works," bypassing limits contact with your partner. But when *you* realize your partner is touching you and pretending you're someone else, does that fill you with desire? Sexual desire problems are difficult to cure when treatment has nothing to do with the eroticism, intimacy, and passion we anticipate and demand.

The same thing holds true for the "squeeze technique," long regarded as a principal method of treating rapid ejaculation. While somewhat effective in stopping ejaculation, it stops intimacy, too. Imagine a man whipping his penis from his partner's body as his orgasm approaches and squeezing it. Long before that he's stopped focusing on his partner, awaiting the proper moment to perform the sexual Heimlich maneuver. This approach has gone largely unchallenged because it teaches troubled couples the same intimacy-incongruent sexual styles used by most people.

Our near-sightedness blinds us to the ways our incomplete views of sex make us feel inadequate: once you adopt the seemingly sex-positive view that "sex is a natural function," the only way to explain sexual dysfunction or disinterest is to look for pathological explanations. When something goes wrong sexually we're set up to ask ourselves, "If sexual response and interest are natural, then why am I not responding or even wanting to respond?" If you remember, this is exactly what Ken was asking himself—and feeling inadequate in the process.

Ken and Karen's therapy sessions demonstrate a new approach that emphasizes intimacy during sex. They realized they often weren't with each other when they made love. Karen was lost in her fantasies and Ken was preoccupied with his anxieties. Ken was shocked to learn just how much Karen was "gone," that he often couldn't tell, and that this had personal meaning for him: it was related to his prior lack of experience being intimate with the people he loved. In treatment, this couple focused on reducing the time their minds were apart while their bodies were together. They even found a new way to use fantasies to bring them closer. Karen displayed a classic example of self-validated intimacy by saying everything she thought while they had sex and letting Ken into her head. She showed Ken her strengths, and Ken let her see his limitations.

Until couples go beyond viewing sex as a biological drive, they presume sexual behavior is a good measure of sexual desire and orgasm always involves high arousal and satisfaction. Common experiences of married couples disprove both assumptions. Both Karen and Ken were regularly orgasmic, even though their sex lacked intimacy and eroticism.

Like the joke about the three blind men who try to imagine what an elephant looks like from feeling its trunk, ear, and tail, we've developed distorted notions about intimacy and sexuality in long-term relationships. We might say our resulting view of marriage is a joke—if it didn't contribute to the social tragedies that half of all marriages end in divorce and many who stay married are sexually unhappy and alienated. Our cherished distortions fuel the even higher divorce rate among second and third marriages. It's not simply that some people don't learn from experience: their feelings of inadequacy lead them to try harder and hold tighter to common beliefs that create relationship problems.

In the midst of marital discord few of us have the courage to consider that the beliefs and practices we share with many couples are the source of our misery. We usually think problems with sex and intimacy are caused by how we're uniquely screwed up. I propose, instead, that they're often caused by being *normal.* If you're well-adjusted to ill-fitting beliefs that permeate society, you're going to have trouble.

When we talk about developing a fuller, deeper understanding of marriage, many people automatically think of unconscious feelings or repressed experiences. We've grown accustomed to looking at life's struggles as a reflection of unconscious processes. When we're unhappy, we look within ourselves for past traumas that incapacitate us in the present. The notion of uncovering repressed feelings has become synonymous with mental health, as if progressively stripping away façades and unearthing unconscious anxieties will liberate our innate vitality and creativity. In this view, therapy is a method of peeling away the layers of your character like an onion. Often, however, the problem is not a matter of peeling away layers but of developing them—growing ourselves up to be mature and resourceful adults who can solve our current problems.

Many marital therapists believe childhood wounds drive marriage, leading us to reenact our family problems with our adult partners. I do not. While I don't ignore unpleasant childhood experiences, I also don't believe they are the only or even the strongest factor shaping a marriage. Childhood wounds have their impact, just like parental modeling and social conditioning. I believe other aspects have at least as much—if not more—impact on marriage than our childhood or unconscious processes. These involve how sex and intimacy operate within marriage as a system with rules of its own. (I'll discuss these shortly.)

Misguided emphasis on childhood wounds does more than send couples off in the wrong direction. The resulting "trauma model of life" ignores everything outstanding about our species' determination to grow and thrive. When Pulitzer Prize winner Ernest Becker said our social "maps" trivialize life and destroy any opportunity to feel heroic, this is an example of what he meant. Likewise, in *Care of the Soul,* Thomas Moore observes "we like to think that emotional problems have to do with the family, childhood, and trauma—with personal life—but not with spirituality." *Passionate Marriage* is about resilience rather than damage, health rather than old wounds, and human potential rather than trauma.

I'm not proposing that we ignore past events that limit our present efforts. Awakening creative effort, however, requires leaving personal tragedies behind rather than constantly revisiting and revising them. This is neither as difficult nor as undesirable as it might seem. Presumably you're reading this book because you're interested in improving your relationship. If you also have important childhood issues to resolve, the approach I will outline can help. It offers ways to *resolve the past in the present* by focusing on what's currently happening in your marriage.

This "non-regressive" approach does not deny the impact of the past—but you don't necessarily have to go back into the past to resolve it. You can work on the past where it's surfacing in the present. This gives meaning and utility to your current difficulties and provides an active way to work on your present and past simultaneously. You don't have to put your marriage on hold while you rework your past; often your current situation won't permit this, and there's no guarantee this will resolve your present difficulties anyway. When working on the past in the present, you're working directly on your current problem, too, so what's of immediate concern to you—your marriage—often improves. You don't have to decide from the outset what's causing what.

Childhood is another place where we've "mistaken a part for the whole." Fifty years ago, child development specialists recognized the importance of infants' drive to bond (attach) to their caregivers. Unfortunately, we've erroneously assumed this is *the* dominant and overriding drive for children *and* adults, and popularized the image of infants being helpless and terrified when no one is there to comfort them. We've applied this same image to marriage and concluded our partner is supposed to soothe us and not do things that make us insecure. However, radically new information emerging from infant research over the last decade shows that infants have remarkable resilience and are able to regulate some of their emotional equilibrium by three months of age. (Chapter 12, which discusses self-soothing, explains these findings.) We've ignored how taking care of your own feelings is an integral part of maintaining a relationship and how it fuels attachment *and* self-direction. We've reduced adults to infants, reduced infants to a frail ghost of their resilience, and reduced marriage to providing safety, security, and compensation for childhood disappointments. In other words, we've eliminated from marriage those things that fuel our essential drives for autonomy and freedom. Common notions of interdependence emphasize our neediness but not our strengths.

There are many ways you can make sense of and respond to patterns and events that surface in your marriage. Our failure to understand the basic ways intimacy and sexuality ebb and flow within marriage has contributed to confusion about how best to use common developments that arise. You can respond in ways that use common "problems" for optimal gain, or you can act in ways that increase problems and minimize any benefits derived.

I believe society has approached marriage the same as we have the environment (until recently): tried to bend it to our will and suffered for it. Today we recognize that the earth's ecology is a complex system of processes that operates as a whole with rules of its own. My twenty years of experience working with couples suggests that marriage operates similarly—if we have the wisdom to recognize and heed its operating principles.

We don't usually think of marriage as a system with its own rules. Like the earth's ecosystem, marriage can operate—more or less—according to whatever template we choose to place on it. ("Wounded child" theory is an example of a template. In this book you'll learn another.) The rules of a system are not mandates—we can bend them by ignorance or design, usually at our own peril. The more we try to force our marriage (or our planet) into a mode of operation that is antithetical to its natural processes, the more likely that it will reach a point of imbalance from which it cannot recover. But it's also possible to remove the blinders of conventional wisdom, discover the processes that govern intimacy and sexuality within emotionally committed relationships, and act accordingly.

What I offered Ken and Karen, and what I'll offer you, is a way to harness the natural processes of sex and intimacy and use marriage in radically new ways. In retrospect you can see that Karen and Ken used their marriage to help them become people capable of having the sex and intimacy they wanted.

Not only do sex and intimacy seem to operate according to some core principles, but they also create predictable sticking points in marriages. Moreover, these patterns can be harnessed in fairly reliable ways that enhance sex, intimacy, personal development, and marital satisfaction.

In other words, marital problems arise for more reasons than our mistaken view of marriage. Mistaken beliefs create unnecessary marital problems, but some marital difficulties aren't "problems" at all. They're parts of marriage that our ill-fitting beliefs don't prepare us to handle effectively. These "problems" are tied into a core process of human development that weaves through marriage. This process is called differentiation (which I'll explain shortly). How you handle *differentiation* gives your marriage its form and flavor. The issues and "problems" of differentiation are inevitable—how you handle them makes the difference.

How could society lose sight of the natural processes of sex and intimacy in emotionally committed relationships? Unfortunately quite easily, since we've hardly looked for them. Only in the last decade have sex therapists and marital therapists seriously attempted to integrate these two fields and to explore how marital sex and intimacy operate as a sophisticated system. This is no simple task because the foundations and working concepts of these fields are fundamentally different and often at odds. I say this from experience, because I've devoted the last ten years of my professional life to accomplishing this very thing.

But what makes this difficult also makes it powerful and useful to do. I found fundamental inaccuracies in contemporary sex therapy by looking at it through the lens of marital therapy and systems theory. Then I used sexuality as a window to see the gaps and inconsistencies in marital therapy. The clinical approach you'll learn here is the first application of differentiation theory from family therapy (developed by psychiatrist Murray Bowen) to problems of sex and intimacy in marriage. In Chapters 2 through 5 I'll share the details of my discoveries with you. But let me point out something now.

In twenty years as a sex and marital therapist, I've seen people achieve levels of intimacy and sexual satisfaction my training never prepared me to expect. In integrating the fields of sex and marital therapy, my clinical approach has pioneered the use of sexuality as a vehicle for personal development. Previously, sex therapy aimed mainly at curing dysfunctions and low desire. Reducing sex to issues of performance pressure, misinformation, and inhibition destroys the possibility of using it to make yourself grow. Resolving common marital problems requires personal development rather than skills and techniques.

What does using sex for personal development look like? Remember Karen's discomfort tasting her own vaginal lubrication but her willingness to taste Ken's penis? Or her rejection of her own body as unattractive? We used both these issues to help her enhance her self-esteem and integrity. We also used them to resolve the past in the present—Karen took these as opportunities to work on her lifelong pattern of self-rejection. She also illustrated another pattern of personal growth: I've seen lots of clients whose fantasies change as they grow. I've even helped them work the process backwards—using their fantasies to trigger self-confrontation and growth, just as we did with Karen tasting herself. Ken showed a similar usage of sex for growth when he realized that always making Karen have her orgasm first was selfish, and that letting her *do* him was an act of integrity that challenged his self-worth. (Highly erotic sexual styles of *doing, being done,* and *fucking* are discussed in Chapter 10.)

Revolutionizing your marriage isn't as simple as learning new touch techniques, improving your communication skills, or rescheduling your time priorities. It involves growing. I hope to do two things in this book: share with you information that's helped many people find meaning and possibility in unexpected places, and offer you the opportunity to find value in what is problematic in your relationship.

As you saw with Karen and Ken, sex can be used as a window into who we are. As Karen said, sex is about who we've been, where we came from, and becoming who we can be. And just as they did, you can use your sexuality as the stage on which you play our your life's drama and rewrite your script. They did this by shifting from the familiar "sensation-based" approach to an intimacy-based approach emphasizing the "tone" and depth of connection rather than technique. (We'll discuss ways to do this in Chapters 6 through 10.)

As stated earlier, many marital problems occur even when we have an accurate picture. The more accurate picture simply allows us to anticipate common difficulties and use them to thrive. Accurate understanding makes it easier—but not easy.

The poorly understood processes of emotionally committed relationships give rise to a common pessimistic view that marriage inevitably kills sex and romance. According to the French philosopher Voltaire, divorce was invented about the same time as marriage—about two weeks later, to be exact! And playwright Oscar Wilde said that one should always be in love and that's why one should never marry.

My work with couples suggests something entirely different: marriage doesn't kill love, intimacy, or sex—it just looks like that at some points along the way. If you use your marriage in a particular way (which I'll illustrate throughout this book), it makes you more capable of keeping these alive in a long-term relationship.

Marriage is often like Procrustes' famous code of hospitality. Procrustes built a bed for his guests the same way we build a marriage: according to his own expectations. Shorter visitors were stretched to fit; taller folks were surgically shortened. Likewise, your spouse will try to change you into what he or she thinks you should be, just as you have fine-tuning in mind for your partner. Barbra Streisand once asked, "Why does a woman spend ten years trying to change her husband and then complain, 'You're not the man I married!' " Marriage is the procrustean bed in which we can develop and enhance our psychological and ethical integrity. It can be the cradle of adult development.

This is partly why my approach to therapy is known as the *sexual crucible approach*. The name describes how it often feels when marriage's classroom is in session. What's an example of a crucible in marriage? How about the fact that *your spouse can always force you to choose between keeping your integrity and staying married, between "holding onto yourself" and holding onto your partner.* These integrity issues often surface around sex and intimacy—about what the two of you will and won't do together. They can just as easily arise over issues about money, parenting, in-laws, and lifestyle. The more emotionally enmeshed you and your spouse are—*fused* in my lingo—the more you will push this choice right down to the wire. Stay in the marriage or get divorced. The key is not to lose your nerve or get overreactive or locked into an inflexible position. I know that's tough when you think your marriage is about to explode—or you're about to sell out your beliefs, preferences, or dreams. But it's actually part of the people-growing process in marriage.

When you're oblivious to ways marriage can operate as a people-growing process, all you see are problems and pathology—and the challenges of marriage will probably defeat you. Your pain will have no meaning except failure and disappointment; no richness, no soul. Spirituality is an attitude that reveals life's meaning through everyday experience; however, don't bother looking for sanctuary in your marriage. Seeking protection from its pains and pleasures misses its purpose: *marriage prepares us to live and love on life's terms.*

Facing relationship realities like these produces the personal integrity necessary for intimacy, eroticism, and a lifetime loving marriage. How is integrity relevant to marriage? Integrity is the ability to face the realities I just mentioned. It's living according to your own values and beliefs in the face of opposition. It is also the ability to change your values, beliefs, and behavior when your well-considered judgment or concern for others dictates it. Putting your partner's goals on par with your own and delaying your agenda accordingly takes (and makes) integrity.

Couples in the Crucible

This is exactly what Ken and Karen confronted when they returned home after our sessions. It wasn't always smooth sailing and their marriage wasn't perfect. But together they achieved a level of intimate erotic connection that neither had experienced or imagined themselves capable of having. They had to get beyond the common, but mistaken, belief that being in their fifties meant they were past their sexual prime; their experience demonstrated that they were just reaching theirs. But they had to do more than just give up misguided information that everyone believes.

Karen kept hoping Ken would dress nicer and act in ways she found sexually attractive—but he didn't. Having faced her own integrity issues and stretched her self-image (by taking off her clothes and putting on a necklace, as well as tasting her own body), she felt new personal pride that made her unwilling to settle for the way things were. Eventually Karen made it clear that she wouldn't keep nagging and hoping Ken would change, but she also wasn't going to be eager to have sex with him if things continued as they had. At first Ken complained that Karen was trying to make him into someone he wasn't, but Karen maintained that he was entitled to be who he was and she was entitled to her preferences.

When Ken realized Karen was serious and this could cripple their "honeymoon," he bought himself a silk shirt—three in fact. And to his surprise and delight, he liked wearing them. It was really to their mutual delight, because Karen not only liked to see Ken in them, she also recognized and respected how much self-confrontation went into Ken's decision. She knew more was involved than his caring enough about her and their relationship to do it. She realized how much Ken had to face his own lack of self-worth and stretch his self-image to get comfortable wearing the shirts.

And rather than feeling like he had capitulated to Karen, Ken felt proud of himself. He could have dodged his anxieties and insecurities by demanding that Karen "accept him as he is." Understanding differentiation (as I'll explain in the next chapter) helped Ken confront himself rather than accuse Karen of trying to tamper with him. He could see she was merely maintaining her right to her preferences. It let him shift from seeing his marriage as a procrustean bed to their spring-board to adult sexual development. Their relationship blossomed in and out of the bedroom.

Couples don't always start from the point Karen and Ken did when they came to see me. They were in their fifties and had struggled through many hard years in their marriage. But if we had seen Ken and Karen in their late thirties they might have looked more like Bill and Joan, another couple who came to see me. Bill and Joan were struggling (and avoiding) issues that younger couples characteristically face.

In our initial meeting, Bill blurts out his worst fears about their marriage. "We got married for the wrong reasons. I really wasn't ready to get married. I let her push me into it." Joan, twisted like a pretzel on my couch, immediately adopts a "Don't blame me again for that, it's your fault too!" expression.

For several seconds it's not clear where things are headed. Then I realize tears are streaming down Joan's cheeks. "Damn! I promised myself I wouldn't cry!" she stammers, trying to gain control, "I've . . . I've always known he never chose me. He just didn't want to give me up. I haven't been able to face it."

Bill turns beet red. "I told you I wasn't ready to get married! You know I've always been afraid to make decisions!"

The session seems to be rapidly deteriorating. And as usually happens, opportunity emerges out of nowhere. I speak to both of them, but I look at Bill. My tone is serious but not hopeless. "If you want to get over your fear of making decisions, then maybe nothing's wrong. That's exactly what your relationship is going to push you to do. I'm curious about why you're defensive about not being ready to get married and marrying for the wrong reasons. Many highly successful marriages start out that way."

Bill lowers his guard and looks interested, "What do you mean?"

"Is *anybody* really ready to get married? I doubt it. Nobody's ready for marriage. *Marriage makes you ready for marriage!*"

Bill and Joan are finally facing the secret they thought would blow up their marriage. Much to their surprise, the long feared devastation doesn't materialize. Instead, there's a reasonable answer and a potential solution to what they thought was an insolvable problem. Bill seems so locked into their pattern of interaction that he hardly notices Joan has stopped crying. She seems to see new hope—but no guarantee—of getting chosen. Instead of berating herself and Bill, she is attentive and composed.

Bill rests his elbows on his knees with his chin in his palms. His fingers hide his facial expression from me; he's used to masking his feelings. He seems surprised that the browbeating he anticipates from Joan is not forthcoming. He doesn't know quite what to make of the fact that she is sitting quietly beside him, eager to proceed.

Why did I tell Bill that highly successful relationships are often launched for the "wrong" reasons? We get married for wrong reasons because we haven't matured enough for right reasons to exist yet. Struggling with wrong reasons for *getting* married can produce right reasons to *stay* married.

What are some wrong reasons to get together? Bill and Joan had a few:

- Both of them had low self-esteem.
- Bill was afraid of being lonely.
- Joan feared meeting the world as a single person.
- Bill needed someone to take care of him.
- Joan needed someone to care for.
- They both needed to be needed.
- They both believed two people can live more efficiently than one.

I've found stunning clarity in every couple's wrong reasons: they show us who we are, where we've been and who we've been with, how we're with our partner now, and where we think we're headed. And more importantly, wrong reasons provide the means to get where we want to go.

We like to believe that "communication problems" underlie most relationship difficulties because we welcome the idea we can literally talk our way out of anything. We love the fantasy that we can "understand" and "express" our way out of our dilemmas.

But this is not what happens. Instead, in unwitting partnership, couples create emotional gridlock. Bill and Joan's relationship was like an intricate Chinese puzzle: one's movement was blocked by the other's equally stymied position. Joan complained that Bill drained her energy by having one crisis after another. Bill was furious that Joan wasn't "supportive." He demanded to be "number one" in her life. She found his neediness unattractive. He became more insecure and accelerated his demands—until they were trapped by their interlocking frustrating and frustrated needs. (In the next chapter I'll show you how Bill and Joan worked this out.)

After seeing this go on repeatedly in my office—and my own home—I've concluded that some dilemmas aren't meant to be "fixed." All problems aren't meant to be "smoothed." The solutions we seek sometimes come from living through them. We spin intricate webs until we have no way around them. We can escape the situation we've created (temporarily), but we can't escape ourselves. Our self-made crises are custom-tailored, painstakingly crafted, and always fit perfectly. We construct emotional knots until, eventually, we are willing to go *through* them. It may sound farfetched, but sexual dysfunctions are blessings to couples who use them well. In like fashion, we sometimes create situations that ask us to risk our marriage in order to receive its bounty.

Approached in this light, committed relationships become epic dramas of heroism rather than soap operas. The suffering and strife inherent in marriage are as purposeful as its delights. Hugh and Gail Prather write in *Notes to Each Other:*

> Did I pick the right person? This question inverts the starting and ending points. We do not pick our perfect match because we ourselves are not perfect. The universe hands us a flawless diamond—in the rough. Only if we are willing to polish off every part of *ourselves* that cannot join do we end up with a soul mate.

This polishing process in marriage is what I referred to earlier as *differentiation.* In a nutshell, differentiation is the process by which we become more uniquely ourselves by maintaining ourselves in relationship with those we love. It's the process of grinding off our rough edges through the normal abrasions of long-term intimate relationships. Differentiation is the key to not holding grudges and recovering quickly from arguments, to tolerating intense intimacy and maintaining your priorities in the midst of daily life. It lets you expand your sexual relationship and rekindle desire and passion in marriages that have grown cold. It is the pathway to the hottest and most loving sex you'll ever have with your spouse. Differentiation brings tenderness, generosity, and compassion—all the traits of good marriages.

Differentiation isn't a trait, however. It's a process—a lifelong process of taking our own "shape." Chapter 2 is devoted to explaining differentiation in detail. It doesn't surprise me that people have successful marriages in spite of our distortions and misguided beliefs—our will to grow and differentiate takes us beyond the obstacles we put in our own way.

Differentiation involves one of nature's basic drive springs, a fundamental life force rooted in the evolution of our species. In subsequent chapters we'll explore how differentiation weaves through the various facets of marriage in the most subtle, intricate, and beautiful ways—including the most exquisitely intense sex you've ever had. You're about to discover that sex, intimacy, and marriage are more elegant processes than you ever dared imagine.

Chapter 2

Differentiation: Developing a Self-in-Relation

Marriage, n. The state or condition of a community consisting of a master, a mistress and two slaves, making in all, two.

—*Ambrose Bierce*
THE DEVIL'S DICTIONARY

You met Bill and Joan in Chapter 1. Let me tell you more about their private world so you can see how they lived out their issues and eventually found the passionate sex and intimacy they thought was beyond their reach.

Bill and Joan got together when they were in their mid-twenties. They have been married twelve years and have two kids, aged eight and six. Bill manages several sporting goods stores in a regional chain his father developed. Before marrying Joan he had dated little and had only one sexual partner. Joan, who first had intercourse in high school, had several long-term boyfriends. After their marriage she gave up her graphic arts career to become full-time mother and homemaker.

Joan is intelligent and emotionally high-strung. Bill likes to think of himself as easygoing, but Joan sees him as too passive in dealing with his family. He is as needy and overreactive as she is, and bristles when Joan criticizes him. Bill refuses to deal with Joan when she loses her temper, which she does frequently. He quietly patronizes her or walks out of the room. He wants her to handle her anger in the way that suits him—by going along in silence.

Both find it painful to talk openly; both are smoldering underneath. Both desperately want the other's agreement and approval. Increasingly, their arguments settle nothing and fuel the next blowup. They are at each other's throats.

Bill complains that he wants more sex. Joan complains that she feels used and wants more intimacy. (Secretly, Bill is intimidated by her eroticism.) Bill thinks Joan is clinging and dependent. Joan thinks Bill is afraid of getting close. She is distant with her parents and sibs but wants closeness with Bill. He is highly enmeshed in his own family, still yearning for freedom and his father's approval. Both are upset by the way the other handles his or her parents; both want the other to do as he or she does. They have lots of fights over who really loves whom.

In retrospect, Bill and Joan had no inkling of the joys that lie ahead for them. At this point, all they see looming is more frustrating years together—or a divorce. Using their struggles to gather information and make changes is the farthest thing from their minds. They're angry at each other and angry at themselves, worried that their problems might be too serious or longstanding to solve. From the way they're bickering in my office, I can see that Bill and Joan feel terrible about their situation. But fighting and feeling inadequate aren't going to help. I ask a question that catches them by surprise: *"What makes you think you shouldn't have the problems you're having?"*

This momentarily derails the bickering. Their look quizzically at each other. "What do you mean?" Bill finally asks. "Why we *shouldn't* have the problems we have? I never thought about it! I just assumed we shouldn't."

"You're both acting like you shouldn't be having your problems. Like something's gone wrong in your marriage—or in you. You're feeling inadequate, and angry, and deprived because this isn't the way you think it should be."

"We shouldn't have this difficulty if we really love each other," Joan huffed.

"That's a pretty common belief," I reply, "and as commonly happens, now you also feel unloved and unloving."

"Other people don't have the same kinds of difficulties we do," Bill countered. Joan nodded in agreement.

"That's another common belief. The couple who left my office before you said the same thing. You've come here believing it's your disagreements that create your difficulties, but it looks to me that it's what you *agree* on that's killing your marriage: you believe you shouldn't be having the problems you do. It makes you feel bad, too."

Bill and Joan settle down briefly, but they seem to need the tumult of an argument to keep everything stable. Within a few minutes Bill is geared up again. "We could hardly keep our hands off each other when we first met. She used to be all over me. Now I'm lucky if we have sex twice a month. We only have sex when I start it—and then only *sometimes*—which really pisses me off!"

"If he spent a little time with me, it'd be more likely to happen! I probably miss it more than he does!" Bill rolls his eyes in frustration at Joan's rejoinder. He doesn't seem to notice she said she misses having sex. Instead, he keeps their interaction on the familiar turf of combat.

"I'm working overtime evenings and weekends to get the sporting goods stores ready for the holidays. Before that it was inventory. I break my ass to show up for the kids' athletics! I'd like a moment by myself, too, you know."

"I'd like some time for myself, too, you know!" Joan retorts. Turning toward me, she adds, "We really don't spend time together. We share almost nothing other than the kids."

I have a very different perspective. "What impresses me is how *much* connection you have between you! I know you feel estranged and alone, but that's what people feel when they're in the thick of a powerful emotional *fusion*. It may not feel good, but I see a strong connection between you—like two candles melting together. And as long as that's the case, maintaining your relationship and being yourself will seem to be conflicting needs, as will your need to be together and your need for time apart."

Finally, I had their attention!

Let's leave Bill and Joan briefly, so I can tell you about what's behind my last statement: I'm actually talking about the process called *differentiation*.

Differentiation: Having Your Cake and Eating It Too

Differentiation involves balancing two basic life forces: the drive for individuality and the drive for togetherness. *Individuality* propels us to follow our own directives, to be on our own, to create a unique identity. *Togetherness* pushes us to follow the directives of others, to be part of the group. When these two life forces for individuality and togetherness are expressed in balanced, healthy ways, the result is a meaningful relationship that doesn't deteriorate into emotional fusion. Giving up your individuality to be together is as defeating in the long run as giving up your relationship to maintain your individuality. Either way, you end up being less of a person with less of a relationship.

In this chapter I'll discuss several ways differentiation dramatically affects relationships. Here's the first and most important one: *differentiation is your ability to maintain your sense of self when you are emotionally and/or physically close to others—especially as they become increasingly important to you.* Differentiation permits you to maintain your own course when lovers, friends, and family pressure you to agree and conform. Well-differentiated people can agree without feeling like they're "losing themselves," and can disagree without feeling alienated and embittered. They can stay connected with people who disagree with them and still "know who they are." They don't have to leave the situation to hold onto their sense of self.

When I was a graduate student studying clinical psychology, I came across the writings of Helmuth Kaiser, a relatively unknown psychiatrist of the 1940s. He described a figure skating performance by identical twins he'd seen as a young boy in pre-war Germany. What captured his attention was not the impeccably choreographed mirror skating but the mesmerized crowd's wild enthusiasm. Precision military drill teams, synchronized swimming, and high-kicking chorus lines, he noted, had the same effect. Kaiser intuited that something about the unison involved in these performances stirred a great many people.

Eventually he recognized what it was: the fantasy of two (or more) bodies appearing to be controlled by a single mind—as if we've given up our separate identities and become part of a larger oneness. He called this a *fusion fantasy.*

Kaiser never forgot what he witnessed in that skating rink, and I never forgot Kaiser's insights. They stirred my appreciation for how our urge to actualize the injunction "two shall become one" dictates everyday interactions.

Years later, when I eventually learned about the psychological concept of differentiation, Kaiser's work was far from mind. But when you stumble upon a deep truth, it surfaces in many ways. As I helped couples work through their emotional impasses and sexual problems, I finally saw how fusion fantasies are the source of much—if not most—marital discord. The illusion that in a good marriage partners are like tightly choreographed figure skaters is impossible to live.

People like Bill and Joan who are emotionally fused are controlled by their connection. They have lost their ability to direct themselves and so get swept up in how people around them are feeling. There's room for only one opinion, one position. Differentiation is the ability to stay in connection without being consumed by the other person. Our urge for togetherness and our capacity to care always drive us to seek connection, but true *inter*dependence requires emotionally distinct people.

Emotional fusion is the opposite of differentiation. Fusion is an invisible-but-tenacious emotional connection. *Notice that the opposite of differentiation is neither connection nor lack of connection—it's a different kind of connection.* You can see this if you don't confuse differentiation with individuality, autonomy or independence. Many people make the mistake of thinking of differentiation as the opposite of emotional relationship, like this:

Think of differentiation as a "higher order" process that involves balancing both connection and autonomy, like this:

Then you can see that emotional fusion is connection without individuality.

Lack of differentiation alienates us from those we love. Emotional fusion deceives us into thinking that we're not connected and we move away in defense. But the deeper truth is that we have to move away to counterbalance the *tremendous impact* we feel our spouse has on us. Or, unable to turn away, we turn ourselves over to the connection, but it feels engulfing.

To Joan fusion seems like security. Any prospect of becoming more separate from Bill scares her. Any mention of individuality sounds to her like prodding to accept Bill's speeches about his need to get away.

"Are you suggesting we become *more* separate?!" Joan blurts out incredulously. "This makes no sense. We're already about as far apart as we could be, on the brink of divorce. I'm telling you there is almost nothing between us except our kids! There's no connection between us, no intimacy, no sex, no talking! Nothing! Don't you understand?!"

I say, gently, "Perhaps I'm saying the things I am because I *do* understand. You decide. Besides, as long as you've tried solutions that seem to make sense, how far have you gotten?"

"Nowhere!" Joan bemoans.

"Then maybe an approach that makes no sense to you in the moment might offer a new solution. Besides, what makes you think there is no connection between the two of you?"

"It sure feels that way. Sex two dozen times a year isn't much of a connection."

"A *dozen* times!" Bill insists.

"You're wrong, but it still isn't much of a connection."

This is the second time Bill overlooks Joan's subtle expression of sexual interest. I choose to make no comment about it. "At the moment, you both feel undesired and undesirable. You think your partner has no interest in you or desire to see you happy. And yet, I've rarely seen couples demonstrate just how important they are to each other as you two."

"*What?!*" Joan's initial outrage is turning into curiosity.

"You both go ballistic when your partner disagrees with you. If you were truly indifferent to each other, you'd hardly care. The very fact that you can't stand your partner's disagreement highlights the importance you place in each other." I direct myself to Bill and continue. "When Joan doesn't make sexual initiations—or declines yours—you take it personally, like it says more about you than about her. But you tell her it's about *her,* not you. [Turning to Joan] And, Joan, you tell Bill that he's afraid of intimacy and that he uses you, but you act like there's something wrong with *you* when he wants sex or wants to be alone. Granted, being so important doesn't feel as good as you'd think. But that's true of many ways you two are connected."

"I never saw it that way," Joan says, softening slightly.

"When you talk about feeling connected, you're implicitly assuming it will feel good. Connection can feel many different ways to different people. There's no absence of connection between the two of you. Many painful aspects of your relationship come from a type of emotional connection we rarely recognize: emotional *fusion.*"

When a person is emotionally undifferentiated, his or her overpowering needs for togetherness can feel like a burdensome neediness to be loved and accepted. Many people who feel this way attribute it to having had an insufficient emotional connection with their mothers or fathers. I've met lots of people who claim that their difficulties are caused by an *absence* of emotional connection. In lots of cases, however, their emotional hunger is caused by the *presence* of a compelling connection that is an emotional fusion.

"So when Bill stays away from me, that's progress? That's differentiation?" Joan's voice drips with sarcasm.

"No, what you're describing sounds more like *pseudo* differentiation. When poorly differentiated people feel the tug of their fusion, they start trying to increase physical or emotional distance to make themselves feel better. Differentiation involves the ability to maintain who you are while you're *close* to people important to you. 'I-got-to-be-me-by-getting-away-from-you' isn't differentiation because the person is unable to choose to get closer. There's a difference between choosing distance and reacting to it."

Bill is starting to fidget, so I speak to him. "I'm not saying you're doing any of this—I never use what one partner says as gospel about the other. I'm talking to your wife from her point of view. I'm not encouraging you to agree or disagree with her perceptions."

"Well, you're going to disappoint Joan," Bill says sarcastically. "She's not happy unless she is disagreeing with somebody: her parents, my parents, even our friends."

"I don't think Joan is happy when she is disagreeing, because she's so hungry for company. But being oppositional is sometimes a way to engage someone we care about—while we fight off the impulse to fuse. I've noticed you do the same with her. It sort of works, but it creates constant tension."

"I argue because at least *I* care about people!" Joan says defiantly.

"Perhaps, but let's not mascarade insecurity as virtue. You told me you feel like you disappear when other people aren't around. You described how you felt that way as an adolescent when you didn't have a steady boyfriend. It happens when Bill goes out of town or your kids need you less. Arguing can be a way of checking that the other person is still there—it serves double duty."

When we have little differentiation, our identity is constructed out of what's called a *reflected sense of self*. We need continual contact, validation, and consensus (or disagreement) from others. This leaves us unable to maintain a clear sense of who we are in shifting or uncertain circumstances. We develop a contingent identity based on a "self-in-relationship." Because our identity depends on the relationship, we may demand that our partner doesn't change so that our identity won't either.

I often use the example of people sitting around the dinner table. In well-differentiated families, people's "places" or roles are fluid. Dad doesn't have to sit at the head of the table to know he's the father. His "self" is not purely in relationship to everyone else. He can sit anywhere at the table and still know who he is.

When I mention this to Bill and Joan in mid-session, Joan sobs quietly. She realizes something new in the sullen childhood family dinners she hated. "My father always had his special chair. No one was allowed to sit in it. One day my brother did, and my father hit him across the face for 'sassing him.' It was no different when we got older. To this day, he's still ranting and raving about respect. And if one of his kids or his wife dares to think they have an intelligent thought of their own that disagrees with his, he tells us we're being disrespectful." Bill sits there quietly stewing, knowing the description fits him too.

As Joan gets over the shock of her insight I talk to her. "People whose identity is primarily dependent upon their relationship don't facilitate the development of those they love. They lose their identity when others change. In poorly differentiated families—as in poorly differentiated marriages—everyone's supposed to stay in his assigned 'seat' so someone can maintain the 'self' he's established in relationship."

"Is that why Bill always lectures our kids as if they were four years old?" Joan still has plenty of fight left in her.

"I guess Bill will have to decide for himself. Maybe it's no different from a woman whose main identity is 'mother.' She loses her identity when her kids grow up, so she gives them 'smother love' to keep them needing her."

Bill and Joan sit quietly looking at each other for several minutes, appreciating how things are starting to fit together. Bill eventually breaks the silence. "If I understand what you're suggesting, I'm not supposed to get my identity from other people."

"No, I'm suggesting that's exactly what you should be doing at this point in your development. I'm just saying that the problems you have are a predictable result."

"Well, if I'm not who people think I am, am I who *I* feel I am?"

"If you thought you were Superman, could you fly?" Bill checks me out to see if I'm belittling him and decides I'm not. He smiles and shakes his head no.

Joan picks up the gauntlet. "If I'm not my feelings, then who am I?"

"Many people assume we are our feelings. It sounds validating and accepting of feelings, but it creates other problems: if you identify with your feelings—that is, if you get your identity from your feelings—then you can't afford to have them change. You'll feel like you won't know who you are. When you have a stable sense of self, your feelings can come and go like the weather. I've seen people who have an identity as a 'hot head' start to get angry when they encounter a novel situation even though they're not really mad. Getting angry reinforces their identity and organizes whatever is unfamiliar into familiar patterns."

Joan glances briefly at Bill and then looks away. Though they're not use to this much intimacy, both are becoming more stable as the session progresses. Joan is still feisty, but less volatile. Her temporary progress is unsettling both of them a little. And then, as so often happens in treatment, Joan and Bill unconsciously play out the very thing we just talked about in session.

Seemingly out of nowhere, Joan launches into a diatribe. "I want Bill to stand by me when we are with his family! I want him to take my side in arguments with them! He becomes their *boy* more than he's my husband when we have dinner at his folks' house. I want him to choose me over them. I'm his wife!"

"You want him to stand on his own two feet?"

"No, I want him to stand on *my* side! I want him to love me that much."

"Is Bill weak?" Bill's watching me closely.

"I think he is!"

"Then why would you want him on your side?" Joan doesn't have an answer.

"Is this another example of your taking the shortcomings of the people you love as a reflection on yourself? Why would you rather believe he's refusing to do something for you that is within his abilities than the possibility that his not standing up has to do with how he perceives his own emotional 'legs'?" After a pause to let this sink in, I offer a seemingly casual comment: "By the way, why are you focusing on this all of a sudden? You were looking more comfortable a moment ago."

Joan bypasses my bid to discuss her improved functioning. "I want his primary loyalty to be with *me!*"

"A frightened man has no loyalty to anyone—except the person he's most afraid of at the moment!"

"Blood is thicker than water," is her disheartened reply. It seems Joan finds it harder to recognize her husband's frailty than to accept her own strength.

I emphasize my last point in the session because I have a clinical hunch. Confirmation comes through additional information about Bill's family. Bill's dominating father is a prosperous self-made businessman who came out of a dirt-poor family but never escaped his fears of poverty. He's used to giving orders to family and employees. Bill's mother, from an equally poor male-dominant family, defers to her husband at every occasion. She draws status from her husband and self-worth from raising her family.

Bill is the oldest of four children and the only male. His sisters' three husbands also work for the family business. Bill manages the largest store and carries executive responsibilities at the corporate central office. However, he's an equal shareholder in the corporation with his sisters. He also receives the same wages as their husbands, whose daily responsibilities in the business are far less. According to Bill's father, this is necessary to avoid "favoritism" among his children, but it certainly doesn't stop jealousy about status and money among Bill, his sisters, and their husbands.

A couple times a month, Bill's father presides over family dinners, which everyone in the extended family dutifully attends. This is where Joan wants Bill to make his "stand" for her. Actually, Joan wants Bill to stand up for himself as well. She repeatedly has watched him regress into a dutiful little boy with his father. This isn't all altruism however: Joan wants Bill to be more of a man, but she wants him to show it *her* way.

Bill usually sidesteps these issues by defending his father and bringing up Joan's family, which seems cold and distant—but no less fused—by comparison. Joan's father travels frequently on business and is emotionally unavailable when he's home. Mom holds the family together, but she's angry about never pursuing own career. Every so often she lets her children know it. Joan has an older brother whom she felt her mother preferred. She's never understood why he and Mom battled throughout his adolescence. He joined the Navy as soon as he was able and has had little contact with the family ever since.

Let me tell you a little more about differentiation so you can see how it applies to Bill and Joan's family: the term actually comes from biology, referring to the ways cells develop. All cells in your body start from essentially the same material, but as they begin to differentiate they take on unique properties and perform separate yet related functions. The greater the differentiation, the more sophisticated and adaptive the life form. More highly evolved forms of life display greater variability in response. Mammals show more variable reactions than amoebae or earthworms. Your fingerprints, voiceprint, and handwriting are examples of highly evolved uniqueness. Biologically and socially, humans represent the most sophisticated differentiation in the world.

When you have a wide repertoire of possible responses, you, your family, your business, and our species have increased versatility and adaptability. Fewer resources in well-differentiated families and marriages have to be rigidly devoted to compensate for the inability of any one member to take care of himself/herself. Conversely, there is less need for anyone to sacrifice growth or self-direction to maintain the stability of the family or marriage. Differentiation allows each person to function more independently and interdependently.

Families are like multicelled living entities, just as your body is composed of many different cells. Families gain or lose differentiation over generations according to the successful struggles of their members to develop. Looked at broadly, human differentiation is the evolutionary outcome of countless generations' struggles to mate and develop. More immediately, your level of differentiation, and that of your marriage and family, results from how well you and your parents and grandparents succeeded in becoming well-developed individuals while maintaining emotional contact with the family.

Differentiation transcends generations because it is partly about intergenerational boundaries. How strong is the emotional umbilical cord between parents and children, particularly during adolescence and adulthood? Have you had to "run away" to other parts of the country to buffer your parents' impact on you (like Joan's brother)? Have family members cut off from each other instead of separating emotionally but staying in touch? Do emotional bonds in your family choke its members development? Joan's comment that "blood is thicker than water" actually describes emotional fusion rather than loyalty. Meaningful sacrifice involves free choices rather than emotional entanglements and guilt. When families (and marriages) have the *use* of us, there's no choice involved.

In Bill's family no one is really an individual; they are like parts of a machine. Neither Bill nor his siblings act like adults with families of their own. Their lives totally revolve around the family business. Their primary identity is as their parents' children. They have little economic or emotional autonomy, and all major decisions in each household are passed by Dad for approval. Their social lives and raising their children are coordinated around Dad's preferences. Although Bill and his sisters live in different houses, they are more like a tribe, with Dad as chief.

When people pick marriage partners, it's not uncommon to pick someone whose family tried the opposite way of dealing with emotional fusion—but who was no more successful. That's what happened with Bill and Joan. Joan's family is equally undifferentiated. But instead of jumping into the emotional fusion, some distanced themselves to counterbalance the togetherness pressure. Joan's father used his job travel requirements to buffer what he felt were his wife's attempts to control him. At the same time, he needed his family to defer to him to reinforce his reflected sense of self and make him feel respected. Joan's mother turned to her son as a replacement for the emotional gratification her marriage lacked. Constant bickering was Joan's brother's way of trying to set boundaries with Mom, but it never helped him establish his own identity. Bickering also reinforced their enmeshment. He never came back after he escaped into the armed forces because he didn't really differentiate. The emotional fusion was never resolved—he probably felt controlled by his parents during long-distance phone calls. Differentiation occurs by maintaining yourself in the presence of important persons, not by getting away from them. The difference between running away and walking away after you're "unhooked" is a critical distinction.

Differentiation is more than what sets us apart from others—it determines how far apart we sit. Highly differentiated people have *strong* emotional bonds. They don't require physical distance, infrequent contact, or totally consuming careers to maintain their separate identities or moderate their reactivity to others. They're not indifferent to others—just the opposite. They can *choose* contact with others out of deep liking, without being compulsively driven toward them or away.

We Confuse Love with Emotional Fusion

We can understand differentiation and fusion from yet another perspective. Jealousy is a form of emotional fusion. At its most severe, jealousy illustrates our intolerance for boundaries and separateness from those we love. Our desire to possess our partner is inherently frustrated by the immutable fact that we are two fundamentally separate (though interrelated) people.

You can see emotional fusion in the mayhem we commit in relationships, in our inability to separate, to leave well enough alone, when we're on the edge. Our most celebrated media events are often tragic tales involving emotional fusion: Mrs. Buttafuoco with a bullet in her brain, who still "loves" her philandering husband and believes in his "innocence"; Lorena and John Bobbitt, who would rather cut it off than call off the competition; Olympic figure skater Tanya Harding's "possession" by ex-husband Tim; the O. J. Simpson murder trial.

Regardless of his other culpabilities, Simpson was guilty of emotional fusion. You can't get more graphic than putting your hand on your wife's crotch and saying, "This belongs to me!" That is, unless you kill her because she's leaving you. It's no longer unheard of that a man stalks and shoots his estranged wife while she's stopped at a red light or sitting at her desk at work. He can't let her start a new life with someone else because emotionally she's a part of him. Such a man loses himself when he loses his marriage—one of the prices of operating on a reflected sense of self.

Emotional fusion also fuels the dramas of less well-known people. Consider a case of a wife accused of cutting off her husband's testicles with a five-inch scissors. She claimed he was often drunk, abusive, and "screwing around." Both husband and wife petitioned the court to have a restraining order against her lifted so they could spend Thanksgiving and Christmas together with their three children. The husband expressed a desire to reconcile with his wife of seventeen years.

Then there's the case of a woman who pleaded with the judge from her wheelchair to drop attempted murder charges against her boyfriend. Witnesses saw him drag her down the street as she hung on to his van, slam her into a utility pole, and then back up and drive over her legs. She lost an arm, a leg, and her unborn baby as a result. The woman grabbed onto the side of the van because she wanted him to stay when he attempted to leave after an argument. Witnesses, including the woman's daughter, reported that the boyfriend held onto her with one hand as he drove her into the telephone pole. The woman, however, accused her daughter of falsifying her account "because she don't want no man in my life." When the judge refused to lift an injunction forbidding contact between the two, the woman said it made her feel like they were both in jail and kept them from putting their relationship back together. A therapist training Indiana police in family violence said this wasn't surprising, even though he characterized the assault as a severe felony just short of murder: "These people are usually not ready to face the reality of a relationship gone bad."

Don't believe for a moment that these are examples of "loving too much." Instead they illustrate how emotional fusion increases domestic violence. Divorces create legal separation and restraining orders attempt to ensure physical distance; yet, many couples fight out their emotional fusion forever by proxy in court. The chilling movie, *Fatal Attraction,* portrays the tenacity of emotional fusion in an extramarital affair. Sometimes one partner feels, "You're not going to get away from me" or the other responds as if "the enemy is coming over the walls of the fort"; sometimes both happen. When one partner responds out of emotional fusion, it usually triggers reciprocal reflexive responses from the other.

Bill and Joan also illustrate why emotional fusion is so tenacious: *borrowed functioning*. Basically differentiation refers to your core "solid self," the level of development you can maintain independent of shifting circumstances in your relationship. However, you can appear more (or less) differentiated than you really are, depending on your marriage's current state. Borrowed functioning artificially inflates (or deflates) your functioning. Your "pseudo self" can be pumped up through emotional fusion, which makes poorly differentiated people doggedly hang onto each other. Two people in different relationships can appear to function at the same level although they have achieved different levels of differentiation. The difference is that the better differentiated one will *more consistently* function well even when the partner isn't being supportive or encouraging.

Before they came to see me, Bill claimed that there was "nothing wrong" with him. As long as he had Joan's "support" and controlled how intimate they were, he functioned well on a superficial level. Joan, however, went through difficult self-doubts and depression. And when she was in her deepest depths, Bill was kinder, more considerate, and empathic. Somehow Bill seemed the more stable of the two.

But things changed when Joan emerged from her unhappiness. As she began to function more autonomously, Bill's functioning seemingly diminished. As she developed more self-respect, he became more insecure. As she needed his validation less, he feared losing her more. Still, Bill wasn't about to support or stroke Joan in ways that didn't enhance his own status or that might require him to confront himself.

Bill and Joan's see-saw pattern stems from borrowed functioning. If it looks like there wasn't room in their relationship for them both to be strong at the same time, you're right! Bill and Joan could pass "selfhood" back and forth, but there wasn't enough to go around. And if you can imagine the powerful emotional connection this "transfusion" involves, you'll understand a lot about emotional fusion.

When we need to be needed and can't settle for being *wanted,* we perpetuate poor functioning in our partner to maintain borrowed functioning. Superficially we may look like we're encouraging our partner's autonomous functioning, but in truth we suppress it on a daily basis. Borrowed functioning differs from "mutual support" because it artificially suppresses the functioning of one partner while it enhances functioning in the other. It feels good—as long as you're on the side that is inflated by the borrowed functioning.

We all experience a difference between our level of functioning when we support ourselves versus when we are emotionally supported by someone else. The wider this difference is, the more our elevated functioning is not a reflection of our "real" self—not without a partner serving as a booster rocket. We latch onto people with whom we function better. Often we call this "finding someone who brings out the best in us"—but it's still borrowed functioning.

Since differentiation is a complex process that is easily misunderstood, let me offer several important clarifications:

People screaming, "I got to be me!" "Don't fence me in!" and "I need space!" are not highly differentiated. Just the opposite. They are fearful of "disappearing" in a relationship and do things to avoid their partner's emotional engulfment. Some create distance; others keep their relationship in constant upheaval. Declaring your boundaries is an important early step in the differentiation process, but it's done in the context of staying in relationship (that is, close proximity and restricted space). This is quite different from poorly differentiated people who attempt to always "keep the door open" and who bolt as increasing importance of the relationship makes them feel like they're being locked up. The process of holding onto your sense of self in an intense emotional relationship is what develops your differentiation.

Differentiation is the ability to maintain your sense of self when your partner is away or when you are not in a primary love relationship. You value contact, but you don't fall apart when you're alone.

Differentiation is different from similar sounding concepts. It's entirely different from "individualism," which is an egocentric attempt to set ourselves apart from others. Unlike "rugged individualists" who can't sustain a relationship, differentiated folks welcome and maintain intimate connection. Highly differentiated people also behave differently than the terms *autonomy* or *independence* suggest. They can be heedful of their impact on others and take their partners' needs and priorities into account. As we discussed earlier, differentiation is the ability to balance individuality *and* togetherness.

The differentiated self is solid but permeable, allowing you to remain close even when your partner tries to mold or manipulate you. When you have a solid core of values and beliefs, you can change without losing your identity. You can permit yourself to be influenced by others, changing as new information and shifting circumstances warrant. Realize, however, that this flexible sense of identity develops slowly, out of soul-searching deliberation—not by simply adapting to situations or the wishes of others.

Differentiation doesn't involve any lack of feelings or emotions. You can connect with your partner without fear of being swept up in his or her emotions. You can evaluate your emotions (and your partner's) both subjectively and objectively. You have feelings, but they don't control you or define your sense of self.

The self-determination of differentiation doesn't imply selfishness. Differentiation is not about always putting yourself ahead of everyone else. You can *choose* to be guided by your partner's best interests, even at the price of your individual agenda. But it doesn't leave you feeling like you're being ruled by others' needs. As you become more differentiated, you recognize those you love are separate people—just like you. What they want for themselves becomes as important to you as what you want for yourself. You value their interests on a par with yours. You can see merit in their positions, even when they contradict or interfere with your own.

What I'm describing is called *mutuality.* Differentiation is the key to mutuality; as a perspective, a mind-set, it offers a solution to the central struggle of any long-term relationship: going forward with your own self-development while being concerned with your partner's happiness and well-being.

When you've reached a high level of differentiation, your view of conflict in relationships shifts dramatically. "What I want for myself versus what you want for you" shifts to "What I want for myself versus my wanting for you what you want for yourself." If you talk your partner out of what he or she wants so you can have your way, you lose. When you participate in the agendas of those you love and sacrifice out of your own differentiation, it enhances your sense of self rather than leaving you feeling like you have sold yourself out.

It might seem that Bill and Joan were destined for difficulty because of personal defects they brought into their marriage. But they were just a normal couple with no unique "pathology."

Part of marriage's elegance is that spouses *always* make ideal sparring partners. When Bill and Joan first came to see me they focused on each other's shortcomings. And like many couples getting an eyeful in treatment, they soon shifted from acting holier-than-thou to thinking they were more differentiated-than-thou. Each thought he or she was more enlightened or better developed than the other. They were confused and dismayed to learn two important principles every married person should know:

First, we emerge from our family of origin at about the highest level of differentiation our parents achieved. Our basic level of differentiation is pretty much established by adolescence and can remain at that level for life. In the process of regulating their own emotions, poorly differentiated parents pressure their children for togetherness or distance, which stops children from developing their ability to think, feel, and act for themselves. They learn to conduct themselves *only* in reaction to others.

Raising our level of differentiation is not easy. We can raise it through concentrated effort (like therapy) or crisis (as commonly occurs in the course of marriage, family, friendship, and career). In general, though, the level of differentiation in a family tends to stay relatively the same from one generation to the next. It changes only when a family member is motivated to differentiate him- or herself enough to rewrite the family's legacy. This reality differs from the popular belief that your spouse is supposed to pull you out of your family's grasp. Eventually, your partner's grasp seems most important to loosen!

Second, we always pick a marital partner who's at the same level of differentiation as we are. If partners are not at the same level of differentiation, the relationship usually breaks up early. Sometimes one partner is a half-step farther along than the other—but it's only a *half*-step. The fantasy that you're "much farther along" than your spouse is just that— a fantasy. If you and your partner argue over who's healthier or more evolved, you'll be interested in three important implications:

- You have about the same tolerance for intimacy, although you may express it differently.
- You and your spouse make splendid sparring partners because you have roughly the same level of differentiation.
- Assume you are emotional "equals" even if you'd like to believe otherwise. If you want to discover important but difficult truths hidden in your marriage, stop assuming you're more differentiated than your partner. Look at things from the view that you're at the same level and you'll soon see the trade-offs in your relationship.

Now I'd like to tell you how Bill and Joan started turning their marriage around. Eventually, they wanted to talk with me about their sex life. Their differentiation started in earnest when they looked at themselves in terms of their sexual relationship.

"What's sex like when you have it?"

"Bill tries to satisfy me . . . like he tries to satisfy everyone in his life so they'll be satisfied with him. I feel like I'm supposed to make him feel like a good lover."

"When you're having sex, how do you know when to stop?"

Bill and Joan look at each other, neither responding immediately to my inquiry. Eventually she breaks the silence. "We stop when Bill loses his erection."

An embarrassed Bill explains, "I have nothing to make love to her with. I lose my hard-on during intercourse."

"Many men with sexual difficulties avoid sex to avoid failure. But you've been complaining you can't get enough."

"I guess I look at it as Joan giving me another chance to redeem myself. You know, measure up. I feel really terrible about letting Joan down—and letting myself down too."

"I didn't know you could let Joan down with your penis. I've never seen a hard-on strong enough to support anyone. And as for needing an erection to 'make love,' how much love have you ever found in a penis?"

"I know, the little head doesn't think as good as the big one." Bill's trying to cover how bad he feels. He's also taken off guard by my response. He expects me to understand and empathize, as most people would. However, that would reinforce his belief that he should measure his adequacy and self-worth by his (loss of) erection and increase his embarrassment. Instead, I want to suggest he's going down the wrong (but common) path and prepare him for what I'm about to say.

"If you want to make love why not use the parts capable of loving—your brain and your heart—and let the rest of your anatomy follow as it will? If not disappointing Joan is important to you, let me ask: when you lose your erection, do you ever find your tongue or fingers go limp too?"

"No," Bill chuckles, surprised by my question, "I can't say they do."

"Then why do you stop pleasing Joan when you lose your hard-on if you're worried about disappointing her?"

Silence.

Joan says, "I really want to hear this one!"

More silence.

"Well . . . I guess I look pretty selfish."

"The question isn't how you look. *Are you?*"

"Maybe I am." Bill quickly changes the topic by asking questions about what could cause his loss of erection (which we'll discuss next chapter). His focus suggests he's interested in taking care of his difficulty—and indirectly, being a better partner for Joan. But when I suggest we stick to his actual experiences during sex, Bill doesn't have much to say. They leave the session with the unstated assumption that they'll try to have sex differently.

Several days later they did have sex. Bill lost his erection soon after he entered Joan (his typical pattern). Bill thought this also meant the end of sex for the night. He expected Joan to get angry and pull away—which was actually okay with him under the circumstances.

But this time our last session was fresh in Joan's mind. She thought, *I saw that split second when Bill acknowledged he was selfish. He knows he is! I'm not crazy in how I'm seeing this! I hate the way I'm always begging and willing to settle, whining like a lap dog wanting to be petted. He as much as admitted he should keep doing things to arouse me if he's really interested in my satisfaction. I don't want to end up like Mom, resentful and bitter because she didn't have the guts to stand up for herself with Dad.* She chewed on her ponderings for long, silent minutes.

Then she had another thought, half black humor and half carnal: *It was so damn obvious in Schnarch's office I couldn't believe it! At least I know one way I can relax and come! And it has been a long time!!* Joan held onto her own needs and took a step toward differentiation: she suggested Bill perform oral sex on her, like he did when they first got together.

Bill was stunned! Truthfully, he was more interested in licking his wounded ego than licking Joan. If he were truly interested in her satisfaction, losing his erection was no impediment—*if* he were willing to grow up sexually. But at this point, he wasn't. He didn't say no, he just lay there in silence until Joan got the message.

Very rapidly, Bill's refusal confronted them both with his selfishness. Normally, Joan would jump out of bed in a huff and move into the guest bedroom for several nights. But this time, she stayed in bed. She didn't make a show of moving to the far edge of the bed to get away from him, and she didn't reach out to reconcile. She lay awake in the dark, alert, saying nothing, but not letting the issue slide. The silence was deafening. Neither of them could sleep.

An hour later, Bill offered to do her orally. In between, he'd gone through lots of feelings: first he thought about criticizing the way Joan had asked him. Then he felt embarrassed and immediately assumed it was because she made him feel like he wasn't good enough—just like his father did. Then he tried convincing himself Joan was being insensitive. Finally, Bill thought about being "independent" and not letting Joan tell him what to do. He'd gone down this line of associations many times in the past.

But this time Bill sensed that he wasn't going to be able to structure their argument along these lines. Her composure, however tenuous, told him Joan knew what she was seeing, and she wouldn't forget it. He felt pushed by Joan, but something deep inside him said she was entitled to ask what she did. Although he was angry at her, he also respected the way she had stood up for herself. He sensed this was somehow a decision point in his life. He was in turmoil—and *alive*.

Joan took Bill up on his offer, but told him she wasn't interested if he really didn't want to do it. Bill made a decision and didn't hesitate from then on: he positioned himself comfortably and put his tongue on her clitoris. Waiting until Joan was ready, he then slid two fingers into her vagina—not too deep, just the way she liked. Then he tried to rub his nose with his fingers inside her, while he pressed his tongue on her clitoris with the same motion. He was never more present while going down on her.

Joan spent the first few minutes struggling with her ambivalence. But the clarity of Bill's struggle to master his own selfishness tipped the balance. In the past Joan might have cut off her nose (and her pleasure) in spite, but not this time. He wasn't just trying to buy her off. Joan's bold step had made him nauseated by his own smallness.

It was actually some of the best oral sex Joan had experienced. She thought, *If I had more of this, I'd sure be interested in sex!* That was just before her orgasm enveloped them both.

I hear about this in their next session, during which Bill adds another delightful detail: "When I got done, Joan returned the favor. At first I had a hard time letting her suck me. It took me awhile to get clear that she wasn't giving me this pleasure with the goal of getting me hard so we could try intercourse again. I realized it was for *me*."

Joan is happier and more settled than I've ever seen her. "He stopped pulling back like he usually does, trying to 'do his job' and satisfy me. He let me suck him good."

"I had this weird thought while Joan was sucking me. . . . I thought about my Dad." Bill thinks there's something wrong with him because this happened.

"Oh, *great!*" Joan is clearly kidding.

"I *said* it's weird! No matter what I do, Dad always takes credit for the business. There's no room for anyone to be competent except him. Then I thought about Joan's dad needing to sit at the head of the table.

I'm watching Joan suck me like she used to, and I thought about the power of letting someone else be competent. Is this what people mean by mind-wandering during sex?"

"I don't think it's weird at all." That's all I said.

A month later I heard about some other interesting developments. Joan called her father and asked him to lunch. Her mother objected to "being excluded" so Joan made separate plans to have lunch with her. But Mom wanted to be at Joan's meeting with Dad, which Joan refused. After a lot of turmoil, Joan's dad made plans to get together with her after his next trip. Bill also spoke up to his father during a family dinner.

In this chapter I've described differentiation and shown you a little about what the process looked like for one couple. How do you actually stop defining yourself by what others think of you or feel towards you? It took a lot of emotional stamina for Bill and Joan to make these differentiating moves with each other and then with their respective families. A lot happened between them in the weeks following the turning point—Joan's asking for oral sex when Bill lost his erection. They went through a similar showdown over their difficulty with intimacy. And Joan took a major step in her sexual development.

When the differentiation process starts, it often occurs simultaneously on many levels and in many areas. I'll tell you more about what happened for Bill and Joan in the next two chapters. I said at the outset that I help people use their sexuality to grow up and become capable of truly loving. I also said I'd offer you a way to resolve the past in the present. There's a subtle and wonderful connection between maturing sexually with your partner and differentiating with your childhood family, which in turn further increases the likelihood of reaching your full sexual potential.

Differentiation: The Most Loving Thing You Can Do

Becoming more differentiated is possibly the most loving thing you can do in your lifetime—for those you love as well as yourself. Someone once said that if you're going to "give yourself" to your partner like a bouquet of flowers, you should at least first arrange the gift!

The problem is, becoming more differentiated isn't easy. The many small steps toward core transformation involve more than a self-indulgent search to "find yourself." Solitary pilgrimages can lead to discoveries, but so can staying with your partner. The end result can bring you the best of what life offers, but that doesn't mean the process feels good. No one ever *wants* to differentiate. You'll probably do it for the same reasons most people do: differentiating eventually becomes less painful than other alternatives. It's what Gloria Steinem referred to as outrageous acts of heroism in everyday life.

So although becoming more differentiated makes your life less painful, it will not be pain-free. The very process of differentiation can be excruciating at times. Loving is both beautiful and painful. Differentiation offers the ability to tolerate it, enjoy it, and see its meaning.

Psychotherapy can do many things. It can aid poorly functioning people and assist those who seek self-knowledge. It can help us affirm ourselves, raise our self-esteem, and remove constricting guilt, doubt, and despair. We function more effectively and efficiently when we're less fragmented and bottled up. But there are many things psychotherapy cannot do. Psychotherapy can "free you up" but it can't give you joy—something Freud well understood, but which we rarely understand about Freud. We've promised ourselves paradise through self-knowledge: love, sex, and transcendence will be easy once we know ourselves and our partner. But that's often when you need to soothe your own heart and calm your own anxieties to take care of yourself. That's what differentiation offers.

By now the paradoxes of differentiation should be clear: while differentiation allows us to set ourselves apart from others and determines how far apart we sit, it also opens the space for true togetherness. It's about getting closer and more distinct—rather than more distant.

What if the key to the best sex and intimacy you've ever had with your spouse is hidden inside your marital problems? What if resolving these problems is a trial by fire that makes you capable of the kind of impassioned connection you assumed your "problems" made impossible? And what if this trial by fire is the integrity-building path of differentiation? Would you, like me, begin to wonder if there was something spiritual about the process?

Chapter 3

Your Sexual Potential: Electric Sex

Marriage is the result of longing for the deep, deep peace of the double bed after the hurly-burly of the chaise-lounge.

—*Mrs. Patrick Campbell*
(1865–1940)

I want to talk to you about the beauty in sex.

I don't plan to replicate "save the beauty in sex for marriage" lectures from adolescence. I have something different in mind: to expand awareness of our sexual potential by taking apart the very notion of "the beauty of sex." In other words, I want to take a deeply sex-positive stance by examining a superficially sex-positive philosophy.

The notion of "saving the beauty of sex for marriage" suggests that the beauty of sex . . . is *in* sex. You can extract it with the one you marry—if you're in love and technically proficient. Share it with the wrong person and you can't get the beauty out, or you damage it forever. Or so this well-worn idea suggests.

Here's my point: *there's no beauty in sex—the beauty is in people.* You can't save the beauty in sex, you have to *put* it in. We all develop inner beauty to varying degrees. Sex becomes beautiful when we bring our personal beauty to it. The issue isn't simply who your partner is, whether you're in love, or how good you can do it. It's who *you* are.

Many people resonate with this thinking. However, some don't realize they've embraced ways of approaching sexuality that make it difficult to live what they espouse. Stop for a moment and ask yourself a seeming simple question: "*At what age do men reach their sexual prime?*"

When I present this query at my public lectures, audiences on different continents call out the same answers: "Seventeen!" "Nineteen!" "Sixteen!" "Adolescence!"

Then ask yourself, "And at what age to women reach their sexual peak?"

If you're like most people I've encountered, the answers tend to be somewhat older: "Twenty-five!" "Thirty-five!" "Sixty!!" When this last response surfaces at my lectures, it's invariably from a sixtyish-looking woman who's smiling broadly.

If you, like many in the audience, think this woman is joking, you'll be delighted and surprised by what you're about to learn. If you know she's very likely speaking the truth from personal experience, congratulations! You've managed to see beyond a widely held belief that negatively affects both old and young.

Most textbooks on human sexuality, adolescent development, and family life teach that men reach their sexual prime before they even hit their twenties. Women supposedly reach their prime several years later . . . and therein lies our problem. Health-care providers make the same mistake as the rest of us: *We've confused genital prime with sexual prime.*

This is another example of the kind of distortion I discussed in Chapter 1 in which we mistake a part for the whole picture. The speed with which your body responds is only one measure of sexual prime. Your sexual peak has a great deal to do with who you are as a person. That's the point about needing to put the beauty into sex. Confusing genital prime with sexual prime illustrates how even those who believe you have to put it in can ascribe to views that interfere with living up to their beliefs—and their potentials. If you're interested in sex with intimacy, there isn't a seventeen-year-old alive who can keep up with a healthy sixty-year-old!

Think about it: if sexual intimacy has to do with disclosing yourself through sex, people who can let themselves be known have more potential for profound sexual experiences. As we'll discuss in Chapter 8, one example involves letting your partner look into your eyes and *see* you while you climax.

Then think back to what it's like being a seventeen-year-old boy—or having sex with one. It can be pretty gruesome! Initial sexual experiences are often disappointing; sometimes the best part is that it's over quickly. Most seventeen-year-olds won't look you in the eye during sex, because you might figure out who they are before they do. If they do let you *see* them, there's often not much there—there's simply not much person inside yet. I'm not saying adolescents' feelings aren't deeply felt (that's often another problem), but few will argue they're anywhere near as developed as they're going to be by the age of fifty.

For males, adolescence marks their quickest erections and shortest refractory period (the time it takes to get another erection after ejaculation). And if you want someone who can pole-vault into bed with a brain-dead erection, then an adolescent boy is hard to beat. But adolescent boys preoccupied with establishing their masculinity aren't very emotionally available in bed.

A sixty-year-old, on the other hand, has more *personhood* behind his eyeballs. Through successes and failures older people know themselves, for better and worse. They may not like everything about themselves, but they're farther along accepting who they are and aren't. They have more *self* to bring to sex, and the differentiation to disclose themselves, unvarnished. A mature man no longer needs to have all the answers in bed and is less threatened by a partner who is a sexual equal. And he can let someone *hold* him.

Likewise for sixty-year-old women. An adolescent girl worries about letting a guy "do it to her," and whom he might tell. She's trying to act sexually interesting and interested but not "easy." A mature older woman is beyond that. She'll *do* her partner *slowly*. She doesn't apologize for her eroticism. *Sexual prime* and *genital prime* occur at vastly different ages.

For many of us, the sad fact is that, according to our *own* beliefs, someone would be crazy to have sex with us! We're supposedly over the hill, sexually! We may think we accept this as an impersonal fact of life, but in truth, we're not exempt from the self-rejection lurking within normal views of sexual potential.

When I give talks, I often ask my audience, *"How many of you are actually <u>better</u> in bed now than you were when you were younger?"* Typically the auditorium fills with belly laughs and delighted surprise. Little by little, a sea of hands come up as people realize this is true for *them*. It is time for anyone over thirty to stop being intimidated by youthful "hard bodies" and stop apologizing for getting older.

When we believe that adolescence is the time of sexual peaking, we are indirectly espousing sex between strangers! This pervasive but misguided view creates topsy-turvy relationships between teenagers and adults. How can parents and educators have credibility about sex when kids are supposed to have *more* sexual potential than we do? When parents hide their sexuality from their kids, it perpetuates the myth that older people don't have sex and makes kids anticipate having as little sex as their parents *seem* to have. Why should they listen to someone who apparently has no recent firsthand knowledge of the topic? When we believe hormones run the show, we send kids the unconscious message that we don't really expect them to control their crotch while they have zits on their face. We give kids a double message: we'd like you to delay first intercourse, but we think it's impossible and you'll be giving up the best sex you'll ever have.

A hormonal model is not an accurate framework for *human* sexual fulfillment. Hormones never determine when you have sex, with whom, and what it means to you. If our models of human sexual response have no component for *intimacy* or *salience,* how do we talk about sex having "meaning" without it sounding like conservative proselytizing or religious moralizing? If we can't show our kids the dynamics of sexual desire or eroticism, how do we explain the sexual advantages of age and maturity?

If we want kids to delay first intercourse, we have to give them a meaningful reason by helping them understand what sex can be. Show them there's more involved than techniques—and much of it's developmentally beyond them. If you want credibility, tell them the truth: adolescents are not potentially missing the best sexual years of their life because they haven't started yet.

Few parents tell their kids, "Your father (mother) and I have been having sex for twenty years—and we're just starting to get it right. It takes a long time. Pay your dues."

Most people never reach their sexual prime, and those who do, don't reach it until their forties, fifties, and sixties. Profoundly meaningful sex is determined more by personal maturation than physiological reflex. *Cellulite and sexual potential are highly correlated.*

"Piece of Meat" Model of Sex

Self-rejection lurks in common views of sex, just waiting for us to get older. Normal people worry about how their bodies look and perform. Men worry about the size of their penis and the firmness of their erections. Woman worry about stretch marks, sags, and varicose veins. Aging stacks the deck against you—unless you realize that it's pushing you to completely revise how you view and live your own sexuality.

Our problem is that we have mindlessly embraced what I call the *"piece of meat" model of sex.* We idolize "tight buns" and flawless skin as the height of sexual attraction, worshipping youth as the essence of eroticism. Although we love parables like *The Velveteen Rabbit* that espouse "becoming *real* only happens after we've gotten loose in the joints and rather shabby," we forget these lovely stories the moment we take off our clothes.

Childhood, adolescence, and adulthood all have their sexual developmental tasks. While there is no advantage in letting your body go to seed, "hard bodies" are frequently emotional light-years and chronological decades away from reaching their sexual potential. The stage of adult maturity has tasks as well, but it doesn't involve "winding down" sexually. On the contrary, that's when important explorations of sexual potential can occur. Most of us aren't ready to differentiate from destructive "normal" beliefs until we're older. Isadora Duncan had it right when she wrote that most of us waste twenty-five or thirty years before we move beyond the conventional sexual lies that permeate society.

Sex *isn't* a natural function—at least, not intimate sex. Intimate sex is a natural *potential* that requires development for its fulfillment. No other species on earth requires as much time to reach full sexual maturity.

Human Sexual Potential

About 400,000 years ago, the newest portion of our brain evolved. With our neocortex, humans became nature's first experiment in *intimacy.* No other species has a neocortex like ours. Language, self-concept, and self-awareness, which make intimacy possible, come from this part of the brain. So does our capacity to impart meaning to sexual behavior, which gives us unmatched sexual *potential.* Our neocortex determines the impact of the physical stimulation we receive, how emotionally involved we are in the experience, and whether or not we reach orgasm. This fact has important—and overlooked—implications:

We are capable of reaching orgasm at relatively low levels of arousal and satisfaction. Orgasm doesn't necessarily involve satisfaction or even high arousal—just ask any man who has chronic premature ejaculation. I've treated lots of women and men who reach orgasm at only moderate levels of physical arousal, desire, and meaningfulness. They have a characteristic in common: they're married.

We are capable of profound sexual experiences not measurable by the nerve spasms or muscle contractions that create the physical experience of orgasm.

Some lucky few in Western society can experience profound sex independent of orgasm; this is a major focus of Eastern sexual approaches. You, too, can learn to do this with your partner, but it's not as simple as taking a Tantric sex course. It's not about strange sexual positions; it's about personal development, which was the original purpose of Tantric philosophy.

Western society's approach to sex has subtly blotted out any vision of our sexual potential. Without realizing it, we've lost touch with, and even given up hope for, the intimate, erotic sex that can occur between partners in long-term relationships. Two common beliefs are largely responsible (on a cultural level) for this erosion of sexual intimacy:

- *"Men trade love for sex and women trade sex for love."* This common belief reflects the fact that girls are socialized to associate sex with love and intimacy, while boys focus on genital sensations. This folk wisdom enshrines an infantile view of ourselves, confusing sexual immaturity with gender differences. The reality is that as women mature, they become more comfortable with their own genitals—they enjoy sex for their own pleasure. Meanwhile, men become more interested in intimacy and emotional connection. Actually, as men and women reach their respective sexual potentials, they become more similar sexually and more "sexually compatible."
- *"Focus on what your body is feeling."* Three decades ago a technique was developed for jump-starting the body's sexual response by teaching people to focus exclusively on their own sensations and tuning out their partner ("remove distractions"). Some therapists taught that "sex is composed of friction plus fantasy." As a result, horizontal, eyes-closed, cadaver-like sex ("sensate focus") has become our society's de facto model. Unfortunately, this approach overlooks several inherent problems: lots of people focus on sensation to avoid emotional contact with their partner. It produces "good enough" sex that subtly emphasizes genital response and orgasm. But it doesn't help couples regain the *hot* sex they may dimly remember from their courting days.

We know we're *supposed* to believe that orgasm is not the most important part of sex—it's being with your partner. Platitudes aside, it's hard to say what this more important "being together" might mean. "Normal" people with "normal" sex may have no personal knowledge of it. We're sure love and passion are important, but most of us are hard pressed to explain how or why.

The Quantum Model

Let's approach sexual potential from another perspective: *the quantum model.* This is my alternative to Masters and Johnson's deservedly famous four-stage model of sexual response.

The quantum model is similar to modern physics' quantum theory, which studies dynamic variables that specify a system's behavior. In both cases, everyday events are understood as sophisticated interactions of small energy sources. When the collection of energy sources achieves a specified condition or level, the entire system undergoes abrupt changes. Giving new meaning to the "big bang theory," the quantum model offers a multilevel view of sexual functioning—how all the complex aspects of *human* sexuality fit together. It considers many dimensions of sexual experience, including depth of involvement and profoundness of sex, intimacy, desire, and sexual style.

At its most basic, the quantum model explains how you function sexually—what's required to make your genitals "work" and reach orgasm. But its real strength is helping people go beyond utilitarian genital function. At the limits of their sexual potential, humans are capable of bringing "high meaning" to sex and integrating sexuality and spirituality in mutually enhancing ways. In short, the quantum model integrates humans' most unique capacities into sexual functioning and experience. The quantum model is easy to learn, and many people have used it to resolve sexual dysfunctions and explore their sexual potential. First I'll explain how you get your genitals to respond and reach orgasm, and then we'll explore how far you can go.

Simply put, your body works like any device that can detect electrical signals. The device reacts when a signal is sent that is strong enough for the device to detect it. The more sensitive the device, generally speaking, the more signals it can detect. There is no more sophisticated signal-detecting device than the human body.

When your body detects sexual stimulation, it responds. The key is when your body detects it. When you are *sufficiently* aroused, your genitals respond. Become more aroused and your body reaches orgasm. At their simplest biological level, genital response and orgasm are reflexes that occur whenever sufficient stimulation has occurred.

Let's develop a mental picture of how this works, so that you can use it to figure out what's going on in your own body. Think of your body as having two sexual trigger points *(response thresholds)*—one for *arousal* (genital response) and one for *orgasm,* as in Figure 1. When sexual excitement exceeds your physiological threshold for arousal, your body

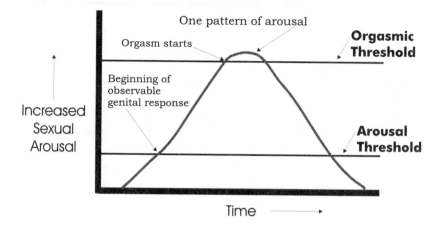

Figure 1. Sexual Response Thresholds

does what you expect: if you are a woman, your vagina becomes lubricated; if you are a man, your penis becomes erect. When your level of arousal exceeds your orgasm threshold, "your brains fall out," according to a friend of mine. We call reaching your arousal and orgasm thresholds "normal" sexual functioning.

The way your body reacts when you reach either threshold isn't very different from the way your leg kicks out when your knee is tapped at just the right spot: they are reflex actions. Except that, compared to the knee-jerk reflex, lubrication/erection and orgasm generally feel better—and make us crazier. That's why a purely "automatic response" view of human sexuality obliterates our sexual potential.

As I mentioned earlier, our species underwent some amazing changes about 400,000 years ago. Females stopped going into "heat" and started having menstrual cycles. From that momentous point on, women had year-round sexual desire instead of being receptive only when they were reproductively "ripe." Men and women started staying together longer; families, communities, and societies emerged; and a totally new part of our brain evolved—the neocortex. Scientists debate how much neocortex apes, whales, and dolphins possess, but no species matches ours and what it lets us do.

With this unique development came unique abilities—and problems. Humans became capable of talking and looking *into* each other during face-to-face intercourse. Human sexual desire now could stem from desire for a specific partner rather than just an urge to reduce sexual tension. But when our ancestors traded hormonally programmed regularity for the ability to bring meaning to sex, we became more susceptible to sexual dysfunctions and "inhibited sexual desire."

Having a neocortex is a liability if you want to be a sex machine. We use our neocortical capacity for self-awareness, which makes intimacy possible. But we can also use it to drive ourselves crazy "spectatoring," that is, watching our own performance during sex. The ability to be with your partner "in the moment" makes lack of connection diminish your satisfaction. Our neocortex has become an integral part of our sexual functioning. That's why the meanings you experience during sex strongly determine whether your body functions and how satisfying that functioning is.

Once our neocortex gave us the capability to modulate our impulses, we transcended any "biological drive" model of human sexuality. If we are going to develop the *human* in human sexuality, we need an approach that takes into account our biologically-based capacity to bring meaning to sex. That's where the quantum model can help.

In humans, sexual stimulation consists of more than exciting the senses. Usually we focus on touch and, to a lesser degree, on sight, taste, smell, and sound. But how you feel about your sensations—and how you got them—has a bigger impact on your overall arousal level than does sensory stimulation itself. In short, *your feelings have a bigger impact on genital function and orgasm than do physical sensations.* That is why learning how to touch your partner is no longer your first priority as you turn your attention to what's going on between the two of you.

We need a new mental picture of what constitutes sexual responsiveness. The *total* sexual stimulation you require to reach either your arousal or orgasm threshold stimulation is made up of the sensory (mostly touch) stimulation you're receiving from your partner *plus* your feelings and thoughts—feelings and thoughts about what you're doing, whom you're doing it with, and what it implies to you. Total stimulation is therefore more than friction on mucous membranes (as it is in more primitive species) and more than friction plus fantasy. So to restate what we said earlier: when the combined stimulation of sensation *plus feelings and thoughts* reaches your threshold for arousal or orgasm, the response you expect occurs. (As I've drawn this in Figure 2, the person is just short of reaching his or her threshold.)

Let's explore both dimensions—physical sensations, and thoughts and feelings—in order to better appreciate the sexual response we take so much for granted.

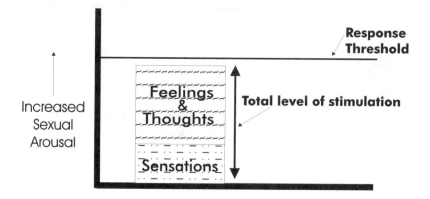

Figure 2. Components of Total Stimulation

PHYSICAL STIMULATION

The part of sex we tend to think of first—its purely physical dimension—has several components, including how much, how long, and how good the physical stimulation you receive is. Your body has to transmit the sensations from where you're being stimulated to your spine and brain and then to your genitals. Anything that interrupts or limits this transmission reduces your total stimulation—and, ultimately, your sexual function and satisfaction. Neurological and vascular diseases, hormonal imbalances, congenital abnormalities, illness and injury, prescription and recreational drugs, surgery, fatigue, and stress can all interfere with your body's ability to receive and process physical stimulation. Vascular, neurological, and hormonal problems secondary to conditions such as alcoholism, diabetes, or kidney failure can also occur. If you suspect any of these difficulties, I recommend you seek a medical evaluation. However, even if you have serious physical problems, remember the power of your mind: paralyzed people often develop new erogenous zones, allowing them to experience sexual sensations in places where they still have feeling.

Your mind also plays a role in your ability to recognize your physiological sensations. Masters and Johnson referred to this ability as "sensate focus" and many people mistakenly think it is a therapeutic exercise. It's really an innate capacity we use constantly, to one degree or another. Gymnasts and dancers develop sensate focus into fine art.

Incidentally, if you're interested in exploring your sexual potential, don't use alcohol to "loosen up." It slows down your nervous system, which means it also slows down the transmission of sexual sensations. If alcohol seems to improve your sexual functioning, it probably means you're trying to anesthetize a certain amount of anxiety. It's better to deal directly with whatever is making you anxious. As you'll see when I tell you shortly about Joan and Bill's sexual development, that's where the process of differentiation comes in handy.

FEELINGS AND THOUGHTS

The role of feelings and thoughts in sexual experience brings the marvel of sexual potential to light. Consider this: some of us experience better erections or lubrication when we are "giving" to our partner than when we are in the "receiving" role. That's because giving lets us avoid feeling guilty about receiving or relieves us of the expectation (pressure) to become aroused simply because we are being touched. *Emotional* stimulation is often a more powerful determinant of genital function and satisfaction than is touch.

The impact of thoughts and feelings on sensory awareness shows up in many ways. Sensations have to be organized, so to speak, into a pleasurable experience. If you're upset, angry, or can't stop thinking about other things, it's hard to imbue your sensations with meanings that add to your pleasure and arousal. You're likely to find the sexual things that usually "work" don't have much impact at these times. If you experience your sensations as chaotic or upsetting—like realizing you're getting aroused in inappropriate situations—the sensations usually become less arousing and the likelihood of genital response and orgasm diminishes. (If you're turned on by the idea of "breaking the rules," however, the same sensations can become highly arousing. That's the case in exhibitionism, fetishism, and some forms of sexual abuse.)

Another source of impact comes from your evaluation of the sexual encounter itself. The meaning of the experience needs to "agree" with who you are. It's not as simple as some situations being inherently better than others—what's important is how the encounter "fits" you. The quality and depth of your connection with your partner, how deeply involved you are in the encounter—even whether you like sex better in the dark or with the light on—all enhance or diminish your physical sensations.

Any unresolved emotional issues will further affect your physical responsiveness. For example, some people function better in a loving context even when the physical stimulation isn't great. If you have difficulty with intimacy, on the other hand, you may feel better if you receive the same sexual stimulation from a casual partner in a one-night stand. People who fear being controlled may experience sexual difficulty in committed relationships but not with uncommitted partners. People who fear rejection might display the opposite pattern.

Clearly, emotional issues have a direct physiological impact on sexual functioning. Generally, the more unresolved issues that intrude during sex, the further away you are from your sexual potential, because these issues limit your sexual preferences and pleasure: you can relax, focus, and enhance the physical stimulation you're receiving only when it fits your dynamics. You might still be able to reach orgasm, but your satisfaction is usually diminished. What's going on in one dimension can add to or take away from the other, potentially increasing or decreasing your total level of stimulation. For example, "poor technique" under the right circumstances can lead to orgasm; the same technique, perceived differently, does not. Notice that what we're saying here negates common notions like "giving someone an orgasm" or "making someone come."

A woman came to me because she was having difficulty getting aroused. When she first met the man she later married, she found endearing the shy and clumsy way in which he touched her clitoris. She could reach orgasm even though he didn't stimulate her in the way she liked. It was fairly easy for her to reach orgasm (low orgasm threshold), and she figured he'd improve with time. Several years into marriage, however, he hadn't. The same physical technique now made her angry and frustrated. She perceived his touch as selfish and lazy, and she no longer could reach orgasm with him. (She remained orgasmic during masturbation.) Their first therapist, who tried to find out "what had changed," could never explain her problem. The real problem was that *nothing* had changed as far as she was concerned! Her confused and defensive husband claimed it must be *her* problem, because he was just doing "what's always worked"!

Many things can interfere with getting enough stimulation to reach your threshold. Keeping the right ambiance both in the room and in your head can be difficult. Consider all the issues you bring to bed in the context of your level of differentiation. Anxiety can have lots of different effects, depending on its intensity and how you perceive it. Massive performance anxiety or serious concerns about your relationship can kill the best touch—both physically and emotionally. Low-level anxiety, however, sometimes helps sex by focusing your attention on the encounter. (Low-level anxiety is why sexual novelty can be so enticing.) One problem in becoming *too* comfortable (emotionally fused) with your partner is that you become sexually bored, which reduces your total stimulation.

We're only just beginning to understand the complex ways anxiety affects sexual functioning and satisfaction. Moderate anxiety, which we experience as tension rather than novelty, can interfere with sexual function. Quite commonly, however, it does not—it only interferes with satisfaction. Many of the couples I see have no idea how much tension exists while they have sex because it's there every time they do it. Lacking any other experience as a reference point, or a symptom such as sexual dysfunction, they have no inkling of the anxiety that exists and how it impairs their emotional connection or sexual satisfaction. Only when they begin to have sex that is both more intense *and* more relaxing than they've ever experienced do they realize, in retrospect, what they've missed of their sexual potential. Only then do they realize how tense they've been all along. (I'll show you how to accomplish this when we discuss *hugging till relaxed* in Chapter 6.)

Your partner's feelings also affect your feelings as well as your sexual functioning and satisfaction. Human sexuality is that subtle. Think of what happens when you're aware that your partner is bored, uninvolved, unaroused, or needs you to reach orgasm to prove his competency. Regardless of how much he touches you, you can't seem to get enough stimulation to trigger an orgasm. That's because the "message" underlying the experience diminishes the impact of the sensations.

When your total stimulation drops below your arousal or orgasm threshold, the corresponding sexual response stops or fails to occur altogether. That's how some dysfunctions seem to come and go. A man may lose his erection just as a woman may become dry midway through sex that seemed fine at the outset. Either gender can have difficulty reaching orgasm with a particular partner or in a certain setting. When total stimulation once again reaches your threshold, the problem seems to go away. The psychological causes of sexual difficulties are as diverse and unique as people themselves. It may be that several small things collectively diminish your feelings and sensations.

Let's see how this works using the sexual problem of the couple we discussed last chapter. We can now explain why Bill loses his erection during intercourse: once intercourse starts, he feels it is time to "put up or shut up" and his anxiety skyrockets. The adrenaline pumps in his veins and he feels acutely inadequate. With dread he anticipates failure and on some level senses Joan's anxiety as well. He hardly notices that his skin is clammy with sweat. Regardless of how aroused he was just prior to intercourse, these factors reduce his total level of stimulation below his arousal threshold once he inserts his penis. No matter how much he thrusts, the physical stimulation is no match for the negative effects of his thoughts and feelings.

Many of us develop "minimalist" sexual styles: we know how to generate just enough total stimulation to reach our thresholds. But sexual potential isn't about merely reaching your threshold. It's about going far above it. Getting defensive about whether you're "good enough" in bed keeps you perpetually vulnerable in the sexual arena, because you settle for "what works." If you can get aroused and reach orgasm the way you usually do it, you might challenge, *why change?* Here's the answer: all you need is a minor variation in touch or meaning to reduce total stimulation below your threshold, and *voila!* Sexual dysfunction! Pursuing your sexual potential makes you less like an accident looking for a place to happen.

After years of working with people with serious medical illnesses and injuries, I've learned how difficult it is for people to make this shift when they *need* to. Although it's often possible to make adaptations that would permit continued function and/or satisfaction, many physically and emotionally challenged couples can't make the shift quick enough to keep their sex intact when they need it the most. Pursuing our sexual potential is prophylactic treatment for us temporarily able-bodied people.

Actually, without realizing it, when a problem arises, most of us will automatically capitalize on the fact that sensations *and* feelings determine our total level of excitement. We compensate for something going wrong in one dimension by enhancing the other—to avoid having to deal with the real problem. I'm reminded of an elegant example: a man who had premature ejaculation married a woman who could have "mental orgasms." Women with this ability can optimize their feelings and thoughts (including very vivid fantasy) until they reach orgasm with little more than tensing their thighs. The wife in this example, blessed with a low orgasmic threshold, could reach orgasm within moments anytime she wished. For years, her husband ejaculated seconds after entering her. She would then bring herself to orgasm several times. She begged him to seek treatment to prolong his ejaculatory control, but he refused. They both came for treatment when she filed for divorce. In our first session the wife expressed her frustration with her husband's rapid ejaculation and his inconsiderateness in not seeking treatment. "Inconsiderate?!" her husband exploded, "Every single time we had sex, *you* had an orgasm! What more do you want?"

Aging and Sexual Potential

As you age, feelings and thoughts must replace biological drive and sensory awareness as the major determinants of your sexuality. Exploring your sexual potential isn't just easier to do; it's a necessity if you want to keep sex a vital part of your life as you get older.

If you're dependent on sex drive to get you started, you will inevitably discover that sex tends to drop off as you age. Couples attending our Couples Retreat have reported this problem. Both men and women had been highly sexually active in their youth, but without much emotional investment in their partner. During the retreat, as they harnessed their capacity for intimate connection and desire for their spouse, they experienced more eagerness and anticipation in having sex.

Masters and Johnson did a wonderful job researching how both men and women need more genital stimulation to experience arousal and orgasm as they age. Men may need longer to reach a full erection, and their ejaculations are not as intense. Menopausal women can experience reduced sensitivity to touch. But the impact of aging starts earlier and more subtly than many people realize. The decrease is gradual, often imperceptible at first. People in the prime of life may begin to notice that their sexual sensations and genital functioning are subtly changing . . . for the worse. Although the changes are hard to describe and embarrassing because we think they are not supposed to happen until we're much older, sex *feels* different.

Men who struggle with rapid ejaculation throughout their youth often enjoy "lasting longer." But men who spend years delaying their ejaculation by thinking of something else (reducing their total stimulation) get good at it—unfortunately, so good that the level of total stimulation they usually experience cannot reach the increased stimulation they need as they age (higher response thresholds). The result is self-induced erectile dysfunction, and it's a lot more common than most men—including urologists—seem to understand.

When our response thresholds begin to rise, we start withdrawing into our own little world during sex, isolated by our fears. The resulting decreased personal contact further diminishes total stimulation, although the impact may go unnoticed if we're not used to emotional intimacy. Full-blown genital dysfunctions and diminished sexual desire may follow.

How do these unappealing realities fit with my saying that people don't generally reach their sexual prime until their fourth, fifth, or sixth decade? Sex at the limits of one's sexual potential can more than offset higher thresholds. Older men and women often report the strongest orgasms and the most meaningful sex of their lives. The very time when many couples despair of ever reconnecting in sex is actually when they can—and need to—make important shifts in their sexual development. Aging is not the inevitable downward sexual spiral we have learned to expect with dread.

Many aspects of your feelings and thoughts can more than offset declining hormonal drive and reflexive responses—if you're willing to grow up sexually. I'll briefly mention three: *eroticism, desire,* and *emotional union.*

EROTICISM

If sex drive is the instinct that preserves the species, then eroticism is the experience of sexual pleasure for its own sake. Eroticism is what turns you on. It makes sex personal, electric, and—well, *sexy.* Eroticism lives in the tone and nuance of sex, the way you engage your partner. It's about "where your head's at" more than what your genitals do and what shape your body is in. Eroticism is a large part of your sexual potential. Remember, you don't "save the beauty of sex"; instead, you have to put beauty into sex. Embellishing sex with your eroticism can give new meaning and pizzazz that adds to your pleasure and arousal as well as your spouse's. As you'll see in later chapters, that's not for the faint of heart.

DESIRE, PASSION, AND LOVE

The misguided message of "save the beauty of sex for marriage" also contains an element of truth: humans have evolved the capacity for love; it's wired into our sexuality. It's a feeling that contributes to your overall arousal—and thus to your sexual functioning and satisfaction. Passion and desire for your partner contribute to your total stimulation in the same way. I'm not proselytizing against sex with casual partners, nor denying that it can include fondness and caring and the thrill of someone new. However, the deeper and more meaningful the level of connection—and the more emotional energy you bring to your encounter—the greater the contribution to total stimulation. We'll discuss this further in Chapter 9, when we consider psychological dimensions of sexual experience.

I'm talking about sexual desire as one source of energy contributing to total stimulation rather than as a biological drive that motivates you toward sexual behavior; that is, I'm talking about desire *during* sex rather than desire *for* sex. The important issue is passion (high desire). When you're exploring your sexual potential, you're no longer focusing on whether or not you have enough motivation to get started. The kind of desire we're discussing comes from maturation rather than infatuation. It's one reason I say cellulite and sexual potential are highly correlated.

EMOTIONAL CONNECTION

Emotional connection is a powerful contributor to high total stimulation. When it's missing, its absence can have a correspondingly devastating impact. That's why I help couples make a deeper emotional connection during sex. This often involves changing their basic sexual strategy. Actually, Ken and Karen (whom you met at the outset of Chapter 1) clearly demonstrated doing this.

By and large, we tend to view sex as an activity that produces a feeling. In the sexual crucible approach, however, partners begin with their feeling of connection with each other and learn to express that feeling through different sexual behaviors. They learn to follow that connection and let it determine what they do sexually. This requires self-discipline and willingness to follow what's happening in the moment as well as a greater sense of self, because there's no technique or sequence to follow. They "simply" follow the connection with their partner right into the unknown.

When I'm working with a couple, I listen to the details of their sexual interactions and track their level of connection. I listen for how they initially make contact (if they ever do), when they lose the connection, and what they do when they lose it. *How you handle losing the connection is always related to your level of differentiation. It is a window into the same differentiation issues that block other areas of your relationship.* I never know what the specifics will be, but the pattern is always the same. In fact, it's so reliable I show my clients how to use it: tracking when they make and break their connection, what happens when they do, and how this sequence reflects their basic relationship difficulties. I'll show this to you in Chapter 5, 7, and 8.

Joan's Self-Mastery

Now I can explain how Bill and Joan took care of his erection difficulty. Actually, it was part of a constellation of dramatic changes in their lives. Their landmark "oral sex night" led Joan and Bill to reexamine their sexual relationship. Both complained that it was dull. It turned out that more than Bill's difficulty with erections shaped their predictable routine. When they had sex together Joan was only able to reach orgasm by using a vibrator, legs together and eyes closed. They culminated almost every sexual encounter this way.

Proud of having stood up for herself, Joan brought up another topic she might have otherwise ducked: she wanted to experience orgasm during intercourse—without additional clitoral stimulation—what's sometimes called "hands off" intercourse. I pointed out that only 30 percent of all women can reach orgasm this way, which surprised her. Like many people, she thought this was the way most ("normal") women did it.

Most people think a woman's vagina is the equivalent of a man's penis. It's not—the woman's clitoris is. Just because humans evolved the same "insert tab A in slot B" way of reproducing as other mammals, that doesn't mean vaginal intercourse is the easiest or best way for women to reach orgasm. We rarely realize that heterosexual intercourse is the equivalent of the man sticking his penis in his wife's "scrotum"—because that's the part of a man's anatomy that's equivalent to a woman's vagina! The fact that some women come during intercourse bears witness to the incredible power of female eroticism. But why use it to drive the remaining women—and their partners—nuts?

As I learned more about Joan's sexuality, a common pattern emerged. In contrast to her description of herself as someone who reached orgasm only with great difficulty, she was actually the opposite: she had started masturbating as a child and became quite proficient. She could bring herself to orgasm with creativity and gusto when she didn't have company. Moreover, she knew from adolescence that she could come "grinding" fully clothed in the back seat of a car. And when Bill was willing to "go down" on her, she reached orgasm within a minute or two.

Without realizing it, Joan had a mental dialogue going on inside when she had sex with Bill, and the emotional "noise" so detracted from her total stimulation that she could hardly reach orgasm. When she drowned it out with her vibrator, she climaxed like someone finally cresting a hill. When she treated herself right during sex by herself—literally maintaining a relationship with herself—she could reach orgasm easily.

Joan was a perfect example of untapped sexual potential—and of how unresolved issues, rather than true preferences or what works best, determine sexual style. Given what she'd already demonstrated, it seemed likely that she could reach orgasm during intercourse. As details emerged, a more personal—and understandable—picture took shape:

although she liked sex and knew how to reach orgasm, she was just beginning to mature sexually.

For example, Joan had hesitantly tried intercourse in the "female superior" position only five times in her life. Women who can orgasm during intercourse often find this position easiest. The position was still new and awkward to Joan in several ways: she hadn't yet integrated this pattern of physical and emotional stimulation into an effective mental framework. She had avoided being on top because it was "too revealing"—in my terms, it might expose her sexual immaturity. She preferred male superior or rear entry intercourse because then, she felt, "Bill is responsible for moving and doing it right."

For Joan, mounting her partner became a landmark in her sexual development—and her differentiation. At first she was happy with herself just doing it, even though she was awkward. She used the "up-down" movement Bill preferred. She had yet to experiment with grinding pelvis-to-pelvis in a circular movement, the way many women prefer. This pattern of progress—from "just doing it," to doing it without anxiety, to eventually relaxing and *feeling* her way through it—is a common path of sexual maturity and differentiation.

Eventually, Joan "held onto herself." She dared to move the way *she* wanted when she was on top. She stopped trying to prove herself with her sexual response—or Bill's either. She "got a hold" of her fears that she wouldn't come and would look inadequate. She allowed herself to move in new and unfamiliar ways, giving herself the acceptance and freedom to experiment. In other words, *she soothed and maintained herself in close proximity to her partner.* It required what I call a "differentiating move." In this case, Joan did it with her hips.

None of this was lost on Bill. Lying on his back so Joan could move *her* way gave him something to focus on besides losing his erection. When he wasn't trying to insert his penis, balance, kiss, thrust, and sustain rhythm, Bill found (for some strange reason) that his anxiety diminished. The first several times they tried this new position, he still worried about it, and he lost his erection after five or six minutes—but both he and Joan noted it was longer.

Eventually a time occurred when Joan's movement suddenly didn't feel wooden to him. He actually *felt* her! Bill looked up at Joan in wonderment and curiosity. Suddenly she saw his expression. Joan *knew* Bill was "in" the experience with her. "Hi!" she said, soft and friendly from deep in her throat. She smiled and rolled her hips. Bill rolled his eyes. They laughed. Then they realized they'd been having intercourse for almost fifteen minutes! Although he didn't know it at the time, the impact of this shared moment would carry Bill through their worst moments yet to come.

Let's look at this in terms of the quantum model. The shift in positions, sensations, feelings, and meanings was enough to keep Bill's total level of stimulation above his arousal threshold while they had intercourse. This significant shift can be further dissected into three parts: (a) the increased jolt of eroticism from their emotional connection, (b) Bill's increasing ability to receive stimulation and enhance it with an aura of integrity and respect, and (c) less pleasure-destroying anxiety. Moreover, Bill's reduced anxiety also meant he could receive more stimulation before he reached his orgasmic threshold. Joan and Bill had intercourse for longer than ever before, tangible proof of their respective successes. Sex now was like literally making love.

Exploring Your Sexual Potential

Now we can use the quantum model to understand the full breadth and depth of your sexual potential. It builds upon what we've said about differentiation and provides a foundation for everything we'll discuss in subsequent chapters: the different dimensions of sexual experience; your personal sexual style; integrating sexuality and spirituality; creating meaningful, mind-blowing sex, and more. Exploring your sexual potential brings your most unique human capacities to lovemaking.

It's possible to raise your total stimulation far beyond what it takes to orgasm. The goal is not a bigger or extended orgasm, because that's still linked to body function. We are all capable of profound sexual experiences for which there are no known physiological thresholds. No doubt one day medical science will find physical processes that correspond to this experience. But don't hold your breath. No one's explained physiologically how we send and receive sexual "vibes"—but that doesn't stop us from doing it.

Pursuing the goals I'm about to outline can help you resolve sexual dysfunctions and low desire and boost your total level of stimulation. The issue is not whether any one area is a "problem" for you; it's how far you can take each recommendation. In this pursuit, you may discover vast unexplored parts of your sexual potential.

But don't drive yourself crazy thinking you should be working on— or have achieved—each one of these goals. These are not the new yardstick by which to measure yourself and feel inadequate. The point is that the more undeveloped aspects of your sex and intimacy you can identify, the more options you have and the farther you can go in enhancing your sex life. All of these goals are more easily said than done, and they're certainly not things you can do all at once. Reaching your sexual potential doesn't occur until late in life because it takes time to work on the many elements that contribute to your total level of stimulation. It also takes a great deal of personal development.

Throughout the rest of the book I'll show you how to accomplish these goals. The five chapters of Section Two will be particularly helpful. Give yourself time to read and digest this material. Pursuing your sexual potential by addressing these issues is not to be taken lightly:

- *Deepen your emotional involvement "in the moment" and optimize the depth and breadth of connection with your partner.* This is the route taken by Karen and Ken, whom you met in Chapter 1. They did this by realizing how little they were "together" during sex and sharing their thoughts while they made love.
- *Broaden the repertoire of sexual "tonalities," styles, and meanings you can use to engage your partner, and increase the duration and variability of your encounters.* Bill and Joan took this path. For them, it involved behaviors and patterns they normally didn't do, like Joan getting on top during intercourse and Bill going down on her after he'd lost his erection. Notice that this and the previous point (and the points that immediate follow) aren't mutually exclusive. We just finished describing the way that Bill and Joan became more deeply connected "in the moment" when she let herself experiment with moving her hips as she liked.
- *Reduce anxiety that interferes with pleasure and connection, increase pleasure-facilitating anxiety (novelty), and reduce situational distractions.* Having an orgasm while you and your partner look into each other's eyes (Chapter 8) usually provides loads of novelty. The point is not eyes-open orgasms per se; rather, it's an example of an intimacy-based approach to reaching your sexual potential.
- *Expand the emotional energy you exchange with your partner through displays of eroticism and sexual "vibes."* Expanding the psychological dimensions and sexual styles in which you and your partner can connect (Chapter 9) is one way to do this. So is *doing* your partner, *being done,* and *fucking* (Chapter 10).
- *Enhance your anxiety tolerance and your ability to soothe your own frustrations and disappointments.* Since this has such important implications for the quality of your sex life—and your life in general— you'll find two chapters of suggestions for how to do it: *hugging till relaxed* and *self-soothing* are discussed in Chapters 6 and 12.

- *Resolve underlying tensions and marital issues, and increase your capacity for desiring and loving your partner.* Each remaining chapter will illustrate a couple doing exactly this. Chapter 14 discusses the poignant realities of love and loss that all couples face.

Notice that each one of these points involves differentiation in one way or another. Making these changes stretches you, but the good news is that increased differentiation makes it easier to handle problems in these areas. Differentiation makes you less intimidated by sexual problems and better able to explore your sexual potential. And exploring your sexual potential in an emotionally committed relationship raises your differentiation.

Wall-Socket Sex and Sexual Potential

What does sex look like at the limits of one's sexual potential? Some people refer to it as *wall-socket sex.* (I first learned this term from my clients.) Wall-socket sex aptly describes the sustained electric jolt of sex on the boundaries. Some people think the term crudely refers to plug-in-and-pull-out "wham-bam, thank you, ma'am" sex—but it's just the opposite. Wall-socket sex involves physical and emotional union in the context of consuming mutual desire, heart-stopping intimacy, and deep meaningfulness. It includes multiple levels of psychological involvement and taps all capacities that are uniquely human, including mutuality, integrity, and spirituality.

Not only is wall-socket sex more than genital response or orgasms, but it often occurs independently of either one. (I'm not saying there's anything wrong with orgasms. I'm rather fond of them myself.) Paradoxically, some people are so taken the first time they experience this kind of sex that they can't reach orgasm. Initial experiences of wall-socket sex can be disquieting when you've spent decades having sex with your spouse without it. Even clients who tell me sex has been a strength in their relationship are shocked and tearful when wall-socket sex finally happens.

It's particularly striking when older people have wall-socket sex because our "piece of meat" model of sex suggests otherwise. Ironically, old age is when it's most likely to happen. Wall-socket sex offers other "shocks": you have intensely erotic intimate experiences that seemingly arise "out of nowhere." And you experience the confusion of watching yourself withdraw from the intense sex you *thought* you wanted. If you've experienced any of the following, you already understand why wall-socket sex is an adults-only event:

- Time stops.
- External reality fades; there is a sense of being transported to another place and time.
- Your consciousness changes, so that, for example, separate acts blend into a single prolonged event. A million delights merge into one.
- Boundaries between you and your partner shift or cease to exist. You *feel* your partner next to you—without touching—as if your bodies are intermingled. Your skin feels open, your pores enlarged.
- Your emotions appear on your partner's face. You see your essence embodied in your partner. He or she knows exactly how to touch you. S/he moans at the exact instant everything seems transcendentally perfect to you.
- Your partner's face "melts," taking on unusual or unexpected emphasis and character.
- You watch your partner undergo age changes. You know exactly what he or she looked like in childhood, or will look like when older. You *see* the child and parent in your partner.
- Profound mutual caring and joy overflow the bond between you. You're moved to tears, appreciating other people past and present, and what it means to be human.

In more rare and esoteric experiences clients have reported "seeing" music or "hearing" feelings (called "synesthesias"). Or an aura, glow, or electricity seems to radiate from their skin. Is it hard to believe we create energy, joy, and beauty beyond the norm through profound sexual union? It's an extreme form of the way your feelings and those of your partner dramatically affect whether you reach orgasm.

If wall-socket sex is unsettling, why do some of us pursue it? In *Constructing the Sexual Crucible,* I suggested an explanation:

> The quest for unfulfilled sexual potential is akin to the quest for excellence in sound reproduction. The pursuit of experiential realism in high-fidelity sound systems is disproportionately expensive, elusive, and difficult to document by scientific measurement. Yet it is the most *salient* portion of the experience to the true stereophile, who willingly spends every penny in pursuit of his or her subjective experience.

The vast majority of people make do with perfectly adequate, moderately-priced sound systems. Without the opportunity for side-by-side comparison, they are satisfied. Even upon initial exposure, the novice is unlikely to discern the subtle differences that mean everything to the person with a developed ear. The stereophile thinks most people don't know what they are missing. The normal individual thinks the stereophile is a nut. Appreciation of sound reproduction, like sexual potential, is an acquired taste and a matter of perspective. Some people enjoy their orifices more than others.

Wall-socket sex is transforming: it changes the way you see life. It challenges your identity and self-worth. It can leave you feeling like a stranger in a strange land of erotic wonders. You feel like you're undergoing another puberty—as transformative as adolescence but nothing adolescent about it—because it pairs intense sexual responsiveness with increased maturity, self-understanding, and self-control. Experiencing wall-socket sex with a long-term partner is a mile marker in your differentiation and also the means to enhance it.

Sexual Transcendence

Forces at work in modern society bode well for greater awareness of sexual potential: AIDS raises everyone's interest in sustaining sexual desire with one long-term partner, and critical issues confronting growing numbers of handicapped and elderly people are the same ones we all face in exploring our potential and enhancing differentiation—detaching self-esteem from our bodies and lifestyle and developing an *anatomy-independent* identity and self-acceptance. The main issue in sexual maturation isn't "use it or lose it." The issue is *grow up* or *give up!*

Sexual potential is a lifelong pursuit. Like heroes and heroines on mythic quests, we have to master ourselves in situations that frighten us: struggling with the mythic dragon—our partner—to become fully human and transcending ourselves in the process.

Where does pursuing one's sexual potential ultimately lead? If thousands of years of Eastern culture are any indication, it can lead to self-transcendence and spirituality. But confusing eroticism with sexual behavior, Western society has gotten bogged down in questioning how much sex we should have—and with whom we should have it. For all our "sexual liberation," we've made sex profane by keeping it mundane.

Without some positive spiritual direction, sexual novelty eventually degenerates into boredom and emptiness.

But one pitfall in discussing wonders of human sexual potential that may be currently beyond you is that you may feel inadequate or despair of ever tasting these yourself. This can seem intimidating to couples who struggle to just make contact during sex or resolve their sexual dysfunctions or low desire.

After talking with thousands of people at public presentations and professional workshops, while teaching in medical school, and during two decades of clinical practice, I've concluded that lots of people are bored and frustrated with their sex life. Many of us are living proof that reaching orgasm isn't inherently soul-satisfying. That's why I refer to those who experience sex and intimacy at the limits of human sexual potential as the Blessed Few. And remember, the beautiful things described above don't happen every time you have sex, even if you're one of the Blessed Few.

Don't worry if you're not there now. You're not inadequate if you're not—remember, by definition, the Blessed Few are not "normal." (Being "abnormal" can be lovely sometimes—but it's not easy.) This whole chapter has taken the opposite position: few of us have the capacity—or the time—to do this when we're young. Maybe it hasn't happened yet if you're older—but now is when it's most likely to. I'll show you how this happens in subsequent chapters.

Although the limits of human sexual potential may seem mystical, the process of getting there isn't. Think back to this chapter's starting point: you have to *put* the beauty into sex—and that beauty develops in us slowly. As we discussed, it often happens later in life—much later than we anticipate.

Wall-socket sex is potentially available to everyone—not just for "beautiful bodies" or double-jointed contortionists. It's not about how your body looks or how you position it, it's about your frame of mind and emotional connection with your partner. It's not about frequency of sex; it's about eroticism. It's not about technique; it's about integrating your head, heart, and spirit with your genitals.

At the end of Chapter 1 I promised you a trip down the sexual road less traveled. Every journey starts with a first step. Next chapter, we'll take a new path through the world of marital intimacy.

Chapter 4

Intimacy Is Not for the Faint of Heart

Marriage is the waste-paper basket of the emotions.

—*Sidney Webb (1859–1947)*
Attributed by Beatrice Webb, his wife

How can you tell the married couples in a restaurant?
I've posed this question to audiences in different cultures and the response is always the same: there's a long pause for introspection, then the sudden realization, "They don't talk to each other!"

"And how do you know the couples who are dating?" The universal answers come quick, now that they've got a frame of reference. "They talk to each other!" "They look into each other's eyes!" Some responses sound wistful. "They touch!!" "They still drink beer together!" (That last one rang a bell with many Australians, although it was new to me.)

Too often new couples talk nonstop while long-married couples sit in silence. As we discussed in Chapter 2, when you haven't achieved much differentiation, you depend on validation from others and you look in their eyes for your sense of self. When you're dating, conversation is designed to reduce anxieties about being rejected and keep open the possibility of a lasting relationship. You search for commonalities and things you agree about. Discussing differences can create awkward silences—not a great strategy if you want a second date. Young couples gab like magpies because they're stroking and reinforcing each other in their quest for commonality and union.

The next question I ask audiences is *"Why aren't the married couples talking?"* Responses are usually slow again. Audience members seem to be thinking, *"Why don't we talk?!"* The answers trickle in. "They have nothing to say to each other." "They've said it all." Some are more idealistic: "They know each other so well, nothing needs to be said."

Then I point out that the silence is more often icy cold than warm and relaxed. This is not the quiet of long-term intimates. Immediately, people see what I'm driving at: we experience this marital silence as alienation and failed communication.

Ask yourself the same question: *"Why aren't the married couples talking?"* If you're married, you know from personal experience that "they've said it all" isn't true. Important things are yet to be said—so why do they remain silent? When I ask this question a second time, a few in every audience eventually call out a difficult truth: *"They don't want to hear what the partner has to say!"*

Now here's the million-dollar question: *"How do you know you don't want to hear what your partner has to say?"* The answer is: *"Because you already know!"* What we call "lack of communication" is often just the opposite: if you truly "can't communicate," you wouldn't know that you *don't* want to hear what your partner has to say. The silence of married couples is testimony to their *good* communication: each spouse knows the other doesn't want to hear what's on his or her mind!

Intimacy, Communication, and Validation: Apples, Oranges, and Pears

While writing *Constructing the Sexual Crucible,* I read almost everything written on intimacy in various psychological disciplines. I found that many notions of intimacy grow out of abstract academic inquiry or research on short-term low-level intimacy. Often the findings just don't apply to marriage (or therapy). Practical understanding of how intimacy ebbs and flows within ongoing relationships is only just emerging.

What we do know about intimacy is that it hinges on our capacity to make self-other distinctions. Self-disclosure involves a capacity for self-awareness, self-reflection, and complex language. In humans, all these processes are mediated by the neocortex. Intimacy is a relatively unique phenomenon within the animal kingdom—something we share with few other species (if any), and one that's singularly sophisticated in humans. Until we evolved a neocortex, humans were not capable of intimacy.

Looking at the big picture, intimacy has existed as a biological possibility on earth for only 0.0007 percent of geologic time! This capacity, which we take for granted, is a relatively new development. Intimacy represents the cutting edge of human evolution—nature's latest experiment. Our knowledge of intimacy, our newest potential, is only just developing.

During this "learning period" we've created intimacy, sex, and marriage in our own image. Emotional immaturity (low differentiation), mediocre marriages, and contemporary social beliefs mutually create and reinforce one another. The result encourages particular views of life, blocking awareness of others. Inaccurate views of intimacy are widely accepted because they keep unpleasant "facts of life" from our awareness, not because they make better relationships. For example, the notion that intimacy requires standing on your own two feet is so alien to our usual way of being that the very thought challenges our mind-set of what's "intimate."

Intimacy is often misunderstood as necessarily involving acceptance, validation, and reciprocity from one's partner—because that's what many people want if they're going to disclose important personal information. But intimacy is not the same as closeness, bonding, or caretaking (all of which bring comfort by emphasizing togetherness, continuity, and shared history). Intimacy is an "I-Thou" experience. It involves the inherent awareness that you're separate from your partner, with parts yet to be shared.

Likewise, our understanding of "communication" is similarly distorted. Communication is about information exchange. Intimacy involves communication (disclosure) of personal information. You can have communication without intimacy—angry accusations are a perfect example.

Couples who complain of "poor communication" or an inability to communicate are often referring to interactions that make them feel bad rather than to an absence of messages. One "problem" of marriage is that you *can't stop* communicating—separation and divorce are often misguided attempts to halt the exchange of "information." When I know you truly think I'm a jerk, we have good communication—but that doesn't mean we feel like talking!

My point is: *communication is no assurance of intimacy if you can't stand the message.* "Good communication" is often mistaken for your partner perceiving you the way you want to be seen or understood. "We don't communicate" is code for "I refuse to accept that message—send me a different one! How dare you see me [or the issue] that way!"

It is easier to believe the problem is one of transmission failure because then the solution would be simple: if your partner's behavior means he simply doesn't understand, then you should send your message again using "I" language and "active listening." However, when you understand that your partner's behavior is a response to your message, which he doesn't accept or agree with, a shift in strategy is required.

Many authors and therapists believe that couples gradually achieve the degree of intimacy they want through accumulated experiences of mutual trust, acceptance, empathy, validation, and reciprocal disclosure. In all my years of therapy, I've never seen intimacy unfold in this idyllic way. Certainly I've seen couples who tried this idealized perspective, but it just doesn't work in the real world of marriage. Ironically, intimacy seems to develop through *conflict, self-validation,* and *unilateral disclosure.*

Couples commonly tell me they can't communicate while demonstrating the most blatant communication imaginable. Remember Bill and Joan? They were your typical "silent" couple when they first came to see me. During their courtship, however, they had talked for hours on end. How did they end up in silence?

I'd like to take you back in time to the start of Joan and Bill's relationship. Their story highlights the way intimacy often progresses in long-term committed relationships. It will give you the backdrop to the night Joan asked Bill for oral sex and her experiments in moving different ways during intercourse. Eventually, I'll bring you up to date and tell you how all of this came together.

From the beginning, Joan was more comfortable with emotional closeness than Bill. She loved long discussions about their feelings, ideas, and values. Bill, though skittish about self-disclosure, enjoyed being the target of her attention; it made him feel desired and important. Joan felt valued for her ability to reveal herself and Bill said she made it easy for him to share his feelings.

At the outset Bill indicated he wanted to "learn to be more open." Joan anticipated he would develop a similar facility for self-disclosure in time and this reciprocal sharing would become the norm in their relationship. So did Bill. In Joan, he thought he had found the solution to his previous relationship dilemmas. Joan's large network of friends became his, too. Eventually, he hoped, he'd develop an interpersonal style that was as easy and sociable as Joan's.

And so both Bill and Joan felt validated, needed, and valued early in their relationship. Each felt lucky to have found such a compatible partner. Conversation came easily and lasted for hours. Each reinforced the other's disclosures with further disclosures of his or her own. They celebrated their ability to talk about "almost anything." They married after a heady six-month engagement, anticipating that things would only get better.

Several years later, however, they didn't talk at all anymore. Although they didn't see it at the time, the very qualities that had drawn them together were now creating contention and resentment. Divorce loomed on the horizon. As far as they could tell, they had "bad communication" and "irreconcilable differences." What was actually killing their marriage, however, were their erroneous but common beliefs about intimacy and communication.

Joan was frustrated that Bill's interest in "developing his ability to be intimate" had tapered off. Hungry for more meaningful conversations, she began to press for "more communication." At first she followed the advice of self-help books and women's magazines: she asked for what she wanted. However, all she got were promises. Then she tried self-disclosure, hoping that the heartfelt expression of her needs might "prime the pump" for an emotional gush from Bill. The books said partners in good relationships reinforce each other and self-disclose as a matter of equity and fair play. Joan set about expressing herself more frequently as a way of pushing her husband to reciprocate. It was the "give to get" strategy she had read about. *Zip.* Nothing came of it.

Bill obviously hadn't read the same books—and wasn't willing to. As far as Joan was concerned, Bill didn't get the message. But in retrospect, it was Joan who wasn't getting it. Bill knew exactly what she wanted— he just didn't want to give it to her. In some ways, he couldn't.

Bill was increasingly aware that he hadn't inherited Joan's comfort with and interest in being intimate. No matter how much they talked and shared, she always seemed to want more. He felt like he could never satisfy her. Eventually, he began to approach "intimate conversations" with dread. Feeling controlled and threatened by Joan's requests, he began to avoid her and discourage discussion.

Bill would say things to create emotional "paper cuts"—things like, "I can't handle this constant soul-searching! And I don't like being opened up like a fire hydrant just because you're thirsty!" Joan, of course, would bristle, get her feelings hurt—and leave him alone. That's exactly what Bill wanted. He didn't want to "wound" her; he just wanted her to back off.

As their discomfort grew, they became more polarized. According to Joan, Bill was "afraid of intimacy." From Bill's position, Joan was "overly dependent and smothering." Arguments became repetitive and positions rigid.

Joan grew frustrated and increasingly less willing to take "no" for an answer. At the same time she felt ever more threatened and insecure, so she embarked on a new series of self-disclosures, but her goal was different. She no longer wanted self-disclosure to know Bill better or to be better known. Instead she used a strategy that had worked in her other relationships: attempting to elicit reassurance and acceptance by self-disclosing. Bottom line: she wanted Bill to dispel her mounting anxieties and insecurities.

Bill fully understood what was expected of him. He fought back by not acknowledging Joan's disclosures, which, in his mind, erased his obligation to respond in kind. His attention was always somewhere else. Joan said she simply wanted him to listen, but when he did that she was never satisfied. Bill knew what she wanted, but he frustrated her by taking her literally. By now, Joan had run out of "expert" advice.

Rather than soothing her insecurities, Bill subtly attempted to stimulate her anxiety. Intuitively he knew Joan wasn't likely to keep sharing her feelings if she became sufficiently defensive. Gradually, she stopped mentioning things she knew he didn't want to hear. Eventually they rarely talked. At this point Joan decided they had a serious problem. More accurately, she thought Bill had the problem. Bill secretly agreed with her, but for the most part he was comfortable. Joan wasn't pushing him to talk all the time. He took their chilly silence as an indication that Joan was in the process of accepting the status quo and things would eventually be okay.

Like many couples, Bill and Joan had reached emotional gridlock. Neither could validate him- or herself in the face of negative reactions from the other. Neither could really make a move—except to react to their partner. Joan wasn't really more differentiated or interested in being known; she just had a different strategy for reducing her anxiety. Bill did it by distancing; she did it by attempting to get close. In retrospect, their emotional honeymoon had been totally dependent on reciprocal acceptance and validation.

Other-Validated and Self-Validated Intimacy

Joan and Bill displayed the irony in marital gridlock: Bill was the one with "the problem"—*and* more control of their relationship. Joan's dependence on his acceptance allowed Bill to run the show. *He* determined whether Joan was "intimate" or not simply by what he did in response. Not only could he control her behavior, he controlled its meaning: if he made a reciprocal response, they were "intimate." If he didn't, then they weren't. Don't mistake this for paradox, however. It's simply differentiation surfacing where it is least expected: *the person with the least desire for intimacy always controls intimacy in the relationship as long as partners are dependent on validation from each other.*

Bill and Joan's relationship might sound uncomfortably familiar— or perfectly normal—and that's the problem. Twenty years ago, sociologists Gail and Snell Putney wrote a wonderful book about what they called the *normal neurosis,* the price of being "well adjusted" in contemporary society. They said our normal neurosis is our need to get indirect self-acceptance by appeasing others. It's what triggers the common post-sex quiz, "Was it good for you, dear?"—code for "Tell me I was good!"

This widespread need for a reflected sense of self has distorted our understanding of what intimacy is and how we're supposed to get it. Enshrined in the popular view is the assumption that intimacy involves acceptance and/or reciprocal disclosure from your partner. We tell ourselves that intimacy (and marriage) takes two people who are willing to work at it—but, unfortunately, we rarely have the slightest inkling of our "job" assignments in this project.

Intimacy is the two-prong process of *confronting yourself* and *self-disclosing to your partner.* It isn't merely self-disclosure. Disclosing familiar and comfortable parts of yourself doesn't evoke the electricity of self-confrontation and personal growth common to intimate experiences. Intimacy also differs from meditation or solitary self-reflection. The interpersonal dimension—particularly the response you anticipate and receive from your partner—is as critical to the process as your feelings about what you're about to disclose.

How do icy, silent couples ever break through gridlock and discuss topics only one of them (or neither one) wants to face? To answer this question we need to look first at the two "types" of intimacy:

- **Other**-validated intimacy involves the expectation of acceptance, empathy, validation, or reciprocal disclosure from one's partner. As noted in Chapter 1, this is what is often mistaken for intimacy per se. Bill and Joan's emotional honeymoon and gridlock were predictable outgrowths of other-validated intimacy.
- **Self**-validated intimacy relies on a person's maintaining his or her own sense of identity and self-worth when disclosing, with no expectation of acceptance or reciprocity from the partner. One's capacity for self-validated intimacy is directly related to one's level of differentiation; that is, one's ability to maintain a clear sense of oneself when loved ones are pressuring for conforming and sameness.

Self-validated intimacy is the tangible product of one's "relationship with oneself."

Self-validated intimacy is a totally foreign concept to "normally neurotic" people—including therapists. Convinced that intimacy involves reciprocity, therapists who write on this topic have broken it down into two different types: "symmetrical" reciprocity wherein both partners disclose in equal measure, and "asymmetrical" reciprocity wherein one partner discloses and the other offers empathy, acceptance, and validation. The possibility that intimacy can occur without some facilitative response was never mentioned in the exhaustive literature review I conducted. In this omission, the type of intimacy most important to troubled marriages is overlooked.

How can you tell the difference between these two types of intimacy? Other-validated intimacy "sounds" like this: *"I'll tell you about myself, but only if you then tell me about yourself. If you don't, I won't either. But I want to, so you have to. I'll go first and then you'll be obligated to disclose—it's only fair. And if I go first, you have to make me feel secure. I need to be able to trust you!"*

Self-validated intimacy in long-term relationships sounds quite different: *"I don't expect you to agree with me; you weren't put on the face of the earth to validate and reinforce me. But I want you to love me—and you can't really do that if you don't know me. I don't want your rejection—but I must face that possibility if I'm ever to feel accepted or secure with you. It's time to show myself to you and confront my separateness and mortality. One day when we are no longer together on this earth, I want to know you knew me."*

How much can you self-disclose without the guarantee of acceptance and validation from your partner? When you've achieved a high level of differentiation, revealing yourself is less dependent on your partner's moods or life's minor ups and downs. You're more capable of expressing who you are in the face of neutral or even negative responses from your partner. You can unilaterally push the boundaries of your relationship, and you feel less threatened when your partner starts (or refuses) to grow.

Self-validated intimacy involves providing support for your *self* while letting yourself be known. Previously, I stated that differentiation is your ability to maintain your sense of self while in close contact with people who may pressure you to conform. That's why differentiation is the foundation of long-term marital intimacy. When you and your spouse try to mold each other to reduce your respective anxieties and keep your identities stable—which normally happens because of our natural tendency to reduce our anxiety through emotional connection—intimacy becomes the living embodiment of "holding onto yourself."

If you are willing and able to show yourself "as you are" and call things as you see them—unilaterally—your partner is less likely to silence you because you're not asking for anything in return—only the chance to say what you feel. Such a relationship can remain intimate even in times of conflict—like when one of you wants less intimacy than the other. Partners who aren't dependent on each other's validation to feel okay about themselves fuel their marriage with their unique strengths, rather than their mutual weaknesses. Other-validated intimacy is the expected currency in many marriages, but *self*-validated intimacy is the life jacket for partners in a troubled relationship.

Emotional Siamese Twins

Fusion fantasies and indirect self-acceptance make intimacy—meaning *other*-validated intimacy—the contemporary Holy Grail. In truth, we've embraced a Siamese twin model of intimacy. The image of two people fused at the hip captures the essence of emotional fusion, as well as our common approach to intimacy. Think about how you would have to treat a Siamese twin. Every single movement would require consensus. If you didn't have your twin's validation and acceptance, you'd be in deep . . . well, let's just say you wouldn't want to frighten or anger your twin. Reciprocity would be the Golden Rule. Empathy wouldn't be a choice. You'd be constantly aware of the tremendous impact your partner could have on you, even by doing self-destructive things.

The image of emotional Siamese twins also conveys how your partner's personal growth might affect you: the more your spouse becomes his/her own person, the more you would feel dominated, controlled, and perhaps torn apart. That's what we saw Bill and Joan exhibit in their use of borrowed functioning so that only one of them could be strong at one time. *In an emotionally fused relationship, when one partner starts to hold onto him- or herself, the other partner feels controlled!*

Expecting trust, validation, and shared reality only encourages fights about "what really happened." If you and your partner are constantly fighting about "reality," you're probably dependent on other-validated intimacy and you're really arguing about whose reality will become the dominant reality and whose anxieties will prevail. As we saw with Joan, the "pro-intimacy" partner is not necessarily the more differentiated of the two. More often than not, the partner pushing for more *other*-validated intimacy is trying to reduce her anxiety and get a reflected sense of self. It shows up as never being able to let go of an argument, either continuing to press one's point of view or demanding an immediate apology or reconciliation. Remember, we pick partners at the same level of differentiation as ourselves.

The same emotional fusion that underlies our Siamese twin model of intimacy shows up in the familiar "we're in the same boat" notion of marriage. This idea gives a false sense of security because once you believe you're in the same boat, the next question is *who's going to steer?!* When you think you're cast adrift with a lunatic—because your partner sees things differently than you—you're likely to try pummeling him/her into steering in the direction you want to go. But when you realize spouses are always in two separate boats—and could sail in opposite directions (unless one grabs all the "supplies")—you're more likely to be kind and friendly to your fellow captain.

Other-validated intimacy occurs spontaneously in long-term intimate relationships between highly differentiated people. The difference is, *differentiated partners are not dependent on it.* Other-validated intimacy is nice when you can get it, particularly when you don't need it—and, paradoxically, that's when you're most likely to get it!

When therapists prescribe other-validated intimacy for poorly differentiated people, they are confusing the *destination* with *the process of how you get there.* It's easy to think a little reciprocal support might get "communication" rolling when your relationship is the pits, but unfortunately, it's not that simple. Other-validated intimacy can artificially improve your functioning and make you feel better when it works, but it has many long-term drawbacks. Let me point out four:

1. *Each partner becomes more dependent on the other's whims and less capable of true intimacy in times of stress.* Reinforcing each other with other-validated intimacy becomes a constant but less viable preoccupation with the passage of time. No couple can maintain the continual other-validation ("support," "mirroring") poorly differentiated people require. Your partner and shifting circumstances can pull the support out from under you at any point. All that's required is a serious illness, a catastrophic event, or even a run-of-the-mill argument. We usually don't feel like exchanging praise when we're embittered or bruised, even when it promises to make things better. At those times, your level of functioning will depend on your capacity for *self*-validated intimacy, which means deteriorated functioning if you are accustomed to other-validated intimacy.

To see how intimacy and differentiation work together as a system in marriage, think back to the point we discussed in Chapter 2 about borrowed functioning. For poorly differentiated people, other-validated intimacy is a form of borrowed functioning. Their level of functioning deteriorates from the level of their pseudo self down to the level of their solid differentiation when not supported by their partner or circumstance.

2. *Other-validated intimacy leads you to hope your partner has his/her act together—at the same time it leads you to hope that he/she doesn't.* Sharing our inner experience satisfies our basic urge for togetherness, but that's not the only reason we push for reciprocal disclosure. Another reason is that we want "ammunition" to use on our partner if he/she should use our disclosures against us. It makes us feel less bad about ourselves knowing our partner isn't perfect—that's what a reflected sense of self is all about. The problem is, it secretly makes us hope the people we love have things they are as insecure about as we are. Without realizing it, we slip into subtle competition.

3. *Other-validated intimacy is inherently limiting because it leads to self-presentation rather than self-disclosure.* When you need a reflected sense of yourself and acceptance/validation from your partner, your most important priority becomes *getting the response you want.* To accomplish this less than virtuous goal, you start misrepresenting, omitting, and shading information about who you really are *(self-presentation),* rather than disclosing the full range of yourself *(intimacy).* Self-presentation is the opposite of intimacy; it is a charade rather than an unmasking.

Self-presentation is one way we adapt to our partner's differences in order to reduce our anxiety. Unfortunately, it never provides the security and acceptance we crave, because we know our partner never *really* knows us. Attempts to cajole someone into making us feel secure only make us insecure, the same way trying to protect ourselves through other-validated intimacy offers no real protection at all. Self-presentation creates an inherent paradox that sets the typical marital squirrel cage spinning. And as you'll see in a few minutes, self-presentation brings us one step closer to emotional gridlock.

4. *Other-validated intimacy allows one partner to manipulate the other's reality.* Earlier we looked at how intimacy ebbed and flowed in Bill and Joan's relationship. Another look at their past dependence on other-validated intimacy reveals how it allows one partner to manipulate the other's experience. This long-remembered painful event occurred the day after their first child, Jena, was born. From her bed in the maternity ward, Joan reminisced with Bill about the moments after the de-

livery. "Wasn't that the most intimate thing we've ever shared?" Joan asked dreamily.

Actually, Bill had been queasy about the blood and mucus on the baby. He also wasn't feeling as bonded to the infant as he thought he should. Trying to mask his true reactions, his response was flat. "Yeah, sure."

Joan immediately felt devastated. She was confused and humiliated to think she could be so mistaken about what she'd felt. *I thought we shared this experience!* she protested inwardly. Then her thoughts turned toward doubting herself. *If it wasn't intimate for Bill, how could it have been intimate for me? Intimacy takes two people, doesn't it?* Her conclusion: Bill had wrecked her experience—a first experience never to be replaced, now a wound never to be healed! She threw this at him in their worst fights. "I'll never get over it! You can't change history!" Joan asserted in one of our first sessions.

Earlier I promised to bring you up-to-date on how things eventually turned out for Joan and Bill. The event I just mentioned is ancient history. But if we fast-forward to the present, history is about to repeat itself. At the point I want to describe, Joan and Bill's landmark "night of oral sex" occurred several weeks ago. Joan is disappointed. She thought surely they would have repeated it by now, but Bill hasn't displayed the slightest inclination to go down on her again. Joan tries to bring up the topic of that magic night, hoping Bill will take a hint. She even puts a positive spin on it by talking only about positives. "Remember that night you ate me and then I ate you? Wasn't that one of the most intimate things we've ever done?!"

To Bill, however, it feels like Joan is closing in on him again, pressuring him for a particular response. "No," he says flatly, knowing he is lying. He thinks, *She'll come around in several days to reestablish contact and we'll have sex again.* He miscalculates that she'll get over her hurt feelings the same way he thought he could get away with being lazy. He is embarrassed and angry when Joan comes into therapy and talks about it. "It's just like what you did to me when Jena was born! How could I be so *stupid* to think you and I will ever be intimate!" Linking her old pain with the new, she proceeds to punish both of them with it in our session.

I decide to speak up. "If you don't want this to end like when Jena was born, then you might want to handle it differently." Joan says nothing, but radiates anger at Bill and at herself. "Did you think the 'night of oral sex' was some of the most intimate sex you two have shared?"

"Yes!" Joan answers emphatically.

"And that experience was almost two weeks ago?"

"Yes!!" echoing her anger that the experience has not been repeated.

"Well, then, you've been happy with your intimate experience for all this time. Your husband says a few words now, and he has the power to change your history. Bill not only determines your reality, he can do it *retroactively!*"

Bill looks at me. "Are you angry that Joan had a better time that night than you did?"

"I had a good time that night. I just feel like she's moving in on me!"

"Where'd you learn to back someone off by making her feel insecure rather than by stating your position?"

Unconsciously, Bill's hand moves to cover his mouth so it's hard to read him. He says nothing, but his gaze becomes hard.

"Wherever you took the course, you sure learned your lesson."

That session had quite an impact on Joan. She thought about it for days, examining every facet for hidden truths about herself and Bill. She tracked parallels in her history with her parents, Bill's parents, and his siblings. Joan could have acted out her experience with her father's unavailability by obeying Bill's indirect message "don't make waves" about his being sexually inconsiderate. Likewise, she could have replayed Bill's family's message to "leave well enough alone" by not challenging his callous response when she was trying to move their relationship forward. Instead she chose to face this as an adult and use it to "resolve the past in the present." She paid more attention to her interactions with Bill and saw how readily she doubted or didn't follow through with what *she* thought. A week later, they experienced what they later dubbed their "dark night of the soul," which I'll describe shortly.

Intimacy is like an orgasm during intercourse—it takes two people to create it, but only one may have it. We tend to be a little crazy when it comes to sex, but our approach to intimacy is even crazier: if Joan were to have an orgasm during intercourse when Bill didn't, we wouldn't tell her she hadn't come. It's quite possible for one partner to have an intimate experience when the other doesn't—it happens all the time. But Joan's lockstep expectations of a shared reality and a reflected sense of self allowed Bill to define her experience.

I realize I'm disagreeing with the way most of us think about intimacy. I'm also fundamentally at odds with marital therapy approaches that embrace other-validated intimacy as their core concept. To me, this gives poorly differentiated people a prescribed way to pry validation and disclosures out of their partners in the name of intimacy. "I have to know, in advance, you won't reject what I'm saying" is dependency, dealing, and extortion—not intimacy. Long-term intimacy within marriage hinges on validating yourself rather than "trusting" your partner to make you feel safe.

This outlook may seem a little strong. After all, aren't we all just human and afraid of rejection? Actually, my stance comes from recognizing this. Living in fear of rejection is terrible. You can never get a guarantee that your partner won't reject you, but distorting intimacy to make it seem possible interferes with developing the self-validation that soothes this inevitable event. I don't think the stance I'm taking is hard—marriage is hard and we need to approach it in ways that work on many levels. The view I'm articulating is compassionate because it allows us to deal with marriage, including necessary issues of differentiation. It seems harsh because the common notion of compassion panders to what I call the tyranny of the weak.

Marital therapies that focus on communication and empathy invariably make certain mistakes: they (a) assume partners are "out of touch" with each other (couples are more often emotionally fused than "out of touch"), (b) confuse intimacy and communication with validation and acceptance, and (c) prescribe other-validated intimacy as a "cure."

Some approaches that recognize emotional fusion still prescribe other-validated intimacy as the cure. They believe encouraging Bill to validate Joan's disclosures and tell her she made sense might eventually instill compassion in him and he might change for her. Their notion is that Bill will recognize Joan is a separate person by validating statements that differ from his own reality. Unfortunately, this strategy renders Joan helpless until Bill undergoes metamorphosis—which doesn't readily occur because Bill doesn't want to hear what Joan has to say to begin with. Moreover, perpetuating Joan's dependence on other-validated intimacy means Bill can "pull the rug" out from her whenever he doesn't like what she's saying. And as long as Joan believes Bill is supposed to accept and validate her, she's less likely to make the leap to self-validated intimacy when they're gridlocked. Therapists with this mind-set don't see this as a problem because they don't believe people can soothe themselves and think the goal of marriage is to soothe each other.

It's not that therapists who espouse other-validated intimacy are "bad" or stupid. They're simply reflecting the fact that psychotherapy in general—and sex and marital therapy in particular—is a relatively young discipline. Often their good intent blinds them to the fact that many widely accepted therapeutic strategies lead people astray. No sane therapist knowingly encourages ideas that seem reasonable in theory but are dysfunctional in practice. They believe they're encouraging people to pursue the very essence of intimacy, when in fact they're pursuing *one* form of it—a form that offers only a temporary solution to the inevitable issues of differentiation and negatively affects sexual desire and depth of connection during sex. No one ever considers the sexual consequences of other-validated intimacy because the fields of marital and sex therapy have operated in isolation from each other.

Functionally, therapies that emphasize other-validated intimacy encourage dependency—not true *inter*dependence: *the "speaker" is totally dependent on the "listener" to accept and reinforce in order for the discussion to go forward.* Remember that when partners are dependent on other-validated intimacy, the partner with the least desire for intimacy controls it. The one who wants more discussion, like Joan, invariably becomes the "speaker," and the one who doesn't, like Bill, becomes the "listener." This creates the same gridlock that brought Bill and Joan to crisis in their relationship. Joan had to shift to self-validated intimacy to break their stuckness. These dynamics have everything to do with your sexual relationship and exploring sexual potential. (Next chapter I'll explain why the partner with the least desire for sex always controls sex, too.) When the high desire partner wants to talk about having more (or different) sex, do you really think the low desire partner is going to offer validation?

Anxiety Is Contagious

We have seen how Bill could define Joan's reality retroactively. Not surprisingly, fusion works both ways, as Bill's revelation now demonstrates.

"I can't handle Joan's anxiety," Bill complains in one of our early sessions. "When she talks to me about her fears, I end up feeling like they are my responsibility to solve."

Joan's response is instantaneous. "What good is a marriage if I can't talk to my partner about what's important to me?! Sometimes I get nervous and I need to talk to someone—it calms me down."

"I know," I say. "That's the problem."

"That I get nervous?"

"No, everyone gets nervous. The problem is that you need Bill to help you calm yourself down. I know that women discuss their feelings more than men, but you're describing something else. You're not just describing a desire to talk. You want to use it to do what you can't do for yourself."

"I keep telling Joan she tries to use me like her security blanket." Bill is trying to capitalize on my statement to buttress his own position.

"Why should she listen to you? You're doing the same thing at the moment—using what I just said to accomplish what you can't do for yourself."

"What's that?"

"Maintaining connection with the people you love without taking on their anxieties."

Basically, the lower our level of differentiation, the more prone we are to engage in highly dependent relationships, where we find ourselves struggling with a chronic urge either to fuse or escape. Remember, the most important feature of differentiation is the ability to maintain a sense of self while in relation to others. As we now look at how humans handle anxiety, you'll see the power behind emotional fusion and why maintaining your own "shape" is so difficult.

Poorly differentiated people have difficulty handling anxiety. As a result, they deal with it through their relationships because emotional fusion can temporarily reduce anxiety and restore a sense of identity and purpose. That's why poorly differentiated people often dive into fusion when they're highly anxious. Consequently, they become increasingly dependent on their relationship and their partner—or avoid emotional contact altogether.

This pattern can only spiral downward. Anything that threatens your relationship creates even greater anxiety because it also threatens your capacity to cope with other challenges. If you are threatened by any tension in your relationship, then you will get anxious whenever your partner does, and you will have difficulty comforting yourself. As you go through repeated episodes of anxiety, you find yourself spending ever more energy trying to reduce the anxiety.

The result is that you feel compelled to reduce each other's anxieties and avoid triggering new ones. In other words, you end up trying to control both your relationship and your partner in order to get control of yourself. Ways of interacting become inflexible. You feel bored and dissatisfied even while you feel obligated to perpetuate the status quo. This is when "commitment" arguments surface. Your efforts to keep things "peaceful" become a knee-jerk reflex even though they are rarely effective for long. Ultimately, your relationship becomes constraining and sterile.

At this point we can underscore a new and important aspect to re-member about differentiation: *differentiation is the ability to soothe your own anxiety and to resist being infected with other people's anxiety.* Anxi-ety is contagious and poorly differentiated people pass it between them like a virus. What we often glorify as empathy is nothing more than in-fection. When you visualize two Siamese twins, it's easy to see how emotional fusion transmits anxiety. Differentiation is your autoimmune defense against this contagion.

Fusion ties people together like a single emotional network that al-lows anxiety to flow readily from one member to the next. In poorly dif-ferentiated families, when one person gets anxious, everyone gets anxious. In common parlance, "When Dad (or Mom) is unhappy, every-one's unhappy." Poorly differentiated people and families can appear to function well—as long as their anxiety stays within a range they can handle. When stressed beyond their limits, people and families become symptomatic.

Differentiated people can modulate their thoughts and emotions when their anxiety start to run wild, and have their judgment prevail. They can *choose* to have feelings and intuitions govern their behavior in a modulated and effective way that fits their goals. Or they can act on reason and intellect. The point is, it involves a *choice*. That's the difference between having feelings vs. your feelings "having you"—being run by your emotions. When you can modulate your anxiety you're neither driven by your feelings nor afraid of them, and you don't need to use your intellect all the time because you aren't "stifling" your feelings.

Marriage Naturally Stimulates Differentiation

We can now explain how the two qualities of low differentiation we've discussed—difficulty managing anxiety by yourself and dependence on validation from others—come together to shape the course of inti-macy in your marriage. The good news is these vulnerabilities form an elegant system in which they can bring about their own resolution.

When you are in the early stages of becoming a couple, you focus on commonalties. As long as you and your partner agree, you feel validated and secure. But in the simple process of revealing yourself and getting to know each other, you eventually disclose sides of yourself that don't agree or fit with your partner. Although disagreement is inevitable in any relationship, your anxiety rises when it happens.

To the degree that you are unable to soothe your anxiety on your own, you try to do it through your relationship. You and your spouse bend your psychological "shapes" to adapt to each other, reinforcing commonalties and masking differences. The result temporarily lowers your anxiety and jump-starts the mutual admiration society again. The problem is that in this natural process of anxiety regulation through accommodation you step back from your real self to adopt a position or posture that fits with your partner's. The price is misrepresenting who you are.

So far this may sound like restating what I said earlier about other-validated intimacy leading to self-presentation. But now things get more complicated: if you are not very differentiated, you go through this process frequently. Many things make you anxious and you can't take care of your own anxiety. You and your partner repeatedly "step back" from disclosing yourselves as you are and adopt positions and identities that keep your connection relatively quiet and stable. Some couples take turns accommodating each other; others assign the responsibility primarily to one partner. Either way, the process moves forward in two powerful ways.

First, *you get tired of the pretense.* Accumulated experiences of "accommodation" gradually erode your willingness to continue to distort and bend who *you* are. You have a vague but growing sense of not being totally honest. You continue anyway, however, because it reduces your anxiety. You glorify this process by thinking of it as compromise and consideration. Eventually, however, you become less and less willing to violate your own sense of self and your integrity.

Since intimacy requires letting someone know you as you know yourself to be, it means you must have some degree of stable identity. These characteristics are often known as your "personality," your external identity. More succinctly, this stable persona is your *solid self,* your unique "flavor" that remains fairly constant across changing circumstances. In Chapter 2, I clarified that this is actually a solid but permeable self. By "solid" I mean in comparison to *pseudo self,* which rapidly fluctuates with circumstance and borrowed functioning.

Solid self also refers to your internal identity—the person you know yourself to be. It's the reference point around which you violate your integrity through self-presentation and diminish your self-worth. Solid self is composed of things you believe and hold dear, your most cherished lasting values, and the deepest truths about yourself. It's who you are and what you do "when push comes to shove." Self-validated intimacy hinges on your ability to present your *solid self* when your partner isn't accepting or validating you.

Second, *the process of elimination eventually leads to a critical situation.* Through numerous repetitions of this shape-shifting dynamic, you create a pivotal situation that makes marriage rigid: through the process of elimination there are no more easy topics that reduce anxiety and evoke consensus. Only the hard ones are left. At this point, neither you nor your partner can reduce anxiety by accommodation, since the fallback positions also increase anxiety. Accommodating your partner means confronting your own unresolved issues. And rather than confront yourself, you are likely to confront—rather than validate—your partner. Many people would rather fight with their spouse than fight with themselves.

When you reach the inevitable point where you are unwilling to adapt to each other and unwilling to confront yourself, you are trapped in *emotional gridlock.*

Actually, I'm describing the natural evolution of any emotionally committed relationship. There's nothing pathological necessarily involved. You don't need to have anything "wrong" with you to hit gridlock—and there is nothing going "wrong" when gridlock hits. It's part of a sequence created by the lack of differentiation that usually exists when we pick a partner: dependence on other-validated intimacy, a reflected sense of self, and regulating anxiety through relationships.

So, what starts the differentiation process? Typically, it is marital problems caused by emotional fusion: sexual boredom, low sexual desire, lack of intimacy, fights about money, parenting, in-laws—and where to spend the next vacation. The particulars of what triggers your differentiation are personal and custom-tailored to your past, present, and anticipated future. The people-growing ecosystem in an emotionally committed relationship is amazingly circular: emotional fusion creates the "problems" that push us to become sufficiently differentiated to solve those dilemmas.

Here's something important to remember when your relationship seemingly grinds to a halt: when you and your partner reach gridlock, neither of you can reduce anxiety through accommodation, and neither of you has any of the old kind of validation to offer the other. Truly validating your partner when you've reached gridlock means accepting that he or she is less likely to accommodate you—and you'll have to confront yourself. At the point of gridlock, your choices are limited:

1. Push your partner to violate himself/herself by accommodating you,
2. Turn yourself over to your partner by accommodating him/her,

3. Separate emotionally or physically, or
4. Confront yourself and become more differentiated.

Gridlocked couples experience themselves as "falling out of love." Ironically, the ability to love doesn't truly develop until the honeymoon is over and gridlock arrives. Gridlock drives you closer to your own core as it nudges you towards differentiation. And as you get more firsthand experience with your own essence, you become more accepting of everyone else, including your partner.

The Leap of Faith: From Other-Validated Intimacy to Self-Validation

Intimacy occurs at different levels of meaningfulness and intensity. It may start with self-disclosure of unimportant or impersonal facts. But as the importance of what we are disclosing increases, intimacy becomes more meaningful—and anxiety-provoking. How important the listener is in our lives has a similar impact: the more important the audience, the more intimate the encounter seems.

Intimacy challenges your sense of self. Profound adult intimacy isn't like "mother's milk"—it's the last thing we want when we feel insecure and, ironically, the first thing we seek. Intimacy is no refuge when couples are emotionally worn out and hungry.

It is inevitable and necessary that intimacy occur without trust and affirmation from your partner. Other-validated intimacy is nice when you can get it. But when you don't, you can attempt to rise to the occasion and validate yourself. Trying—and succeeding—to validate yourself when your partner doesn't validate you isn't as improbable as it might seem. In Chapter 12, we'll discuss how infants by age three months do the equivalent process for themselves. Being out of synch with their caregiver stimulates their ability to regulate their own emotional equilibrium. This forces you to draw upon what is solid within yourself. Intimacy involves your "relationship with yourself" as well as your relationship with your partner. If you're strong enough (sufficiently differentiated) to master your own anxieties and maintain your position, you will feel better about yourself. This is self-validated intimacy, which is part of the process of increasing your differentiation. In other words, it's a circular process: differentiation is both the basis for, and result of, self-validated intimacy. Self-validated intimacy is the means to *two* ends: becoming more of a person and developing a more resilient intimate relationship.

Getting Ready to Leap

Perhaps this differentiation stuff sounds great for someone else, but not for you and your partner. Many of my clients say, in essence, "I'm not ready for that yet! Just let me get a little more reinforcement! *Then* I'll have the faith to stand up on my own." However, getting one's fill of other-validated intimacy doesn't guarantee an automatic transition to self-validation. No amount of a reflected sense of self adds up to self-validated intimacy. A solid sense of self doesn't develop that way. Differentiation grows slowly from the inside through self-confrontation. Pseudo-self changes quickly from the outside through borrowed functioning. This is where the leap of faith comes in: at some point you have to become a hero or heroine in your own eyes by doing something that requires you to self-validate. And, inevitably, emotional gridlock will offer you plenty of opportunities to take this leap.

Sooner or later, you'll be challenged to make the critical transition: "letting go of your partner" and "holding onto yourself." The shift to self-validated intimacy happens suddenly in its first several appearances and then more gradually over the course of a lifetime. It fundamentally changes the dynamics in your relationship in the same way—suddenly and then gradually. This isn't simply a matter of "renegotiating" your marriage. Self-validated intimacy completely shifts the way your see yourself, your spouse and children, marriage, and life itself.

Earlier I said you need to develop your capacity for self-validated intimacy in order to break through emotional gridlock. Emotional impasse arises because partners become overly dependent on each other's validation. Now consider what generally happens over the course of time in relationships:

Even if you don't really like your partner, he or she becomes increasingly important to you over time as a central reference point in your life. As you become more dependent on his or her validation and acceptance, you become less willing to risk disagreement and rejection. While your partner's importance increases the potential meaningfulness of your exchanges, it also heightens the threat to your sense of self when he or she doesn't concur. The very fact that you love your partner makes it harder and harder to maintain yourself with him or her.

When the importance of your partner exceeds the strength of your relationship with yourself (your differentiation), you stop disclosing. Whether the result is withdrawal, "communication problems," "lack of intimacy," or "alienation," emotional fusion is at work. Several important facts follow from this simple but elegant development (although it doesn't *feel* elegant):

1. If you want to keep intimacy alive, your level of differentiation must keep pace with your partner's increasing importance to you.
2. The point at which your partner's importance exceeds your level of differentiation results in another layer of emotional gridlock.
3. Gridlock caused by your partner's growing importance sets the stage for your shift to self-validated intimacy and enhanced differentiation.

This is what the sexual crucible approach is all about—using the connection between intimacy, sexuality, and differentiation to facilitate the growth necessary to free yourself from emotional gridlock and experience profound sex and intimacy. You can't stop taking care of yourself once you're married, although that's what we tend to do. It doesn't hurt to marvel at the inherent paradox that it's our partner's growing *importance*—and not indifference—that creates problems (and new solutions) in long-term relationships.

Joan and Bill's Leap

The notion of "emotional Siamese twins" suggests its own necessary solution: differentiation is gut-wrenching emotional surgery—and what's worse, you have to perform the operation on yourself. There is often some fear that one or both of you won't survive the procedure, an operation that is painful and slow because fusion is tenacious.

You've already heard about three powerful experiences Joan and Bill went through that enhanced their differentiation: "the oral sex night" (after Bill lost his erection), Joan's experimental movements during intercourse, and Joan's desperate attempt to speak about "the oral sex night." But in spite of these developments, the relationship didn't move forward the way Joan hoped. Bill remained comfortable with their status quo. Now, she felt it was a matter of personal integrity.

The night they now call their "dark night of the soul," Joan tried to talk with Bill about her sense they were losing their hard-earned progress. It had been a week since she first tried to talk about it and he'd shut her down. That was the time she tried to ease into the problem area by talking wistfully about "the oral sex night."

Now, a week later, Joan brought up the topic by suggesting that Bill was lazy in bed. He liked their new position for intercourse—all he wanted was for Joan to get on top of him. Joan was glad to oblige some of the time, but his inflexibility felt selfish to her.

Bill reflexively tried to deflect her criticism: "You're going to run me off the same way your mother made your father eager to travel on business!" Joan was stung by his cutting remark, but this time she didn't simply crawl back under the covers to lick her wounds. She lay in bed in the dark, staring at the ceiling. Thinking. She replayed in her mind the part of our last session when she realized Bill could redefine her reality retrospectively.

In the hours before dawn she revisited a line of thought many times. *At the end of our last session I told Dr. Schnarch, "I know too much to turn back now." He said, "Don't kid yourself. It's never too late to sell yourself out." I'm there right now! I don't want to spoil what seems to be on the verge of flowering with Bill. But if I take this crap, he'll do it forever. I'll be damned if I'm going to be like Mom, and I'll be damned if I'm going to live in fear of Bill's anger—or my dad's! I'm worth far better treatment, but if I don't take a stand, I won't think so—I'll think I deserve exactly what I'm getting. This isn't just about what I'm not getting with Bill. It's about me!* Joan suddenly realized that to preserve her own integrity, she had to go to bat for herself.

At breakfast the next morning, Joan expressed her feelings without focusing on Bill's reaction. "I'm no longer willing to accept how rarely we talk," she said, "and I'm no longer willing to push you to do it. But don't assume I'm accepting things the way they are because I won't be nagging or criticizing you anymore. For myself, I don't want to be pathetically grateful just because my partner talks to me. Or has oral sex with me. And for you, I don't want you feeling pressured all the time by a screeching wife. I'll interpret what you do from here on as indicating your decision about how *you* really want to live. I'll make my decision about my life accordingly."

Bill was stunned! He scrambled to get the conversation on familiar ground. "You're telling me what to do! You're pressuring me! Threatening me!"

"No," said Joan quietly. They both noticed her unusual calmness. "I'm telling you what *I'm* going to do. I have no idea what you're going to do. That's why I'm scared stiff. I'm threatening *myself!*" Joan expressed her dissatisfaction with the marital part of her life and her ambivalence about possibly ending their relationship. She didn't give Bill an ultimatum, but she made her own priorities and desires quite clear.

This was Joan's shift to self-validated intimacy, her leap of faith, and it pushed Bill. As I said earlier, when one partner in an emotionally fused relationship holds onto himself or herself, the other feels controlled by their fusion. Joan wasn't trying to control Bill, however. She had to speak up and express herself or violate her own integrity yet again.

Bill was confronted with a totally unfamiliar situation. Joan wasn't just acting different; somehow, she was changing the rules. Unilaterally. Without asking him. He could feel he was losing control of her, of their situation, and of his emotional equilibrium.

Bill had the impulse to escalate his responses until Joan backed down, but then he realized that's exactly what he'd always seen his father do! Bill thought about what being on the receiving side of his father's tactics had done to him. Then he came to two difficult realizations: he couldn't do that to Joan if he really loved her (his own integrity issue), and it was no longer safe to even try such behavior! He was watching Joan do what he'd never been able to accomplish with his father.

Bill no longer had the choice of holding onto Joan—he hadn't been able to hook her into a fight. He now faced a life-changing choice: he could really lose his cool and unleash his worst qualities, or he could "get a grip" and reach for something better. Although he could never have explained it, Bill sensed something was happening between them that he couldn't stop. And, actually, he was right. If Bill chose to hold onto *himself,* the differentiation process in their marriage would move forward. If he tried to control Joan to regain control of himself, differentiation would still move forward, but in a very different way: it would push Joan further to hold onto herself. If she continued on her current path, she'd be even harder to overpower in the future.

When Bill realized he'd finally reached the crossroads of his life, he rose to the occasion. He'd already done something like this on their famous "oral sex night." Once again, when the chips were down, he showed himself he didn't always "weasel out" of his fears. After terrible days of self-examination, Bill won some measure of self-respect by admitting he tried to hurt Joan's feelings to silence her, and then apologizing for it. He also struggled with his willingness to disappoint her if that allowed him to avoid dealing with his own issues. This was as much a "dark night of the soul" for Bill as it was for Joan.

The less Bill replicated the way he'd grown up, the more accessible were his feelings. He burst into tears in our next session—not as a wounded child but as a man confronting the reality of his own actions. Even Joan could hear that he wasn't being self-indulgent in his torment. To use Bill's phrase, he was on his knees and not sure he would be able to stand up.

These powerful experiences—"oral sex night," daring to move the way she liked during intercourse, their "dark night of the soul"—in close succession had a tremendous impact on Joan's growth. As is usually the case, differentiation had positive ramifications outside the relationship. It was shortly after this Joan asked for, and received, the pleasure of her father's company at lunch.

This difficult period had similar impact on Bill. In a later session he told me about a time he held onto himself with his father and spoke up about his role in the family business. "We were at family dinner. Then I told Dad I wanted to speak to him privately. I told him I wanted to be with my family during the upcoming holidays, that I was not working overtime anymore, and that I wanted to be compensated proportionately for my work."

Joan crowed, "He took his dad on!"

"You took your dad on . . . or you took yourself on in front of your dad?"

"I . . . I guess I took myself on. All the action was basically over by the time I spoke to him. I didn't do it to get a particular response, although I still cared about what he thought. I did it because *I* thought, *If you don't speak up now, you'll have no self-respect!* I didn't stand up to my *dad,* I stood up to my *fears!*"

Bill stopped for a moment in the session to put something together in his mind. "Maybe that's partly why dad took it better than I anticipated. I wasn't trying to get one over on him. I just wanted to stand on my own two feet—not on his toes if I could help it. Maybe he sensed that: he said fine to no overtime and that we'd 'talk about' the finances. I sensed he felt angry and proud at the same time."

Resolution and Transcendence

As often happens, Joan and Bill's "dark night of the soul" led them places they never imagined. Joan stopped criticizing Bill or trying to mold him. She let him see who she *really* was, even when the implications for him weren't likely to be welcomed.

Bill didn't like everything he heard, nor did he like the feeling of losing control of their relationship. He couldn't hook Joan into frustrating but familiar arguments like he used to, and he couldn't intimidate her into backing off. Although he got angry and felt insecure sometimes, he secretly began to respect her more. And much to their surprise and pleasure, their relationship improved.

Joan and Bill no longer expected each other's validation—and, paradoxically, that's how they got it. They didn't hesitate to reveal themselves in ways the other might not like. They stopped trying to "gain ground" in arguments by pushing their partner's vulnerabilities (having found that it no longer worked). They became more uniquely themselves and brought new resources to their marriage.

I sit in awe of couples who seek my help. I watch people who think they've ruined their lives grab hold of their own collar and pull themselves upright to their true potential. They end up respecting themselves. And I respect them, too. How can you not like people who do what Joan and Bill did? It's actually this possibility in all of us that I relate to in my clients from the first time I see them. It allows me to sit quietly through horrendous struggles because I know where they can lead.

Joan and Bill eventually got to explore their sexual potential. Going through gridlock wasn't easy, but they were thankful for their journey. It's what allowed them to lie in bed some months later, basking in warm silence. Peace. No anxiety. Not even when Joan rolled over toward Bill with a sexy grin. She stroked his forearm lightly with her nails. It made his penis and the hair on his arm stand up.

"You have familiar hands. I know your touch!" Bill was feeling her nails move over his body. He reflected for a moment on his own observation. That's when he realized he "knew" her in the biblical sense. *My God, I finally understand what that means! Joan's part of how I found out!* For a minute he felt overcome with gratitude, finding it hard to swallow.

His reaction didn't disturb the connection between them. In fact, Bill marveled at the way Joan unselfconsciously reveled in her eroticism. As they lay in bed, he noticed she was methodically stroking her own pubic hair. Neither would have imagined it when they started treatment. When she realized he was watching, Joan's moment of embarrassment melted into a warm smile that was becoming familiar to Bill. In the past her response to being *seen* would have been a half hour of "All you care about is sex!" and "You have to be patient and make me feel more secure!"

"I *love* your goose bumps!" Joan understood Bill's comment perfectly. He was one of few people who knew Joan got goose flesh on her butt and back when she really allowed herself to be *done*. It had taken years for Joan to stop pulling back from the power of her own sexual response. That's why Bill was stunned by what unfolded in their bedroom. He was having the best sex of his life—with his wife no less—without having intercourse. And, to his amazement, he was thinking about God.

Thank God! he thought reflexively at first, remembering years of frustration and anger. Then he realized he really meant it! He wasn't angry anymore. He was just thankful.

"I'm glad you and I have this opportunity to share what we now have," he said turning serious. "It really means a lot. To think we almost passed this by frightens me!"

"Well, come on over here!" Joan smiled and reached for his penis. "I think you'll be less frightened if I take you in my mouth." Bill knelt on the bed, the way she knew he like best.

"I'm flirting with believing there's something spiritual in what we've found! Do you think it could be true?"

"Of course!" said Joan as she moved into position. "That's what you're always telling me when you come! 'Oh, God! Oh, God!!' "

A little while later, kneeling in a way he hadn't previously associated with prayer, he told her again.

Chapter 5

Sexual Desire:
Who *Wants* to Want?

Courtship to marriage is as a very witty prologue to a very dull play.

—*William Congreve*
THE OLD BACHELOR (1693)

For most of Western civilization low sexual desire has been considered a goal rather than a problem. Since the early days of Christianity people's self-worth was measured by their ability to destroy their sexual desire with their mind. (Sex was not a sin if done without desire.) This attitude continued undiluted through the turn of this century, when the temperance movement held power and George Comstock, U.S. Postmaster General, declared war on sex. In fact, Kellogg's Corn Flakes and Graham Crackers were originally marketed as a cure for carnal strivings and masturbation. Honest!

Society's view of sexual desire has reversed in the last three decades, but whether we've become more enlightened is debatable. Today's notion that "sex is a natural function" is a step forward from the moral degeneracy theory that previously prevailed. But we've gone beyond making it okay to want sex. Now, you're *supposed* to want it (unless you're excused for a medical or mental condition). Low sexual desire is almost always considered a problem. (I've found it often reflects good judgment: healthy people don't want sex when it's not worth wanting.)

When I was trained as a sex therapist, I was taught that low desire was a personal characteristic of people who were poor candidates for treatment. Two decades later therapists see low desire as a treatable disorder—and a lucrative industry. But in their rush to be helpful, therapists have espoused views of sexual desire that create unrecognized problems.

Once it was socially sanctioned, the belief that sex is a natural function reinforced another widely held but erroneous idea that sex therapists dispute: that good sex just happens. Many couples assume good sex should happen naturally, especially if they love each other. It's true that sexual response is biologically programmed for all species but that doesn't mean human partners will necessarily enjoy the experience.

In my years as a sex therapist, I have found that the "naturalized" view of sex is not so liberating because it pressures people to have sexual desire and sexual response, and makes worrying about sexual performance seem inappropriate.

In the late 1970s the fact that some people had orgasms just fine but had little desire for sex upset the entire field of sex therapy. Problems in sexual desire violated basic assumptions about the "natural" way sex worked. But rather than change directions, sex therapists made sexual desire "natural" too, comparing it to the desire for food. Low sexual desire was thought of as "sexual anorexia," a kind of illness.

Viewing sexual desire as a "natural" hunger masks its complexity and encourages people to see themselves as defective. One couple I worked with is a good case in point. Carol and Warren were an attractive couple in their mid-forties. They looked like the ideal couple everyone else thought them to be. Their presenting problem was Carol's lack of sexual desire: they had had no sex in the last six months of their ten-year marriage. Before that, it had been infrequent.

This was Carol's second marriage. She had two children with Warren and she didn't want a divorce. In fact, I was the third therapist they had seen in their quest for a solution. "Sensate focus" sex therapy and marital therapy had already failed.

Trying to joke about her fears of being too emotionally damaged to sustain a sexual relationship, Carol referred to herself as "romantically challenged." Prior relationships with men had broken up because she lost interest in sex once the relationship developed. A similar pattern unfolded in each sexual encounter: she would become aroused during foreplay and initially during intercourse. But her desire would "vanish" during the middle of sex. From that point on, she didn't want to be touched at all. She would become passive and "tune out" and eventually Warren would explode in anger.

"I know you may not be able to help me, Doc," Carol said in a quavering voice. "I'm pretty twisted. First I want sex and then I don't. I'm driving Warren crazy. It just makes no sense."

"I've never worked with someone whose sexual desire didn't make perfect sense. Why do you think you have the pattern you describe?"

"My prior therapist thought it might have come from a bad childhood experience. I was close to my grandparents and often stayed with them when my parents were on the road. My father was a nationally prominent lawyer and my mom often traveled with him. Once when I was five, Grandpa took off his pajama bottoms and encouraged me to touch his penis when we were alone. I started to cry and Grandpa put his pants back on. Nothing really happened."

"Do *you* think that accounts for your lack of desire?"

"No, I don't. But my therapist said I was 'in denial.' "

"I'm more interested in what *you* think."

"When I was twenty I got married the first time. My husband was selfish, arrogant, and crude. He had a violent temper. He pushed and shook me. Maybe that's it."

"Did you have this pattern of 'start-stop' desire before these experiences with your first husband?"

"Yup."

Carol seemed alert and perceptive, yet her words lacked emotional charge. She rarely made eye contact with me; it seemed to make her uncomfortable. It would have been easy to label Carol a sexual abuse victim. But I sensed that Carol would accept *any* label I put on her. I didn't rule out sexual abuse as a contributing factor, but I've learned to look for more complex answers.

"Couldn't Carol's reactions be caused by abuse?" Warren sounded as though he'd be relieved if I were to say yes. Then Carol's difficulty wouldn't have anything to do with *him*. He held dear the fact that she'd had this difficulty with other partners.

"It could, but that doesn't make it so. Many other things could be involved." Warren said he understood, but I sensed he wasn't thrilled. Except for making brief comments, he was happy to let Carol be the focus, with him as her support. He wanted her "to get as much out of the session as she could." But he also seemed afraid I might ask him more about himself. He was content for Carol to carry the feelings of inadequacy for both of them, which she was quite ready to do.

"What else should I know?"

"Well . . . I've never had an orgasm. Maybe that's why I don't want sex?" Carol sounded apologetic. Warren shifted uncomfortably in his chair. "I've never had an orgasm with anyone—even when I've tried by myself."

"When you're masturbating, how do you know when it's time to stop?" I asked.

Carol's brow wrinkled. She had never thought about it.

"When it's past the time something should happen. . . . When most people would reach orgasm."

"How many people have you watched masturbate to orgasm?"

Carol blushed and laughed. "No one! I just think I should have come by a certain point so I stop."

"How long do you give yourself?"

"Oh, about five minutes." The speed of Carol's response suggested her last attempt wasn't years ago. Warren seemed surprised.

"It sounds like you test yourself to see if you can 'measure up.' "

"Yup."

"Is that the way you generally live your life?"

"Why . . . yes! I never saw the similarity!" Carol was surprised—and not just by the way her sex mirrored her life. Her sexual pattern suggested that she *felt* inadequate. She had thought it meant she *was* inadequate.

"Tell me how this pattern fits who you've been."

Carol teared up. "Daddy" was hot-tempered, emotionally distant, and often critical of her. He belittled her efforts to win his praise while bragging about Carol's older sister. Carol's role in the family was "the stupid, cute one." Carol's mother was a chronically unhappy housewife with a country-club lifestyle. Like many children, Carol interpreted not receiving her parents' approval as a sign of her own unworthiness.

Carol craved acceptance. She had grown up trying to please people in order to feel lovable and worthwhile. In her own words, she was raised "to serve others." She often overspent her credit cards, buying presents for friends and relatives. Her lack of desire interfered with playing out this pattern with Warren: she couldn't ingratiate herself sexually.

"So what's wrong with me, Doc? Why don't I want sex?"

"What makes you think something's wrong with you?"

"I must be defective. Everyone wants sex."

"What makes you think *you* should want sex?"

"It's a natural thing. You're supposed to want it.

"Do you want sex more when you feel inadequate or defective?"

"No. It makes me want to avoid it. I don't want sex when I feel defective—but I wouldn't feel defective if I wanted it."

"From what you've told me, I doubt that. If *you* wanted sex, you'd probably think you were a horny, defective person. You're using your lack of sexual desire to prove what you already believe about yourself."

Warren nodded. He thought that was right on. But where Carol might have felt belittled she was now rather bemused. We were talking about her feelings of inadequacy, but she was feeling less inadequate.

"Do you want to have sex because you and Warren feel horny?"

"I get horny—but it doesn't last! . . . Wait! Now I'm confused! I thought the problem was that my horniness didn't last. But I want making love to *mean* something. I don't want it to be just horniness. Maybe I don't know what I want."

"That may be true. But it also makes perfect sense to me that you don't want sex. I haven't heard anything in your personal experience that would make you want it. I suspect if we put someone else into similar experiences, they might not want sex either."

"They wouldn't?"

Carol seemed amazed and relieved. Warren looked a little afraid, as though he thought I was giving her permission to never have sex again. He had thought that if Carol accepted the "fact" that there was really something wrong with her—that her past was causing her problem—she'd "work on herself" and resolve it. He never considered that therapy might help her accept herself as she was.

"Are you telling us Carol is so damaged by her past we should forget this?" For a moment I couldn't tell which answer Warren wanted.

"Not at all. I'm saying Carol's pattern makes sense—I'm just not certain about what sense it makes. One part already seems clear: Carol's assumption that she should want sex might not be warranted scientifically, but it's a true picture of who she is."

Warren seemed satisfied for the moment. I turned to Carol.

"You start with the common assumption you should want sex and conclude there's something wrong with you if you don't. You use that to pressure yourself, which partly kills your desire. But it's not true you don't want sex at all. You wanted it at the start of this relationship— and other relationships—and at the start of many encounters."

"That's right!"

"Then you might want to phrase your question differently. The question isn't 'Why doesn't Carol want sex?' It's 'Why does Carol want sex initially and then lose that wanting?' The problem is less global than you say it is. I guess you say it the way it seems."

"It seems pretty overwhelming! But why do I stop wanting sex?"

"We don't know *yet*. But I know it will make sense—*good* sense—when we figure this out. I've never seen a single person where it didn't. And that doesn't have to mean we'll discover you're screwed up!"

What Is Human Sexual Desire?

Human sexual desire is the most complex form of sexual motivation among all living things. It's a combination of genetic programming and variables of life experience, producing the utmost sophisticated nuance and variety of sex on the face of the planet. After several sessions Carol began to appreciate how she, like most people, focused on only three characteristics of sexual desire:

- *Biological programming to reproduce our species.* All aspects of sexual desire have some bio-evolutionary basis. Even while our understanding of how hormones, smells ("pheromones"), and mating displays affect our brain chemistry remains incomplete, we assign this biological basis great importance; in fact, we overestimate the influence of biology on sexual desire. Biological factors act primarily on the primitive parts of our brain we share in common with other mammals and reptiles.
- *Relieving tensions.* This is commonly referred to as "horniness," "blue balls," or a "sexual itch."
- *Craving for sexual gratification.* This is like Sigmund Freud's notion that we are driven by an instinctual sexual energy (*libido* or sex drive) and organized around a "pleasure principle"—we seek pleasure and avoid pain.

If you believe sexual desire is only the result of a "natural" biological drive, you may expect to want sex all the time. Such beliefs shape our picture of sexual desire per se. For instance, consider how we ask each other, "Do you want sex?" The question is about wanting a particular type of *behavior* and *willingness to get started*. It has nothing to do with desire *for your partner* or desire that lasts throughout the encounter. The real question is, "Do you want *during* sex? or, "Do you want *me?*" The whole notion of desire during sex isn't clear in many minds because it isn't something you think about if you assume sexual desire is primarily biological. Some people expect that you're not supposed to want *during* sex, you're suppose to be *satisfied* (if you're partner is any good). And yet, particularly if you're dependent on a reflected sense of self, don't you want your partner craving and panting for you while you're together? Others see desire during sex as a tension buildup that's finally satisfied by climaxing. But, as pointed out above, this is one of the basest ways people understand sexual desire. We're just not used to thinking of sexual desire as something inherently interpersonal and deeply affected by what happens while couples have sex. The ways we approach sexual desire steer us away from the very thing we miss and seek.

Humorists James Thurber and E. B. White observed, "Understanding the principles of passion is like knowing how to drive a car; once mastered, all is smoothed out; no more does one experience the feelings of perilous adventure, the misgivings, the diverting little hesitancies, the wrong turns, the false starts, the glorious insecurity. All is smoothed out, and all, so to speak, is lost." Desire during sex restores the adventure and the passion. But as Thurber and White point out, it's not as simple as shifting gears—as our biological view of sexual desire makes us think, unfortunately.

Here are six often overlooked aspects of sexual desire that have everything to do with sexual potential and the waning of desire:

- *Sexual desire is part of our interpersonal communication system.* Since prehistoric times, when men and women first lived communally, humans have evolved the ability to sense each other. In modern parlance, this is known as "sexual vibes" or chemistry. Not only can we sense each other's sexual interest, but under some conditions we enjoy that feeling.
- *Sexual desire partly reflects our longing for pair-bonding.* Our need for "togetherness" surfaces in our hunger for the touch, warmth, smell, and taste of physical contact.
- *Sexual desire expresses an eagerness to exchange meanings with another person through sex.* Just as our ancestors developed language as one type of communication, sexual "languaging" has also evolved over time; it's how we know the message in a one-night stand is very different from exchanges between long-term monogamous partners. Sexual desire expresses our capacity for intimacy. We enjoy playing with I-thou experiences during courting and sex.
- *Sexual desire includes the intensity and depth of our involvement in sex while we're having it.* Our capacity for *passion*—healthy lust, sexual aggression, carnality, ardor, and enthusiasm—is part and parcel of our sexual desire. Many complaints about low desire actually refer to our (or our partner's) lack of passion. Passion goes beyond biologically-driven "urges." It comes in delicious flavors of craving,

longing, fire, and fury reflecting emotional desire for your partner—affection, ardor, amorousness . . . love.

• *Sexual desire is eroticism in action.* Eroticism involves the *ways* we want to engage our partner—our preferred sexual behaviors and styles. It reveals the way sex is encoded in our mental world. Family and life experiences all leave their mark.

• *Sexual desire—like satisfaction—is partly determined by our culture.* Society shapes what arouses us and how we experience our own desire. Women's bare breasts are "sexy" in Western culture but merely pragmatic in African tribes. In past centuries, Japanese men found women's powdered necks and petite bound (crippled) feet alluring. On an island off the coast of Ireland, people rarely have sex, and when they do, they almost never remove their clothes. Imagine an Irish islander marrying a Polynesian islander whose native culture celebrates sex. Every society defines sexual satisfaction—and it becomes part of our normal neurosis.

Human sexual desire is complex. Although the most fundamental aspects of our sexuality are rooted in biology, hormones don't run our desire as much as we think. In fact, modern research suggests that some "bonding" hormones *follow* rather than precede sexual behavior. With such complexity, it is not surprising that the delicate dynamics of desire are easily disrupted.

Marcel Proust said there's nothing like sexual desire to keep your words from having anything to do with your thoughts. Or, in our cruder times, "A hard-on has no brains; a wet crotch has no conscience." But just because many people live that way doesn't make it true. The physiological connection exists; using it is optional. Getting the thinking part of our brain (our neocortex) in charge of our sexual desire is a spectacular (and uniquely human) achievement.

In Chapter 3 we saw how feelings and thoughts contribute to one's total level of stimulation. Desire is an important case in point: our *brain* is our largest sex organ. We've noted three ways in which the neocortex affects sexuality (and desire):

• The neocortex's ability to modulate sexual impulses means that understanding human sexual desire requires more than a purely "biological drive" model.

• Our ability to attribute a variety of meanings to sex increases our susceptibility to sexual dysfunctions and low sexual desire.

- Our mental world is a large part of our sexual potential, and the nature and nuance of our sexual desire play a big role.

Now let's consider other parts of the brain in relation to sexual desire so you can see the big picture. Basically the brain comprises three parts that have increasing evolutionary sophistication: the *reptilian* brain, the *mammalian* brain, and the *neocortex.* We share the most primitive part, the *reptilian brain,* with reptiles by virtue of our common evolutionary path (it's the back of the brain, which sits on top of your spinal column and controls basic functions such as breathing, digestion, and excretion). As humans evolved, the brain's large mid-section *(mammalian brain* or *cortex)* emerged. In later evolutionary steps the forehead enlarged to make space for the *neocortex,* the latest (and most "human") part of our brain. This three-part structure of the brain is why intimacy and sexual desire in humans are a breathtakingly complicated matter.

Human sexual desire has roots in all three parts of the brain. The part of the brain that is engaged determines the character of our desire. Realistically, we experience a mixture of all three levels, but it's still useful to distinguish between "neocortical," "mammalian," and "reptilian" desire. It's the difference between choosing your partner versus rutting or going into heat; creative sex versus preordained mating/breeding; and loving union versus natural selection. It's all a question of emphasis.

Hormones and horniness primarily involve mammalian and reptilian parts of your brain. We can see society's emphasis on mammalian/reptilian sexual desire in how the legal system views eroticism as something that is contagious. Legislators argue that society must restrict sexually explicit material to shield those who might become "inflamed" and lose control—human reptiles running amok. While some restrictions are necessary, the emphasis is misguided. Sometimes we *wish* the legal view were true. Wouldn't you love to be inflamed by your partner's passion? Don't you wish you could ignite him/her? It's just *not* that easy—that's what usually burns us up.

In Chapter 4, I pointed out that differentiation determines how much (and what kinds of) intimacy we can handle—how much we can risk in love. Differentiation also permits the kind of desire most of us think we want: *"front-brain" neocortical desire.* It's what makes sex personal. We want to be *wanted* (chosen). Only a neocortex can do that. Your neocortex determines *whom* you have sex with (or don't), *how* you do it (or won't), *why* you're doing it (or not), and *what this means* to you—that is, if the neocortex is the part of your brain that's running the show. Unfortunately, that's often not the case.

Under most circumstances, you want your neocortex determining your behavior because it possesses the greatest adaptive sophistication and variability. When prehistoric mammals' lives were at stake, fast primitive responses served best. Unfortunately, threats to our identity and emotional security often trigger similar responses. When interpersonal pressure is high enough and we get anxious, survival reactions "hard-wired" into the reptilian and mammalian parts of your brain take control from your neocortex. Your anxiety increases your impulse to fight, submit, or run away. The more anxiety and pressure to adapt, the more this tends to occur. When this happens frequently we label it being "poorly adjusted."

Roughly speaking, the part of your brain that predominates determines the characteristics you display. When you're severely anxious, as though your life is at stake, you behave like a reptile. Reptiles and badly frightened people have two characteristics: they have no sense of humor, and they eat their young. Relationships aren't peaceful or stable. Although you're responsible for what you do at such times, the notion of "choosing" is erroneous because the part of your brain that chooses (your neocortex) is no longer in control. Lessons in "fighting fair" are usually forgotten because reptiles don't fight fair.

When you have your anxiety under better control, you stop going for your partner's jugular vein. You act like mammals do: you're capable of mother-infant nurturance and pair-bonding (like geese who "imprint" on their partner)—but not intimacy or *choosing* someone and being *chosen*. Human sexual desire is only possible when your neocortex is running the show. The mammalian and reptilian parts of your brain follow the 1960s free-love anthem, "If you can't be with the one you love, love the one you're with!"

In Chapter 4 we said differentiation is your ability to soothe your own anxieties and emotional immunity to infection from others' anxiety. This reduces the likelihood of anxiety-triggered regression in functioning, which limits your capacity for intimacy or wanting your partner. Differences in sexual desire in an emotionally committed relationship are a prime example of "pressure to conform" that generates anxiety. That's why spouses commonly act like reptiles when arguing about sex.

It takes lots of years to develop the necessary differentiation to keep your neocortex in charge. That's one reason why humans have the longest (and most sophisticated) postpubertal sexual development in the animal kingdom. Another reason: *neocortical sexual desire has to be developed.* Having your neocortex run your desires doesn't just mean controlling them. It also involves *creating* them: fantasizing and thinking up new things to do. So-called mindless submersion in eroticism actually takes thought and creativity—it is a "thinking person's sex."

You probably don't want lizard-level sex (or mammalian sex either). On the other hand, sometimes you might wish that your partner could be a "real animal" in bed. Having sex with a "sexual predator" can be fun if the "predator" is well-modulated; subtlety and variability go a long way. That's where differentiation and your neocortex come in.

This clarification about your brain and your sexual desire has important practical utility; you need to keep this in mind as you read about "tools" for connection in the next five chapters. If you don't appreciate the neocortical aspects of sex, you may reduce these tools to mindless "sensate focus" exercises.

For Carol, understanding the neocortical basis of desire had practical effects. She stopped expecting herself to want sex and became curious about her pattern of desire. Rather than seeing abuse as a compelling force from the past that explained everything, she began looking for other factors that could be involved. She no longer focused on the sexual feelings that were present at the beginning and then vanished. Instead she began watching for other feelings that showed up during sex that possibly interfered. She even went a step further: maybe the "interfering" feelings were really present all along? Maybe they were strong in the beginning but she was too turned on at first to notice?

All of these were possible. Each one might reflect a different emotional possibility. Carol didn't have a clear map, but at least she knew there were places to look. Before, her desire—or lack thereof—was just an immutable given. Now Carol and I could look for nuances together, though neither one of us was sure what we were looking for. I contributed my expertise on sex and marriage; Carol contributed her hunches and reactions, especially her reactions in bed. We started discussing what she and Warren did in great detail: who did what to whom and how each felt about it. Warren was uncomfortable with our "freeze-frame analysis," but it paid off.

In a general sense there was no surprise. Carol's problem boiled down to the inevitable truth: she approached sex the same way she lived her life. But how this pattern played out in bed had an elegance most scriptwriters would die for. Like at the end of a good murder mystery, you want to slap your forehead and say, "Of course!" What if a particular pattern of response emerged as Carol's relationships—and sexual encounters—evolved? What if the same pattern, developed over months or years, replicated itself in microcosm in any given sexual interaction?

Carol's issue wasn't learning to like sex. She already did. Carol entered sex with Warren—and relationships in general—with the thought, *"Who would really want me?"* That's when she was "interested in sex." Actually, her sense of inferiority mobilized her to start having sex—but it really wasn't a desire for sex: it was a desire for a reflected sense of self. That's why she initially "desired" sex at the beginning of each sexual encounter (and each relationship). Her partner's sexual desire for her relieved her anxiety and made her feel worthwhile and secure, temporarily banishing the nagging thoughts.

However, once solidly engaged in sex—or a relationship—Carol's fears of rejection quieted down, and so did her motivation to have sex. Her focus shifted to another core issue waiting in the wings: *feeling like she had to serve others in order to be loved.* In Carol's case—and many others I've seen—her quest for a reflected sense of self played havoc with her sexual desire. It got her into sex, and once satisfied, it also pulled her out. (This is, in part, why I said earlier that dependence on acceptance and validation from your partner has tremendous negative impact on sexual desire.) It illustrates how anxiety can "facilitate" sexual motivation in some circumstances, but it has nothing to do with desire for your partner, or for sex, either.

In the midst of this melange of factors affecting Carol during sex, the struggle of differentiation was occurring: Carol was developing a solid sense of herself. Anxiety initially propelled her into sex, and then her resentment and attempt not to sell out to her fears took over. Carol's mysterious but consistent loss of desire was her way of daring to say "No!" to her partner (in this case, Warren)—no to giving in order to get, no to exploitation and isolation, no to past abuse. What Carol thought of as her "problem" was really the healthy part of herself attempting to stand up and hold onto herself.

Carol didn't realize that her "problem" was really a developmental task everybody faces. She saw it only as damage from her past that needed to be repaired. She never suspected she was in the process of "resolving the past in the present." If this seems extremely complex, it is—that's what I've been trying to show you about sexual desire!

I asked Carol what she felt when she wanted someone to touch her. She couldn't have answered more clearly. She changed the topic to "Why would someone want to touch *me?*" She had difficulty hearing, let alone heeding, her own voice because she lived her life according to how she thought other people saw her. Warren, in contrast, acted as if he were the center of the entire world, demanding that Carol cater to his every whim. Carol was jealous and resentful of his selfishness.

"When Warren has an orgasm, he seems to go off into his own world!" she complained.

"Maybe that's an inner world you can't validate for yourself," I suggested. "If you are cut off from your memories and emotions and devalue your perceptions, where do you have inside *yourself* to go? You tune out from yourself. It's not someplace you want to be . . . yet."

Carol's issue was basic: developing an *internal* sense of self she could value, maintain, and live by. In the end, this developmental task proved to be her pathway to a lot more than just "good sex." But even the complex process just described didn't fully explain Carol's pattern of desire. Other issues were involved—and not all of them were hers.

Desire Always Has a Context

Sexual desire within marriage isn't reducible to two sets of the various aspects of sexual desire outlined earlier (one for each partner), or two sets of reptilian-mammalian-neocortex brain systems, or both partners' unresolved individual differentiation issues. There's more involved than each partner's thoughts, feelings, past histories, anticipations, replays of parental dynamics, or unconscious processes. That any single issue seems to "fit" isn't the point—it may indeed be involved. The point is that sexual desire in marriage involves all of these but is more than any of these parts.

Growing social consciousness highlights forces and factors surrounding and shaping marriages that transcend individual characteristics (for example, intergenerational family loyalties, gender roles, economics, sexism). But we have to expand our view further: we must consider individual and social factors *and* recognize the unique forces within the interaction itself. Try keeping neocortical desire alive while your partner is in full reptilian mode and you'll see what I mean. Think back to Carol's pattern of shifting desire: notice that *elapsed time* in her relationships and sexual encounters was a significant factor. *Duration* is a property of an interaction, not a personal characteristic. Sex in marriage forms a *system* that is more than the sum of its parts.

Marriage is a system the same way families, government, and corporations are self-adjusting, self-perpetuating systems. Some aspects of sexual desire are properties of "the system" of marriage. Couples allude to this reality when they speak of their relationship as if it were an independently existing entity (for example, "I think our relationship is in trouble").

Carol and Warren each had their own differentiation issues, some of which reflected their particular histories. Their childhoods had shaped who they became, which partner they selected, their patterns of sexual desire, and what surfaced when they hit gridlock. Like most of us, they tried to handle their marital problems in accordance with widely held beliefs. But this perspective doesn't consider the process of marriage itself: any move Carol made to differentiate had an immediate impact on Warren and "the relationship," which reverberated back through these component processes. (The fact that childhood issues heat up in the boiler room of marital conflict doesn't mean they "cause" the sexual difficulty.)

Think of marriage as similar to ecology. Every little part (species extinction, shrinking rain forests, oil spills, etc.) affects the operation of the earth as a whole, which in turn affects every little part. You and your spouse are complex entities made up of physiological subsystems (for example, endocrine, respiratory, excretory), as well as emotional/psychological ones (for example, unconscious processes, family of origin issues, and anxiety regulation and brain functioning as discussed above); in loving and living together you create a new and larger entity (marriage), which itself is part of larger entities (extended families, communities, societies), giving rise to still larger entities (nations, human evolution). Each higher level contains parts not found in the lower one; each higher level is more than the sum of its parts or the operation of its components.

Here's the point for sexual desire: the common tendency to reduce sexual/marital problems to any single underlying process (or a simple collection of processes) overlooks the complexity of marriage and human sexuality. Reviving sexual desire is not as simple as "resolving past hurts." Some aspects of sexual desire problems are inherent to the system of marriage and can't be fixed, rebuilt, or resolved; they are part of marriage's people-growing machine. In the latter half of this chapter I'll show you why low sexual desire is a normal developmental stage in the evolution of an emotionally fused couple.

In marriage, we create a new process beyond ourselves—and become an interacting part of that process. The ebb and flow of sexual desire within marriage is the end result. You have to deal with marriage on its real-life level of complexity. Can anyone track all levels of human operation at the same time? No, but that's not the problem. The problem is that we erroneously view each individual piece in ways that are actually contradictory to or isolated from the others. We don't have to figure out how to put all the levels together because they already *are*. Our task is to remain open to seeing how the levels interact and shape the whole system.

The Person with the Least Desire for Sex Always Controls It

If sex is supposed to be satisfying and anxiety-free once we are safely ensconced in marriage, how come that's when many of us stop wanting it? Part of the answer involves the *system* of sex in marriage.

Some processes are simple but powerful. Consider that it takes only one partner's preoccupation with an actual or anticipated sexual dysfunction to desynchronize both partners during sex. Men with rapid ejaculation often take this a step further. They condition their partner to be sexually inert and unenthusiastic. It's done by verbal request or it's the wife's automatic response to her husband's "shooting off" when she gets aroused. This is the sexual version of the systemic reality that it takes two people to make a marriage but either one can unilaterally create divorce.

There is a still bigger sexual conundrum that affects all relationships. It holds true in every bedroom (unless physical force is involved): *the person with the least desire for sex always controls the frequency of sexual contact between spouses.*

For example, early in their marriage Warren wanted sex more often than Carol did. Although he made most of the initiations, Carol actually determined when sex happened: she chose which offers she accepted. Warren acted as if *he* made sex happen (and didn't like the burden), but Carol was the one in control, whether she liked it or not. In fact, Carol controlled the content and style of their sexual contact as well: Warren felt he had to accept sex on her terms—since she might not want it at all. When Carol lost her desire during intercourse, for example, Warren felt he had to "hurry up" and reach orgasm.

When they came for treatment Carol was "the identified patient"— the one with "the problem" of low desire. But long before they visited me, Carol's identity in their relationship had been established as "the one with the sexual problem." Warren's role was "the sexually normal one"—and the resident sex expert. Together these rigidly assigned roles created several powerful processes:

1. Carol had actually been more sexually active and erotically inclined than Warren before they met. So while Warren was flaunting his superior sexual status, Carol had a different view of things, and her husband's inflated view didn't exactly inflame her with desire.

2. Warren tried to make Carol want sex. Warren needed Carol to respond to his advances because it gave him indirect validation and a positive reflected sense of self. As a bachelor he measured his desirability by how many women wanted him and how aroused they became. So Warren repeatedly tried to "cure" Carol to prove *his* desirability. When he was unsuccessful, he blamed her and told her she was inadequate instead of facing his own feelings of sexual failure. Warren's reaction is an excellent example of social programming (culture as a system). In response to the cultural belief that "a good lover satisfies his partner," men try to establish their sexual adequacy by pleasing their partner the same way a boy (supposedly) becomes a man by "scoring." Unfortunately, women aren't pleased or interested when their partner is more eager to demonstrate prowess than to be with them. The men are then unable to explain their partner's sexual disinterest—until they think it's her gender training that's in the way—which blinds them to the truth about themselves.

3. Warren's attempts to make Carol want sex made her want it (and him) even less. Carol had less "status" than Warren regarding sexual ability, desire, and initiative. Furthermore, she couldn't "gain" status by increasing her desire because any success would accrue to Warren's competency. It would also validate that Warren had been right all along.

4. With little to gain and little to lose, Carol was relatively unmotivated to improve their sex. After all, she had already forfeited her sense of sexual competency. Warren was the one still afraid of looking inadequate, which fueled his desperate attempts to keep her interested in sex. When Warren berated her she became more passive—and resentful. Carol had greater control over their sex life by doing nothing and looking helpless.

5. Warren escalated by alternately becoming more indifferent to Carol or more insistent. His goal was to keep Carol from having an impact on him or their sex, but he just struggled and suffered more. (Differentiation gives you the option of *letting* people affect you.)

6. Warren's dependence on a reflected sense of self indirectly put Carol in control of whether or not he felt adequate. As a consequence, she had the paradoxical experience of feeling simultaneously inadequate and powerful. When she was angry, she could "jerk his chain" by simply not responding. Even when she wasn't angry she found his "lit-

tle boy" neediness unappealing. On the surface Carol accepted her position of inadequacy but secretly smoldered underneath.

Carol's behavior didn't always reflect withholding from Warren; it was often a matter of holding onto her *self*. However, that's not the way it felt to either of them. At his reptilian worst, Warren attacked Carol's adequacy with greater frequency, which made their marriage worse. We dealt with this in our sessions:

"You must think Carol is a masochist," I said to Warren.

"Why? Because she's married to me?"

All three of us burst into laughter at Warren's unexpected honesty.

"No. Because you act as if hurting Carol's feelings makes her more likely to have sex with you."

My comment wasn't lost on either of them.

"You two have created an elegant sexual gridlock: Warren, *your* efforts to increase Carol's sexual desire make you powerless. Your frequent invitations allow her to remain passive. She can have all the sex she wants, when she wants it—without ever initiating. Blaming Carol and disowning any responsibility don't help because you make her angry and give her total control. If her low sexual desire is totally of her own making, then you are totally dependent on what she does. Every so often, you can pressure Carol into having sex more frequently or staying in it longer, but you can never pressure her into *wanting* you. In fact, the more you demand sex the less she wants sex—or you."

Warren started to realize why he was so frustrated. The fact that it was partly his own making and partly the system of marriage at work frustrated him more. The fact that the person with the least desire (in this case, Carol) controls sex is part of marital systems. Having that person also control your sense of adequacy is optional. Warren digested this for a minute and nodded in begrudging agreement. I turned to Carol.

"At the same time, *you're* conditioning Warren to badger you. Aside from 'rewarding' him when he whines and cajoles, you're teaching him what really motivates you: you don't have sex with Warren simply out of desire. You do it when he gets you to feel sufficiently guilty or frustrated— or when you start to feel afraid he might not want you. You're training Warren in the chicken-pellet model: the chicken that gets a pellet of food when it pecks at a lever in its cage—not every time, but after a large number of pecks. Like any smart chicken Warren thinks he'd starve if he waited to peck (initiate) when he was hungry (horny/needy). Now he's just like that chicken pecking away while he still has food in his mouth. You've trained him to initiate more frequently than he wants to. He knows he has to get enough pecks (initiations) in before you feel guilty, frustrated, or insecure enough to have sex with him."

Warren didn't know if he should be offended by the analogy. Carol started to laugh uproariously. It was clear she was laughing at both of them. Warren chortled in spite of himself—it did describe the way he often felt. He took some pleasure in seeing that Carol was as trapped in her own way as he was in his. We laughed for several moments. Discussing such prickly issues as *withholding* and *controlling* could have gone a *lot* worse.

"Some of what's happening isn't personal or intentional, although it feels that way. You're both up against the realities of sex in marriage. That's why some aspects of this pattern don't change. For example, even when your relationship is wonderful, the partner with the least desire will still control sexual contact, although it will probably feel quite different to both of you. Some couples try to approach this dilemma by fighting over who's going to want sex—or the other person—the least. *Wanting* your partner more than he or she wants you means giving up a pivotal position of choice, unless you become more differentiated."

Carol chuckled at the thought of fighting over who wanted sex the least. It hit home differently for Warren. For the moment, he focused less on what he thought Carol was doing to him and more on how he was going to deal with his situation.

"What are you telling us to do?" Carol asked.

"Yeah," said Warren, "are you telling us we're doing something wrong?"

"I'm not telling you to do—or not do—anything. I'm just pointing out conundrums of sex in monogamous relationships. What you do with it is up to you. I think the solution usually involves holding onto yourself. You both seem to think the solution is getting your partner to accommodate. What you've got is sexual gridlock. Neither of you can take the pressure off yourself without taking on some issue you haven't resolved or giving your *self* up altogether."

Carol and Warren Move Forward

There was a lot more going on in this relationship than the possible aftermath of Carol's childhood abuse. At best, her traumatic experience was a piece in a much larger puzzle. In any case, it was easy for me to couch our discussions in ways relevant to someone who'd been abused, because resolving their current issues and Carol's past abuse involved similar trials of differentiation. It simply meant we had to approach this so that past and present issues "lined up" in overlapping ways. This isn't hard to do—that's how dynamics in marriage usually occur. We used their presenting problem: Carol had already begun the process of "resolving the past in the present" when she "lost" her desire in the middle of sex.

Carol needed to establish a stronger relationship with herself, to learn how to *not* give herself up to *anyone*. Once she approached sex (and therapy) with that goal in mind, she moved forward relatively quickly. From the outset she had shown interest in sex: some initial interest in their encounters was genuine. She was experimenting with masturbation. And she seemed eager to have her "disappearing" sexual desire stick around.

Carol, Warren, and I continued to meet for therapy and to watch and discuss the process of their sexual relationship. Carol and I started focusing on masturbation as a useful tool. Warren was delighted because his exposure was minimal—he declined my offer to discuss masturbation in the same way. Little did he realize what was to come next.

We chose masturbation because it was something Carol was already doing. It was also a picture of her relationship with herself: what she did sexually was totally up to her. We *didn't* focus on masturbation because she was most likely to reach orgasm that way (although this is also true). In fact, we confronted *pushing* herself to orgasm as self-abuse and selling out to her fears—not good practices if Carol wanted to have "a good place to go inside her." If Carol believed she wasn't inadequate, there was no need to *try* to reach orgasm (not that she should avoid it if it happened). The point wasn't to go looking for an orgasm or focus on her sensations—it was to watch how she dealt with *herself.*

Masturbation became the place where Carol answered the question, "What do you think you're worth?" She struggled with herself in real time. Telling herself "You deserve it!" wasn't enough. She had to live it—giving to herself and receiving like she meant it. Was she worth enough not to cut her time short? Was she deserving enough to touch herself any way she wanted—and ways she'd never done? Was she a slave to her perceptions of other people's standards? Was she just rubbing her crotch and trying to measure up?

The sex and the impact on her development were electric. Carol started having orgasms—and a lot more. She felt better about herself. She felt less defective and enjoyed her sense of mastery. But it wasn't from having orgasms as much as how she got them. She took on self-worth issues *before* she had her orgasm.

It wasn't too surprising that Carol became more interested in sex with

Warren. She was excited by her development. She was starting to come alive. She started staying present throughout their sexual encounters. That's when the entire system of their marriage started changing.

Did you take Warren's sexual desire for granted, as if only Carol's required explanation? That's the mistake therapists and couples make when they assume sexual desire is a given—a "natural function." Carol and Warren were surprised by what happened next, but I've seen it many times: Warren stopped wanting sex.

To understand this you have to keep in mind the multiple aspects of sex in marriage we discussed above. Warren was shifting strategies in response to a shift in their marriage, instigated by the changes in Carol. Now he tried the strategy of trying to be the partner who wanted sex the least. The rule "the partner with the least desire for sex controls it" always applies, even when spouses switch roles. We approached Warren's about-face in treatment on many levels. I'll point out two of them, one *systemic* and one *individual* (realizing the distinction is somewhat artificial).

Borrowed functioning—the systemic process that occurs through emotional fusion—can help us understand Warren's puzzling disinterest in Carol's rejuvenated sexuality. I had helped Carol move forward sexually by changing the meaning of her sexual progress. It now had to do with differentiation (her relationship with herself) rather than her relationship with Warren. Carol's progress didn't validate Warren's contention that she was defective—in fact, quite the opposite.

Carol wanted sex now, but not because she loved Warren more or because she realized he was a great lover: it was because she liked *herself* more than she ever had in the past. Her new attitude didn't do much to enhance Warren's reflected sense of self. (Warren and I discussed how it takes strength to watch your partner grow, but it didn't help. That wasn't really what he wanted.) Carol had done more than increase her sexual functioning. She had changed the world inside her head. In the process she took a big step in changing her marriage: borrowed functioning was coming to an end.

Borrowed functioning artificially inflates one partner's performance beyond the level he or she can maintain in the face of adversity. The inflated partner looks more differentiated than he or she really is. (This is *pseudo* differentiation versus *solid* differentiation.) The other partner's functioning is correspondingly reduced. This decrease in functioning is the basic difference between borrowed functioning and mutuality. Mutuality involves one partner sacrificing his or her own goals to facilitate those of the partner—but the sacrifice *enhances* both people's functioning.

Borrowed functioning is like an emotional transfusion that "fills up" the receiver but drains the donor. Its vampire quality may not be readily apparent because the donor is quite willing to donate—at first. (Often he or she reports very pleasurable sex, security, and romance for a while.) But when the partners hit gridlock, the erotic aspect ends and both sides struggle for emotional survival. Often the donor feels sucked dry and his or her emotional functioning declines. This can go on for so long that it's mistaken for the donor's real level of ability.

When gridlock intensifies, the donor's functioning can plummet precipitously, especially if the partners decide to divorce. This is commonly described as "going through a rough time around the breakup of a relationship." During this time, the donor takes the breakup as a negative reflection upon him/her. The receiver takes the donor's difficulty functioning as vindication of personal culpability in the marital problems and "proof" of deserving somebody "better." The receiver's reflected sense of self is inflated by the donor faltering, and the donor's functioning is further diminished by the receiver's apparent lack of distress. The donor looks terrible and the receiver "does great"—unless differentiation takes place. Once the emotional fusion is lessened, both partners return to their unilateral level of functioning (solid differentiation). The donor improves, the receiver "gets worse"—unless he or she finds another relationship on which to "feed."

Without borrowed functioning, Warren "fell apart" as Carol "got on her feet." Without Carol "underneath" him to lean on, Warren started to go downhill. "Helping" Carol from his one-up position had helped Warren sustain a comfortable self-image. When Carol started helping herself, Warren lost his equilibrium in the relationship, and in his head. He didn't like Carol controlling his sense of adequacy, but he liked having responsibility for it even less. His anxiety was going up and his ability to reduce it through his marriage was going down. His neocortex was losing out to the parts of his brain programmed to take over in life-threatening situations. Warren was becoming a frightened reptile.

As Carol became more interested in sex, Warren said he didn't want her at all. Partly he was poking her where she had previously been vulnerable. But there was something to what he said: Warren didn't *want* to want her. This wasn't just about not wanting what he could have or being intimidated by Carol's sexuality. Let me explain by looking at his background. As you read about Warren, keep in mind the two basic "rules" about differentiation mentioned earlier:

- We come out of our family of origin at about the highest level of differentiation our parents achieved.
- We pick partners at the same level of differentiation as ourselves.

As a young boy Warren grew up with his erratic alcoholic mother after his father died. Warren ran the house as soon as he was able—and tried to keep Mom sober. She could be a fun drunk but got spitting rageful in an instant. She was frequently depressed for days. Warren was embarrassed to be seen with her in public—and afraid to leave her at home. In fact, Warren was nervous, insecure, and "all alone" most of his life—at the same time he was emotionally fused to his mother. There was never enough stability at home to start differentiating from her.

Warren tried to stop wanting his mother to change. *If I don't care, I can't be disappointed* became his childhood mental litany. Warren tried to suppress the part of him that *wanted*—wanted her to stop drinking, wanted to feel secure with her, and wanted to respect her. He never succeeded. Warren suffered every time his mother stumbled or her speech slurred, and it affected how he treated Carol from the outset.

Warren found little "faults" in Carol. He insisted that she didn't do enough to please him. Actually Carol was *too good* for Warren's comfort. Warren thought he'd feel safe with Carol, but the opposite occurred: he felt endangered by his very love for her. His fears of losing her grew the more he enjoyed being with her. He feared she would manipulate him with his desire for her . . . or withhold herself from him . . . or worse—she'd die.

Warren didn't *want* to want Carol because it made him vulnerable in a way he had never learned to tolerate. Finding "flaws" was Warren's attempt to "reassure" himself that Carol *didn't* love him and prove she wasn't so special and could be replaced. Warren probed for things Carol wouldn't do, which immediately became the subject of his next diatribe. His outbursts led Carol to back away from him and intimidated her to a level he could deal with. He felt destructive and selfish, but he wasn't about to let her get close.

Sometimes Warren encouraged Carol to talk him *out* of his fears of wanting her. He wouldn't let her alone until she tried—and things really went crazy when she did:

"I don't trust you."

"Why don't you trust me?"

"I don't know. I just don't."

"What can I do to make you trust me?"

"Nothing."

"Well, then, what's the use of my even trying?"

"See, you don't really care! I knew I couldn't trust you!!"

Warren was trying to reject her so he would have nothing to lose. And at the same time, he was trying to engulf her so she couldn't control him and he couldn't lose her.

Carol tried harder to please Warren, but the more she tried the worse things got. The more she pleased him, the more he wanted her. The more he wanted her, the more vulnerable he felt. The more vulnerable he felt, the more he had to find fault with her. The more he complained, the harder Carol tried (at least for a while). They were caught on the merry-go-round of marital paradox. To understand the power driving this kind of pattern, you have to keep in mind the complex interplay of two people's unresolved issues as well as the larger context of their relationship system. I'm describing a systemic conundrum, a mind-boggler arising from the essence of human relationships—not simply individual craziness.

Throughout their relationship it looked like Warren wanted more sex than Carol. What he really wanted was a "transfusion" of borrowed functioning. That changed when we reached a particular point in treatment: when Carol no longer occupied a one-down position in the marriage, Warren became "disinterested." He could have sex, but not with the same borrowed functioning and reflected sense of self. And without the benefits of borrowed functioning Warren was "overextended." He was exposed to his lurking fears of *wanting* in ways he couldn't soothe on his own. He had to pull back.

The Politics of Sexual Desire

Lots of things are set into motion when partners start to differentiate, including their unresolved childhood issues. Specifics are as diverse as people's experiences growing up. However, many adults adopt a strategy every child knows: *not wanting to want* is an attempt to protect against the pain of wanting, longing, caring, and depending—and not getting. Parents like Warren's mother control their family with the threat of self-abuse. It was as if she put a gun to her head and said to Warren, "Give me what I want or I'll kill myself!" (You don't have to be a "horrible" parent to do something like this. People who refuse to have medical checkups and those with serious illness who are "negligent" taking medication are using the same strategy.)

Once you appreciate what that's like as a child, fighting with your partner makes more sense. It's easier than wanting him or her. Besides, fighting *makes* it easier not to want your partner. Like Warren, we'd often rather fight than *want*. The politics of *wanting* are truly powerful—and volatile. Low differentiation requires a rather tricky balance: it's only safe to want your partner as much as your partner wants you. On the other hand, it's only safe to *not* want your partner when your partner wants you. If your partner stops wanting you while you don't want him or her, you might end up divorced.

We can't delay *wanting* until we know our wants will be fulfilled. Marriage and life offer no such guarantees. Wanting, as an adult, takes strength. The "too much" in "wanting/loving/caring too much" is code for "more than I can self-soothe and maintain my sense of self." Differentiation (your ability to calm your anxiety and soothe your own heart) makes *wanting* tolerable, though still not safe.

People who don't *want to want* are unable to tolerate the vulnerability involved in choosing their partner. One fateful session I asked Warren and Carol the question that usually brings this issue to light: *"Who chose whom when you were deciding to get together?"*

Carol realized that it was she who had chosen Warren. And Warren married her because he never had to choose. Realizing she had never been chosen—not by Warren, her first husband, or her parents—profoundly affected her. Carol was back in her crucible once again.

Spouses' interlocking crucibles are an inherent part of the *system* that is marriage. Carol wanted Warren to want her—to choose her deep down in his soul. But this meant Carol had to face the possibility that he might not pick her now if he had a choice. If she couldn't live through that gamble, she would never be wanted the way she desired.

There was another level of gridlock: the only way Warren had a choice was if he *didn't* need Carol. But that challenged Carol's bottom line: she wanted to be wanted *but she needed to be needed*. Warren needed her as long as he couldn't take care of himself—at those low times he had no choice. Carol had the impulse to "help" Warren with his unresolved issues—to make herself indispensable as she had in the past. (This is the role Carol had assumed in their prior days of borrowed functioning.) But then she would never be certain Warren *wanted* her. As long as she pandered to her need to be needed, she would never know if she was wanted for herself.

Carol's crucible fit snugly with Warren's struggles. (Remember, that's the essence of gridlock.) He had much the same issues of wanting to be wanted but needing to be needed. And there was the twist that the only way Carol could be wanted was if he exposed himself to the vulnerability of wanting and choosing. They both benefited when Carol let Warren struggle with himself. In the process Carol had to struggle with herself, too. If Warren went through his crucible and came out wanting her, *then* she would know he had truly chosen her.

(We'll find out what happened to Carol and Warren in the next chapter.)

The Strength to Want

Sexual desire shares three commonalities with intimacy in marriage: *borrowed functioning* often mascarades as either one; dependence on *other-validation* causes problems with both; and we mistakenly think *indifference* is the culprit when sex or conversation stops. *Not wanting to want* contradicts the "indifference hypothesis" because it expresses *importance,* not indifference. Paradoxically, emotional fusion is the foundation of *not wanting to want.*

One property of marital systems is the *vulnerability of increasing importance of one's partner:* your partner's increasing importance over time naturally increases your vulnerability, which in turn fosters sexual boredom and low desire. Two fears bring this about:

- *Fear of losing your partner's acceptance.* No one wants to be rejected by a valued and needed partner. When your partner's acceptance means more to you than your own integrity, you only reveal your eroticism in ways that will receive acceptance. Your spouse becomes "too important" for sexual experimentation. You can't create sexual novelty or expand your repertoire for fear of disapproval. The resulting boredom contributes to low desire.

  It's a lot easier to introduce sexual novelty and undisclosed aspects of your eroticism in a one-night stand or an affair than in your marriage. It's a greater challenge to your sense of self when you're with your spouse. That's why sexual boredom (and affairs) are so prevalent. We demand stability in marriage—and when we get it, we complain that things are always the same. This is not quite the benefit we anticipate when we yearn for being important to each other.

- *Fear of losing your partner altogether.* The longer and better your relationship with your partner, the more you stand to lose if you want something important your partner doesn't want—or if he or she dies. When your partner's importance exceeds your differentiation (your ability to self-soothe), your partner becomes too important to *want*. The end result is *not wanting to want*. It's a matter of time and personal development. Warren and Carol are a poignant example. The problem wasn't that they became dependent on each other. It's that poorly differentiated people can neither tolerate nor maintain true *inter*dependence. The realistic dependencies, contingencies, and vulnerabilities of long-term emotionally committed relationships frightened both of them.

I've seen lots of people try to dodge this issue of *wanting*. There are those who say, "I'm dying to really want somebody again! I just keep picking the wrong partner!" But they pick the wrong partner because they don't want to want a *person*. Wanting someone gives that individual unique importance and leverage in your life. Wanting a *person* involves spending time with him or her, which diminishes the credibility of repeated "bad picks." This complaint about picking the wrong person reflects the cravings of an unresolved emotional fusion.

Others have no illusions about wanting their partner: they simply make sure they don't. It never gets to the level of *not wanting to want*. They don't *want*—period. They don't have much capacity for wanting, and they like it fine that way. Their partner is always replaceable. But don't confuse lack of significance with lack of connection. There's still lots of emotional fusion in these couples as well. Borrowed functioning is central to their relationships; it's just harder to see.

Are you among those who might dare to *want* your partner? Then you have additional reason to remember what we discussed about intimacy, because it applies to desire, too: *if you want to keep desire (and intimacy) alive in your marriage, your continued differentiation must keep pace with your partner's increasing importance. When your partner becomes more important to you than your relationship with yourself, you have four choices:*

- Withdraw emotionally.
- Engulf your partner.
- Allow your partner to engulf you.
- Raise your level of differentiation.

The first three options attempt to avoid wanting your partner or to reduce the vulnerability of wanting rather than increase your capacity for it. Differentiation makes the difference between love deepening and saying, "I love you but I'm not *in love* with you anymore." In this code, "being in love" involves *wanting,* "loving" simply means caring for and good wishes.

Give it some thought and you'll see society holds paradoxical expectations of marriage: we think it creates passion *and* sexual boredom. The irony is, it actually works that way! Some sexual boredom in marriage is inevitable (given the way differentiation moves forward). *Long-term* sexual boredom, however, is not. Resolving sexual boredom depends on your willingness to tolerate pain for growth (another facet of differentiation).

Sex often improves on vacation for more reasons than reduced interruptions and pressures. When removed from things that define one's persona, the sense of being unknown in one's environment significantly disinhibits displays of eroticism. You *can* capitalize on novelty of the situation to compensate for inability to innovate in your sexual relationship. But you'll have horrendous hotel bills—or only have hot sex when you travel. The inability to "really get it on" at home reflects a need for greater differentiation rather than a change of scenery.

Low sexual desire can't be cured with provocative lingerie or sex toys (if such items increase your interest, that's fine). Low sexual desire is no fun, but it does have a *purpose.* It's part of marriage's intricate people-growing machine: it invites you to stretch yourself and your relationship. Whether you accept the invitation to change from within—or just "dress up"—is your choice.

Section Two

Tools for
Connection

Chapter 6

Hugging till Relaxed

Certainly sex can be "I will do that for you if you will do this
for me," but what a lonely arrangement.
A caress should say "I love you," not pay off a debt. An
embrace should fill the heart as well as the arms.

—*Hugh & Gail Prather,*
Notes to Each Other

Weddings are great for people-watching. In but a few minutes of observation you can see the language of hugging in action: one-arm hugs,
bear hugs, side-arm hugs, "let's be civil" hugs, long lingering hugs, pat-
on-the-back hugs, and seductive hugs. Each has a different style and
meaning. How did Aunt Sally learn to hug in ways that perfectly express who she is?

You can conduct an interesting study of hugging by also keeping
track of time. As a child I learned to say "one-Mississippi" to count off
seconds. Count "one-Mississippi, two-Mississippi, three-Mississippi,
four-Mississippi" to yourself as you watch your relatives embrace. You
can do the same right now: imagine hugging a variety of people you
know. At your hugging peak you probably get to about four-Mississippi
when they—or you—let go. Some folks can't finish one-Mississippi
with parents or relatives.

Four-Mississippi is a long hug. Beyond that, someone usually pulls
back. Why does the average hug last for only four or five seconds?
Many people shudder or at least stiffen when they're held longer. Up
to four-Mississippi, a hug can mean almost anything. As long as it's am-
biguous or innocuous, everything's fine. After four-Mississippi comes
the realization, "You're *really* holding me!" Or, "This is getting
serious—or sexual!"

When people suddenly realize it's not a "casual" hug, they often have a reaction I call the *jolt*. Jolting says, "That's enough! It's time to let go!" If you break off the hug before four-Mississippi—before either person hits his or her limit—you never know the jolt is there. Lots of people "jolt," although occasionally you can feel a person do the reverse—melt. Signaling in hugging is amazing.

When you put your arms around your partner, *how do you know when to let go?* Many people answer, "When I'm through!" But how do you know when that is? The real answer for many couples is either one partner jolts and starts to disengage—or the other does it first.

If you're the one in your relationship who likes to hug longer, you may be all too familiar with what I'm describing. You can *feel* your partner pull back, if just by a slight shift in muscle tension and balance. In contrast to the common wail, "we don't communicate," hugs demonstrate just how well couples do. (If you didn't communicate, you might still be in your last hug rather than reading this.) Hugs show—visually and physically—"who wants whom more."

I've made a conscious study of this with my own father. Twenty years ago hugging my dad was like embracing a tree trunk; he was stiff and awkward. Then he went through the stage of not wanting to miss a hug if one were offered, but not wanting to make the first move and be rebuffed. Then he started to relax into our embrace and wasn't the first to let go. The first time he wanted to hold longer than I did was a delightful shock. Then he progressed to walking toward me and wrapping his arms around me without hesitation.

Recently my parents greeted me at an airport near where they live. As I walked off the plane my dad grabbed me, hugged me, kissed me on the neck, and said, "Have I told you recently that I love you?" Dazed, amazed, and slightly embarrassed, I stammered, "I think we need to let the other passengers pass by." We still managed to hug for several seconds. No one who saw us seemed upset by the delay.

Two days later my Dad wanted to talk. He said, "I want to apologize if I hurt you in any way when you were growing up. My own father wasn't physically affectionate. We never touched. When you were growing up, I wasn't comfortable showing the kind of affection we now share. I hope you and your brother know how much I love you. I'm really glad we can do this now and I'm real proud of you. I only wish I'd known about this earlier because we've wasted so much time."

Although I'm rarely at a loss for words, it was hard to say anything at first. Dad hadn't bothered to mention that he'd been in a German prisoner of war camp for almost a year during World War II, an experience that must have affected his parenting. I was overwhelmed with love and admiration for my father. I'm thankful things have turned out as they have. I sustained no damage and have no regrets. Not bad progress for twenty years—for either of us. With chagrin I thought back to my adolescence, when I was sure I was born to the wrong parents because mine didn't ski!

Have you ever watched a group of women pass around a newborn baby like they were sharing a drug? Give yourself at least four-Mississippi to imagine holding a smiling, freshly washed and diapered baby against your chest. Sink and slouch into the experience. Let yourself make the "molding response" where you and baby melt together. *Feel* the soft flesh and *smell* the unmistakable baby aroma. Maybe you want to stroke its soft skin or feel its little fingers curl around yours.

Now keep this mental/emotional mind-set but change the picture slightly. Let's say that snugly baby has suddenly reached puberty. You probably feel yourself withdraw, even if you haven't moved a muscle. Notice how the baby's gender suddenly makes a difference. When pubic hair starts to grow, hugging starts to change: both parents and children start hugging as if they were broomsticks.

Now, in your mind, change the person you are holding—this time it's your less favored parent. Feel the difference! Even with your arms still around him or her, you can break contact if you don't want to *feel* him or have her feel you. Have you mentally shifted to an "A-frame" hug—shoulders together but hips apart? Is your body stiffening? These are two common ways to keep from feeling while you're hugging.

Clearly it's possible—and common—to hug without emotional contact. Think about superficial social greetings, the perfunctory clasp where hands and arms keep you from getting close. The point is, even when we embrace, we can enforce a sense of distance.

Couples often find they have deeper, more relaxed hugs with their young children than with each other. This often skews the family dynamics and makes spouses (rightly or wrongly) conclude that they love their children more than they love their mate. This is fueled by the common lack of "electricity" or sexual vibes when spouses touch. Few couples realize that both problems arise in part because it takes more personal development to maintain a deep, relaxing connection—or a hot, erotic one—with a long-term marital partner than it does with one's kids. The problem stems from a lack of differentiation: both partners' inability to stand on their own two feet, figuratively and literally when near one another.

I want to show you a special use of hugging I've developed for my clients that I call *hugging till relaxed*. I'm not referring to any old kind of hugging; I'm talking about something special.

Is hugging till relaxed just a technique for relaxing and focusing on your sensations (sensate focus)? Only if you insist on doing it that way. Techniques make you a technician, but not a lover. Used to its full potential, hugging till relaxed becomes a tool: a living tableau of your differentiation—your ability to hold onto yourself in close proximity to your partner—and a way to enhance it. Even if you don't have "difficulty" hugging, the underlying issues in your marriage (and your life) play out in your hugs, in the particular style you and your partner have worked out.

Given that sex therapy generally progresses from easier to more difficult steps—trying to progressively "desensitize" people's anxiety—it's easy to assume hugging till relaxed is a "baby step" compared to intercourse. My approach differs in that you generally get the hardest things first. Hugging till relaxed isn't easy to do with real depth. It's like intercourse in that neither is too difficult if you only do it superficially—but profound hugging till relaxed is harder to fake. Once you've learned to make deep contact through it, you can extend the connection to intercourse. (That works better for many people than the other way around.) It's not uncommon to be moved by the experience—more respect for our resistance to being truly known and held—tasting what we're missing during sex. Hugging till relaxed has both sensitizing and desensitizing aspects, among others.

It's something almost everyone can eventually do, and it doesn't require nudity or genital contact. It's beneficial to couples who have widely differing comfort levels with (and motivation for) sexual behavior. Hugging till relaxed is effective with a wide range of sexual difficulties, including lack of orgasm (in either gender) and rapid ejaculation. While it doesn't necessarily resolve these problems, it sets the stage for resolution and greatly enhances the tone of the couple's sexual interaction. Much can be gained by a single attempt (if you understand it) in very little time. It's simple enough to be worth a try. That's exactly the way Carol and Warren, the couple with the sexual desire problems you met in the last chapter, approached it.

Hugging till relaxed is elegant and simple. The basics require four sentences: stand on your own two feet. Put your arms around your partner. Focus on *yourself*. Quiet yourself down—*way* down.

The real power of hugging till relaxed comes in realizing that it's both a window offering a clear view of the level of differentiation in your relationship and a useful tool for developing more differentiation. It's a perfect example of using touch (sex) to grow yourself up by learning to enjoy togetherness *and* separateness. Remember, that's exactly what we saw in the diagram of differentiation in Chapter 2—balancing togetherness and separateness (individuality).

Differentiation is your ability to stand on your own two feet, physically and emotionally, when you are close to others. It allows you to stay close while your partner "bounces off the wall." If you can quiet yourself while your partner is flooding with anxiety, you don't have to move away or make him or her feel differently in order to control your own emotions. You can stay near—all you have to do is calm yourself down.

This is consistent with the advice child development experts give parents about dealing with kids. Rather than rush in to comfort and soothe every discomfort and emotional "wound," world-renowned pediatrician T. Berry Brazelton says it's important for parents to stay near, quiet themselves, and not interfere as their children learn to "repair" themselves.

If your spouse is your support system, when he or she gets nervous you have to grab onto him, physically or emotionally, or let go of him all together. If you depend on your spouse to "be there for you," you have to be wary all the time. When your spouse is upset, you can't relax when he's holding you, and you can't relax when he isn't.

Hugging till relaxed provides a tangible way to learn to self-soothe, to quiet yourself, to maintain yourself in close proximity to your partner. It's the literal embodiment of how well you can do that. You can also feel how "holding onto yourself" eventually brings connection with your partner. You can feel how that connection differs from lockstep emotional fusion.

If you want to see what happens when spouses are rigidly linked (emotionally fused), picture two people standing a foot apart. They are leaning on each other in an "A-frame" hug, literally getting their support from each other. When one partner starts to "wobble," the other has to prop him up or make him stop wobbling, in order to stabilize both of them. The "wobbling" partner often complains that the other partner is very controlling or not "supportive" enough!

Now picture two people standing on their own two feet supporting their own weight, loosely holding each other with their arms. In this position one partner isn't as affected if the other starts to lose equilibrium. If the stable partner remains quiet and still, the wobbly partner is more likely to find a new balance, since (a) there's no static from the quiet partner to amplify the initial disturbance; (b) the wobbly partner realizes that it isn't the stable partner's responsibility to fix the disequilibrium; and (c) it's actually easier for people to maintain equilibrium if they know they can/have to do it on their own. In hugging, as in life, the best thing to do when your partner starts to "lose it" is hold onto *yourself* and quiet down.

If you often complain that your partner is too dependent ("You're always leaning on me!"), you will probably like what you've just read. But I won't argue with those who complain, "But I *like* leaning on my partner while we're hugging." It happens with my clients frequently. "Leaners" usually expect me to argue that they shouldn't want to lean. Instead, I encourage them: "Do what you want. Just notice if leaning really lets you relax—or if you find yourself complaining about your partner. When you both stand on your own two feet, leaning on each other isn't a problem. There certainly is a place for it when it is appropriate and invited, but often there's no room for it in marriage. Is now that time?"

You can check this out with your partner. William Doyle, Ph.D., developed my description of hugging till relaxed into what we now call the *differentiation stance*. Stand face to face about two feet apart. Place your palms against your partner's with your elbows comfortably against your ribs. Align your weight over your legs. Take a moment to relax and feel the "tone" of the connection with your partner.

Now see what happens when you place your "trust" in the stability of your relationship and your partner: take a large step backwards (keep your palms together, elbows against your sides) and lean in. If the impact on your connection isn't clear—or if you believe mutual support, trust, and commitment are the keys to a stable relationship—take another large step back and experience those beliefs in their physical form.

How does this position feel? Do you like it? Does it feel different from your expectations of how marriage works? If you and your partner both step forward to take responsibility for individual support, how does *this* position feel? Isn't it curious that the differentiation stance, a position that allows your partner to walk away, also makes your "relationship" feel and function better? More curious is that emotional tug that makes us most want to lean when it's unwise to do so. While discomfort is the most common reaction to the pressure of "trust" built on dependency, it is by no means the only one. Many people say they *like* the way this feels. They feel more "secure" with their partner pressing against them, and I wouldn't disagree. These same people often pick fights to "get a reaction." In other words, pressure and tension in the relationship reassure them that their partner is still "there."

When Warren and Carol were about to try hugging till relaxed, Warren looked like someone realizing he's about to be trapped. "How long and how often should we do the hug?" he asked in a tight voice. That seemed like a simple question. But hugging till relaxed and the differentiation stance are tools (with unpredictable outcome) rather than techniques used to create an expected result. They are part of an *elicitation approach* that uses your experience as a perfect window into who you are. I didn't tell Warren "how long" or "how often" because then we wouldn't be able to *see* him in the way he did it.

"I have no idea. I'm sure that however long you do it, it will be the right amount. But at this point I can't even tell you 'right' in what sense." Warren looked at me in disbelief. I added, "I can tell you this: it's hard to get profoundly relaxed and deeply connected by four-Mississippi. The more often you do it and the longer you do it, all things considered, the deeper it gets."

I'll tell you about Warren's reaction to doing "The Hug" in a moment. But first I want to show you a little more about an elicitation approach: take the time to visualize what happens when you're hugging your partner in your typical way, and you feel you're both losing your equilibrium. Notice what *you* do.

Emotionally fused people strain and struggle to regain their equilibrium without letting go. They literally give up feeling safe and secure in order to maintain connection with their partner. Whether or not they actually fall over, they are off-balance and their connection is tension-filled. If this happens repeatedly, people dependent on a reflected sense of self sometimes decide it doesn't feel good to hug, or they're "not a hugger," or they picked the wrong partner. They don't realize it doesn't feel good to hug *the way they are doing it.*

It never occurs to emotionally fused spouses to let go of their partner in a hug (or discussion) gone sour, allow both to center themselves, and then return to hugging (talking). They worry far more about hurt feelings than regaining balance.

It's true that leaning on your partner in an A-frame hug can stabilize the system. ("My spouse is the center of my existence, my support system.") But when your spouse is your support system, you have to keep one eye on him or her at all times. (Not during sex, though; that's when you will probably close your eyes.) If he or she "moves" emotionally or physically, you immediately feel off-balance, even threatened. That's when you become preoccupied with issues of "trust" because any unilateral shift is a violation of sorts. Your equilibrium depends as much on your partner's shortcomings as on his or her strengths. When you draw your sense of stability from your partner, you have to try to control him or her at all times. In short, you can never relax.

In contrast, partners whose sense of stability comes from themselves are aware of, but relatively unaffected by, one another's shifts. They don't "upset" each other as much and can even encourage each other to move as they wish. (Remember, differentiation includes nonreactivity to other people's reactivity.) Herein lies a suggestion for hugging till relaxed: if your partner is pulling or pushing you off-balance, leaning too much or withdrawing, it's no big deal if you are standing on your own two feet. Just let go while remaining in place (take a step back if you have to), recenter yourself, step forward, and hug till relaxed again. You don't have to get away. Just let your partner go, focus on yourself, and calm yourself down. Then reach out from a place of stability.

The pattern of see-sawing says, in essence, "Only one of us can be comfortable at any given time. Only one of us is going to be happy, and it will be at the other's expense." We act like we believe there's only enough room for one and a half people in a relationship; the only question is, who's going to be the half? The point isn't, "Do you love me enough to sacrifice yourself for me?" Your partner's refusal to stay bent over or off-balance so you can be comfortable eventually makes you capable of valuing his goals on par with your own.

When Warren described the details of how he and Carol usually hugged, it was like he was saying, "I want you to come to me so I don't feel one-down. So I'll get almost next to you and yank you the rest of the way toward me. I can't take that last step. I can't come all the way to you."

Breathing Life into Your Relationship

There are other subtle lessons in the way couples characteristically hug. Consider your breathing for example. Sometimes couples feel "together" breathing in unison when they hug. But there is a difference between how couples accomplish this sense of togetherness.

Emotional Siamese twins achieve unified breathing by means of an unspoken accommodation: one breathes more slowly than normal and the other breathes more rapidly. The resulting "togetherness" leaves one starved for air and the other hyperventilating. (That's a good metaphor for how Carol and Warren felt about their sexual frequency!) Most importantly, both feel disappointed and ill-at-ease when their breathing inevitably gets "out of synch."

When you first try hugging till relaxed, I suggest you first do it any way you like—see what your personal style is. That's the elicitation approach. Then try a particular strategy to achieve unified breathing I'm about to describe. Keep in mind the pattern I'll outline doesn't have to happen—but something will! For example, you might feel you *have* to create the described pattern and are "not good enough" if you don't. Or you may feel angry, as if pointing out this strategy somehow becomes a demand that invalidates any other experience or outcome. Granted, my attempts to describe a pattern may sound like this is the "right way," despite my disclaimers. But looking beyond this, is there any merit to the notion that your personal reaction reflects something about how you go through life?

If both partners "hold onto themselves," quieting themselves and breathing at their own rates, they, too, eventually breathe in unison. However, the quality of their togetherness (breathing) is entirely different: their connection is relaxed, free of the constant tension about the anticipated "separation" of their breathing patterns. They have arrived at a natural point of overlap in their breathing, possible only when neither person sacrifices his or her "shape" (in this case, natural breathing rhythm) for togetherness. This kind of union is warm, peaceful, deep, and meaningful.

If both partners continue to breathe at their own pace, they will inevitably go in and out of synch. In terms of their relationship, being separate doesn't feel lonely or painful because they haven't alienated themselves *from themselves* in order to be together. Being together is easier and so is being apart. What else could you wish for someone you truly love, but to be happy when he's with you and also happy when he's not? (So many hope that their partner feels pain during separation just so they can feel valued. That is not love; it is emotional fusion.)

The breathing pattern I've described reflects the natural cycle of two separate but related people going in and out of synch. "In synch" celebrates two life forms who have found each other—and "out of synch" does the same. Neither state is "better" than the other. This is what true love and mutuality are all about: the *choice* of putting your partner's goals ahead of your own.

After I talked with Warren and Carol about hugging till relaxed, Warren returned to our next meeting to report his experience doing the "breathing exercise." Hugging till relaxed is neither an exercise nor really about "breathing," but Warren was pretty much on track. He had a hard time understanding how his report mirrored his life and relationships.

"Togetherness is togetherness. What's the big deal? What difference does it make *how* we breathe?" Never having experienced anything but tense connection with the people he loved, Warren didn't know it could be anything else.

"When you were around people important to you when you were growing up, did you 'breathe easy'?" I asked.

"I must have breathed enough, I'm still alive!"

"If that's your criterion for a relationship, you must be delighted with your marriage. You said a moment ago that 'togetherness is togetherness.' How did the connection with Carol feel?"

"What do you mean 'feel'?! I stood there and we did The Hug."

"Is that the way you live? Going through the motions—nearby but not in contact with those you love?" That stopped Warren cold.

Finally he said, "People don't get angry at you if you just do what they expect."

"Yes, but do they love you?"

"How would I know?"

"That's an interesting point."

The type of reaction Warren had is common among people who have never made contact with themselves—or anyone else: he complained that he didn't feel much when they first tried hugging till relaxed. "It's not that it feels bad. It doesn't feel like much of anything—and *that* feels bad."

"This isn't designed to give you an overpowering feeling," I assured him. "Besides, that's exactly what you're afraid will happen if you get close—you'll be obliterated. If you're looking for a sense of connection, hugging till relaxed starts off as so mild that you'll overlook what you're experiencing if you're not tuned in and relaxed. During intercourse you can be totally distracted but not realize it because of the intense physical stimulation. Hugging till relaxed can help you learn if you're tuned out during sex.

"If you quiet your anxiety, you might feel something or *someone*. You might start by trying to feel *yourself*. You asked me about sexual potential—well, here's where it starts. Do you want to give into your fear that you'll never feel anything? Or would you rather see what it's like to quiet yourself and believe that you can?"

Warren looked genuinely perplexed. "I'd rather believe in myself. . . .

I know this will sound odd, but how do I *feel* myself? And how do I ever get in touch with Carol?"

The Paradox of Intimate Connection

Hugging till relaxed highlights how connection with your partner requires solid connection with *yourself*. We can't avoid this inherent paradox: when you're alienated from your own experience, you have no basis to feel or connect with your spouse. You have to go inward first to make a connection with yourself.

We also see here how a reflected sense of self works. This plays out as, "I can't get more involved with you, because when I do I lose myself." Another example: someone who can't allow himself to be held says, "I need to be able to trust you first." Translation: "I can't let you hold me because I don't trust you, and if you do something to make me trust you, I'll still feel insecure (or even more so) because I'll have even greater fear you might stop."

You have to learn to stand on your own two feet if you want to let yourself be held. You can make a big show of being fiercely independent, but the deeper truth is that you are still trying to convince yourself that you *can* stand alone. Hugging till relaxed involves standing alone . . . in connection with another. This is the key to interdependence. It is only safe to focus on your partner when you have an unshakable center within yourself. The ultimate paradox is that your self-centering ability (differentiation) gives you the ability to do this.

As with sex, you can do hugging till relaxed at different depths of involvement. You can go through the motions superficially—and for some, that's an important first step. They get through it without freaking out (like their first intercourse). Though this may be an initial step, it's definitely not the goal.

You can reach a stage where you center yourself effortlessly. You stop focusing on your partner; you stop wondering what he's thinking or worrying he's having a bad time. You do more than contain your jolting and twitching. You quiet yourself to profound calm. It wasn't like this when my wife Ruth and I started doing hugging till relaxed. Now doing it for ten minutes is better than two martinis. Many a time I didn't realize how wound up I was until Ruth said, "Come on, honey, let's do The Hug."

You can use sensory awareness to center and quiet yourself—that's a standard Eastern technique of self-realization. But becoming aware of your body is only a first step. There is a key part of Eastern practices we often forget: *self* awareness leads to realizing we're all part of a larger oneness. In some ways hugging till relaxed develops the "quiet mind" Buddhism emphasizes. It involves clearing your mind and having your emotions—not "blanking everything out."

How relaxed and quiet can one get? You can hear your blood pulsing in your ears. You listen to the sound of air going in and out the back of your throat. Your jaw goes slack and your eyelids get heavy. You realize your ears were tense. You *hear* the quiet, not an absence of sound, but the presence of *peace*.

When the noise in your head finally quiets—it can take weeks, months, or years—you may experience a sense of self-transformation. It often shows in your face. Participants at our Couples Retreats so often comment on the change in each other's faces that we've started photographing them.

Once you finally *relax*, you may experience the curious impulse to stop hugging. The jolt in hugging we discussed earlier is often caused by anxiety about relaxing. Although this seems at first contrary to common sense, relaxing is harder than we realize. People who complain of being tense sometimes don't want to relax, just like some want desire and passion but don't want to want.

Pushing your own reluctance to relax can enhance your differentiation. It's a way to "resolve the past in the present" and increase your ability to self-soothe. The resulting tranquillity sets the stage for such intense intimacy that, paradoxically, it can challenge your self-image and self-worth. This shows up lots of different ways. Remember what we said about an elicitation approach to hugging.

We all carry a base level of tension. Many people ignore their anxiety about sex and intimacy as long as they can reach orgasm. If you've never experienced sex without anxiety, you don't know the difference—you just assume it's inherent in the act. Examples abound of women who "strain" to have an orgasm, feeling inadequate if they don't, worrying about their partner's reaction, worrying that they are taking too long, or that their partner will "give up on them." Or men who ejaculate too rapidly. Or people who need to turn the lights out to reduce their anxiety (but call it "more romantic"), or close their eyes and ignore their partner so they can climax. Calming down enough so you stop having sexual dysfunctions or anxiety attacks is one thing—it is quite another to *really* relax. As Warren and Carol learned, you can carry a level of anxiety you don't know is there. Only when your anxiety drops *below* your baseline do you realize in retrospect that you were anxious.

If you are not centered in yourself, the longer you hug and the more you relax, the more you may suddenly feel anxiety break through your relaxation. For some the anxiety builds gradually as hugging till relaxed proceeds in a single experience. For others it surfaces suddenly, when their ability to soothe themselves is finally exceeded. They feel the discomfort that comes with trying to turn off their emotional radar. That's what Warren ran into when he finally started to relax. It caught him by surprise—something he didn't tolerate very well. I tried to help him use his own reaction: "You've made enough progress to realize what you've accepted as 'being relaxed' is really a baseline of tension you carry like body armor. Martial arts experts don't stay at 'red alert,' ready for battle at any moment. They are perfectly relaxed because they know they can take care of themselves. Their 'safety' doesn't come from trusting other people; it comes from knowing they can trust themselves. They've shown themselves they can respond effectively when the situation warrants. They focus their energies and act decisively when need be, rather than squandering energy reacting unnecessarily to things better off ignored or self-soothed.

"When you are constantly clanking around in your emotional armor, you are a sitting duck for anyone who wants a fight. You can't move quickly because you are stressed out all the time. You keep your radar going full strength, but you can't see anything new. Being tense offers little protection, increases your vulnerability, gives a false sense of security, and increases your reactivity. If you relax and quiet down, you can 'go to war' if you have to without squandering your resources. I'm not trying to lull you into dropping your defenses; I'm suggesting you defend yourself in a smarter way."

Warren expected me to encourage him to "lower his defenses" and make himself vulnerable, as if this were a virtue. I knew that would only make him more reactive and defensive. He seemed surprised and relieved that I spoke of better ways of reducing his vulnerability. He looked calmer when he turned from me and held Carol's gaze for several pregnant moments.

For such an innocuous activity, hugging is loaded with meaning and emotion. Some people tell themselves their anxiety is about letting someone come close to them—when actually they *wish* that were the problem. It's stressful being physically close to someone from whom you feel totally emotionally distant. In quiet embrace we realize how far apart we are.

The nice thing about hugging till relaxed is that you can trigger emotional issues that limit your depth of involvement in sex and intimacy—while you have your clothes on. People are more likely to become "reptilian" when they drop their drawers. Becoming profoundly quiet, deeply connected, and at peace while you're touching your partner—in a hug or through intercourse—reflects your personal maturity and paves the way for the flowering of your full sexual potential.

Self-Soothing

Self-soothing involves turning inward and accessing your own resources to regain your emotional balance and feeling comfortable in your body. Your breathing is unlabored, your heart slows to its normal rate; your shoulders are relaxed, no longer hunched to ward off an anticipated blow. Self-soothing is your ability to comfort yourself, lick your own wounds, and care for yourself without excessive indulgence or deprivation.

Many people ask how I "teach" self-soothing. I have two answers: first off, I don't teach. Life brings situations requiring self-soothing and we teach ourselves. Hugging till relaxed is a good learning situation.

My second answer involves two true stories: when my daughter Sarah was five years old, she wanted me to watch her jump off a "scary" diving board into a swimming pool. Rather than walking to the end and leaping once she had my attention, she sat down in the middle of the diving board. "I'm not ready," she said seriously, "I have to get myself quiet." Profoundly impressed, I said, "Take your time, there's no rush." Thirty seconds later she stood up with a grin and an exuberant squeal, and flung herself off the end of the board.

Later that night, as I put her to bed, I reminded Sarah of what she had done on the diving board. "I hope you remember how you calmed yourself today. That's an important ability. If you take care of yourself like that whenever you feel scared—about how things are going, or being pushed by your friends to do something—you'll enjoy life a lot more." I wasn't quite sure how much she understood.

Several minutes later she allowed me to enter a new place in her inner world: she told me she was afraid of the dark. I said, "Remember what you did on the diving board? That's the trick when you're afraid of the dark."

"That's the trick?!" she repeated in wonderment.

"Yup, but knowing the trick isn't the same as being able to do it. If you practice and get good at it, the dark won't scare you anymore."

A week later Sarah came home in tears, heartbroken. Several playmates had banded together against her, pretending she was "invisible." "My feelings are hurt! They were mean to me!" she cried. I commiserated with her for several minutes, but this seemed to make her hurt more. Then I stopped acting like a nervous parent.

"Do you remember what you did on the diving board, quieting yourself?" Distracted from her painful reverie, she nodded as her tears ceased. "If you do that right now, you'll probably feel much better."

"But they were *mean* to me!" she wailed.

"That hurts, and it also hurts to think your friends probably *wanted* you to feel bad. Even people who love you occasionally do that. It's not good, but it happens. It helps if you can be nice to yourself when others aren't nice to you. If you do now what you did on the diving board, you won't hurt as much."

I sat inches away from her and imagined myself doing hugging till relaxed with her, although we never touched. I was close enough that she could feel me, even though she couldn't verbalize what was happening. To our mutual relief, after sitting quietly for a few minutes, Sarah leaned over and whispered in my ear, "Want to hear a secret? . . . You don't have to stay with me tonight after you read me my bedtime stories! I don't think I'll be as afraid of the dark anymore."

You can develop your ability to soothe yourself, like Sarah did, in your marital relationship. While Sarah is learning every day from her relationships, she is also the beneficiary of what my wife and I have accomplished. As a couple you can pass along similar benefits to your children. Start experimenting with hugging till relaxed in private, where you won't be distracted. But when you get good at it, do it in your livingroom and kitchen so your kids can see and feel it. Modeling intimacy and interest in physical contact is only one benefit. You can also change the atmosphere in your home. Since families with young kids are an inherently undifferentiated emotional network, being near parents in a soothing, intimate interaction often has the impact of calming children.

The second story is about my mother: Mom's father died of a heart attack when she was twelve years old. The following year her mother and two of seven siblings were killed in an automobile accident. Not surprisingly, she grew up seeing the world as a dangerous place and anticipating losing anyone she loved. She married my father when they were both twenty-one and a year later he was missing in action during World War II. For the next ten months my mother didn't know if her husband was dead or alive. After he returned a year later, they went through a difficult period while Dad suffered from post-traumatic stress syndrome and medical complications from his prisoner of war experience.

As her first-born child, I was the recipient of Mom's anxieties. For most of my childhood and adolescence I kept her at a distance, trying not to get infected with her perpetual concerns. Being as controlled as she was by her fears, I found it hard to feel she ever really took care of me—although she was intrusive and hovering. I never doubted her good intent, though, which made my distancing behaviors difficult for both my parents and myself. They thought I was complaining that Mom was criticizing or taking out her frustrations on me (which she didn't do), when, in fact, I was reacting to her difficulty managing her anxiety.

(Going over this portion of *Passionate Marriage* with my parents prior to publication, we found tremendous value in this important clarification. It brought us to a new level of ease with each other. Estranged children and parents often experience the same benefit when they recognize they've interpreted interactions in overly personal ways and mistaken each other's intent. The difference between "My parents (children) criticize me"—taking things "personally," which a reflected sense of self encourages—and "My parents (children) are acting out of their own anxiety" is small but significant. It creates a different world filled with new opportunities.)

My mother did not develop much ability to self-soothe until she was in her seventies. (Things between us actually started improving a decade earlier when, much to my surprise, she told me "go screw yourself" one time when I was badgering her. I never heard my mom talk like that.) It took going through challenges she (and I) never thought she could handle: both she and my father developed forms of throat cancer and my dad had prostate cancer, too. You might assume that, given her age, Mom would respond to these dangers by intensifying her lifelong patterns. But she took them as her wake-up call rather than "freezing" in fright; she learned to soothe herself—in part because she needed to. It was also the generous thing to do: it would help her husband and two sons cope with what might lie ahead. (Two main points of *Passionate Marriage* are that people are more resilient and driven by what is good and solid in them than we think, and going through—not around—crises often triggers differentiation.)

For their fiftieth wedding anniversary, my folks took my and my brother's families to Jamaica to celebrate. In contrast to being afraid of everything, my mother tried every activity the resort offered—reef snorkeling, open ocean swimming, kayaking, and being dragged behind a jetboat seated in an inner tube! Mom was the only adult to line up with the young kids who tried jet-tubing. The boat driver was so impressed he gave her an extra-long ride—a half-hour tour up and down the coastline!

The finale was Mom asking me to take her out to the reef in a small sailboat. As fate would have it, a gust of wind capsized us directly over the reef, dragging me over it with inches to spare as I held onto the boat with one hand and kept the removable rudderboard from floating away with the other. My mother drifted off in another direction behind me, where I couldn't see her. I was terrified Mom would panic and try to stand on the reef, where she would be cut by sea urchins and sharp coral. As I became more frantic, I suddenly heard a calm voice behind me say, "Don't worry, David, I'm fine. I'm just floating behind you. I won't do anything until you tell me to." I burst into tears!

This was a memorable time in my life. My mother hadn't burdened me with her anxieties. In fact, she gave me an enormous gift—one only she could give—by "simply" taking care of herself and allowing me to respect her. The waterfront lifeguards eventually used the jetboat to rescue us. But my mother was the one who saved the day. It was a turning point in our relationship—I felt my mother really took care of me, simply by soothing *herself*!

Self-soothing involves meeting two core challenges of selfhood: (a) not losing yourself to the pressures and demands of others, and (b) developing your capacity for self-centering (stabilizing your own emotions and fears). Sometimes we miss the chance to become self-*centering* and self-soothing because we fear becoming self-*centered*—selfish, self-preoccupied, and indifferent to others.

Conventional wisdom suggests that the ease with which we lose our equilibrium with someone ("I'm head over heels in love," "she knocked me off my feet") reflects our degree of caring. Maintaining equilibrium is interpreted as indifference. Conventional wisdom, however, ignores reality: people who lose their equilibrium become completely self-centered until they regain it. Our ability to maintain ourselves in close emotional proximity to our partners doesn't lead to self-interest at their expense. Differentiation helps us tolerate the tension in recognizing our partners as separate individuals with competing preferences, needs, and agendas.

Emotional Siamese twins aren't so lucky—they often feel compromised to the point of obliteration. If they finally start to self-center and self-soothe (often only when on the verge of divorce), they overshoot the mark by asserting emphatically, "I am going to be who I really am, and my spouse can take a hike if she doesn't like it!" This, however, is still the attitude of someone who either easily loses himself/herself or is self-centered.

Someone who is self-centering (that is, willing and able to hold onto oneself) has no need for the "I don't care what you think" mind-set. The point is not to thumb one's nose at one's partner or deny his reality: if yours is the only permissible reality, differentiation loses its meaning in theory and practice. People who are clear about who they are and what they believe are able to value and listen to others' opinions and feelings without losing their own position.

The solution to marital problems isn't becoming more heartless or hard-hearted—it's taking better care of your own heart. Once you learn self-soothing, you can apply this to everyday life when you are tolerating pain for the sake of growth (differentiation). This comes in handy if you're a parent or a spouse.

Holding On and Letting Go

For the first several weeks practicing hugging till relaxed, Carol did all the initiating. Sometimes Warren participated; sometimes he begged off as being "too tired." Carol was the "pursuer" and Warren the "distancer." Eventually she got angry about making all the approaches. The same dynamic surfaced in the hug itself: when they hugged, Warren wanted to break off the hug before Carol did.

In a session, Carol asked, "What if he wants to stop and I don't? Warren *always* stops before I'm ready." Warren winced in embarrassment.

"Well, you could hold Warren whether he likes it or not, or you could let go."

"You mean *he* determines how long we hug—forever?!" Carol thought I was placing Warren's interests above hers; Warren thought I was offering him a way out.

"Are you saying Warren has to hug because *you* want to? Do you really mean you'd take his hugs on that basis?"

"No . . . I don't want to force him. I want him to *want* to hug me and get pleasure out of it."

"You think I'm taking Warren's side, but I'm saying this for *you*. If you want to feel desired—feel Warren's own motivation to be with you—then you may have to let go when Warren wants to. I'm not saying you should do this forever or that you have to do everything Warren's way. Quite the contrary. It's probably in your best interest to consider how important this is to you and if you're prepared to give up what you want."

"What do you mean?" Carol decided I wasn't selling out her interests.

"It may be that you will never get to be intimate with Warren the way you want. That's just the deal—the way intimacy plays out in marriage. Your partner *can* stop you from ever being intimate with him. Each of us has a monopoly in this way. But he can't stop you from sharing that with *somebody* for the rest of your life. If you can't tolerate that notion, pull Warren into a hug or hold him even when he wants to let go."

"I've tried that. It feels terrible! I hate that!!"

"I don't doubt it. But I'm wondering why you'd even be willing to try? Where did you come from, and who have you been with, that you're willing to chase after someone to hold you?"

Carol burst into tears, and talked about her childhood experiences with her distant father and rejecting mother. Seeing this pattern surface in the way she hugged gave her a taste of her past—and new resolve that her future would be different.

"You sound like you feel rejected when Warren pulls back."

"That's the way it feels!"

"You're taking Warren's lack of desire to hug as a negative reflection on you. Did you do the same with your folks?"

Carol sobbed convulsively several times. "I thought Daddy would pay attention to me if my grades were better than my older sister's. Mom was always angry at me. I figured it was my fault. It wasn't until high school that I started to realize that Daddy had difficulty letting anyone close. Being an attorney and often traveling to litigate cases around the country really suited him. I always thought it was me."

"Well, if you want it, you've got a real-life opportunity to unhook your sense of self from how you perceive yourself reflected by others. There isn't much difference between what you're describing with your parents and what you're doing when Warren wants to end the hug or he doesn't want sex." Carol stopped crying and looked at Warren.

"If you want to spend the rest of your life chasing Warren, hold on when he wants to end the hug. It's like saying 'I'm not going to take NO for an answer! I'm going to make you give me what I want!' Watch Warren's response."

"What about Warren? Doesn't he have to confront why he wants to run away?"

"Maybe he does—but it won't occur by your holding on when he wants to stop. If you grab him and won't let go, Warren never has to confront himself—he just confronts *you*. He jumps to the side of his ambivalence that doesn't want to hug or be intimate. You embody the side of him that does, and he counts on you to pull him into it. Warren gets to hug and have sex without *wanting*, because you do the wanting for both of you. You make it safe for him not to want you. For all your complaints and demands about being wanted, *you* make it possible for the relationship to continue without getting what you say you want. If that's what you want, hold on when Warren wants to end the hug. But if you ever hope to be *wanted*, let go of him when he's ready to stop."

Carol didn't like what I was saying but she saw its merit. She feared Warren wouldn't confront himself and work it through. She settled down, which (predictably) made Warren nervous.

I turned to Warren, "Warren, 'running away' is Carol's perception of your behavior; I don't assume you necessarily see it that way."

"I feel like you're telling her to push me away. She already does that when I want to end our hugs."

"Actually, I'm suggesting the opposite. If Carol stops taking personally your lack of desire to hug, she doesn't have to push you away. Your reaction doesn't have to be a rejection of her; it's simply your reaction. If it's a reflection on anybody, it's a reflection on you."

"When you say it's a reflection on me, it sounds like you're saying there's something wrong with me."

"I don't think you were put on earth to hug or have sex with Carol. You have a perfect right not to do either one. That doesn't make you defective. You are entitled to your preferences, but you're not entitled to make Carol live in accordance with them. That's your two-choice dilemma. When I say your reaction to hugging is a reflection of you, that doesn't mean it's a *negative* reflection. I'm just saying your reaction makes sense in terms of who you are and where you've been. I said the same thing when we looked at why Carol was willing to chase after you to hold her. People have good reasons how and why they hug or don't, although usually not the ones they think."

Warren became a little less defensive. "Is there a way I can use hugging till relaxed like you showed Carol? I'm not good at doing it. I'm going to want to break the hug."

"Is there something wrong with that?"

That caught Warren by surprise. "What do you mean?"

"Maybe at first you won't do it for as long as you think you 'should.' But think of things you now do with ease that you didn't think you could do. By the way, looking competent at all times is pretty important to you, isn't it? Do you need to be competent to feel lovable?"

"I . . . I don't like doing things I don't do well. How'd you know?"

"I got it from your reaction to hugging. Even your thoughts about doing it reveal who you are."

Warren's attitude changed as he saw how I approached hugging till relaxed. "What should I do when I want to let go but Carol doesn't?"

"Do what you think is in your best interest. You have several options. One is continuing because you're afraid Carol will be angry with you or you may lose her. You can see what kind of hug that produces."

"I know all about that kind of hug. It's awful. What if I want to get through this for *me* but I still want to let go?"

"For starters, stop being afraid this reaction will come up. You can almost count on it—but it doesn't have to be a problem. You can stand there and quiet yourself down. Either you'll have a better time than you've had before, or you'll find out what's always been in the way. Actually, I wish you a little of both. If you stop fearing your reaction and *use* it, you can't go wrong."

"How do I use it?"

"When you get it through your head that Carol is willing to let you go, you may find yourself more willing to stay. If you want to let go, let go. But if *you* want to work this through, you can stay in the hug even though your guts are screaming, *I've got to get out of here. I can't breathe. I feel like I'm suffocating.*

"I know that feeling! But I don't know how to get rid of it!"

"Instead of trying to kill off a part of yourself—in your words, 'get rid of it'—maybe you can talk to yourself like a friend. Maybe something like, *I'm driving myself nuts! This is not the end of the world. This is a hug. I'm acting like this is bigger than life. Even though it has lots of meaning, if I really don't want to do this, I don't have to. But if I want the benefit, I need to stop complaining and get on with the process. I may end up getting divorced, but that, honestly, is the deal. So let me stop driving myself nuts with "what if" and just relax for a moment. If "what if" happens, I'll be better prepared to face it if I'm calm. If my world is about to end, at least let my last moments will be relaxed.* If you try this self-soothing, listen to the tone of voice you use with yourself. Keep your arms around Carol and quiet yourself down. Eventually you may begin to hug for longer and quieter periods—and it might even feel good!"

"What if I don't quiet down and relax? What if I still feel like I've got to escape?" Warren's anxiety was palpable.

I realized I needed to take a moment to quiet myself there in the session. My heart was starting to race. Warren's anxiety was getting to me.

After a long relaxing exhale I said slowly, "It can go that way—but you don't have to be afraid of it. Do you know what that feeling is really about?"

"No . . . I really don't."

"Well, then there's some advantage to not getting rid of it—quite yet. As you stand there in the hug, you may find your guts don't quiet down. They may get louder . . . AND LOUDER . . . **AND LOUDER**. And what has always been in the way of your being intimate and relaxed with Carol will get clearer in your awareness. If you finally allow it to get loud enough, you may figure out what's chasing you."

"What if I don't want to do The Hug at all?"

I took another long breath, and deliberately spoke slowly and gently. "If you don't want to do The Hug, don't do it. I have no difficulty encouraging either of you to hold onto yourself, regardless of how you define it. There's no gift in buying Carol off and then being resentful about it. People who resist hugging because they 'need space' or fear 'losing themselves' often have to go through openly saying NO. If you finally say 'I'm not doing The Hug'—without any guarantee of Carol's response—it may reassure you that you won't lose yourself. I've seen this refusal paradoxically free people to hug deeply. But let me warn you, this doesn't happen if you do it to manipulate yourself—or Carol."

Warren turned to her. "You're not angry with me, are you?"

"I'm worried we might not stay together, but I'm not angry with you. This is what I said I always wanted. I feel scared. How do I seem to you?"

"You seem calm and quiet." *That* had Warren worried.

Don't kid yourself that this session turned everything around. Insight doesn't set us free—it just lets us know where the fight is. The question remains whether we are willing to fight it out—not with our partner but with *ourselves*.

Warren never initiated hugging till relaxed between therapy sessions, but Carol no longer nagged or initiated like he expected. She was preoccupied, struggling with the fact that Warren had never actually chosen her. That, combined with her insights about her parents, made her determined not to initiate. Carol wanted to be chosen. Warren thought she was "testing" him. Had he realized she was testing *herself*, he would probably have been less defiant and more worried.

Without realizing it, Warren started our next session true to his image of himself by announcing, "I didn't do what you told us to do."

"What did I tell you to do?"

"You know, hugging till relaxed."

"You *wish* I had told you to do it. Once you have your back against the wall, you know how to respond. My guess is you are on unfamiliar ground. . . . By the way, nice try! I admire competency in all forms!"

I grinned at Warren. At first he was uncertain what I meant. He truly was on foreign turf. I watched him process each piece of what I had said. When he finally digested my last statement, he looked at me. Then he smiled back. I knew he still had a chance.

"What if I never get around to doing The Hug?"

"Then you never get around to doing it."

"Well, if I don't do The Hug—or we never have sex—Carol's going to think I'm not motivated and we might get divorced!"

Once again, I had to calm myself down in session with Warren. Slowly I said, "I understand that. I still have to encourage you not to do The Hug or have sex if you decide you don't want to. If you just do it out of fear—or because I tell you to—you're likely to get divorced anyway. You can soothe yourself doing The Hug or soothe yourself that refusing to do it may result in Carol's saying good-bye. You can learn to soothe yourself either way.

"You're not going to get anywhere if you won't confront your own ambivalence. Carol can't trap you long enough for you to learn to master yourself. She has to let go of you for you to do it. You may interpret this as meaning that she is giving up on you or she doesn't love you anymore. Although you don't like being trapped into The Hug—or sex—it makes you feel secure (for the wrong reason) when she asks for either one. If you want your feet held to the fire, they are your feet—hold them there yourself.

"When you hug from this *emotional* position, hugging is different. It isn't how you move your body, it's about your internal stance. We're talking about literally putting your arms around your partner—or not—and holding onto *yourself*."

Warren decided to see if he could hook Carol as usual. "You're not angry at me, are you?"

"I'm angry you're asking me. Decide for yourself. I've got my own problem: am I going to live with someone who takes me for granted, doesn't respect me when I'm kind to him, and has never chosen me?"

Carol and Warren left the session shaky and uncomfortable. Gridlock had reached critical mass. Both were struggling with their two-choice dilemma. They were in their crucibles.

Carol sagged for a week and then found herself. Warren started picking at her again, but she didn't try to appease him as she had in the past. Carol's noncompliance threatened Warren the same way her compliance had frightened him before. Warren regressed to his knee-jerk emotional response: attempting not to want, while demanding more from her. He escalated his provoking behaviors. Carol didn't react. Warren escalated more. Carol still didn't react. And in a strange, predictable, and wonderful way, the pressure went up in Warren but not in the relationship. Carol didn't get infected with his anxiety and didn't take his discomfort as a reflection on herself. She knew he was testing her resolve and recognized the importance of not overreacting. Actually, it was getting easier not to take Warren's diatribes personally. She could stay in emotional contact with him and remain cordial—even friendly—without taking a load of abuse from him. She was becoming more differentiated—and Warren could feel it.

At their next session Carol looked remarkably unburdened. Warren, however, was distraught. Carol said with no malice, "My husband is having a fight with me—by himself. I'm having an okay time with him. He didn't initiate hugging till relaxed and I didn't push him."

Warren's mounting fears of losing Carol had crystallized into a suspicion that she might be attracted to someone else. She was clearly less dependent on him for a reflected sense of herself—it was as if he preferred to think she was getting it from another man than realize she was getting it from herself. Warren missed the control, attention, importance, and illusion of security this had offered him.

"You don't care anymore!"

Carol didn't even bother defending herself. When he realized she wouldn't take the bait and argue, Warren turned to me. "I must really be screwed up!"

"What makes you think you're so unique?"

"I don't think other people have the difficulty I'm having."

"I hate to puncture your narcissism, but that's just not true. I've seen this with lots of people—people who've been sexually abused, for instance. You think *you* have fears of being engulfed or abandoned? They have a hard time believing that their body belongs to *them*, especially when they are close to someone they love." Warren silently took this in.

"How about people with disabilities, or women who have had mastectomies? What do you think it's like for them to let themselves be held? Make your own decision about doing hugging till relaxed. Hold onto yourself. Only when you're at home inside yourself do you have someplace good to invite your spouse to visit. You don't get that by giving yourself up—it comes from holding onto yourself. Holding yourself. It makes it safe to relax."

"I have a real block about relaxing and letting go!"

"Then why not stop trying to do that. Maybe you should be thankful for your 'block.' Maybe it's a sign of health. You need to get better at holding onto yourself rather than letting go. You seem to think the price of love is giving someone else the use of you."

"That's what my mother wanted me to do with her." Finally! Warren let me know he'd put together the historic level of what was happening for him in the hugging.

"If you're smart enough to figure that out, maybe you don't have to do what you think your mother wants." Warren was starting to pull himself together.

"I can understand you think you're supposed to 'relax and let go.' Many people think that's what they are supposed to do. That's exactly the misguided notion therapists tell women who have difficulty having orgasms. It makes sense on the surface, but it backfires. When people with experience like yours—or those who've been sexually abused—try to follow the 'relax and let go' guideline, they have predictable difficulty. Your own experience says 'letting go' of yourself is a disaster. It's no wonder you're reluctant to do this. It *should* fill you with anxiety.

"One of the biggest roadblocks to 'letting go' is the misguided suggestion to 'relax and let go.' 'Letting go' requires a stronger grip on oneself than many people have. It takes *more* self-control, not less, to really 'let go.' It's the proverbial 'tight grip on a loose rein.'

"Do what you want, but you might try getting a better grip on yourself rather than trying to lose control. If you get clear you are not turning yourself over to *anybody*—not to your mother, your wife, your fears, not even to your therapist—*then* maybe you will feel safe and be able to relax!"

"Is there something I can do to help Warren?" Carol asked.

At first I wondered why Carol was making this offer at the moment Warren seemed to be at his strongest. Was this her ambivalence about Warren standing on his own two feet? But from what transpired at home and in my office, she didn't seem to be asking because she was caving in. She was asking from a position of strength; she genuinely wanted to help.

"If you have faith in Warren, when you are hugging till relaxed don't rub his back or try to soothe him. If you want him to relax, stop focusing on him. If he's nervous and you try to *make* him feel better, two things happen: he feels pressured to feel better—which usually means neither of you feels better or relaxed. And you take the fact he doesn't feel better personally—then you don't feel good. That's the price of sat-isfying others for the purpose of feeling good about yourself or know-ing who you are.

"If you want to do something helpful, put your arms around War-ren, hold onto yourself, and quiet *yourself* down. If you want to soothe him, give him someone to hold who's already quiet."

Well-differentiated couples hold onto each other and try to make one another feel good. The difference is that the outreach is a choice rather than a necessity; it is done from a place of stability rather than insecu-rity, and done for the other person rather than one's own needs. The re-laxed, warm tone between such partners and the richness of their connection differ drastically from a poorly differentiated couple. The difference is not in the behaviors; it's inside the people doing them.

Remember the little baby you imagined holding at the beginning of this chapter? If the baby is crying and you are calm and quiet when you pick it up, the baby is likely to quiet down. Now imagine picking up the crying baby while your hypercritical parent is in the room. You need the kid to shut up, you're not sure it's going to, and you're ready to die of embarrassment. You pick up the baby—and the baby cries more! That's because the baby can *feel* you.

We are "prewired" with an interpersonal communication system—it's how we broadcast both anxiety and sexual vibes. Anxiety is infec-tious; many people don't have enough differentiation (emotional immunization) to not "catch" it from their partner. (That's what started to happen to me in session with Warren.) Usually we either get anxious in their proximity or we move away. But if the partner who is calm doesn't get infected with anxiety and stays in connection with the anx-ious partner, the anxious partner calms down—unless the anxious one insists the partner join in the anxiety as a sign of "caring," "under-standing," or "empathy."

I asked Carol, "Are you strong enough to *hold* Warren—not hold him up or 'support' him—just hold him, while each of you supports your-self? Supporting someone's emotional growth sometimes requires de-manding that he carry his own weight in a relationship—and you carry your own. Can you allow yourself to be *held* the same way?"

"In the past I would have said, 'Sure!' Now I'll say I'm willing to find out."

"Then you might want to take time to process your experiences with hugging till relaxed in private, separately. You can always tell Warren what you've found. The point is, don't try to arrive at the same reaction or a single reality. Each of you needs to understand your own experience, past and present, and your own position in your gridlock issues."

If relaxed connection isn't a common occurrence in your relationship, you may find that you feel "all kinked up" when you start hugging till relaxed. You'll probably be tense and so will your partner. It's part of getting in touch with what's been in the way of really connecting. Putting your bodies together when you are tense may not seem like a smart idea, but you may find you "fit together" in surprisingly familiar ways. Relaxing sounds great in theory, but it can create a new problem: you don't fit together anymore—literally.

As you start to relax, you'll probably have to readjust your position so you're comfortable on your own two feet *and* better "fit" your partner. But if you and your partner are highly reactive to each other, he may misinterpret this as meaning you want to stop. He may break off the hug—when that's the exact opposite of what you wanted. Hearts are often broken.

If you are insecure and dependent on your partner's validation, what do you do when this happens? Probably nothing at all—except perhaps get angry at your partner for "rejecting" or misinterpreting you. You stop hugging even if you weren't ready to stop. Who wants the vulnerability of saying "I want you" at that moment? While these are understandable reactions, it works better to stay in the hug, soothe yourself, and gently say, "I'm just shifting position to get more comfortable. I want to linger here with you a little longer."

Attendees at our Couples Retreats report a new sense of freedom when we suggest they may need to shift their position whenever it becomes awkward in the midst of hugging till relaxed. A surprising number feel they need "permission" to do this, not realizing it's actually in both partners' interest.

There is no room for anyone to readjust his or her "position" (in the hug or the relationship) when partners take each other's movements as personal rejection. If you think rapid ejaculation makes sex "over before it's over," that's slow compared to the speed of muscle tone Morse code. Calming yourself, you might hold an internal conversation: *Let's stop this 'you're going to reject me' nonsense and see what's really between us.*

You can put your arms around your partner and continue your internal dialogue. *Maybe you don't want to be with me—but that's not the same thing as rejecting me. You, my partner, have a right to choose whom you want to be with. You can vote about whether or not you want to be with me, but you no longer get a vote about whether or not I'm okay. The whole point is, I need to hold onto myself—especially if you don't want to hold me.*

You might want to remember this when you partner jolts, lets go, or wants to adjust his position. One or the other inevitably happens when you hug till relaxed past four-Mississippi. A two-minute hug is eternity for many, but it usually takes at least that long—and sometimes ten or twenty minutes—to reach a deep, relaxed connection.

Warren waited two more weeks before he asked Carol to do hugging till relaxed. They did it several times each week for several weeks, and each time *wasn't* better than the last. Some were more relaxing than others—those "others" allowed us to resolve the issues between them and within them. The tone between Warren and Carol became more collaborative. They used their own reactions to hugging to work on themselves, rather than on each other. Their growing respect for themselves and each other kept pace with their reports that hugging was "getting better." They had no genital sex (without a word about this from me) until they had their "breakthrough." Six weeks into hugging till relaxed on a regular basis, Warren and Carol finally experienced a quiet, solid connection. Hesitantly, Warren told me about it: "I realize now how much I haven't wanted to relax. It frightens me. As long as there is tension between Carol and myself, in a funny way it organizes me. In The Hug when I start to feel quiet, I get afraid—afraid of being happy because it might go away. I begin to enjoy Carol and I get afraid she will go away."

Warren turned to Carol with tears in his eyes. "The self-centering starts to feel so good I get afraid I'll miss it or I'll never have it again—or I'll miss sharing it with you. . . . I have a feeling I don't deserve to feel this. I struggle with an impulse to provoke an argument. I fight my feeling that you deserve someone better than me. Then I start to get quiet again and I let myself feel profoundly good . . . and sad."

Warren allowed Carol to hold his hand as he continued to cry. The air in my office was filled with "clean" pain; the absence of anxiety was remarkable. It was quiet and respectful.

After a minute I asked, "How did you do it?"

"Well, first I mentally talked to myself in a nice way and calmed myself down. Then I used your suggestion for scanning my body to see where I might have stored up tension. My face and buttocks were tighter than I ever imagined. I also gradually deepened and slowed my breathing. I surprised myself that I could do this. I realized my tongue was relaxed in the back of my throat and my breath came easily. Then two things happened automatically: I was aware of Carol's breathing—but it didn't throw me—and then suddenly all these parts came together and I had a totally different experience. We were—I was—just *quiet*! "I previously thought we'd been doing hugging till relaxed, but we were really just standing there with our arms around each other. We've been 'practicing' for a month. Last night we did it for the first time. Now I understand what you mean by *depth* and *feeling* each other. It's entirely different!"

"What it would be like to have that feeling when you and Carol have sex? Would that be more like making love?"

"I can't even imagine it—much less imagine myself doing it!"

"Well, you couldn't imagine ever feeling what you do through your hugs."

"I couldn't imagine being where Carol and I now are, either."

Carol didn't imagine Warren would initiate sex in the following week, but he did. The "peace" wasn't as good as they experienced doing hugging till relaxed, but they applied what they'd learned. Now they knew what to look for. As their connection during sex became calmer and deeper, it also became more erotic. Warren began to look forward to sex with Carol and initiated more frequently. Having watched Warren refuse to initiate until he was ready, Carol finally got it through her head that Warren was *choosing* her. Choosing Carol meant that Warren had finally chosen himself.

Appreciating the subtleties of hugging till relaxed prepares you for using what follows in subsequent chapters. Doing these suggestions is self-validated intimacy in action. Discovering the untapped potentials within even a simple hug expands your opportunities for deeply fulfilling sexual connection.

Hugging till relaxed is one milestone on the sexual road less traveled. It embraces the paradox that "boundaries" both block and facilitate intimacy. As intimacy and differentiation increase, your ratio of "time in synch" to "time out" will probably increase—but time out becomes increasingly important too. Poorly differentiated people envision time apart as an insignificant shadow of their time together.

The fact that disengaging is one key to intimate connection may seem surprising at first. But remember: your primary level of differentiation (which controls your ability to maintain yourself in close proximity to others) is heavily determined by the degree to which your own parents achieved some disengagement from their own parents, and how much this occurs between you, your parents and siblings, and important others. This is true of subjective experience doing hugging till relaxed, and true to the basic nature of intimacy: it involves awareness of self in the context of other, and not simply "knowing your partner" or "being close."

The fundamental link between disengagement and connection is even evident between infants and mothers. Infants disconnect to "re-fuel" in preparation for the next connection with mother. This is so well documented that it has been quantified on a ratio of eight seconds "in" and one "out." During disengagement the child looks away and breaks the gaze with mother. Mothers who can't tolerate this discontinuity be-cause of their own anxiety "drain" the baby.

Hugging till relaxed is one pathway to integrating sexuality and spirituality—and the link between disengaging (from your immediate environment) and connecting on a deeper level is evident even here.

Let me end with a quote from a contemporary Jesuit monk, Sebast-ian Moore:

> The simplest form of awakening to God is . . . a new, intense sense of self, accompanied with a desire . . . with the feeling of being a des-tiny. This condition . . . cannot be induced. It simply happens. But from time immemorial, in different cultures and religious climates, people have used a method for quieting or simplifying consciousness so that a person may be better disposed for the moment of awaken-ing.

Chapter 7

Love and Foreplay Aren't Blind, Unless You Insist on It

Though I know he loves me,
Tonight my heart is sad;
His kiss was not so wonderful
As all the dreams I had.

—Sara Teasdale

Several years ago *USA Today* carried a full page of my suggestions on improving marital intimacy. The Lifestyle feature by Karen Peterson included the idea of opening your eyes during sex. The next day, passing through several airports on my way to conduct a workshop, I observed several people reading leftover copies of the newspaper and watched them read the article. Their facial reactions seemed to match the range of comments I received from people at my workshop who saw the piece when it ran. Some thought, "I can't do that!" Others hoped their spouse saw the article; still others prayed theirs didn't. In all likelihood many readers became uncomfortably aware they didn't want to kiss with eyes opened.

This was exactly the article's point: normal sexual styles typically don't include intimacy-promoting behaviors, since we often don't want to do the most intimate things. That's why a couple's sexual style is typically designed to keep intimacy to tolerable levels.

Shortly after the *USA Today* article appeared, a San Francisco radio station followed up with a telephone interview. During the five o'clock drive home listeners heard the interviewer ask, "Dr. Schnarch, why on earth would you want to see who you're kissing?"

Why, indeed!

The question is funny, understandable, and yet a sad commentary on sexual normality. I responded that many people *don't* want to see. They'd rather make love to the fantasy in their head than the partner in their bed, only to complain five years hence, "You're not the person I thought you were!" It's inevitable when your unwritten prenuptial contract stipulates, "I won't really see you if you won't see me. I may demand you look at me when I talk to you in the living room, but don't look at me in bed!"

Why do we think eyes-closed kissing (and intercourse) is "more romantic"? For many, love is blind—and we're grateful that it seems that way. We are afraid we wouldn't be loved if we were truly known. We tune out our partner (or ourselves) to tolerate getting close enough to touch.

Sometime later I chatted with Helen, the director of a television show on which I was about to appear. She demurely reported that her personal experience confirmed the power of my suggestions in the *USA Today* article. With laughing eyes and an embarrassed smile, Helen confided that she and her husband had enjoyed an erotic leap in their sexual encounters.

Much to her surprise, however, Helen found that her married women friends had no intention of doing likewise. Their reasons varied: some had no desire to make sex more intimate with their husbands; they were smoldering with resentment, locked in wars of mutual withholding— in short, they *liked* making sex unpleasant for their spouse. Others were unwilling to tolerate the discomfort of trying something new, no matter what the benefits. And still others were "emotionally divorced"— staying with their husbands only for financial and social reasons: they were heeding the adage, "Keep you friends close, but keep your enemies closer."

Given the chance to see (or be seen), many of us prefer to close our eyes. We live like sexual ostriches, afraid to look *into* the one with whom we copulate and procreate—but there is always a reason for ostrich-like behavior. It is as if we fear our fate is sealed and find it easier not to examine it too closely. We don't want to be seen *not wanting to see*, however. Everyone's supposed to be eager for intimacy. That's another reason we kiss with our eyes closed!

Don't misunderstand my point. I'm not saying that Helen's friends are kissing the "wrong" way. From working with hundreds of couples, I know they were doing it "right." It took me a while to comprehend this. I had to throw away much of my professional training and what I'd learned growing up. In short, I had to stop telling my patients what to do and be willing to learn from *them*.

Once you understand that Helen's friends were doing it "right," you'll have a new perspective on foreplay that could revolutionize your marriage. I know this shift totally changed my personal and professional life.

These couples weren't kissing the "wrong" way because the issue isn't about technique. They were doing it "right" because it expressed what was and *wasn't* occurring between them. Their foreplay was a form of communication. Eyes-closed foreplay is like sexual "braille"; we all become good "readers." Helen's friends were well aware of their spouse's attitudes. They knew they were ignored by—or at least cut off from—their partner. Some of the men may not have known the difference and others may not have cared. Some may have wanted more intimacy during sex but accepted their wives' "take it or leave it, I'm doing you a favor" attitude. In each case, their wives may have sensed this and been further disinclined to be sexually generous.

Consider a couple who consulted me for longstanding sexual and marital difficulties. When I asked them to describe what their foreplay was like, the wife looked embarrassed. The husband said, "She always turns her face to the side and won't kiss me on the mouth. I end up kissing her cheek! Then she tells me to just get it over with." The wife countered, "He always insists on sticking his tongue in my mouth! Besides, I don't feel like kissing him when we can't communicate—we can't even hold a meaningful conversation."

Knowing that couples *always* communicate, I asked them, "What do you think you are saying to each other during foreplay?" After a minute the husband said, "She's telling me I'm inadequate, that I don't know how to kiss. She doesn't want me! She's just going through the motions."

The wife had a different response: "*He* wants to tell *me* how to do it! He's going to do what he wants to do, whether I like it or not!" I said to her, "I know there's a good reason, so tell me: why are you willing to have intercourse if you're not willing to kiss him?" Without hesitation, she replied, "He's less of a pain in the ass if I have sex with him. Besides, I like having orgasms!" So much for keeping romance alive in marriage.

We have been taught that foreplay is important because women find it "necessary." True, research has shown that a sexually aroused woman's vagina lubricates and swells out—*tenting* in Masters and Johnson's terms—making intercourse comfortable. But it isn't necessarily true that this takes a long time: it turns out that women respond physiologically as quickly as men when emotionally and erotically involved in the experience. So, foreplay cannot be laid on women. It isn't even true that women necessarily want longer foreplay. Think back to Helen's girlfriends and the couple I just mentioned. These women were telling their partners, "Get on with it."

Marriage manuals of the 1930s, '40s, and '50s dictated laborious foreplay and machine-perfect technique. Men were told to touch their wives like they were polishing their cars. Caught up in prescriptions for rubbing every nook and cranny, conscientious men were as estranged from their partners as if they'd skipped foreplay altogether. Trying to rub your partner the right way often rubs her the wrong way, since she's likely to feel you're just "doing your job."

It may sound obvious that foreplay isn't amenable to a skill-building approach—but you couldn't prove it by the hordes of contemporary self-help books. Now we're supposed to "communicate" and reveal what we want, as if foreplay is nonexistent unless we're moving our lips. But like the wife who refused to open her mouth when kissing her husband, we *always* communicate through foreplay.

Since learning to ignore my training that said sexual problems are caused by ignorance, ineptitude, and ineffective technique, I have approached my patients with far greater respect. I start by assuming their sexual behavior is purposeful and rich in meaning—no matter how painful those meanings, or how severe or longstanding their sexual and marital difficulties. No longer do I dismiss sexual styles as faulty or inadequate, to be immediately replaced by my superior techniques. Now I understand, in retrospect, why couples didn't act on the sexual prescriptions I used to give—or get the results I (and they) thought they should. And my clients now get better results.

Foreplay Always Exists

Through experiences with my clients I have arrived at a totally new understanding of foreplay: *foreplay is where we negotiate the levels of intimacy, eroticism, meaning, and emotional connection (or lack thereof) in what follows next.*

Foreplay is important because it's *inevitable*. Foreplay *always* occurs. Whether gentle or rough, extended or momentary, foreplay is a fact. Foreplay is the conscious and unconscious negotiation process that sets the emotional tone and meaning for the remainder of the encounter. Once established, it's often difficult to change in a particular sexual exchange and resistant to change in successive encounters in an ongoing relationship, too. (I'll explain why shortly.) The sameness of meaning—and not simply the same behaviors—gives marital sex its boring, repetitive quality.

How is it that so many couples argue over foreplay, despite the fact that we are bombarded daily with magazine articles on "Ten Ways to Improve Your Love Life"? Shouldn't we have "the answers" by now? We try to accept simple answers to complex questions because the full magnitude of the problem frightens us. We like to think that, in the best of circumstances, foreplay is where couples establish emotional connection and instill feelings of love, arousal, and desire in each other. More commonly, however, foreplay establishes *disconnection*. It's where we recognize there won't be much emotional intimacy when we're rubbing genitals together—and that more isn't necessarily desired.

Kissing Styles

When clients tell me they "have foreplay" without offering further description, they are assuming everyone generally does it the same way. They don't realize *nobody* does it the same. You get a picture of different people in different relationships just by "seeing" them through their sex.

Kissing styles flavor every sexual encounter and reveal more than we think. For some of us, kisses are joyous mouth-fruits, planted and harvested with all too little frequency. At one time or another, we all may have experienced:

- The soft but electric kiss of a familiar lover.
- The hard kiss of passion.
- The breathy, languid kiss of tasting and smelling each other's body.
- The gentle bite on the lip from someone begging to be "rode hard and put away wet."

The differences are amazingly subtle and important. Then there are the all-too-familiar kisses that convey the thorns of one's marriage:

- The mushy, limp kiss of passivity and withheld eroticism.
- The perfunctory kiss on the way to the office.
- The sloppy, soupy, wet kiss that triggers anger rather than desire.
- The rigid-tongued kiss of the mechanical lover.
- The smothering kiss that rekindles childhood fears of an intrusive, engulfing parent.
- The impatient kiss of a partner preoccupied with more important things.

- The bad-tasting kiss of the inconsiderate partner, whose "If you love me, take me as I am" attitude becomes the bludgeon for take-it-or-leave-it lousy sex.
- The begrudgingly given kiss of the "you can't take me for granted" lover who demands tooth-brushing and mouth-scouring (not to mention shower, shave, and pedicure) before a meeting of the tongues.

It's not too surprising that Mr. Natural and Mrs. Clean often end up married to each other (the genders can be reversed). Isn't there a place for kindly telling your partner about his/her odors, saving both of you the frustration of a reluctant, angry, breath-held kiss? Sure there is—just like there's a place for salty, freshly sweating bodies. Deep down, these people often would like to call a halt to the oral sparring. But they have other things in common besides their mouth-to-mouth combat: neither believes he or she is ever really loved. Their sexual inconsiderateness makes them feel neither loving nor lovable. It takes differentiation to fine-tune techniques without triggering issues of power, identity, or boundaries. That's why they keep fighting over mouthwash and toothbrushes.

The inevitable and necessary "You're not going to control and shape me" struggles of marriage surface through lips long before they are played out through hips. But the message of foreplay isn't confined to the lips. Where are your partner's (or your) hands? Do you gently touch each other's face while kissing? Does your hand softly stroke the back of your partner's neck, sending electric shivers down his or her spine? Does the way your partner's hand cups the back of your neck convey, "Don't go on to something new, I'm getting into this," or gruffly demand, "Press harder, you fool! You're making me angry! Put more into this!" These are all part of the elusive language of foreplay we intuitively know—and try to ignore.

Osculating (kissing) becomes a sophisticated language long before folks intentionally say what they mean with a smack, a peck, or a darn good smooch. Someone with serious intent to *do* you kisses differently from an angry, impenetrable partner or a self-preoccupied, anxious one. All three often give tight-lipped kisses. But kissing styles can't be determined by a lip rigidity meter.

Kissing reveals more than we realize—and more than we like. Kissing always contains the emotional "signature" of the kisser and kissee. It contains our reactions to who kissed us and how they kissed. It reflects how intimacy, sex, love, and our personal history are pictured in our conscious and unconscious inner world. Kissing makes a great Rorschach test—but remember, your interpretations about your spouse may say more about you than him or her. The history of your life (and marriage) determines how a kiss feels as much as the lips (and emotional dynamics) of your partner. All that is 100 percent certain is that *you* experience it the way you do—the safest interpretation to make about your reaction to foreplay is what it says about *you.* "I feel that way because of you" is emotional Siamese-twin style. Try, "What does it say about me that *I* feel this way?" Interpretations about your partner are best kept unsaid—unless you want to poke at each other's sexual blind spots in the guise of being "helpful."

As I've said, foreplay is where boundaries of intimacy and eroticism are negotiated. People read nuances of how much of either one is desired. A most revealing example is the signal that foreplay is over. Even couples who prefer oral sex to intercourse to bring each other to orgasm have a mental marker between intimate "playing around" and goal-oriented "getting down to business." In contrast to euphemisms about "making love," the end of foreplay is the end of anything to do with love in many bedrooms. To help couples see this, I use their own experiences. I ask them (and let me ask you): *"Who decides when foreplay's over and it's time for the 'main event'?"*

This question shocks many clients. People act as if the question never occurred to them. "I just know," is the common initial reply, meaning they get the message but they don't know how.

I usually have to ask twice. "So how do you know when it's time for intercourse? If you didn't know, you'd never have gotten to it last time you had sex!" Typical answers include:

- "When he/she seems impatient."
- "When he/she touches my genitals for a while."
- "When he gets an erection or is afraid he'll ejaculate."
- "When I'm bored (or my partner is)."
- "When he/she wants to get it over with."

I can always tell when I'm talking to the partner who controls the decision: he or she says, "We both decide."

Notice that none of these answers has anything to do with intimacy; they reveal sexual performance concerns or impatience. They have more to do with *alienation* than with intimacy. It's rare for either partner to say, "Foreplay's over when we're so hot and full of desire that I think we'll explode if we don't go on to something else!"

Foreplay reflects the politics of intimacy and power in your relationship.
The shift from foreplay to intercourse doesn't "just happen." Becoming aware that it involves a decision often has an impact. Couples realize foreplay is a negotiation process. This realization allows both partners to make decisions more deliberately and take more control of their sex—and their lives. Foreplay involves lots of signaling, countersignaling, and unconscious "pushing and shoving." It's hidden under common problems like low sexual desire, lack of arousal, and problems with genital function.

We never realize much of what eventually happens has already been determined before we "move on" to touch each other's breasts and genitals. By the time kissing stops and fondling begins, someone often gives up in disappointment and lumbers through "the main event."

John and Mary

When Mary and John entered treatment, the presenting problem was her lack of desire for sex. As their problem unfolded in our sessions, it turned out that Mary liked sex—what she didn't like was the way she and John went about it. One of Mary's longstanding dissatisfactions was that John repeatedly put his finger in her vagina before she wanted him to. She felt rushed and interpreted his behavior as meaning, "He's only interested in screwing me."

John felt chastised if Mary moved his hand away. He read this as meaning, "She's always criticizing me! Nothing I do is ever good enough." This imagined rebuke often prompted John to bristle and defensively tell his wife he'd had sex with lots of women and they always liked what he did. Needless to say, this did nothing to heighten Mary's desire.

Emotional fusion between John and Mary was surfacing in their foreplay. John's "contribution" was his attempt to get a positive reflected sense of himself. He was playing the common adolescent game: "If you love me (and if I'm lovable and desirable), you'll let me do it." Like a lot of men, he'd been playing at sex in this way ever since adolescence.

John was also making the common mistaken assumption of *communal genitals.* Fusion in couples often turns monogamy into an unspoken compromise depicting how emotional Siamese twins operate: *"If I'm not going to have sex with anyone else, then your genitals half belong to me. They are part of your body, but you have to make them avail-*

able to me on demand." Some women believe in communal genitals too: one insisted on sleeping with her husband's penis in her hand; he reacted exactly as Mary did.

Mary was fighting back. More than simply angered by John's attitude, she was asserting her sense of owning her own body. She didn't like being his "property," to do with what he liked. Though she had cherished the notion that "two shall become one" in their wedding vows, she hadn't foreseen that such merger would also destroy her sexual desire.

As I listened to the details of their sexual interaction, it became clear that John and Mary's behavior during sex was determined long before he ever touched her genitals. It wasn't just that they couldn't agree on timing and meaning for touching her vagina. The dynamics that destroyed the possibility of a pleasurable connection in sex existed as pervasively outside the bedroom. They experienced little connection at other times either—except via emotional fusion, which was hardly satisfying. By the time Mary complained about John's way of touching her vagina, she had long given up in disappointment, frustration, and anger. She wasn't eager for sex with John, because past experience taught her she wasn't likely to get what she wanted.

Subtle psychological distinctions in their foreplay "dialogue" affected what they did and how they felt about it. Foreplay was "for Mary." What followed was "for John." Foreplay tended to be "too brief" according to Mary because this was the part she enjoyed. To John, foreplay lasted "long enough"—and sometimes went on "interminably." These differences led to repeated arguments no stopwatch could ever settle.

I asked John and Mary, as I usually do, how they had tried to resolve their problems on their own. Their responses were typically revealing. Taking suggestions from a best-selling "sex book" they had read, Mary had tried to tell John what she really wanted from him sexually. Unfortunately, she didn't have the insight to say she wanted more connection with him—and John wouldn't have known how to touch her in a way that would have produced it. Then she followed the book's mistaken advice and tried to show John how she liked to be touched. The book said he wouldn't feel criticized if she verbalized her suggestions in a noncritical way, but John still did.

Taking another of the book's suggestions, John and Mary tried "compromising" and "win-win" negotiations about how they had sex. They tried, "I'll do a little more of what you like if you'll do more of this for me, and both of us will be happy." But that wasn't very successful, either. John and Mary were too good at reading each other during foreplay. Neither ever got what he or she *really* wanted because both felt each other's disinterest during his or her "turn." John tuned out during foreplay; Mary tuned out during intercourse. Mary could sense John felt he was doing her a favor or paying his obligatory dues; John felt like Mary just barely tolerated him during intercourse.

Actually, their experience highlights the importance of differentiation in the foreplay process. John and Mary were thoroughly emotionally fused. They were surprised when I pointed this out, because they felt so alienated and withdrawn. Like many poorly differentiated couples, they were beyond the point where simple suggestions to communicate and compromise could work.

Mary often felt she was losing control of herself and John felt entitled to the use of her body. She became withholding and less sexually desirous as she attempted to reestablish her emotional boundaries. John felt controlled whenever he tried to follow Mary's suggestions. As far as he was concerned, he'd be admitting he was wrong and she was right. Even when he waited longer before inserting his finger, Mary could feel his anger and resentment. John thought she should just let him do it and "she'd see that she liked it." He accused her of setting her mind not to like it just to make him feel bad. Even when Mary "went along with him," John was frustrated by her lack of passion and interpreted it as a negative reflection on his adequacy. He then blamed her for his bad feelings. Together, their reactions gave rise to perfunctory foreplay and lackluster sex—a situation that's painfully familiar to many couples.

Foreplay is an elegant arena in which we enact the common quests for validation and identity we discussed in Chapter 2. Unfortunately, such quests ultimately kill foreplay. The effects of low differentiation are manifold:

- As we discussed in Chapter 4, the less differentiated the couple, the less tolerance partners have for intimacy. In their sex life, this translates into superficial and brief foreplay. Couples like John and Mary eventually avoid foreplay altogether because it's too intimate and revealing.
- The often overlooked point behind "telling your partner what you like" is more than getting the stimulation you want: it's the resulting mind-to-mind contact. (That's why people don't do it.) Poorly differentiated couples are more likely to focus on technique than emotional connection.
- John and Mary illustrate that poorly differentiated couples don't

have much flexibility in altering foreplay behaviors. The problem is
that their self-concepts depend on doing things in familiar ways—
even if they don't work. It often shows up more with men than
women, due to the traditional emphasis on men having "responsibility" for orchestrating foreplay. It shows up in women when they
are asked to become more active than they are used to.

- Emotionally fused couples have difficulty tolerating the subtle—and
  sometimes not so subtle—"sign language" of foreplay. Negotiations
  are indirect, with much "pushing" and "shoving" and sexual power
  plays. Given their difficulty soothing themselves, they are likely to
  get their feelings hurt in the process of working things out.
- Poorly differentiated partners typically use foreplay to extract a positive reflected sense of themselves. This puts extra pressure on the
  spouse to "moan and groan" and get turned on—which paradoxically makes the "designated groaner" less likely to feel genuinely
  aroused. The resulting cycle is likely to diminish both partners' sexual desire.
- People have the "right" to more foreplay—and more intimacy—but
  like many rights, this one is only as useful as your willingness and
  ability to exercise it. People in poorly differentiated relationships cave
  in easily and blame their partner when they don't get what they want.

Open Your Eyes

Changing the ambience in your marriage and becoming more intimate
is sometimes no further away than hugging till relaxed and kissing in
a way I'm about to describe. Since we've already seen how complicated
hugging can be, you know I'm not trying to market an easy fix. Your
style of foreplay—just like your style of hugging—is connected to what
is inside you, and changing that is *always* a significant (but not necessarily unpleasurable) matter. Changing foreplay has far-reaching
impact—particularly once patterns in your marriage have become rou-
tinized. (In fact, that's why this topic of eyes-open sex continues in
Chapter 8.)

How do you broaden your kissing language and change the message
in your foreplay? The method is eye-opening. Literally.

Do you ever have foreplay with your eyes open?

It's amazing how many people haven't. The very question surprises
some folks, highlighting the fact that many of us are not intimate during sex—and that sex itself isn't inherently intimate.

It takes a specific kind of effort to avoid looking into each other's eyes, and when that effort is exerted, the quality of interaction is noticeably different. Recall, for instance, your family dinners when you were a kid. Were faces uplifted and animated, or did everyone stare awkwardly at their plate? Was eye contact natural and comforting? Or was it cold, vacant, disinterested, or threatening? Even little children can tell—until it gets so painful they train themselves not to notice what they are seeing and feeling.

If foreplay is the negotiation period for intimacy and eroticism in sex, think of the message you are giving if you change from street clothes to long flannel pajamas and turn off the lights before your spouse gets into bed. What about people who undress in the closet and never let their partner see them nude? Even for those with more tolerance for intimacy, the ante goes up when they open their eyes during foreplay.

Kissing with your eyes open is often a path to intensely intimate and erotic sex—although the route differs depending on what your particular need is. For some, it's an immediate turn-on; for others, it's more diagnostic and therapeutic at first. Eyes-open kissing uses foreplay's natural negotiation process in a *deliberate manner*. It helps you see what's lying under the surface of your relationship. It can also raise your level of differentiation and increase your tolerance for intimacy and passion, if that's what the two of you need.

What's it like kissing with your eyes open?

Beyond feeling a little silly and awkward at first, initial reactions are often so dramatic you can't begin to focus on your mouth. All you're aware of is *eyeballs*. Actually, eyes-open kissing makes us acutely aware of *ourselves*. You have an extreme sense of proximity and exposure to your partner. Often you want to "back off."

Paradoxically, an acute sense of yourself as a separate individual occurs when you are pressed this way against your partner. Your focus of attention rapidly oscillates inward and outward, highlighting boundaries between the two of you. You become acutely self-*conscious*—that is, you become aware of your own thoughts and feelings. The process can be a little unpleasant at first. Interestingly, this experience mirrors what I said about intimacy in Chapter 4.

When you open your eyes the first several times, you may have difficulty keeping your genitals functioning. This demonstrates how we have learned to tune out our partner *and* ourselves in order to function sexually. In Chapter 3, I pointed out that focusing on sensations (sensate focus) is the most common sexual style, and this is why: intense intimacy is hard to tolerate; eye contact just makes it apparent. The recognition helps you see what you need (and can grow) to do. The notion that "intercourse is the most intimate thing that two people can do" can be seen for the farce it is (for most people). Even those who devote their lives to "gaining insight" often don't open their eyes during sex. Many couples are not really together when they "make love."

All this was true for Mary and John. They achieved wonderful sexual connection using eyes-open foreplay, but it wasn't as simple as changing "techniques." It started with Mary confronting her feeling that John tuned her out and focused only on her body. The way she did this itself constituted a critical step in Mary's shift from other-validated to self-validated intimacy. For one thing, she never asked John to confirm or deny her perceptions. Another was the way she put eyes-open foreplay into action.

Initially, Mary considered talking with John about eyes-open foreplay before they got into bed. On the one hand, she thought he might be more willing if he had time to consider it and didn't feel "pushed." On the other hand, her general tendency was to "test the waters" about what John wanted about *everything* and then model herself accordingly. She detested how she hid in fear of his disapproval and vowed to do things differently. Mary briefly considered asking John about eyes-open foreplay in the "safety" of our therapy sessions. But she recognized that she'd never really feel "safe" if she couldn't do it on her own.

Having made this momentous decision, Mary realized that she didn't need "permission" to change herself or her marriage. It *doesn't* "take two," as the old saying goes. It takes two to keep your marriage the same; it only takes *one* to change it. When you change, the relationship changes. (The difference in these philosophies is the difference between emotional fusion and differentiation.) When this realization shook up Mary's cherished views of marriage, eyes-open kissing was already "working"—even though she had yet to do it.

Mary implemented eyes-open foreplay in one of the "cleanest" ways possible: with very little fanfare. She just opened her eyes during foreplay and saw what was going on. She wasn't staging an "ambush" or a failure so she could say she "tried." She wanted to become sufficiently solid in her sense of herself that she would stop living in fear of John's response. John often kept her off-balance with his anger, making her easy to maneuver. He would keep her hanging while he "made up his mind" about things that affected them both. He maintained control as long as he remained "undecided." If she finally refused to wait idly by, he would refuse to cooperate and blame her for "not waiting." Actually, Mary was daring *herself* in a way that made her heart leap to her throat.

Mary tried a method of kissing with intermittent pauses for eye contact I call *kissus interruptus*. It's a cute name for a sophisticated process many clients have used with great gains. While couples use *coitus interruptus* for various reasons, the same style of kissing and foreplay is almost unheard of. (It shows where most people focus.)

Tantalized by a new sense of freedom and the prospect of more self-respect, Mary stopped kissing John long enough to move her head back and take a look. In the process, she confronted self-doubts: *What if I see things I don't want to see? What's going on in my own head? And in John's? What kind of reaction am I going to get? What if his eyes are open? What am I afraid he'll see in me? What if his eyes are closed? Will he open his eyes and look at me if I ask him to? And what will I do then? What if I like this and he doesn't? Or vice versa?* Mary learned how a "little" thing like opening your eyes during foreplay can be a heroic act of bravery and self-acceptance.

John wouldn't look at her. Mary was doing more than violating his vision of "swept-away" passion. He didn't want to be "checked out." He knew her eyes were open—he peeked when she stopped kissing him long enough to get his attention. He lay there with his eyes closed without saying a word, deliberately waiting her out. Mary got anxious and started kissing again as if nothing had happened. John figured she would have learned her lesson and that was the end of it. Later he complained Mary was "testing him" and "making him jump through hoops" to get sex. But the truth was John never let anyone get emotionally close.

At first Mary thought she had failed, but she actually stood to succeed one way or another: if John had done eyes-open foreplay with her, their sex and intimacy probably would have improved. When he didn't, it challenged her to self-soothe and validate herself—to become more differentiated, which was her goal.

Eyes-open foreplay can be *real* sexy from the outset if you are almost ready for it. But such readiness often comes later for emotionally fused couples like Mary and John because the process works differently for them. Becoming more differentiated is gut-wrenching work. Getting the best sex of your lives—especially after years of lousy sex together—isn't easy or simple.

The next time they had sex Mary tried *kissus interruptus* again. But this time she did more than stop and look. She gave John a hesitant-but-friendly "Hi!" She hoped he would at least smile. Mary tried to have fun with it, saying, "Hello, are you in there? Can you come out and play?" She wanted John to join in the game, but he misperceived her words as sarcastic and hostile. John tried waiting her out again. When she didn't kiss him after several minutes, he pounced out of bed and stormed out of the bedroom—and pouted for several days.

In our subsequent therapy session Mary didn't get an outpouring of "support" and encouragement from me—and neither did John. If I "supported" Mary too much, she would never accomplish her goal of *self*-validation. John and Mary's desperate need for mutual validation was killing their sex and marriage. Shifting that dependency to me offered no real metamorphosis. John's refusal to immediately agree to Mary's request actually facilitated the process: it was vital to the differentiation process for *both* spouses to hold onto themselves, neither turning himself/herself over to the other.

What was occurring went beyond a mere battle of wills—and beyond the stubbornness and heel-dragging that characterize emotional fusion. John and Mary were each building selfhood, using each other as the testing ground. While this may sound like recipe for divorce, it's just the opposite. The pressure for togetherness between undifferentiated people—like John's demand for "communal genitals"—often blows couples apart in reaction. The paradoxical realization that your partner can never completely control you—and yet can have an impact on your life just by exercising self-control—often comforts couples enough to make new solutions possible. This is what differentiation is all about. Neither John nor Mary wanted to destroy their relationship. They wanted to improve it—but not give themselves up in the process.

Neither a bizarre nor "kinky" activity, eyes-open foreplay taps the natural and inevitable people-growing machinery of marriage. With John and Mary it brought long dormant feelings and issues to the surface. It happened "simply" by both spouses refusing to sacrifice their integrity as they experienced it in the situation at hand.

The strength and seriousness of Mary's resolve weren't clear to John until she stopped kissing during their third encounter. He opened his eyes and demanded, "What's wrong now?! Why'd you stop?!" unwittingly inviting her to criticize him. (Like many couples, John and Mary only talked during sex when "something was wrong.") Mary gave neither complaint nor defense—just a "simple" request: "Nothing's wrong," she said. "I just want more emotional contact with you. I want you to look at me while we're making love."

Emotional Siamese twins expect their partner to coerce them—which was how John experienced Mary's request. He angrily complained, "You're changing the rules without asking me!" "*I'm* changing," Mary said, "and I'm not willing to do it the old way anymore. I'm not kissing you if you won't look at me." John responded by calling her "a manipulative, controlling, withholding bitch!"

Wedlock is not always peaceful or blissful (as every married couple knows). This is particularly true when the people-growing machinery is working. Sooner or later you hit up against the fear that there won't *be* a marriage unless one of you remains willing to violate himself/herself "for the good of the relationship." That fear is part of the differentiation process.

Eyes-open foreplay is one key to the treasure chest of marital sex and intimacy. Like any key, however, it doesn't work unless you put it in the lock and turn it. Contrary to contemporary emphasis on "understanding more" or "being more understanding," differentiation doesn't occur unless you *do* something. (Don't kid yourself that just reading this book will free you or your marriage from the shackles of fusion.) Differentiation involves taking a stand that defines *you* and, at first at least, may evoke ominous responses from your partner. You are likely to hear accusations such as "You're making a mistake" or "You'll destroy our relationship" more than once before the benefits kick in.

Becoming more differentiated doesn't mean that the stand you take is "right." It means that the stand you take is *yours* and that you are responsible for your actions. Both Mary and John were struggling with difficult questions, like:

- "Am I being too rigid and demanding, or too 'easy' and a fool?"
- "Am I destroying my marriage, or trying to make it worth saving?"
- "Should I listen to reason, or am I dealing with a terrorist?"
- "Is my integrity really on the line, or am I just being selfish and stubborn?"

Grappling with such issues, with your marriage and future at stake, creates turmoil—and eventually makes you stronger. Marriage's "polishing process" uses each spouse as the abrasive to finish the other's development.

Initially, Mary was hurt and defensive about John's comments. Painful soul-searching helped her realize that she really didn't want to withhold, reject, or control him. Once she concluded that John's accusations weren't true, for the most part, Mary quieted down. In spite of everything that had transpired between them, she was still willing to try. She stopped arguing with him, which made John more worried. As long as she was upset, he knew she "cared"; now he wasn't sure. When she stopped trying to make John do what she wanted, he wasn't sure what it meant.

In Mary's fourth attempt at *kissus interruptus*, she took a more differentiated stance. When John wouldn't look at her she said: "Continuing sex this way makes me feel like I'm selling myself out. I don't respect myself, I get angry at you, and I won't do it that way anymore. You don't have to do it the way I want—I'm not going to attack or coerce you. I want a happy partner and I'm sure you do, too. Who wants sex with someone who's unhappy, even if he has his eyes open? To get what I want, you have to do it willingly, not just resentfully. It won't work if either of us gives up what we want for the sake of the relationship, because we'll just be miserable. I just hope we end up at a point we both want."

Mary's development destroyed their old style of "foreplay for Mary and intercourse for John." "Willing" wouldn't suffice anymore. Both of them would have to be *eager*—and we all know you can't force enthusiasm. As it dawned on John that Mary wouldn't—and couldn't—coerce him, he began to feel he was losing control of her. In a last desperate attempt, he accused her of "turning the tables" sexually—trying to control him as she had complained he did when he touched her vagina.

But Mary didn't fall for it. Dealing with John's accusations and barbs had made her more self-reliant and self-assured. Finally strong enough to persevere in the midst of his tantrum, she said, "I'm not trying to control you. I want a chance with you, to relax and savor the moment between us. I want to be with you, and what's happening between us is breaking my heart!"

This time, however, Mary wasn't fuming when she said it. And John could hear she really meant it. She wasn't verbally attacking him anymore. Before she would recount all the things she did for him and how he never reciprocated. She would complain about how she felt sexually misused. She would diagnose his problems with intimacy and communication. He was used to Mary comparing him to his stoic father—although it still made his blood boil. But she wasn't doing any of those things this time.

The difference wasn't lost on John, but it didn't make him happy. He was having his usual tantrum, but she wasn't having hers. It frightened him that Mary was really growing—and maybe leaving him behind.

That just made him angrier, but it seemed less safe to take it out on her. He couldn't make her do what he wanted anymore. The only real choice was to get more control of himself. Yes, he could decide to withhold from her what she wanted so that neither one would "win." But that would mean he'd probably have to give up sex—or the relationship—and that wasn't what he wanted.

When he really thought about it, he finally realized Mary wasn't trying to deprive him. She was willing to do what he wanted to do—she just wanted to go *beyond* that. The whole thing made him feel very insecure and unsettled.

John and Mary's marriage had reached a life-changing point. The truths of their lives were laid out as clearly as the boundaries that remained between them. More fighting wouldn't bridge the barriers any more than it could mask them. John and Mary each had to assess what he or she really thought was happening and decide what to do. They did it separately and, paradoxically, together. Each partner's refusal to cave in created the necessary crucible for the other.

Mary's new behavior so negated John's image of her that he felt embarrassed to have misjudged her sexual interest all along. While he wasn't about to acknowledge this to Mary, he calmed down enough to try eyes-open foreplay. Much to his surprise, he liked it—and Mary did, too. It ignited the hot sex he thought touching genitals was supposed to achieve; it was also the pathway for the warm, solid connection they both had been wanting. Eyes-open foreplay was daring and loving. John was shocked at how quickly Mary got aroused this way. They had sex a *second* time that night, accompanied with tears and laughter. They shared long-held secrets with their newfound best friend.

At their next session, John and Mary looked different. Their eyes shone brightly and they sat holding hands. They talked proudly of themselves and each other, almost in disbelief. Mary was her own person and John was willing to acknowledge it. He asked what else he could do to signify the end of "communal genitals." He decided to use an approach that "works" when people are ready to send that message. In their next sexual encounter, when Mary was ready, John moved down by her legs. He covered her vagina with the palm of his hand and his fingers rested on her pubic hair. This "palm over labia" position made it physically impossible for him to insert a finger suddenly and gave her the message that "your vagina belongs to *you*." This conscious use of foreplay changed the emotional dynamics between them—and lying as he was, they could see one another.

This position became a frequent part of their sexual encounters for a variety of reasons: Mary liked the broad pressure on her labia, not to mention the underlying message. John liked to watch Mary grind her pelvis and feel her labia pushing against him. They would start out soft and slow, but things could get hard and fast, too. Sometimes, when on her back, Mary would slip her hands beneath her buttocks and raise her hips to grind his hand. Through their connection, John could feel the difference between when Mary was pressing because she wanted more pressure and when she was "leaning into the connection" and wanted everything to stay the same. He could feel her interest and energy—he described it as Mary *doing* him. Her wetness and scent flowed onto his hand before he ever inserted a finger.

Both John and Mary started using variations of *kissus interruptus* throughout their sexual encounters. Mary used it if she felt John tuning her out and "going faster" than she wanted. John used it when his attention started to drift. He'd stop kissing briefly and say, "We have to stop for a moment. I'm losing it. I'm not really here." Mary took it as a sign of his investment in making real contact with her.

John and Mary began to look at each other frequently during sex. Eye contact would come and go. At first it was awkward. But soon both anticipated seeing a friendly smile or a sexy look when they opened their eyes. Sometimes they saw a questioning frown or an inner-focused gaze. They talked about it and kept in touch. There were plenty of opportunities to close their eyes and revel in their sensations. When Mary wanted more eye contact, she asked for it. The ease in her voice made John more eager to open his eyes.

For his part, John put to rest the pictures in his head. He realized he had always been competing with his fantasies of Mary's prior lovers. He'd imagined she let them do to her whatever they wanted. He'd always pictured it as if they were so good in bed—and he was inept. Now he saw it differently: Mary wanted him enough she was willing to struggle through difficult times to make things better. He knew this was the best sex either of them had ever had. He had fewer temper tantrums, in part because he knew Mary wouldn't put up with them anymore. But the bigger reason was that he didn't want to jeopardize the great things happening between them.

The constant tension in their relationship was dissolving, replaced by mutual begrudging respect: not "begrudging" in the sense of discontented or resentful as they had been in the past; begrudging as in hard-earned admiration from seeing Mary not cave into his tantrums or her fears. It was mutual respect based on strength and actual events, rather than lofty ideals that wither when things get tough.

Increasingly, John and Mary anticipated good times in sex. John became more willing to be "known" and less afraid of being inadequate. That openness came in handy when he eventually faced his fear that Mary liked sex more than he did. They became more flexible with each other and more generous. And equally important, both began to feel worthy of being loved.

Peekaboo!

Many people feel ill-at-ease the first time they open their eyes during foreplay. I sometimes half-jokingly suggest that if opening both eyes is too much, spouses can open just their *left* eye. That way, they can experiment with seeing each other without feeling watched or seen. It still looks as if your partner's eyes are both closed! Some couples reply that they are willing to open both eyes and "chance it." Others take the suggestion seriously. There is lots of humor and pathos in foreplay "peekaboo."

One couple demonstrated how we live side by side with our partner-for-life, well synchronized but never really touching. Long before she'd heard about eyes-open foreplay, the wife would sneak a peek every now and again, knowing her husband's eyes always remained closed. You can imagine the interesting conversation they had when this pattern was revealed. There was humor, a little awkwardness, and eroticism—all the elements of an intimate sexual experience.

Laughing nervously, the husband asked his wife, "When do you do it? . . . and what do you look at?"

His wife's response was playful and provocative. "Open your eyes and find out!" It was clear she was ready to meet him eye to eye in a loving way.

Those more skittish about intimacy completely reject opening their eyes simultaneously. Another troubled couple had *excellent* communication but less humor: their synchrony was so sophisticated they hardly bumped into each other in bed (except with their bodies). During sex they alternated peeking, only rarely getting their signals confused, making eye contact inadvertently. Usually one might briefly open his or her eyes, secure in knowing the other's would shut if the first one's started to open. Sometimes they "caught" each other looking during the switchover. These would be awkward moments as they saw each other's eyes, cold and guarded. Both claimed they didn't care that their partner never spoke of it, but their attempts to look indifferent didn't camouflage their pain and anger.

It's hard not to laugh at how successfully our pursuit of intimacy masks our avoidance of it. Almost without exception, foreplay peeka-boo helps couples realize how the intimacy they've been looking for is right under—actually, right *above*—their noses. We need to use sexuality to see ourselves, literally and figuratively.

Remember, the strategies I've described are merely suggestions—not "homework assignments." I never give my clients assignments—and I wouldn't do that with you. I've extolled the virtues of eyes-open foreplay, but I wouldn't presume to tell you to do it. That would take away the benefit of making this crucial decision for yourself and diminish the advantage to your own differentiation. Only you know when—if ever—it feels like the right time for eyes-open foreplay.

Must your eyes be open every moment? Do four staring eyeballs constitute the ultimate intimacy? Should you never kiss "until you see the whites of their eyes"? Certainly not. But let's not slough off the intensity of eye-to-eye foreplay, either.

Can one partner lie back and be *done* by the other? Sure! Sometimes it's nice to close your eyes, tune into yourself, and let your partner work you over. Focusing on your own body isn't antithetical to wall-socket sex—in fact, it's often part of it. The question is: does this stem from active involvement or from laziness and inconsiderateness? Lying back and being *done* in wall-socket sex is a very active process—and a hard one to tolerate for the many people who have difficulty "receiving." Next chapter we'll discuss the difference between lying back with your eyes closed while you're tuned into your partner and using the same behavior to tune him or her out.

We are talking about a freedom to explore that makes certain sexual styles optional rather than forbidden. Many who argue that eyes-closed sex is "better" are really defending their personal limitations: it's "better" not to feel their *discomfort* with eyes-open contact. The point is that it's nice to be *able* to enjoy both!

There is a difference between having sexual preferences and settling for the limitations of your sexual development. If you lack the ability to have eyes-open foreplay, calling eyes-closed contact a "preference" is really fudging: a preference involves choice; an inability does not. People don't simply prefer eyes-closed sex like some prefer vanilla ice cream over chocolate. Choice has everything to do with differentiation. "I prefer not to" often covers up "I can't—and don't want to face what might be involved in becoming able to." (This is one reason why paper-and-pencil questionnaires about sexual "preferences" are often worthless.)

Not everyone has to "go to war" to have eyes-open foreplay. The higher your level of differentiation, the less pressure and anxiety are necessary for you to move toward more satisfying solutions. Fused couples often require an emotional atomic bomb to get things dislodged enough to start some movement. It's possible to negotiate new ways of doing things, but deeper connection usually involves increasing your differentiation. That's why verbal negotiations often don't produce significantly better sex and intimacy.

Paradoxes of Foreplay and Marriage

Some people honestly wonder, "How can you see *anything* when you're kissing?" (This is not the same as, "Why would you *want* to?") Kissing with your eyes open is often electric and a little "wild-eyed." You're right *there*! It has its time and place. Lots of people enjoy it and it's good for a laugh!

But the answer to the question touches on a physical reality with a deeper message. Because of the way eyes focus, you can't see much when you're up too close. Without a little distance, you can't see your partner clearly. *Kissus interruptus* lets you stop long enough to catch your breath and move your head so you can *see* and *be seen*. The same is true for emotional fusion: differentiation enhances awareness of your partner. You have to step back from your loved ones to truly see them. Being more separate—rather than farther away—actually brings us closer.

Paradoxes like these show up constantly in marriage (and this book). When we attempt to analyze and subdue these paradoxes to a level we can handle, we generally create even more unsettling paradoxes. Indeed, emotional fusion is one way of attempting to eliminate the inherent paradoxes of marriage. Emotional Siamese twins wonder, "Won't we be more likely to separate if we no longer *need* each other?" It's hard to convince them that that's exactly what's needed if they want to stay together. And, paradoxically, trying to persuade them of this undermines their differentiation process and makes their efforts to self-validate less effective.

Differentiation provides more tolerance for current paradoxes and those that lie ahead. As marriages, families, and people mature, they don't become simpler. They become more complex—with *more* inherent paradoxes. As we grow, the paradoxes of life and marriage don't go away; they just bother us a lot less. Old contradictions now look like flip sides of a more complete whole. Inherent paradoxes look like contradictions if you need simple answers and cannot stand internal conflict.

We've touched on some paradoxes while discussing sexual foreplay, although we didn't label them at the time. These sexual paradoxes capture some of this chapter's most important points:

- We fear our marriage is threatened when we refuse to give up our integrity—and yet it actually strengthens it.
- Having a marriage worth cherishing requires the willingness to challenge it; maintaining the status quo is a good way to kill it.
- One partner can always make the other choose between loyalty to the marriage and loyalty to oneself.
- Sexual crisis doesn't necessarily mean your relationship is falling apart; it can be a crucial part of the people-growing process.
- "Compromise" and "negotiation," long extolled as marital virtues, may actually impede decisions of differentiation, which make us capable of true compassion.
- Emotional Siamese twins, though symbiotic, are not really nice to each other; common strategies involve domination and intimidation, placating submission, or emotional withdrawal—none of which is nice.
- *Kissus interruptus* may sound like coercion but it leads to freedom in bed and feeling wanted by your partner. John and Mary's nonerotic hardball foreplay negotiations led to the most intense sex of their lives.

Eyes-open foreplay works particularly well at both ends of the marital continuum—for deeply troubled relationships as well as harmonious couples pursuing the limits of their sexual potential—because it taps the profound ways differentiation and paradox affect our daily life.

Do you lie alone in silent darkness wondering about your partner's thoughts? Are you millions of miles apart while your mouths are pressed together? Do your tongues search out signs of life in a desert of alienation? Millions of couples know the thundering silence of dead sex. Very little can make you feel more lonely. Eyes-open foreplay and differentiation can bring you an entirely different type of stillness: the centeredness of a profoundly intimate connection.

Within Eastern approaches to sexuality, it's common practice for partners to look *into* each other during sex. It's been done by millions of people for thousands of years; it takes practice and self-discipline. It's not easy—but then neither is most of what's meaningful in life.

Chapter 8

Eyes-Open Orgasm: Making *Contact* During Sex

True vision is always twofold. It involves emotional comprehension as well as physical perception. Yet how rarely we have either. We generally only glance at an object long enough to tag it with a name.

—Ross Parmenter

The saleswoman at Frederick's of Hollywood taught me a lot about eroticism. As she rang up my purchase, she asked kindly and gently, "Can your wife pull this off?"

I was stunned. I have a long history of purchasing garments for Ruth and myself, and have yet to pick out something she didn't like. I wasn't expecting someone else to be concerned that I'd bring home an item Ruth would be horrified to wear. This wise woman helped me understand the source of countless fights triggered by men blindly pursuing their fantasies: they don't recognize the challenges and clash of meanings they present—gift wrapped—to their partners. As I stood at the cash register, I looked at other people in the store with new appreciation and interest.

I watched a woman stroll the racks unselfconsciously, stopping occasionally to hold up lingerie that caught her attention. Several times, she held one against her body for a minute or two, as if trying it on for size emotionally as well as physically. She seemed to feel these more "suited" her than the styles she passed over. As I watched her, I had a sense of knowing how this woman saw herself sexually—not just her "sexual self-image" but what style of sex she had in mind and what she might be like in bed. From years of working with people's sexuality and seeing how it expressed their inner world, I didn't think I was merely seeing my own projections about this woman (although that could certainly have been the case).

Just when I felt I was violating her privacy, she saw—or felt—me. There was instant connection between us—I nodded and she smiled warmly. Everything was okay. We acknowledged each other's interest in sex the same way people do who share a common hobby or a love of fine wines. We left it at that. I felt very mature.

I noticed two women in their thirties looking through bikini underwear, laughing and complaining about how long it had been since they'd "been laid." They obviously hoped to end the drought.

In the next aisle a man and woman were looking for something they both liked. They teased each other with various items, trying on different "tones" of sex. As they walked towards the cash register with their choice, it was clear the "harlot" had won out over the "baby doll."

In every case, it was like staring into people's bedrooms—and their heads. I suddenly felt a kinship with each of them. I wasn't the only one looking around. Browsing through the store was like having group sex with our clothes on—a club for adults celebrating human sexuality.

Unfortunately, the party ended for me when I noticed three men in suits joking among themselves like schoolboys. They radiated bravado and lust—and fear. They seemed to tarnish the clothes they ogled, the way some men demean the women they pursue. I thought they'd probably be scared shitless to encounter any of the women in this store, one on one. The spell broken, I went to the men's section to buy some hot underwear to wear for Ruth.

Driving home I recalled a decade-old experience that seemed almost from another world. I was standing with a dozen tourists inside the eleventh-century "erotic temples" of Kajuraho, India. We were in a tall narrow circular chamber standing around a small stone bed. Statues engaging in every imaginable sex act (and some I'd never imagined) adorned the outside walls of the tower; inside, the room was barren. I remembered *smelling* everyone in the room. We were all sexually aroused—men and women, gay and straight, young adults and old. We weren't turned on to each other, we were just turned on—moved by the sacred sexuality. As in Frederick's of Hollywood, we exchanged acknowledgments and smiles. I never touched a single person, but I *felt* each one.

I want to pick up last chapter's discussion of making contact during foreplay. Let's take a stroll downtown to consider something that has everything to do with what happens in the bedroom: sexual vibes.

We encounter sexual vibes daily walking down the street. Eyes meet. People realize they're making contact—really *seeing* each other, and liking what they see. They *feel* each other. It sometimes happens without even looking. Just stand near someone in an elevator, ostensibly watching the floor numbers light up.

Sexual vibes involve true interpersonal exchange, but not always between consenting partners. Vibes are something one person can direct towards another. Subtle forms of family sexual abuse and harassment in the workplace are examples of wrongfully directed sexual vibes. One person can feel another's (unwanted) sexual interest even when "nothing (physical) ever really happens."

Most people know the icky feeling of being "undressed" or violated by someone *looking* at them (icky if you don't want it from that person). You know when to avert your gaze when approaching an "intruder" on the street—you can *feel* it. On the other hand, under the right circumstances, prolonged eye contact can be a form of "safe sex": there is no exchange of body fluids, only an exchange of vibes.

The politics of sexual vibes, eroticism, and sexual attraction are part and parcel of everyday life. There's nothing magic about sexual vibes. As a species, we've sent and received vibes ever since we became social animals. It's no different from sensing another's joy, or sadness, or being "infected" with their anxiety, pain, or anger. Sexual vibes are an erotic form of emotional contagion—the interpersonal broadcasting of emotion found in many species. Researchers have documented the intricate and subtle interpersonal "ballets" that occur around sexual vibes. Psychophysiologically, however, we can barely explain how we do it.

Sometimes we are aware of sending and receiving sexual vibes, sometimes not. Men and women can often sense others of their gender whose sexuality is well developed and well harnessed. Their vibes feel different from those of the hysteric, whose sexuality screams this is all she thinks she has to offer, or of the "macho man," whose posturing flaunts a totally narcissistic lust. For teenage boys, leering at girls is part of male-bonding and "acting like a man." (Some men never grow up.) Girls learn that making eye contact is tantamount to accepting a sexual proposal. Society has dictated men are "senders" and women "receivers"—until recently.

Modern women feel freer to send vibes too—leading men and other women to experience varying degrees of relief, flattery, and intimidation. A recent Diet Pepsi ad created a stir by depicting women in an office building gathering to ogle a well-built construction worker several stories below. Each woman's ogling style was as different as her personality. This was eyes-open sex on national prime time television. Some viewers may have recognized a less obvious facet of the scenario: these women may have felt free to "send" sexual vibes because the man in question *wasn't* likely to feel them. In reality, they probably wouldn't send the same vibes at close range.

This brings us to the real point of discussing sexual vibes: remember that sizzle of "electric" eye contact with a stranger across a room? *When was the last time you felt that with your partner?* Probably not recently if you've been together long. Married couples often wish they had in the bedroom what they feel just walking down the street. Reciprocal sexual vibes make casual encounters feel like hot sex in public. But few long-term couples exchange sexual vibes *during* sex.

Spouses acutely sense the loss of sizzle. Complaints of "alienation" often refer to lack of sexual vibes. It's a subtle message that sexual aggression, desire, and "intent" are gone. Some fights about lack of sex are really about lack of *quality:* the absence of sexual vibes. (A few people grow up so alienated from their sexuality that they wonder what their partner is complaining about.)

Why is this such a common problem? It's because, as with intimacy and sexual desire, it takes differentiation to keep sexual vibes alive with an emotionally committed long-term partner. Your eroticism is as personal and unique as your genitals. Simply acknowledging you have erotic sensations may feel like you are revealing a big secret. And giving your partner a peek at your erotic map may feel as if you are showing him how to steal your sexual "stash." This was part of my lingerie-buying lesson: if the item taps an aspect of sexuality that the wearer can validate in herself or himself, you get to play; if not, you fight.

Revealing your eroticism through sexual vibes is a powerful form of self-validated intimacy when done with your spouse. After a while you won't be able to send sexual vibes if sex with your partner has been a pit stop for other-validated intimacy. Once marital fusion grows cold, differentiation is critical to keeping sexual vibes alive with your spouse; this arises from simple things:

- We may not want to be *really* known, sexually or otherwise.
- We don't tend to risk disapproval from our increasingly significant other.
- We often depend on other-validation of our attractiveness/sexuality, and our partner's response becomes less effective in "pumping up" our pseudo self over time.

- It becomes increasingly difficult to maintain (or change) our "shape" in the presence of our partner and see ourselves (or our partner) as sexy.

Exchanging sexual vibes with a long-term partner eventually becomes an act of will and integrity.

The important issue is not just that absence of sexual vibes creates many disappointments, like low sexual desire, decreased intimacy, and not feeling attractive or attracted to your mate. Sexual vibes provide a way to stay in synch with your partner moment by moment during sex. If you're trying to let the emotional connection with your spouse determine your behavior as the encounter unfolds, you have no "trail" to follow if you're not exchanging sexual vibes. I'm not saying you can't have some connection with your spouse if you don't have sexual vibes—but "caring" doesn't point to a specific path when you're getting it on.

Theresa and Philip

Let me tell you about a couple who illustrate what we've said about sexual vibes and how far these issues extend. Theresa and Philip had been married almost thirty years. Theresa was plagued with lifelong insecurities; she was preoccupied with her appearance and constantly anticipated failure, disappointment, and rejection. She couldn't believe that Philip really loved her. Her constant fears that he would leave her undermined the reassurances she demanded and received. Not surprisingly, Theresa had difficulty reaching orgasm, too. For his part, Philip was approaching retirement and worrying what the rest of his (married) life was going to be like. He was also starting to have difficulty reaching orgasm and secretly wondered if a new partner would get him more turned on. Neither spouse ever believed they would end up seeing a "shrink"—until Philip revealed he was having loads of fantasies about being with younger women. The next day Theresa made an appointment for herself and Philip to see me.

Theresa and Philip could hardly remember what it was like to have some sexual sizzle. Philip admitted this was what he thought his fantasies were about. Theresa pointed out he didn't do much to "light her fire," either. But there was more involved here than lack of passion and feeling inadequate; there was also something rather sad: after thirty years of cohabitation and copulation, Theresa and Philip were isolated from each other when they lay in bed. Like many couples, they no longer kissed much during sex, although they had intercourse about once a week. Theresa and Philip bypassed the painful emptiness in their kisses and instead focused on touching each other's genitals. Each felt the other's skin, but had no sense of the other's essence or feelings.

In the course of discussing how they had sex, I learned that Theresa always kept her eyes closed. Philip occasionally opened his, but they never made eye contact. This didn't seem significant to them. Seeing them through their sexual style, I contemplated the self-understanding, intimacy, desire, and differentiation that eyes-open sex could offer them later on. I didn't comment on this at the time because they would have thought I was suggesting new sexual activities to add novelty. But I had an inkling it could change their relationship

This is what Theresa and Philip badly needed. The mechanical quality of their physical exchanges in and out of bed were worse than routine and perfunctory. Theresa's insecurities limited their sex and intimacy, and Philip was too unsure of himself to push her on this. Besides, he had his own ambivalence about being more intimate with his wife. All manner of touch lacked energy and enthusiasm because they didn't put any of *themselves* into it. On the surface they were bored and lazy during sex; underneath they were isolated by their concerns and fears. On the rare occasions that Theresa and Philip's bedroom came alive, it was with anxiety rather than passion. Sexual vibes hadn't made an appearance in twenty-nine years.

This contributed to one of their main points of contention: Theresa complained that she had to keep telling and showing Philip how to touch her. She said he didn't care enough to learn what she liked. Philip claimed that she complained when he did the very thing she told him to do last time. In our therapy sessions Theresa accused Philip of not caring enough to pay attention to what he was doing. Philip replied that Theresa was never satisfied with anything he did for her—in his view she was "spoiled" and he blamed this on her parents.

"He's wrong. He doesn't care enough to give me what I want!"

"I guess you see Philip as insensitive. The way you are describing this, it sounds like you're leading someone who can't feel what he's doing."

"You got that right!" Theresa seemed elated that I could understand and took the opportunity to voice her dissatisfaction.

Philip was a perfect demonstration that a man can rub a clitoris the way his partner instructs—side to side, up and down, or elliptically— but still not make contact with her. To Theresa it felt like Philip thought his finger was an eraser and he was trying to remove a mistake. She resented having to give instructions like "a little to the left and slower." She said it was like she was leading the blind. The point is, she was!

Philip was "blind" because he had no vibrational link to guide him; he *had* to do it as a technique.

"Philip, it sounds like you're touching Theresa with no sense of what you're really trying to do. My guess is that you're trying to rub her skin a particular way, in a specific spot with a specific pattern of pressure and motion." Philip wasn't sure whether I was joining with Theresa to gang up on him.

"I'm not sure I understand you."

"It sounds like the two of you don't *feel* each other when you touch. I don't mean this in some abstract way: when you touch her, the sensations only seem to go one way—from you to Theresa. You use a part of your body to try to give her the sensations she wants, and you feel your body touching her so you can tell what that part of you is doing. But it's like you're not *feeling* Theresa as you're touching her—getting no sensory feedback to know how Theresa's experiencing it."

Philip was surprised I could describe exactly how he did it. He was also curious that I was suggesting there might be some other alternative. But he didn't want me to see that he didn't have all the answers, any more than he wanted Theresa to sense this when they had sex. "I keep asking her to tell me how what I'm doing feels to her. She says 'it's good' and then doesn't say anything else!"

Theresa looked embarrassed. "I shouldn't have to keep telling you what to do. I feel like I have to order you to do it. If you cared you'd pay attention."

"I don't think the issue is telling Philip what to do, or having to compel him to do it. I think it has to do with Philip trying to touch you the way you want when he isn't able to *feel* you. It sounds like it's part of your mutual issues of caring and connection—who cares for whom and why. I think it's a question about, 'Will Theresa let anybody really know her?'—*feel* her in this context—and 'Has Philip ever had enough real contact with the people he loved to even know the difference?' "

"This has to do with why I have to keep telling Philip how to touch me and why he never seems to learn?"

"And why Theresa won't talk to me during sex like I ask?"

"I think it may have everything to do with both these things. It's as if Theresa is saying to Philip, 'Don't you dare *feel* me during sex!' and Philip is saying, 'OK, if that's what you want, I'll touch you without feeling!' "

Like many couples, Theresa and Philip were surprised by this distinction between touching and feeling. Let's leave their story briefly so I can clarify this by sharing a lovely vignette about a different "couple."

Touching without Feeling

Do you touch your partner when you have sex?

The question may sound ridiculous at first, but I'm underscoring the importance of *feeling* your partner. Do you touch her, heart and mind? Although our reasons for breaking (or never making) emotional connection while touching are unique, the ways we do so are not. Some are so inherent in human nature that, when teaching, I am reliably able to have students show them to themselves.

For many years I taught human sexuality to medical students at Louisiana State University Medical Center in New Orleans. In an amphitheater of several hundred almost-doctors I would solicit two male volunteers for a "demonstration about touching." I'd ask one to take the other's hand and caress it while they stood in front of their classmates. (I deliberately picked two men because I knew that common homophobia would make them try to comply with my request without really *feeling* each other.) Invariably the "giver" rubbed the other's hand briskly, mechanically, and repetitively. I often "helped" by suggesting, "Why don't you slow that down a bit?"

"I'm *trying*!" was the common response.

Usually the giver continued to scour the partner's hand. Occasionally one slowed down his touch enough to *feel* his partner. You could tell the instant it happened: they stopped touching all together! In debriefing we discussed how this applied to what they did with their lovers and patients. The way they defended against making contact applied to heterosexuality and homosexuality alike.

I'll never forget one time I did this demonstration: one student I chose was a more mature man who hadn't come to medical school straight from college. I was amazed watching him slowly and deliberately touch his "partner." (The other man was dying of embarrassment and homophobia.) I said I'd never seen anyone successfully *touch* a "partner" in a decade of demonstrations. "It's taking all the willpower I have," said the student, who continued touching his partner as we talked.

Several days later this student ran down the hall to catch me as I was leaving my office.

"Do you remember me? I was part of your demonstration."

"Remember you? I'll never forget you!"

"Well, I want you to know what's happened for me since your class. I started thinking about my five-year-old son. He's always complaining I'm too rough with him—that I hurt him when we roughhouse.

After the demonstration I realized I touch him roughly because I'm afraid of really feeling him and enjoying it. I've been afraid of turning him into a sissy—or making him gay—if he enjoys being touched by a man. All my life I've been afraid I was a latent homosexual. I realized that I'm playing out this fear with my son."

He continued, "My son has always been wound up, hard to discipline—he was even diagnosed hyperactive. Well, after I thought about what happened in class, I *touched* him—not sexually, of course—but I just let myself *feel* him. That was a few days ago. My wife and I can hardly believe the change. My son is *quiet* . . . like someone drained the charge out of him! I just want to say thanks!"

Neither of us said anything for several seconds. We just looked at each other. Finally I said, "Do you mind if I write about you and your son one day?"

"Why? Are we different?"

"Yes, but in a beautiful way! I think your experience will help many people."

When couples stop sending and receiving sexual vibes, they are touching without feeling. This pattern surfaces in the myriad repetitive patterns of touch that wear out your skin (and your patience). Being on the giving end isn't much better. Touching your partner while he or she is mentally "absent" is living proof that sex isn't inherently intimate (or erotic).

Blocking emotional connection while touching isn't as contradictory as it sounds. In fact, we do it all the time in sex. You can block feeling during kissing and foreplay, intercourse, and even oral sex (imagine doing it while you don't like the taste). We exploit our "ability" to touch without feeling when we perpetrate *normal marital sadism* (discussed in Chapter 11). It's how you withhold yourself from someone even while you're bringing him or her to orgasm. Emotional connection while touching makes quite a difference to people who can afford to want it (Chapter 5). Some can't stand acknowledging—and missing—it, some people can't feel the difference, and others simply don't care.

Feeling—or not feeling—the people you love isn't just about sex. At our Couples Retreat, people tune into *feeling* when I suggest they reexperience what it was like to sit at the dinner table with their childhood family. (Take a moment to try this for yourself.) Reactions are visceral: some people shudder, and many flatly decline to do it! Forty years later they can still feel the "bad vibes" permeating their house. (This is one reason I suggested doing hugging till relaxed in the common space of your home if you have children, once you are comfortable doing it privately.)

It isn't true that all people who seem tuned out sexually don't know what they're missing. The ones I just mentioned (who didn't want to "go back home") had to feel what went on to know they didn't want to feel it again. People who act like they wouldn't know a feeling if it bit them are not necessarily "insensitive": often they are still trying to kill the part of them that feels. (They are trying to kill the visceral link we labeled earlier as "vibes"—trying *not* to feel the people they love.)

Time and again I've worked with couples who can't explain their sexual problems or lack of desire or satisfaction because they're blocked by their assumption they are in touch with each other. They usually can find new ways of getting the sex and intimacy they want—but the price is giving up the fantasy that they've been in contact all along. They begin to understand what they don't feel during sex, and why/how they avoid it (and stop blaming their busy work schedule). Like Theresa and Philip, they have to soothe the emotional impact of realizing what has (and hasn't) been happening for years. It embodies of another aspect of differentiation: tolerating pain for growth.

Just as for Theresa and Philip, an common initial response is to feel stupid for not recognizing the lack or believing it was otherwise. That's because you can be regularly orgasmic, have no "dysfunctions," and still not make contact. When you really *feel* your partner, the difference is electric. (I referred to this as wall-socket sex.) You can tell if and when this happens for many men: that's when they ejaculate.

This is how it originally showed up for Philip. He struggled with rapid ejaculation for most of his life. Early in their marriage he and Theresa kept foreplay to a minimum and conditioned each other to have no emotional contact during sex in order to prolong it. When Philip *felt* Theresa during sex (or if she ever became animated), he ejaculated—not because he wanted to deprive her, but, rather, because he just wasn't used to the intensity. Philip only had ejaculatory control during emotionally disconnected sex (if he had any at all): he spent years trying to tune out from himself and his partner in order to be a "better" lover.

After thirty years, the games they played with emotional connection caught up with them. Decades of trying to reduce his arousal, paired with increasing emotional estrangement and loss of sexual vibes, now kept Philip's total stimulation from reaching his orgasmic threshold, which continued to rise as he aged (see the quantum model in Chapter 3). This insidious aggregate was why Philip was increasingly unable to reach orgasm at all.

The fact that Theresa used a sexual style that interfered with establishing a vibrational link with Philip during sex didn't help any. Her style happened to be *the* most common sexual style: instead of tuning *into* her partner, Theresa closed her eyes, tuned out Philip, and focused on sensations in her body.

This approach "works." It makes your body function. It's the "normal" way. If you're planning to be married only several years, maybe this strategy will work well enough for you. But if you're hoping to celebrate your golden anniversary with a smile on your face, you need to move beyond this style. Bypassing your partner blocks profound sexual experience. It creates minimally satisfying orgasms and boring sex in marriage. And it makes your partner more likely to rub faster or harder—or stop rubbing altogether—because he or she can't *feel* you. Theresa was amazed how much sense this made when I explained it in one of our sessions.

"Is this what happens when I try to reach orgasm?!"

"Very likely. Check it out for yourself by seeing what happens if you really make contact with Philip during sex. But feeling while touching doesn't happen automatically once you have insight. It takes time and effort to *know* each other the way the Bible suggests happens in a single act of copulation. Many of us are living proof that you can bang away with the same partner for years and not *know* him.

"Lots of people withdraw into their sensations when they're having sex and break contact with their partner, who becomes a travel agent sending them on a trip. They give instructions like they are sending back travel postcards saying, 'Everything's wonderful. Rub just a little to the left. Glad you're not here.' The same people may complain, 'I don't like sex when it's just a technique.' But the deeper truth is they're uncomfortable with the alternative."

Theresa and Philip looked at each other with slightly embarrassed smiles. I had spoken their truth. Theresa was relieved that we could identify their problem, but she was getting worried that it couldn't be fixed. "Can you give us some exercises to use that will help us correct the situation?"

"Are you making a joke?" I said this to ease the mood and shake her mind-set. Theresa contained her fears of disappointment for a moment and reflected on my question. Then she broke into laughter.

"You mean, we just talked about the problem with techniques and here I am asking for some?"

"Exactly! I don't have a preset bundle of techniques in mind for you to do. That's one way this approach differs from traditional sex and marital therapy."

Philip found this a little too unsettling. "Well, isn't there something we can practice—you know, get good at doing?"

He and Theresa wanted to "perform" in bed and make themselves feel less inadequate—to master behaviors to keep the flaws they feared lurked within them from being discovered. Philip wanted to be competent in bed and a good partner for Theresa, which, for Philip, meant she'd have an orgasm and stop complaining about his ability. Theresa wanted to have an orgasm, in part, for the same reason her clothing, makeup, and home furnishings were always perfect: appearance was everything. (It was remarkable when Theresa eventually came to therapy without makeup.)

"The kind of techniques you want me to prescribe are the antithesis of what you're looking for. You're still operating under the misconception there is a preordained 'right' way to touch Theresa—and you think that if she can't teach it to you, perhaps I can. The whole point about connection is that when you focus on your technique, you aren't focused on your partner—even though you're doing the technique for her. Doing something *to* or *for* your partner isn't necessarily the same as being *with* her.

"We all begin our sexual careers by focusing on technique—that's part of every adolescent's developmental task. The problem is that many of us never stop. Remember your earliest curiosities and experiences with sex? The first thing you probably wanted to know was 'how to do it.' I remember trying to get it right before I ever really kissed someone. I remember thinking, *How should I hold my lips? Do I breathe? Where do I put my arms? Should I open my mouth? How do I move my tongue? What if she sticks her tongue out first? What if she has braces on her teeth?* I didn't want to be seen as a lousy kisser, inexperienced and inept—exactly what I was at the time. Like many people, I focused on technique and not my partner. My goal was to *avoid* intimacy and contact with my partner, although I thought I was pursuing it at the time. Maybe you 'know' foreplay isn't a system of mechanical touching to be perfected, but this doesn't guarantee you will avoid this trap once sex starts. Someone once said we've tried to reduce sex to simple technical skill, as if the secrets of life could be learned on the dissecting table!

"Lots of books, magazines, and therapists tell women it's their responsibility to be explicit about how they want to be stroked or kissed, so their husbands aren't responsible for translating what they want into technique. This sounds fair and reasonable, but people rarely experience connection this way. Technique only transmits the flow of connection that already exists between partners. Trying to improve your partner's technique rarely works because people hide behind technique to avoid making contact. As long as partners focus on technique instead of each other, they won't produce the feeling they yearn for—and often fear. I know this is contrary to common belief that sex is a way to *establish* connection."

"That's what I've tried to tell Philip! I have to feel some connection with him if he wants me to have sex."

"I've heard other people say that. You're talking about needing connection to feel desire. I'm talking about a related point: that connection dramatically affects behavior and experience *during* sex. And as I understand it, you've been dodging that kind of connection." Theresa saw my point and stopped trying to take the moral high ground with her husband. Philip was impressed and wanted to hear more.

"The issue is making contact *through* behavior. Focusing on technique per se interferes with making contact. It's often more like 'parallel play' of young children—occupied in the same room but not really together. There is often minimal love in 'lovemaking' because partners don't have sex with each other; instead, they pay attention to their technique. The common 'skill-building' approach is one way couples keep intimacy to tolerably low levels. You relate to your roles and behaviors instead of to your partner. Everything is so well choreographed, you might convince yourself you are in contact."

There is some legitimacy to "practice makes perfect," but the important issue is *what* you're practicing and *why?* Many couples only "master" a sexual behavior well enough for one or the other to reach orgasm; they don't focus on profound connection and settle instead for minimal function. Through a progression of suggestions (which I'll describe shortly), Philip and Theresa developed a sense of mastery that included making contact during sex. This involved three main aspects:

- *Mastering the anxiety triggered by (new) sexual activities or styles.* This is more than eliminating discomfort or aversion. There is a level of comfort and pleasure beyond "desensitization," merely "OK," and even "good" that brings sighs of relief, release of tension, relaxing your defenses—and profound connection. At this level your partner feels different and so do you. (You can see the difference if you think about experimenting with anal sex. There's a big difference between tolerating it to get through it and relaxing and connecting through it.)

• *Mastering yourself while mastering "something new."* Trying a new sexual behavior is always a stretch. It challenges your self-worth and expands your self-image. It involves—and enhances—self-mastery and self-soothing. It takes both to engage your partner at profound emotional depth.

• *Mastering a variety of sexual styles.* This permits multiple tones of emotional engagement and sexual encounters that incorporate the context of the moment. Beyond making it easy to "connect," a broad vocabulary (i.e., repertoire of behaviors and meanings) makes sexual communication far more interesting. Sex becomes "feeling your partner out" rather than simply "feeling him up" (we'll discuss this in depth in the next chapter).

Drastic changes in behavior aren't always involved in feeling each other while touching. Theresa and Philip accomplished this by considering how they already touched, rather than focusing on a specific way to do it. We talked about this as establishing a "vibrational link" without describing a particular pattern or location.

True, I gave them "simple" suggestions to make deep contact, like *slow things down.* It's usually not too hard to make connection when you do, which is why many couples don't do it. Remember how hard this was for students in my medical school demonstration. Slowing down enough to make a vibrational connection—letting your partner *feel* you and vice versa—is not easy to do. But it's often beautiful when it happens: just think back to the story of the medical student father who made contact with his young son.

The real issue in sexual mastery is *self*-mastery. We need more respect for the power of a positive vibrational link between people. If it can affect your immune system (as research now reveals), it can surely impact your emotions. I've seen the power personally and professionally.

Participants at our Couples Retreats work on feeling while touching because almost half report they feel "nothing"—that is, they feel skin but not their partner. (Lack of "presence" contributes to low sexual desire in women regardless of their sexual orientation. At our retreat for lesbian couples we found it particularly destroyed sexual interest.) We offer additional sessions for couples who can't feel each other. Their remarkably consistent responses are illustrated by one couple I remember clearly. The wife had great difficulty slowing her touch. She was "brittle" and never let anyone hold her, physically or emotionally. The daughter of Jewish refugees who barely escaped during World War II, she was riddled with anxiety. She moved her hand woodenly against her husband, who had his own history of problems with touch: as an adolescent he had contracted a disease that destroyed his athletic career and isolated him from human touch for many months. After several minutes of the wife stroking her husband's hand, an instant arrived when it looked like she had allowed herself to *touch* him. At that moment, the man burst into tears! In finally feeling the connection they had always wanted, they experienced the pain of what they'd missed. When people finally make contact the usual reaction is tears of joy and more respect for sex. (Several days later other couples at the retreat spontaneously remarked how much softer and approachable they both seemed.)

The key here is to establish this kind of vibrational link and feel each other any way you can. It lets you use your own experience as a *tool*: once you recognize what you're looking for, you can "follow the connection" into any sexual behavior, rather than just doing it to get stimulated. We've already encountered many couples who used this approach, although we didn't label it at the time: Karen and Ken, the very first couple you met in Chapter 1, who followed the connection by doing whatever Karen fantasized about while they had sex. Bill and Joan (Chapter 4), who realized that he "knew her touch." And Warren and Carol, who finally achieved profound connection doing hugging till relaxed (Chapter 6). "Following the connection" is another tool for connection.

I often try to find some way a couple already makes contact. It makes absolutely no difference what it is—it can even be while they're dancing. What's important is that they have some tactile/emotional cue they can follow that tells them when they are "on" or "off." This way couples don't feel like they're starting from scratch—they can use what's already there. More importantly, they can follow their own internal processes instead of following me. Often they use hugging till relaxed and kissus interruptus to deepen their connection, but it's not necessary. Following the connection means you're together, and that's supposed to be what's really important, isn't it?

Couples who have no existing way of making contact often start with hugging till relaxed to create one. But connection isn't inherent in hugging till relaxed or any other behavior. You have to connect *through* the behavior—hugging till relaxed is just a tool to encourage it to happen. In this case, you can use it to get a feeling link you can track when you move on to other things.

In the course of our meetings, I discovered that Theresa and Philip had a feeling connection when he ran his fingernails lightly across her arm as they watched television. For many couples this involves mindless touching or "gentle scratching," but it turned out they both relaxed and mentally followed their point of connection as it moved down Theresa's arm. They could feel when one of them "tuned out" and focused on the TV. Theresa was so afraid they did everything wrong, she was surprised and delighted they were already doing something right.

"At least you can do it some way," I pointed out. "I know couples who have no way at all. Can you maintain contact if you look at each other or do you have to be facing the TV?"

"Facing the TV." There was no doubt in Philip's voice. "I never realized it. Why is that?"

"It means you don't want to see me." Theresa was always ready to think the worst.

"It doesn't have to. It could simply mean questions surface for both of you when you look at each other: Will you let someone really know you? Be with you? Not just inside your body—inside *you*. Will you let someone love you?"

"What did you mean, know me?" Theresa seemed unsure what I meant.

"Will you let Philip *hold* you—and deeply open to it? You say to Philip 'have sex with me and bring me to orgasm,' but the message in the way you have sex is *stay away from me—and reassure me you're not going to leave.*"

"Does Philip have issues like this?"

"He does. His words say 'I'd be competent if you didn't find fault with me,' but his behavior says, *Please help me feel competent in a way I've never felt. Someone has to make me feel better about myself! Maybe a younger woman might do it.*"

Theresa leaned forward to read Philip's reaction. Her own expression was inscrutable. It took me a moment to appreciate the elegant demonstration. "That's a perfect example of what I mean!"

"What is?"

"You're turning to Philip to see his reaction, but you're not showing yourself to him."

"OK . . . you caught me!"

"I think the question is, are you going to have to be 'caught' for the rest of your life? Or, are you ready to let yourself be seen—and welcome it?" That stopped Theresa cold.

As if nothing had happened, Philip asked, "Any suggestions about how to get a 'vibrational link'? This is all new to me."

"Some people do it by playing 'mind games' with tongues, passing the 'lead' back and forth. You might even consider having sex with your eyes open. A vibrational link demands attention to your partner and staying present in the moment. Eyes-open sex is one way to do it. . . . By the way, is your question a signal that you're going to avoid the same issues of 'opening' and 'welcoming in' I just raised with Theresa?"

". . . Honestly . . . I . . . I don't know if I can." Philip's sudden forthrightness stopped them both. "I assume when you say 'eyes-open sex' you also mean being really open with each other."

"Indeed."

"If I were that open to Theresa, I don't think I could keep an erection."

"I know I certainly can't orgasm with my eyes open that way!" Theresa was as worried about sexual performance as Philip. They also shared a common worry about letting anyone that close.

"Then I guess you'll have to choose what's really important to you."

Eyes-Open Sex

At the time, Theresa and Philip thought they might have to give up erections and orgasms if they chose to be together during sex. I didn't say anything to reduce their conflict over priorities, because they were on the path to not having to choose between sexual function and emotional connection: following the connection through eye contact is a form of energy exchange. In terms of the quantum model (Chapter 3), the combination of sensory and emotional stimulation can contribute to your total stimulation. However, you have to get to the point of comfort where having your eyes open contributes to your arousal, rather than distracting you or creating pleasure-reducing anxiety. Visual contact can put you in touch with your partner, but many people find that this interferes with awareness of their sensations.

Having sex with your eyes open builds on foreplay as the time where you establish the level of intimacy and meaning of the sex that follows (Chapter 7). If you are emotionally distant during foreplay, the likelihood diminishes that you'll want to open your eyes during sex—or enjoy it if you do. Conversely, emotional connection during foreplay makes you more eager to open your eyes and increases the likelihood it won't be awkward. Following the connection established during foreplay allows you to remain in synch with your partner when you open your eyes during sex. Seeing your partner becomes a natural extension of your emotional link rather than a distraction. Your physical sensations and emotional connection become an integrated whole rather than separate dimensions that interfere with each other. Following the connection makes your sensations and thoughts and feelings flow harmoniously. It makes eyes-open sex simple and delightful rather than complex and uncomfortable.

However, if you go into sex focusing on sensations to bypass thorny relationship issues, your emotions and your sensations are more likely to go in opposite directions, requiring you to give up awareness of one for the other. To feel comfortable looking each other in the eye, you'll probably have to confront conflicts you've swept under the carpet, which is why some couples continue to have sex with eyes closed. You aren't likely to let your partner look deep inside you until you've done that yourself. If you're avoiding your partner (or yourself) when you're out of bed, you're not likely to act differently between the sheets.

Many people are fascinated with eyes-open sex—and well they should be. Think of all the eye shadow and lip gloss used to make us to look at each other's faces. In native cultures men decorate their faces, too. Facial displays are central aspects of human courting and mating. The highly developed facial muscles of primates and humans permit more complex emotional expression and visual communication than in other vertebrates. Eye contact has also evolved to be an important aspect of how we initiate sex. Eye contact ("flirting") is a sexually arousing, "phylogenetically ancient" trait that transcends culture. Our anatomical ability to sustain eye contact during face-to-face intercourse facilitates our uniquely human capacity for intimacy during sex. And yet couples ignore how vision taps into our innate emotional connection with other humans.

Absence of eye contact during sex is particularly striking when you consider other cultures where the opposite is courted. For centuries Eastern cultures studied facial expressions during sex to understand emotions associated with eroticism. A seventeenth-century painting of a Taoist couple having sex shows the woman looking into a mirror to examine her facial expression. Many Tantric sexual positions utilize prolonged eye contact to gain spiritual transcendence. So does the *Kaballah*, a book of Jewish mysticism.

There are even common examples in Western society: sexually explicit videotapes usually depict couples having sex with their eyes open. Granted, the people often look bored, but when they have a hot erotic connection it's most evident in their eye contact. Even popular TV shows and movies convey hot sex by prolonged eye contact between partners.

With all this in mind, it's striking that sex in the dark with eyes closed is so common. And given our pursuit of the ultimate sensation and daredevil thrill in bungy-jumping, recreational drugs, and foreign travel, you'd think more people would open their eyes when they have sex. On the other hand, it's perfectly understandable. Some people have issues about body-image. Even more have issues about being seen on the inside. They have to "tune out" to get close enough to copulate, because being seen "behind the eyeballs" is hard to tolerate. They have what you might think of as autistic sex. I often joke with workshop audiences that many of us don't like masturbation because we find it lonely—we want to have sex with someone else so we can ignore him (or her).

I've even had clients who pretend they don't know what it means to be "seen behind the eyeballs" and don't know how to do it. This denial is their way of avoiding having to do it with their partner. I know it's denial because they've done it with *me* (emotionally) in session. Openly discussing why someone fakes not knowing about *seeing* and *being seen* is invariably intimate and poignant.

Experimenting with eyes-open sex helps couples become more differentiated, enhances their relationship in general, and increases contact during sex. Theresa and Philip experienced this kind of benefit. Like many couples, they had never seen each other during sex. Theresa never watched Philip give her oral sex during thirty years of marriage. It wasn't due to lack of opportunity and it wasn't exactly going on behind her back! She felt too embarrassed to open her eyes and see what she was getting. Philip occasionally opened his eyes during intercourse to watch their genitals, but never focused on Theresa's face.

However, after some "peekaboo" experiments with opening her eyes, Theresa became engrossed in the drama. There was some initial awkwardness but they soon grew to enjoy seeing each other during sex. They liked looking, talking, the change in pace, and the remarkable reduction in anxiety and increased connection that occurred.

The first time Theresa watched Philip give her oral sex, it had quite an impact. They recognized the significance of what was happening and it electrified their connection. Philip got really excited—but instead of rubbing faster or harder as he often did, he moved slower. He let his tongue drag over her labia, feeling their smoothness and feeling her react. She shuddered at some points and relaxed into it at others. Philip found Theresa's erotic "magic spot"—and it turned out not to be a spot at all! It was an emotional connection that existed independent of body parts. He *tasted* her with his eyes as well as his tongue while they looked into each other.

The way Philip was kneeling between her legs, Theresa couldn't see his face below his nose. She was about to say she wanted to see his whole face, when she realized she didn't need to. Philip's eyes were smiling and twinkling in a way she hadn't seen in years. Theresa didn't need to see Philip's mouth to believe it was smiling too. Besides it felt good exactly where it was.

It moved Theresa to realize she *wanted* to see all of Philip—and for him to see her. In our next session she described the exhilaration and terror of eye contact with him during sex. "It was like Philip was looking into my core. It scared me. I don't like everything about me, and I didn't expect him to, either. I felt *vulnerable*. I like sex, but I don't like being vulnerable. I felt like he could see all my inadequacies. I also felt . . . touched. Quite honestly, I'm surprised he wanted to see me. We've been together all these years and we've never done that. I never realized how much we've taken each other for granted."

Theresa had her first orgasm in a subsequent encounter soon thereafter. Her eyes were closed when it happened, but progress with eyes-open sex contributed to it. Theresa and Philip had been looking into each other's eyes while he rubbed her clitoris, occasionally bringing his fingers to his mouth to keep them wet. The emotional and physical stimulation was wonderful. She had no doubt Philip was really enjoying himself—and enjoying her, too. She closed her eyes for a minute to let the sensations wash over her—and she climaxed.

Theresa and Philip started opening their eyes during sex, adapting their usual sexual behaviors and positions to permit eye contact—like when Philip received oral sex from Theresa, or while having rear-entry intercourse in front of a full length mirror. Theresa got over her fear Philip was just watching her body instead of making contact with *her*: she realized he used the mirror to look intently into her eyes. She even found she liked watching their bodies move together, too. It was *sexy*. Philip remarked, "Eyes-open sex does more than add another dimension to our lovemaking: it makes 'familiar' behaviors seem like new things we've never done. But it's not easy! I always thought our problem was that Theresa was uptight. I never realized how hard it can be to let someone you love get that close to you!"

Theresa and Philip had set the people-growing process in their relationship into gear. Gradually, Theresa became emotionally stronger, less narcissistic, and more secure. She went through a series of intense emotional crises: she confronted her prior selfishness and her attempts to protect herself by withholding from Philip. She even maintained herself as a grown woman with her infantilizing parents and tolerated the disappointments of seeing them more realistically. Theresa stopped feeling like a phony little girl masquerading as an adult—and her orgasms became more frequent and more varied.

Eventually, Theresa pushed sex beyond Philip's comfort level: like lots of clients who experiment with eyes-open sex, Theresa now wanted to see as much as she could. She purchased contact lenses so she could see Philip's eyes in sharp focus during sex for the first time. This wasn't as frivolous as it might sound at first—it made their connection more intense and Theresa benefited from the self-confrontation involved in purchasing contacts "just for sex."

Although Philip admired this, he wanted to pull back. He was intimidated by Theresa's growth. He was faced with his own selfishness and his fears of really loving her. She confronted Philip on this and he rose to the challenge. Much to his own surprise, he started feeling *less* vulnerable than ever before. He stopped being "wounded" when Theresa disappointed him, and business problems and minor frustrations stopped "getting to him." But he wasn't sure he could match Theresa's new goal. Having come this far, she wanted to see how far she could go: Theresa wanted to have an orgasm while she and Philip were looking into each other.

Eyes-Open Orgasm

There seem to be two types of people in the world: those who are shocked that others can have orgasms with their eyes open, and those who are shocked that others don't! Neither group believes the other exists. A female gynecologist recently told me she thought it was physiologically impossible to have an orgasm with eyes open. A cab driver in Melbourne, Australia, told me just the opposite:

I was sitting in the front seat next to the driver because that's what a "good bloke" does in Australia. The driver was a mathematician from Pakistan unable to find other employment. As he drove me to the airport, he asked for advice about a serious concern. He revealed that, like many men in his culture, he had been a virgin when he married his Australian wife three years earlier. Now exposed to Western culture, he felt bad about his "lack of experience." He wanted to know if I knew of some esoteric sexual practices his wife might be missing. I told this gentle man that I don't teach techniques, but I do help people have orgasms with their eyes open.

As often happens, the man looked incredulous. But I wasn't prepared for what followed. He said: "You mean there are people . . . who *don't?*"

I was filled with sadness and admiration. Here was a man apologizing for himself, feeling inadequate, when he'd accomplished something relatively few people do. In three years' time, he and his wife had spontaneously developed the ability to have orgasms with their eyes open.

It's hard to describe the impact of looking into the eyes of someone you love as you reach orgasm. It's difficult for me to convey the richness of eyes-open orgasm between Ruth and me. Everytime it happens it brings to mind how far our relationship and our love—and our personal development—have come. Looking into each other and climaxing can be electric, tender, forceful, and nurturant, all at once. It's truly amazing how the human mind can integrate this cacophony of sensations, thoughts, and emotions, into a cohesive—*delicious*—experience.

I realize eyes-open orgasms can sound intimidating and maybe even unnatural (remember, though, they were quite natural for the Pakistani man). If this makes you self-*conscious*, ask yourself if that's really a bad thing. As we discussed in Chapter 4, self-consciousness is inherent to intimacy. And according to Tantric sex experts, self-awareness during sex is part of our sexual potential and the goal of sex. They say this helps partners focus their minds and emotions, channeling their energy and transforming their unity into ecstasy. Eyes-open orgasm highlights how close people (and sex) can get, and how far apart so many of us are. At the moment of orgasm—the supposed peak of the sexual encounter—we're on separate worlds: we tune out each other in order to climax. In comparison to eyes-open orgasm, simultaneous eyes-closed orgasm seems sort of funny.

Eyes-open orgasm builds on many topics we've discussed previously, like sexual vibes, feeling while touching, and following the connection. You have to be open to the inherent intimacy and eroticism, open to being *seen*, *felt*, and *tasted* emotionally. And everything we've said about open connection in eyes-open sex holds true for eyes-open orgasm—only more so. Having an eyes-open orgasm usually requires a level of partner engagement so profound that your spouse becomes an integral part of your arousal pattern (rather than a distraction from your sensations). This kind of emotional transparency requires a high level of self-acceptance based on knowing who you are and what your partner is likely to see. You can't be carrying a lot of anxiety or a load of unresolved issues to bed. You have to feel pretty good about yourself to let your life-mate look inside you. You don't "blink" when he looks. You invite him "in" and *want* him there. That's what differentiation lets you do.

These generalizations about intimacy and emotional contact hold true for couples who want to develop their ability to have eyes-open orgasms. Occasionally, however, I've worked with people who could keep their eyes open, but without partner engagement or openness; in fact, they were so distant from their partner that looking eye to eye during orgasm was, for them, like viewing a porno flick and masturbating. Eyes-open orgasm doesn't always mean intense connection, but it's a terrific opportunity for couples who want connection to find it.

One client said, "I think I'm like lots of people. I learned to have orgasms through a certain pattern of stimulation that included closing my eyes. I guess I started it for various reasons: because I heard it was romantic and because it worked. I had to shut out my partner so I could focus on my sensations. Now this routine has developed into the only way I know how to climax."

She continued, "When I first experimented with eyes-open orgasms it was hard. I had to make my eyes stay open. They seemed to close automatically. Sometimes I made myself do it; other times my partner encouraged me. It got easier, but at first this lessened the likelihood of my reaching orgasm. Sometimes I got pissed, thinking, 'What kind of nutty idea is this anyway?' But with experience it changed into a pattern I really enjoy—it's *different*! I know I'm doing it right when I feel a little awkward, weird, exposed, and very intimate with my partner. If I find myself averting my gaze, I refocus my attention: I ask myself, 'Am I hiding? Why?' Sometimes I just get nervous—'twitchy'—like it feels *too* good or something!"

I'm aware that there's a pitfall in discussing eyes-open orgasm: it can sound like I'm suggesting that you're supposed to be able to do it. Or that you're not in real contact with your partner if you can't. My intent is to highlight the complexity and depth of your sexual potential, increase your differentiation, and offer you a way to pursue both. Discussing eyes-open orgasm accomplishes all of the above, but I want to avoid establishing the eyeball Gestapo in the process! (You *will* keep your eyes open! That is an order!!)

For this reason, let me highlight several reasons why you *shouldn't* feel inadequate if you can't reach orgasm with your eyes open. First off, you have a lot of company, since most people *can't.* From informal polls taken at my lectures and workshops I estimate only thirty to forty percent of us have sex with our eyes open and only seven to fifteen percent can reach orgasm that way. In other words, it's technically *abnormal* to have an eyes-open orgasm. (Some people see this as proof that being "normal" is not all it's cracked up to be.)

Another reason you shouldn't feel inadequate is that eyes-open sex and eyes-open orgasm are ignored in sex therapists' textbooks, training, and professional practice. Most therapists didn't consider either topic until five years ago, when I made it a professional issue for the first time. Many still don't. Consider a small survey I conducted just before *Constructing the Sexual Crucible* was published in 1991: I was presenting a workshop at the annual conference of the American Association of Sex Educators, Counselors, and Therapists—the national credentialing body for these specialties. I asked the overflow crowd of certified sex therapists if they helped clients have sex with their eyes open, including being able to reach orgasm that way. Not a single therapist raised a hand! In fact, a renowned sex therapist rose from the audience to demand*, "Who says that's important, anyway?!"* (In an act of self-validated intimacy, I said, "I do.") This challenge is understandable once you realize eyes-open sex is antithetical to the "sensate focus" approach on which modern sex therapy has been based. Focus on eyes-open sex and eyes-open orgasms is a unique feature of the sexual crucible approach. So you could argue that these are esoteric things of interest to few people.

A third reason you shouldn't feel inadequate about not having eyes-open orgasms is that many therapists can't do it either, if clinicians who've attended my workshops are any indication. (One lovely man called me three weeks later to tell me he'd just had his first.) I half-joke with fellow therapists that we teach clients to have sex as bad as we're having; the part that's not a joke is that it's often true. If the "pros" can't reach orgasm with their eyes open, why should you expect yourself to? (I realize this borders on encouraging a reflected sense of self.)

Recognizing these points can help you remember that eyes-open sex and orgasm are about exploring your sexual potential rather than about setting benchmarks of adequacy or normality. These are not new hurdles you have to jump over; they are abilities, not dictates. You don't have to! The issue is, *can* you? If you can't, the notion of "choosing" or "preferring not to" doesn't really make sense. Previously we said that the limits of your development greatly determine your sexual preferences (e.g., you avoid what makes you nervous). Eyes-open orgasm is another example of this notion: we don't do what we can't yet do. The issue here is choice: being able to orgasm with your eyes open doesn't mean you have to do it that way every time. People who can have eyes-open orgasms sometimes close their eyes too!

If you can't have eyes-open orgasms, it doesn't mean you always tune out your partner when you climax (although that's what some people do). You could have a vibrational link with your partner when your eyes are closed and be unable to orgasm with eyes open because it involves another level and type of contact—another dimension of following the connection between you and your partner. This doesn't mean you're not "really" intimate if you can't, but there's merit in recognizing how much farther you might go.

Eyes-open orgasm is more than a skill, a behavioral technique, or a boudoir "trick." Simply keeping your eyelids apart signifies nothing in itself—this you can accomplish more quickly with scotch tape than through differentiation. Keeping your eyes open makes little difference if your "emotional shades" are drawn. Your partner won't see any more of you than if you kept your eyes closed. Some rapists and voyeurs can orgasm with their eyes open but their victims can't see past their retinas; and unfortunately the same holds true for some spouses. The eyes-open orgasm I'm discussing is an invitation for your partner to look inside you. Your differentiation makes it possible to extend the invitation.

It's really about "I-contact"; eye contact is just the vehicle. I'm describing "I to I," "I-open" orgasm. That some people fake orgasms and others worry about being "faked out" reflects how little I-contact many couples have during sex. I-contact is the vibrational link described earlier. There's no question when it occurs. You're aware of only yourself and your partner. Reality extends no farther than the edges of your bed. It takes integrity to get it, tolerate it, and acknowledge its occurrence.

Eyes-open orgasm is more than just esoteric sex. It can be a milestone in your differentiation and a way to get there. It shouldn't surprise us that this form of sexual connection tends to occur more often as people mature. It's another example of what we said earlier: most people don't reach their sexual potential until the fourth, fifth, or sixth decade of life (if they ever do). When intercourse is *really* intimate, you've reached a pinnacle of human development. That's what eyes-open orgasm can be, and what differentiation lets you do.

Theresa and Philip See the Light

As I mentioned earlier, Theresa's interest in seeing if she could climax with her eyes open was a natural progression in enjoying her abilities. Philip wanted to see if he could reach orgasm that way too, but Theresa's eagerness surpassed his. Given that she originally wanted to have orgasms to "measure up," this could have merely been her switching her ruler for a yardstick. Occasionally Theresa did feel inadequate because she couldn't climax this way, but pushing for an eyes-open orgasm diminished the connection with Philip she now regularly enjoyed. Recognizing this put Theresa on back on track. It was another example of following the connection—or, in this case, its absence.

Instead of berating herself for falling into her old pattern of feeling inadequate and trying to "perform," Theresa took pride in her recognition of the pattern. She realized her supposed "inadequacy" was about something she never thought she'd even try just a short time ago. She refocused herself by attending to what she and Philip were doing. *Trying* to have an eyes-open orgasm is self-defeating because it spoils emotional contact, but you have little to lose if you keep focusing on connection with your partner. You'll have a great time whether you reach orgasm or not.

Still, Theresa's wanted to know what an eyes-open orgasm felt like and wanted that depth of connection with Philip. Both Theresa and Philip reported getting "close" to orgasm this way on several occasions, but neither could quite "get there" (i.e., to orgasm threshold). We *didn't* look for something that might be "blocking" them, because then we'd be acting as though they were supposed to orgasm with eyes open. They were exploring their sexual potential and we proceeded on that basis. For example, we considered the fact that not being able to orgasm with eyes open now was not a good predictor of whether Philip or Theresa could do it in the future: we couldn't rule out the possibility that opening their eyes still "distracted" somewhat from their sensations since eyes-open sex was relatively new. Time and experience might be all they needed. With this in mind, we also tried to optimize their physical stimulation and thoughts and feelings as part of exploring their sexual potential.

For one thing, we explored their pattern of interaction. It turned out that Theresa and Philip were using a pattern couples often stumble across spontaneously. They could reach orgasm when they closed their eyes, so that's what they did—they just kept them open longer and longer before closing them to have orgasms. They focused on foreplay as a conscious eyeball-to-eyeball "negotiation" to establish the depth of connection and intensity they would have later on. They often didn't touch each other's genitals until they had a solid connection. Over the course of their encounters, the time between closing eyes and reaching orgasm shortened and the time between foreplay and "I'm ready to finish up and have an orgasm" increased. It became a period of peace and communion. Their overall level of stimulation and satisfaction increased, but not enough for either one to orgasm looking into the other's eyes. So next we looked into nuances of their subjective experiences. I began with Philip.

"Last time, what were you thinking while Theresa was doing you?"

"I don't know. . . . I was just thinking about her."

"In what way?"

"I'm not sure. Why?"

"Because thinking about your partner isn't necessarily the same as being *with* her or being in the moment."

"I guess I was thinking about how I was going to do her after I had my orgasm."

"That can help or a hinder depending on what's happening. If it's a hot, erotic image it can help—but it also means you're thinking about the future, and perhaps not fully available to what's happening in the moment. If it's a fantasy you like, you might try bringing the fantasy into the present by talking to Theresa about it. Some people find talking to their partner a distraction—like patting their head and rubbing their stomach at the same time—it's one more thing they have to do. That's because they approach it like they're a court reporter reading a transcript. But other people find it becomes effortless and automatic because it's another form of following the connection. That's more likely to happen when the tone of your encounter and your fantasy match."

"Tone?"

"Sex always has a tone: a style and flavor that conveys emotional meaning. If your talking about erotic behaviors but your eyes say, 'I'm frightened,' or 'I'm angry you're making me do this,' or 'I'm not really here,' I don't think either of you is likely to climax. It's more likely to happen if the tone of your eye contact says, 'I want to be with you. I'm proud of us. Let's get into this.' " Philip was struck by the different meanings that could be occurring in *his* sexual experience.

"Let's also consider how much connection really exists between you two. When you look in Theresa's eyes, are they focused like she's 'there' or do they seem glassy and vacant?"

"She's definitely there! Her eyes are bright and smiling."

"Theresa, what about when you look at Philip?"

"He's really present at first, and then he gets glassy-eyed. I feel like he's not really there."

Philip looked surprised. He stared at the floor and then at Theresa. "You can tell?" It was half question, half admission.

"Only recently. When I got my sense of self from you, I tried not to pay attention to when you tuned out because I thought it said something negative about me. Lately I've become aware that there are times you touch me in repetitive motions, like your hand is moving but your head is somewhere else." Theresa's tone made it clear she wasn't "unloading" on Philip. She was speaking her experience and confronting herself as much as she was confronting him.

Philip's momentary defensiveness melted into a rueful acknowledgment. "I didn't think it showed. . . . I felt like you had shut me out, too. We were so far apart emotionally and you were so lost in your anxieties. I didn't think you even noticed."

"I noticed. But I've spent a large part of my life trying not to notice what I don't want to see—with you, with my parents, and even our kids. I've been so preoccupied worrying about how I look to others, I never realized how I avoid *seeing*. Now I understand what Dr. Schnarch means when he says we can't stop communicating."

"I do, too. . . . So here's the message I want to send now: I want to get lost in your deep brown eyes the next time we make love. I love you."

"Tell me that when we're in bed!"

"Tell you that I love you?"

"No. Tell me with your eyes and mouth, *'I want you to take me inside you.'* That's how you can take me inside *you*." Philip blushed. It was another time Theresa wanted to go beyond his sexual comfort level.

Not long thereafter, Theresa reached orgasm with her eyes open for the first time. Optimizing the tone and depth of their connection was all she needed to increase her total stimulation beyond her threshold for orgasm. Their emotional energy increased and became harmonious with the physical stimulation she received.

When it happened, Theresa wasn't trying to reach orgasm. She and Philip were deeply engrossed, looking into each other's eyes. It sort of "snuck up on her"; in fact, she was surprised when she recognized sensations that signaled her orgasm was underway. Theresa suddenly realized she was well into her orgasm—her buttocks and thighs were in spasms and her head rose automatically from the pillow, moving her closer to Philip's face. His was the most beautiful face she had ever seen.

Philip had his first eyes-open orgasm several weeks later. He usually liked Theresa to get on top of him during intercourse while he laid back and "went into orbit." He liked it best when she was fully upright, "riding" him. Sometimes he'd imagine she was his "slave girl," eager to serve his every pleasure. Theresa liked this position, too, but sometimes she felt Philip was tuning her out when he closed his eyes. Many times she didn't do anything about it because she did the same thing to him. Other times she'd lean forward, taking her weight onto her elbows, bringing her head near his. She'd kiss him and start talking to draw him out. Sometimes Philip would tell her to be quiet and let him concentrate on his "feelings."

On one particular sexual "ride" Philip opened his eyes. He saw Theresa watching him. It was like she was _doing_ him with her eyes. The connection was _electric_. She never took her eyes off of him as she put her hands next to his chest and put her weight onto her outstretched arms. She stopped moving straight up and down on Philip's penis; her hips now made a sensuous sideways swish in mid-stroke. The force when their groins met was firm without bruising; she brushed him with her pubic hair as her hips moved slightly side to side. Philip could feel Theresa feeling it, too. There was no doubt in his mind. _This_ was wall-socket sex!

They didn't break eye contact for a moment. Theresa contracted her perineal muscles to tighten herself around him. Philip involuntarily grabbed her hips in response, making it hard for her to move. She gently moved his hands to the back of her thighs so he could lift her.

"Don't let go!" Philip knew she was talking about their eyes.

He smiled back. "Don't worry, I'm enjoying the ride."

The smile in Theresa's eyes deepened. Philip loved the feeling that she was drawing his penis inside her, like she was sucking him in rather than just making room for him. She did it just as he was thinking it. Philip thought, _She's doing me from both ends at once!_

Philip got lost in her eyes and time stopped. As he watched, Theresa's face seemed to change. It melted in the nicest way; she became softer and younger. Suddenly Philip realized this was how Theresa looked as a young girl. He'd never seen this part of Theresa, and he'd never seen such a dramatic and visible transformation in anyone. Rather than the spoiled "princess" he always imagined, he saw a clear-eyed little girl who wanted to be loved and hadn't yet become guarded.

Theresa saw Philip's expression change. She said, "I love you!"

Philip came without a moment's hesitation. He never closed his eyes. It was the first time he'd ever seen the light of day in the middle of his orgasm.

Chapter 9

Where's Your Head during Sex? Mental Dimensions of Sexual Experience

> When a girl marries, she exchanges the attentions of many men for the inattention of one.
>
> —*Helen Rowland*

What do you think about during sex?

Well, what *do* you think about during sex? You'd probably sooner disclose every sexual position you've ever used than utter one word about the content and flavor of your thoughts while you're doing it!

What you think about during sex reveals *you* in a way that your behavior may not. Two bodies can be entwined or inserted in relatively limited ways, and you can always blame your behavior on your partner in the name of accommodation. Variations on the mental aspects of sex, however, are infinite. What you think about during sex is totally up to you. We often don't allow our partner access to our mind and genitals at the same time. Has your spouse ever asked during sex, "What are you thinking about right now?" If you're like most people, you've probably lied, and said, "Nothing!" or "I'm thinking about you, dear!"

This chapter is about your hottest erogenous zone. We're going inside your head to explore the mental dimensions of your sexual experience. Modern society gives lip service to the philosophy that "your brain is your biggest sex organ"—if we really lived up to this, "giving head" would have entirely different meaning!

Wandering Minds and Sexual Fantasies

How often does your mind wander while your having sex? What does your mind wander to? Notice I'm not asking, "*Does* you mind ever wander?" Mind-wandering is so common it's enshrined in our humor: have you heard the joke about the two people comparing what their partners say at the height of sexual passion? The first one says, "My partner says, *'Oh, God! Do me, baby!'* " Crestfallen, the second one says, "Mine says, *'I think we'll paint the ceiling mauve.'* "

Some people don't realize their mind is wandering while they're having sex. It occurs so often that they just take it for granted. In other cases mind-wandering shows up disguised as sexual fantasies. Either way, it means you're not emotionally connected with your partner. In society's rush to assure people that sexual fantasies are "normal"—meaning *okay*—we have lost sight of the fact that they can nonetheless interfere with intimacy during sex. Sharing fantasies with a partner can be intimate, but curiosity and open-mindedness often wear thin when your partner finds out what you're *really* thinking. A lot goes on in the brains of two people when they are between the sheets—and differentiation plays a crucial role in these mental activities.

Consider the example of Florence and Stan, a young couple with numerous marital complaints. Their current fight: Stan revealed that he sometimes thought of other women while they had sex. Florence felt "used" and "wounded."

In our session Stan defended himself by accusing Florence of thinking of past lovers or possible new partners, just as he did. "Everyone does it! I don't think I'm abnormal!" Stan was snorting his "For heaven's sake, Florence! Grow up!" attitude.

At first, Florence denied having any such fantasies, but eventually she acknowledged "occasionally" thinking of someone else. She was quick to point out that *she* always knew the person in bed with her was Stan. She wanted it known that she didn't pretend he was someone else. She just "thought about it." This didn't end with Stan feeling vindicated, however. He became enraged!

"You raked me over the coals for doing the same thing you do!"

I pointed out that Stan was acting as though her admission had come as a big surprise. "If you believed what you said when you insisted that Florence thought about other partners too, why are you so upset when she finally agrees with you?" I knew his answer would be important.

Stan quieted down and thought for a minute. He said with chagrin,

"I guess I wanted to believe her denials! I knew she must do it, but having it confirmed makes me feel insecure. I feel like I've lost something! I feel stupid, too! I knew better! I shouldn't be feeling like this!"

"I think you're feeling the only way you could feel, given who you two are. It makes little difference what the front of your brain 'thinks.' The back of your brain has taken over. Emotional fusion is painful until you give it up—and it dies a painful death."

We insist on being our spouse's *one and only*—even in fantasy. On the surface it may seem like we're following the commandment, *"Thou shalt not covet thy neighbor's wife,"* but underneath it's our narcissism demanding, *"Thou shalt have no other gods! Worship only me!"* Even though Stan and Florence "knew better," the emotional recognition that this mental level of fidelity wasn't true was a bitter pill to swallow. We don't want our partner fantasizing about anyone else! It's not easy to accept, even if we do it, too. Realizing they're doing it during sex with *us* adds insult to emotional injury.

Research indicates that, of all sexual fantasies, thinking of someone other than your partner is the most common. These are called "partner-replacement" fantasies. When confronted about their fantasies about other partners, many people assume it's better to deny everything and be glad it's hard to prove they are lying. They think partner replacement fantasies belong to the category of "the few things *not* said each day that improve a marriage."

Wanting to be our partner's "one and only" *in fantasy* is not just an extension of the principle of monogamy. It has to do with being dependent on our partner's validation. Our mate's sexual fantasies play havoc with our reflected sense of self. Validation from our partner evaporates while he or she fantasizes about someone else. We can tell ourselves we don't have to take it personally. But if we've spent our lives pursuing validation from others, we don't really have much choice *but* to take it personally when we are not the focus of our partner's fantasies.

What I'm describing isn't a problem if you handle it properly. Granted, it doesn't feel good at first. But it's part of marriage's people-growing machine. You can persist in hating the fact that your spouse's fantasies don't always include you, or you can develop a more stable sense of yourself.

For several chapters we've looked at what happens to marriages dominated by other-validated intimacy. To review the general characteristics of partners in these marriages: (a) they have difficulty introducing novelty into their sexual relationship, (b) they experience anxiety and resist change when their partner does something new, and (c) they have difficulty with maintaining a clear sense of self when out of synch with their partner. More important to our current discussion, they are likely to tune out their partner during sex and focus on body sensations to reach orgasm. Over time, they are more likely to experience sexual boredom and resort to partner replacement fantasies for sexual variety.

Here's the paradox: the very thing that makes poorly differentiated people go crazy over their partner's sexual fantasies predisposes them to do the same thing themselves! People wounded by the discovery that they are not their partner's "one and only" are likely to be fantasizing about someone else. Being dependent on validation from others, they have to lie about it even while they are complaining about their partner. And in the midst of all this, they want their partner to validate them and make them feel secure. Like the exercise wheel inside a squirrel cage, this process drives marriage's people-growing machinery.

If this pattern rings true for you so far, consider the impact during sex: desire to fuse with your partner actually increases the likelihood of experiencing *less intimacy* during sex. Your heads are inevitably in different places. You can *feel* your partner tune you out even if you're "in synch" enough to grind.

I'm not saying that there is anything "wrong" with mind-wandering and partner replacement fantasies during sex. I'm putting them in context so you can use them productively. Mind-wandering during sex is probably inevitable—but you can reduce it significantly and increase the intimacy and potency of your sex. The benefit can generalize to the rest of your life, because it involves increasing your level of differentiation.

Humans will always fantasize; that's not necessarily a problem. The difficulty is that the *way* we fantasize (and hide it) interferes with intimacy and wall-socket sex. Like hugging, kissing, desire, and monogamy, fantasies operate differently depending on your level of differentiation.

Magazines and media therapists suggest that you share fantasies with your partner—but most people don't. They know their spouse will go ballistic if the truth comes out. Poorly differentiated people don't include their partners in the *content* of their fantasies—which could lead to new ways to do the same old sexual things—because they aren't very flexible in their sexual style. (I'll explain this in a moment.) They use partner replacement fantasies to create novelty in their heads because they can't innovate in their beds. They fantasize to tune *out*—to escape the "togetherness pressure" and boredom of emotional fusion. Highly differentiated people can use fantasies to tune *in*—creating new psychological links in bed (and out)—and tolerate the jolt when profound connection occurs.

Some partners who "share" fantasies do so for the wrong reason. Poorly differentiated people sometimes flaunt their sexual fantasies and mind-wandering to deliberately tamper with their partner's reflected sense of self. Their spouse usually feels hurt and backs off—creating the intended reduction in "togetherness pressure" and inflicting revenge for boring sex. (We'll discuss this in Chapter 11 as *normal marital sadism*.)

Dimensions of Psychological Experience during Sex

Let's explore some psychological dimensions of sexual experience and see how they determine what you do or don't like. These preferences are the source of unending fights about sex. Previously we looked at the psychology of hugging, foreplay, and eyes-open sex. Now let's discuss sexual *styles* in more detail.

The advice to "tell your partner what you want" doesn't involve simply a vocabulary of words. As noted previously, it also requires a vocabulary of sexual behaviors. But the range of sexual behaviors you desire isn't as important as the vocabulary of emotions and meanings you express through these behaviors. Cunnilingus, fellatio, or intercourse in different positions isn't enough to keep sex from being boring. It's the *style* of doing these that contains the real communication. For example, the *Kama Sutra* discusses sixty-four coital positions *plus* subtle nuances of biting, scratching, and sexual noises. Taoist texts consider "nine styles of moving the Jade Stalk while inside the Female Crucible."

Let's divide sexual mind-sets into three categories: *sexual trance, partner engagement*, and *role play*. (Psychologist/sex researcher Donald Mosher originally developed this framework and some of the insights that follow.) These dimensions broaden the quantum model's premise that what you think about during sex affects how your genitals function and whether you reach orgasm. More importantly, they help explain how an optimized mind-set can produce profound sexual experience and increase contact with your partner. (However, remember that these categories are just artificial labels for digesting your own experience. They are useful for putting words to common experience and finding new ways to talk with your partner. They can help you discuss what's really going on when you're fighting over who likes what.)

These three dimensions—sexual trance, partner engagement, and role play—differ in a dozen ways. Each has its own preferred physical technique, emotional tone, and style of engagement. Which psychological dimension of sex you prefer determines what you fantasize about, what you think "good sex" is, and what sex means to you. It determines how and when you want to be touched by your partner.

Sexual Trance

Sexual trance primarily involves focusing on body sensations . . . feeling yourself get aroused . . . the tingling in your loins . . . feeling your orgasm about to happen (or wondering if it is).

If this is your preferred sexual style, you like sex in private settings with few distractions. If you have your wish, the mood is relaxed and serene. It allows you to focus inward on your sensuality. You probably like "taking turns"—you get to focus on "giving" or "receiving" and devote yourself to one or the other. You like being touched in slow-paced repetitive motions and you want your partner to be non-intrusive. You don't want a lot of mutual kissing (although you might enjoy having your lips stimulated).

You certainly don't want your partner sticking his or her face in yours, saying, "Tell me you love me!" You prefer relatively little talk during sex, mostly limited to guiding your partner about where and how to touch. For the most part, talking seems like a distraction because it interferes with focusing on sensations.

If you enjoy sexual trance, sex is like an altered state of consciousness. To you, "good sex" is a great vacation in a strange land to which you are transported on a magic carpet of sensations—like a drug high. Sometimes it can be like simultaneous drug experiences, both you and your partner groaning in unison. "Great sex" is like discovering the sensual secrets of the ages. Sensations seem to have their own illuminating meaning. Profound sexual experiences can be almost hallucinatory— like your body flowing in a river of petals. Your orgasm can be so strong you see stars or a whirling nebula, or momentarily lose your hearing. (People joke about this as "the earth moved.")

"Bad sex" is a lousy trip to an unpleasant place where transportation is unreliable—you can't communicate with the "locals" upon whom you're dependent. You may be "on vacation," but you can't relax for a moment. You wonder if the trip was worth the effort!

Fantasies are hard to share if you like sexual trance. They are mostly wordless visual or sensory images and sharing them doesn't necessarily let your partner be there with you.

If this style sounds like yours, consider what happens as you become involved in sex: sexual trance requires that your awareness of the "real world" fades. At low levels of trance, you can't abandon your day-to-day reality. Maybe you're thinking about unreturned phone calls, or the argument with your boss, or the possibility of the baby crying. The content really doesn't matter—except that it mirrors who you are—but the impact is the same: you never get into the experience and you don't connect with your partner.

At moderate levels of sexual trance distractions fade. The sexual encounter grabs your attention. An altered state of sexual reality increasingly takes over. You're still vulnerable to external interruptions (like the sound of a police siren). Distracting thoughts and feelings surrounding the sexual encounter can still interfere—like worries of being sexually inadequate, or that your partner will tire and leave you hanging just when you're about to come. For the most part, however, you're "there."

At profound levels of involvement you are totally absorbed in the sensations of sex. You are "in the moment" and oblivious to everything else. Short of an emergency, you are unaware of extraneous events.

Superficial sexual trance is the style of sex to which Masters and Johnson's "sensate focus exercises" are erroneously reduced. Their approach involved teaching this trance style (which lots of people use spontaneously) to couples with sexual dysfunctions. However, the part of their approach that has escaped general attention—making *contact* with one's partner—doesn't often occur spontaneously with this sexual style. That's because focusing on yourself and your "internal" experience is inherent in sensate focus (sexual trance), but contact with your partner isn't. Particularly for those who aren't good at recognizing their sexual sensations, sensate focus is antithetical to awareness of your "external" partner. Recognizing this, Masters and Johnson instructed clients to "tell your partner what you want" to draw connection with the partner. However, many people find *this* distracts from sensory awareness, and others don't want to be intimate during sex to begin with.

Trance state sex can be intimate if both people enjoy it and are good at it. But it can just as easily leave you feeling "used" and ignored—like your partner is using you as a fleshy sex toy—and he just tunes you out and focuses on his (or your) body. If he achieves only a low level of sexual trance, he probably *has* to tune you out. He has to close his eyes to focus sufficiently on sensations to enable his body to reach orgasm. This autistic outcome isn't inherent in this sexual style. Whether or not this occurs depends on how well either of you can engage in sexual trance.

There are two directions you can go in to establish a better connection. One is to draw your partner out of the sexual trance and demand that he pay attention to you. The other is to allow him to get in *deeper* and/or learn to do this, too. If you can do trance state deep enough, you can open your eyes without losing awareness of your sensations. If you develop your own ability to use this sexual dimension, it becomes something you and your partner can share. We'll talk more about this once we outline the other two sexual dimensions.

Partner Engagement

If your sexual mind-set emphasizes your emotional bond with your partner, you are into *partner engagement.* The important setting for you isn't the isolation tank of sexual trance or the theatrical "props" of role play. It is the psychological setting of a relationship and its mood. You prefer affectionate sharing and mutual pleasuring in contrast to the turn-taking of sexual trance. You like foreplay with eye-gazing and lots of kissing and hugging. You want full-body contact and face-to-face positions (although you may think that sex is more "romantic" with your eyes closed). Your sex talk revolves around romantic endearments, and your sexual fantasies involve courting, romance, valentines, and love songs.

Partner engagement is the sexual style idealized by Madison Avenue and epitomized by romance novels. If this is your preferred style, you cherish sex as loving union between warm, tender, caring partners. "Okay sex" is a way to get acquainted in the midst of a romance or to satisfy your curiosity about someone's sexual "flavor." "Good sex" is when you merge with your partner and feel, "I know you at your essence and you know me!" At least briefly you experience the two of you "becoming one." Orgasm feels like surrendering yourself to your "oneness" as a measure of your affection. "Great sex" feels like a spiritual rebirth and a mutual celebration of life. In all cases, emphasis remains on the connection.

The way you actually use partner engagement reveals a great deal about you. There are different depths and ways of focusing on your partner. Each reflects how you relate in general. The tone of your connections may vary from event to event, but the overall character tends to be stable; it is determined more by your personal development than by how you feel about your partner at any given moment.

Let's consider six levels of partner engagement reflecting different levels of differentiation. Let me warn you that the initial examples may seem somewhat extreme, distasteful, or hard to identify with. They are examples of primitive sexual partner engagement and reflect the unfortunate realities of contemporary society. By understanding the many faces of partner engagement we can more fully comprehend human sexuality and develop more respect for when it is beautiful and uplifting.

- *Sexual predators* focus somewhat on their "partner's" reactions but for purely sadistic reasons. These are the most poorly differentiated people—their "partners" are merely puppets who must give the desired response. For example, I once treated a man who was a sexual sadist. His children "took turns" going with him to their vacation home, where he tied them spread-legged to a chair. He would draw a pen knife lightly around their genitals as ritualistic "punishment" for some concocted misdeed. He described his own behavior as "monstrous." He was driven by his overriding hostility and desire to revenge past events in his own life. He was redressing in fantasy— and replicating in reality—his experiences with his own mother. He *enjoyed* seeing pain and terror in his children's eyes. It enhanced his pathetic sense of power. His "sexual partners" were like props— his wife was no more a real person to him than he was to her. In his fantasies, he presided over an underground citadel of faceless slaves who followed his every whim. This man's profound lack of differentiation surfaced in his indifference to his children's pain and his reflected sense of "power."

- The next step in development is a style of partner engagement that involves *opportunistic encounters* between consenting adults. I don't necessarily mean "one-night stands" where people "fall in love" for the night. One woman I treated was more a scavenger than a predator. She had sex with people she had no shred of interest in—or they in her. For her the connection was purely one of shared sensory experience, using her partner's genitals for stimulation because she didn't like to masturbate. In her best relationships, the bond was a shared craving for contact-comfort with another human being. This was as much emotional connection and investment in another human being as her differentiation allowed. Although you might imagine people like her are single, I've worked with many who are married (and having affairs).

  I'm not saying opportunistic sexual encounters always involve this degree of exploitation. Casual sex, at conferences or on a college campus for example, can be based on shared pleasure or companionship. It can involve even more partner engagement, such as friendship between "fuck buddies." Sometimes fondness for a familiar sex partner is all that connects spouses—whether married or divorced. These varying degrees of selectivity, intimacy, and caring reflect higher differentiation than the woman I just described. (Just realize that exploitive sexual relationships can masquerade as a casual friendship—whether between college students, work colleagues, or spouses.)

- For some people, sex partners provide *narcissistic self-reflection*—ego strokes, a body on which to demonstrate sexual prowess and attractiveness. At this level of differentiation people have some emotional investment in the relationship—although it's primarily to get a reflected sense of self. Their sexual fantasies are like private pornography, often involving unflattering power motifs with their partner. In worst case scenarios, partners are "playthings" and "boy toys," to use modern parlance: this partner engagement involves borrowed functioning in which the "plaything" provides an emotional transfusion of pseudo self—until he or she feels drained and develops low sexual desire (Chapter 5). (Opportunistic sex—for example, between friends and former lovers—sometimes reflects a higher level of differentiation.) This kind of partner engagement often underlies short-lived "movie star" marriages, but some are fairly long-term when the "drainage" isn't so high. These frequently (but not always) involve "trophy wives" or "May-December" marriages between rich older men and financially dependent younger women.

- At the fourth level of partner engagement the sex partner is recognized as a *real person*, not just walking, talking genitals. In contrast to the prior category (investment in the relationship), the greater differentiation involved here surfaces in investment in the other person. However, there's not enough differentiation for the partner to be fully recognized as a separate individual. This is the partner engagement of dependency on other-validated intimacy. There's awareness that the other has feelings and needs of his/her own. Satisfying some of them and not inflicting pain (beyond normal marital sadism) becomes important, in part, because it contributes to one's reflected sense of self. The sex partner is one's mirror—making sexual trance attractive as time-out from monitoring one's reflection (meaning sex with eyes closed).

The preceding four examples describe emotionally fused forms of partner engagement. The other person is a non-person—an extension of one's own needs. Moving from the first to the fourth level, people demonstrate greater differentiation, culminating in the partner emerging as a real person—although not a truly separate one. Psychologically, at the fourth level there are finally two people—or more accurately, one and a half. There is still a tendency for partners to function like emotional Siamese twins. Until the partner is more than just an extension of one's ego, there isn't a genuine basis for caring about him or her.

Notice that it's taken four of the six steps to reach this degree of personal evolution, which reflects how little true caring goes on even in partner engagement sex. The remaining two levels are ones we'd like to believe apply to us (and most people). They're what we optimistically expect and demand from modern marriage. More realistically, these forms of sexual relatedness increasingly occur as we live longer and acquire more personal growth. Turning these potentialities into realities is both the result of—and the reason to pursue—your own differentiation.

- The level of partner engagement we now address probably came to mind when I first mentioned partner engagement. It involves *unique connection*. At this level of differentiation, the partner stops being one's mirror, a reflection on oneself, or an extension of oneself. He or she emerges as a bona fide separate person, and occupies an unrivaled place in one's life. His/her happiness and satisfaction become as important as one's own. Compassion, consideration, mutuality, and integrity steer the interactions, made possible by one's ability to calm one's anxiety and self-soothe one's conflicts and hurts. Partners realize and appreciate each other's deepest core personality and potentials—pushing themselves to disclose their most private and personal truths. It isn't easy or comfortable, yet nothing is deliberately held back. Looking into each other during sex is commonplace. Acceptance is based on true knowledge of each other—it's not a mutual validation pact predicated on fantasies and projections. Partners share a profound and irreplaceable love.
- The ultimate stage of partner engagement reflects a level of differentiation few people reach. Here partners come to grips with the barriers of existential separateness and experience *oneness with each other and humanity*. Their sexual encounters heighten self-awareness *and* interconnection. Normal boundaries between self and other dissolve. Partners see themselves in each other (and vice versa) during eyes-open sex, but this doesn't stem from emotional fusion or reflected sense of self. It comes from appreciating the essence in each of us that connects all of us (and encourages social and environ-

mental consciousness). Sex becomes a form of spiritual communion celebrating the mysteries of life.

These six categories of partner engagement illustrate once again how differentiation facilitates the highest forms of emotional union. But the last two uplifting forms are hard to achieve, periodic at best, and their absence can be painful. The more primitive and exploitative forms of emotional fusion are commonplace in daily life.

Differentiation determines the availability of the following ingredients that comprise partner engagement:

- the strength and meaningfulness of your bond,
- how much "self" either of you has to invest (to what degree are you self-validating),
- the degree to which either of you is willing to invest your "true self,"
- and the degree of profound meaning in a particular sexual encounter.

Differentiation plays another role in partner engagement: as you strive for deeper partner engagement, the range of potential sex partners narrows. If all you want is minimal engagement, almost any partner will do. Casual engagement—recreational sex—simply requires an available, socially appropriate partner. But from this point on, increased engagement narrows your field of choices. Personal characteristics of the partner and the nature of the relationship become important. Fewer people meet your selection criteria. If you want profound partner engagement—particularly with any regularity—it usually involves a single partner with unique status in your life. It also involves a partner who can engage you on that level.

My saying that deeper levels of partner engagement demand restrictive selectivity might sound like a condemnation of casual sex, especially to those who argue that casual sex can be just as rewarding as monogamy—or more so. I have no argument with people's personal experience, but let's be honest: you can't deeply know the fullest potentials of a large number of sex partners. *Knowing* one all-important person probably involves not tasting lots of others.

Our discussion of sexual styles brings us back to the question from Chapter 5: who really *wants* to want? The fact that profound sexual partner engagement narrows your selection highlights the vulnerability of establishing a profound bond. It isn't just that your partner is irreplaceable: there aren't many suitable candidates even when you have numerous volunteers. (We'll talk more of this in Chapter 14.)

Role Play

We have one more sexual style to discuss: if you like sexual drama and acting out erotic script-like fantasies, you're into *role play*. People who enjoy role play like to share fantasies—indeed, the whole encounter revolves around fantasy. Rather than just whispering secret desires, role playing involves *acting on* them. Many couples find it more difficult to connect using this style than the other two.

If you delight in role play, sex is a stage. You like your settings dramatic and exhibitionistic. Your bedroom and bathroom become theaters for your performances. Perhaps you prefer sex on the kitchen counter, or outdoors, or someplace you might be discovered. Such settings would never do for people into sexual trance or partner engagement—they would interfere with losing awareness of their environment or focusing on their partner. For someone into role play, however, setting is vitally important. Anyone who enjoys good theater knows props set the mood and create a believable alternate reality. If you are into role play, you value sex toys for more than physical stimulation, and you know clothes *do* make the man (or woman). You want eyes open and lights on to appreciate the performance—unless it interferes with the script.

If you like role playing, sex captures you like a good novel. When sex is mediocre, you (and/or your partner) move through a lackluster role like a high school performer. Lousy sex is like a bad movie—you want to walk out!

When sex is magic, you and your partner are like method actors. You "become" your roles to such a degree that your behaviors and expressions are automatic. In fact, the distinction between you and your role ceases to exist. The role play becomes a means for expressing a very real part of you. Orgasms tend to be dramatic and expressive.

People who like role play want different qualities in a partner than those who primarily like sexual trance or partner engagement. They pay attention to more than their sensations and tire of always playing *Romeo and Juliet*. They want a partner who has a broad repertoire of sexual positions and "tonalities" that lets him or her play a variety of roles. Technique has to match the plot being enacted, and sound, action, and facial expression are important. Both roles must coordinate because it's no fun being Scarlet O'Hara with Walter Mitty, or Rhett Butler with Little Bo Peep.

If you consider depth of involvement in role play, the fit between the role you are playing and your sexual self-image (the sexual "self" you know yourself to be) is terribly important. The closer the fit, the easier it is to *become* the role (and thereby connect with your partner). However, your level of differentiation makes the biggest difference. Just as your ability to maintain a clear sense of yourself allows you to get closer without fear of losing yourself, it also gives you the flexibility to take on a variety of roles without running into the awkward feeling, *"That's not me! And I won't do it!"* The clearer you are about "who you are," the easier it is for you to take on, temporarily, a different persona—you can "blur your identity" without feeling phony. At my workshops I often tell a story to dramatize this point:

Daniel and Gwen have been next door neighbors to Bernard and Susan for years. After a day of male camaraderie, Daniel and Bernard each told their wives of a secret fantasy they had in common: having sex with a $1,000-a-night call girl.

Daniel and Bernard separately asked their wives to surprise them by purchasing a sexy garment appropriate for the role play. Gwen and Susan were asked to wear it the next time they had sex. Both women agreed. And there the similarity ends.

Daniel's wife Gwen was excited by the prospect. She went shopping at her first opportunity—the very next morning. At the lingerie shop, Gwen saw a garment displayed in the window. It was more blatantly erotic than anything she'd ever worn before. She had no difficulty imagining a self-assured courtesan wearing it and wowing her "date." Trying it on felt wickedly daring. Gwen liked feeling the smooth silk against her skin. There, in the dressing room, she became sexually aroused. She was even a little embarrassed by the scent and warm moistness she left on the garment. Flush with great expectations for that evening, Gwen purchased her selection and hurried home—after stopping briefly to pick up great bath oil for a long hot soak in the tub.

In contrast, Susan, Bernard's wife, was angry. She interpreted Bernard's request to mean that he found her unattractive—something she'd felt about herself for years. Feeling demeaned, she ruminated that Bernard was treating her like a "sex object"—something she never thought she was good at being. She took her sweet time getting to the lingerie shop—she got there barely before closing time the next evening. Actually, stopping there was only an afterthought when she found herself driving by it.

Susan went to the same store as Gwen and the same garment caught her eye. She, too, knew it was perfect for the role—but it sure didn't fit her sexual style. Susan wore modest nightgowns that left everything to the imagination. The garment in the store clearly "wasn't her." But she knew it fit the kind of woman Bernard had in mind.

This brought up feelings she'd struggled with all her life: being intimidated by women who were comfortable with their sexuality. On her way to the dressing room, a man shopping in the store made eye contact. She imagined him fantasizing about her having sex in the garment she was holding. She felt embarrassed and exposed when he smiled. Susan was quick in the dressing room. She made her purchase and left as fast as possible.

On the way home, Susan was angry at Bernard. She was angry at herself. She was angry at her mother who had taught her that sex was all men wanted—and good women didn't.

Later that evening, Gwen was luxuriating in her bath, Daniel was sitting on their bed in the adjoining room, reading his newspaper. Comforting sounds of Gwen singing to herself came from the bathroom. Realizing the singing had stopped, he looked up and turned around. Gwen was standing in the bedroom doorway dressed in her new lingerie. Daniel realized he hadn't heard her standing there—he'd *felt* her presence.

Gwen didn't say a word. She stood there leaning against the doorjamb. A dark spot gradually appeared as she rubbed the silk against where her legs met. She never took her eyes off Daniel.

"What?!" said Daniel. He had a sly smile on his face.

"Pay me," Gwen said seductively.

"Pay you? Pay you for what, Gwen?" Daniel was laughing gleefully.

"The first thing I learned when I entered 'the life' is always get my money up front! And don't call me Gwen. My name is Candy. What's yours?"

Daniel couldn't think of anything to say at first. But the look in Gwen/Candy's eyes and the way she touched herself made him smile in anticipation of what (and who) was to come next.

"My name's not important. Call me Bob. Why don't you come on over here, Candy!"

"Not until I get paid, Bob."

Daniel/Bob loved it!

Things weren't going quite as well at Bernard and Susan's house. Susan put on the same lingerie and walked into the bedroom. Bernard could tell she wasn't happy.

Susan said grudgingly, "Okay. Tell me what you want me to do."

Bernard was hurt and disappointed. "Tell you what I want you to do?"

"Yes! What do you want me to do? I'm not really a $1,000-a-night hooker. I'm not comfortable with this. But I said I'd do it because *you* wanted it. So, here I am in *your* outfit—so what do you want me to do?"

Bernard was so frustrated he could spit. "If you were really a hooker, you wouldn't ask me what to do!"

Susan was equally furious! "I'm *not* a hooker!! Besides, this is *your* stupid fantasy—now do *you* want to have sex or not!"

"I don't!" Bernard was seething.

"Well, just remember that I've done what you wanted, so don't ask again!"

"You haven't done what I wanted! You're not putting anything into this!"

"I think this is just another of your little boy tantrums about sex! You want me to turn myself into a sex kitten. I find that degrading and cheap! I don't think you know how to handle getting what you said you wanted, either!"

Bernard and Susan would fight over that night for years to come.

O bviously, Susan didn't want to get into the role play, but Bernard's performance wouldn't win an Academy Award either. *Both* partners have to get in role. Men are often as uncomfortable as Susan was about wearing silk lounging pajamas or sexy underwear. Sometimes it's as subtle as a man refusing to shave and shower before sex because it isn't really "him." Women are expected to fuss and prepare and wear the props, although in other species the male displays the plumage.

Your sexual self-image and level of differentiation together determine how deeply you can get into a role and which roles you can play. When the Frederick's of Hollywood salesperson asked me if my wife could "pull off" the outfit I was going to buy, she was addressing this very point. The roles you "come alive in" reveal something significant about you. Your eroticism—not just your "acting ability"—makes your part in the sexual drama come alive. When you are immersed in the role play, it becomes a fluid source of self-disclosure. Role play isn't something you can do well when you're feeling bad about yourself—unless that's part of your erotic map. Some people's sexual template involves feeling bad about themselves. The rest of us need to feel pretty good to get into being *b-a-a-d* in a hot, erotic way.

Notice that role play requires you to use your neocortex. It permits unmatched sexual variety (and meaningful engagement) *with the same person* over a lifetime. Contrary to the belief that sexual boredom results from time spent together, the reverse can also be true: it takes a lifetime to explore the available sexual scripts. It probably takes that long to differentiate enough to do it!

Sexual Potential: Putting It All Together

I've described sexual trance, partner engagement, and role play as if they were more or less mutually exclusive—as if people use a single one and neither of the others. I did this, in part, to differentiate the three "camps" on the mental map of sex, but also because we usually limit ourselves to a single dimension. And our depth of involvement in this preferred style is often pretty minimal—good enough to reach orgasm. Sexual development frequently stops at the point we are "nondysfunctional," leaving ourselves just a step away from problems with arousal and orgasm.

Inability to use your preferred sexual style at significant depth does more than limit arousal and satisfaction and ensure eventual boredom. It limits how deeply you can connect sexually with your partner. In other words, your limitations using sexual trance, partner engagement, *and* role play limit sexual intimacy with your partner. If you can use only one (or two) sexual style(s)—and only at superficial depth—sex never becomes profoundly intimate.

Conversely, attaining simultaneous profound connection in all *three* sexual modalities has some lovely qualities:

- Arousal and orgasm come effortlessly. Orgasm almost seems secondary because it is no longer your focus of attention.
- You become acutely aware of every sensation in your body—not just in your genitals. You're alive with the sounds, smells, and tastes of sex.
- Your sexual encounter becomes the only possible reality. The world ceases to exist beyond the edge of the bed—or whatever defines your sexual space. There is only you and your partner. Time stops.
- Bonding is solid and profound. There is a sense of commitment conveyed through action rather than pledges. You may find yourself moved to tears by the happiness and love you thought yourself incapable of feeling.
- You do things you've never done before as if they were second nature to you. You see universal aspects of your partner (and yourself) you've never seen before. Jungian therapists would say you've tapped into our "collective unconscious"!

- When orgasm occurs, it's explosive *and* illuminating. New and lasting insights emerge, providing leaps in personal development. It goes way beyond "I'm coming! I'm coming!"—it's an ecstatic "I've got it! I've got it! I *am*!"
- Orgasm doesn't define the end of your encounter because your desire is driven by fullness rather than deprivation. (We'll discuss desire out of fullness in Chapter 14.) As the sexual reality fades, it leaves behind a sense of connection and personal renewal.

In *Flow: The Psychology of Optimum Experience,* Mihaly Csikszentmihali observes that peak experiences like this occur when the hard work of adding increased complexity eventually yields an effortless mastery. The repetitive, boring, utilitarian sex created by limited sexual styles is the exact opposite. All along I've said that normal sexual styles are determined by developmental tasks you're trying to avoid, rather than by things you're really dying to do. In other words, the styles you are *not* comfortable using determine your sexual signature and your relationship's sexual "flavor." (Sexual relationships develop by each partner ruling particular behaviors and meanings off limits—and the couple doing whatever sexual options remain.) Someone with truly balanced sexual development is equally comfortable with all three psychological dimensions of sexual experience. Such a person has no sexual "pseudo preferences"—that is, preferences based on limitations. Two such people are capable of having the kind of sex described above.

Unfortunately, most of us aren't there yet. Men's and women's differing socialization leads to preferences for different sexual styles. Neither gender is encouraged to develop all three. Women generally have greater comfort with partner engagement. Men more frequently prefer sexual trance. Role play scares almost everyone. (Obviously these characterizations are merely illustrative. Some women get into sexual trance more than men; in fact, women are capable of deep sexual trance—if they can validate their interest in sex as an end in itself.)

The time-worn saying that "women trade sex for love" is misguided and false. Women enjoy eroticism as least as much as men do—I believe more. In the couples I've worked with, wives are often more willing than husbands to try role play. But women—and indirectly, men—don't move forward as long as they hide behind partner engagement and don't broaden their range.

There are also men whose capacity for partner engagement outpaces many women. They enjoy this level of relating without labeling it as their "feminine" side. That's a flaw in contemporary views: we still stereotype aspects of human development as belonging to one gender or the other. When men and women can use all three dimensions of sexual experience with equal facility, we will be a step closer to true equality. But the "problem" in many marriages is that we're not yet there.

When sexual behavior steps outside gender sex-role stereotypes, people often question their identity and adequacy. I remember a women telling me, "I have the sex drive of a man." She meant that she engaged in sexual trance with many partners. Her marriage was important to her, but she didn't need much partner engagement—or emotional commitment—to enjoy getting into bed with someone new. She knew what she liked—but she didn't feel entirely good about it.

It's safe to say most people haven't achieved "balanced" involvement in all three dimensions of sexual experience. A couple's particular pattern of "unbalanced involvement"—the psychological dimensions and depth either of them *can't* use—gives their encounters a repetitive style and flavor, and predisposes fights about sex. Our limited sexual styles create the rigid quality so characteristic of long-term sexual relationships. We channel our sexual expression into dimensions we know how to use. Using a sexual style we haven't developed creates anxiety—which makes differentiation a critical factor.

An unfamiliar dimension of sexual expression is frightening or exhilarating, depending on our level of differentiation. Poorly differentiated people have difficulty self-soothing their anxiety and like to stick to the familiar. It makes them feel "safe"—for the moment. This reflexive response isn't "wrong," however. It is actually part of the process.

Over time, these unfulfilled potentials create routine patterns of insipid sex—and arguments about technique and meaning. It's the end result of "tyranny of the lowest common denominator." Boring monogamous marital sex has its own built-in solution: partners' unbalanced involvement in sexual trance, partner engagement, and role play produces arguments about preferred sexual styles. It's easy to think your marriage is failing when it gets to "my (sexual) way versus yours." Ironically, it's a sign of marriage at work. "Pushing and shoving" about sexual styles drives both spouses' differentiation forward. The paradox of differentiation surfaces once again: the road to greater commonality and connection involves refusing to relinquish your differences. (I know this defies common logic and society's sermon that compromise is the heart of marriage.)

Using Sex to Grow

In Chapter 2 I said a couple's sexual repertoire grows through conflict rather than compromise. Our current discussion fleshes out this idea. Sexual conflict in marriage is not just inevitable—it's *important*. Both partners' sexual maturation is at stake. The conflict looks like it's about whose limits (of sexual development) will control the relationship. Lots of accusations of "You don't love me!" fly around the household. But the process makes both people grow up.

The resulting friction stretches you. If either partner's style dominates the sexual relationship, you both lose because you stop growing. Remember, this "growth" is the differentiation that has to keep pace with your spouse's growing importance in your life—if you want to keep intimacy and sexual desire alive as you stay together longer. Poorly differentiated people mistake the absence of open conflict to mean that everything is okay.

The struggle over sexual preferences/limitations may lead you to ask, "What's wrong with me the way I am?" While often said defensively at first, this is really a productive question. You may not want to answer it because it means facing things about yourself you know need changing. Your response to the question unmasks your reluctance to become what you can be—just as it unmasks your rejection of who you are now. Your response also reveals how you interpret your partner's difference as reflecting some personal shortcoming. Finally, the question itself highlights the unspoken assumption that if people love you, they'll be satisfied living within your limitations.

As we learned in Chapter 5, people become alligator-like when they get anxious; the reptilian part of their brain takes over. They lash out to protect themselves and snap at whatever they deem threatening. But alligators don't use partner engagement or role play—they have sex but they don't make love. If you want to have *human* sexuality, you have to soothe your reptilian responses so that the "thinking" part of your brain stays in control. Growth is often uncomfortable, but you won't accomplish much if you never push each other's sexual development. It's been said that evolution is self-realization through self-transcendence. The miracle of differentiation is that the path to being more than an alligator lies in refusing to be a sexual "one-trick pony"!

If you allow it, the people-growing machinery of marriage results in the simultaneous development of your sexuality, your personhood, and your level of intimacy with your partner:

- Venturing into unexplored dimensions and depths of sex exposes you, your partner, and your marriage.
- Both of you run into your unresolved issues and lack of personal development.
- Working through—rather than avoiding—these sexual styles leads to self-mastery, integrity, and pride.
- New dimensions and depths of sexual experience permit increased contact with your partner.
- Issues about intimacy and eroticism inevitably arise.
- Resolving these issues removes emotional "underbrush" and makes possible new meanings and increased pleasure in sex.
- At this point you are beginning to explore your sexual potential, which means you are bumping into the limits of your sexual development once again.
- You start mixing and matching sexual styles from two or more dimensions (at a time), coming up with novel combinations of behaviors and tones.
- Your level of differentiation is measured, stretched, and used every step of the way.
- You've earned the privilege of returning to the first step and beginning a new cycle of growth in yourself and your marriage.

Aside from reducing boredom—both general and sexual—this process helps develop your strength to love. This is the people-growing machinery of marriage. It drives—and is driven by—your current sexual development. Marriage can fulfill—rather than frustrate—your sexual potential.

The people-growing machinery of marriage generates a cycle with no distinct end. It loops back on itself recursively. It takes a leap of differentiation to open your eyes during sex and increase your intimacy. Your increased differentiation then makes you more capable of intimacy. It's not just that you have more "skill." You have more inner ability—and more interest in putting it to use. The cycle moves forward as you reinvest your increased ability. Sooner or later, you push against your partner's limits, becoming the stimulus for his or her process—and eventually, your partner pushes yours. As differentiation increases, this push-pull process stops feeling adversarial and starts feeling more like you are "worthy opponents"—friendly training partners. It leads to being true lovers and best friends.

Chapter 10

Fucking, Doing, and *Being Done:* It Isn't What You Do, It's the Way You Do It.

I want to ball. Like I never have balled before!
I want to ball! Like I never been balled before!
I may never get a chance like this in Life no more!

—Musician Ry Cooder
"LET'S HAVE A BALL"

This chapter concludes our exploration of ways to connect with your partner during sex. In the final section of *Passionate Marriage,* our perspective shifts from micro to macro: from tools for connection to the process of marriage. But before that, let's take one last leap into the wilds of human eroticism—to *doing, being done,* and *fucking.* "Good sex" and "a good fuck" aren't quite the same.

I realize I'm skating on thin ice here—ice most modern sexual scientists have skirted. When Masters and Johnson studied human sexuality in the 1960s, they adopted the sterile aura of medicine to escape censure. Their dry approach was by design. Talking about *doing* and *fucking* goes entirely in the opposite direction. It's *wet*—it has everything to do with eroticism (and intimacy). Let's hope we've matured enough in three decades to stop hiding from ourselves.

In *Talking to Your Children about Sex,* the grandmother of sex education, Mary Calderone, notes that questions about *fuck* turn up at about age five or six. Lexicographer Hugh Rawson notes that the English language lacks another transitive verb expressing the basic idea with any degree of vividness. *Having sex* reinforces sex as behavior rather than as part of our nature. *Sleeping with* is self-contradictory. *Making love* and *meaningful relationship* don't always live up to their label. *Fucking* and "making love" differ subjectively and behaviorally. Rawson observes that the taboo we place on this term, combined with our lack of suitable synonyms, results in a fair amount of hypocrisy. Our euphemisms denote how we avoid eroticism.

I agree with many who think we've gone too far liberating the use of this word. Our pattern today was previously observed among soldiers during World War I. They found that their usage of the f-word was ". . . so common indeed in its adjectival form that after a short time the ear refused to acknowledge it and took in only the noun to which it was attached."

I always experience trepidation bringing up the topic of fucking in public lectures and professional workshops. At one workshop I conducted, a woman stood up and said, "Speaking as a woman, I dislike your language! Everything in society today is f-this and f-you! I don't mind talking about 'making love' or 'having sex,' but I find the way you're talking offensive!"

What could I say? I knew that anything I said would look like a defensive male authority figure discounting this woman's perspective. While I was pondering, another woman stood up.

"Well, *also* speaking as a woman, I agree about all the dirty mouths. Everything is m-f-this and m-f-that. But I also know it's taken almost twenty years for me to get into bed with my husband and say, '*Come on, lover, fuck me good!*' "

That sure broke the tension! The audience erupted in laugher and the workshop moved on.

It is now acceptable to teach young girls the mechanics of their bodies. "Nice" women and "good girls" are allowed—if not pressured—to be crazy about sex. The trouble is, the kind of sex it is acceptable to be wild about is "making love." People—women, in particular—are not suppose to *fuck*. In the last chapter you saw how couples fight when straying into styles and meaning outside their sexual comfort zone. Much public fury surrounding this word and this style of sex stems from that process on a society-wide scale. I use the word *fuck* here because:

- It's the label millions of people use for this subjective experience.
- In many people's minds, it represents one polarity on the continuum of "making love."
- It keeps issues of sexual intent and aggression center-stage.

To ease our discussion, I'll use terms like *doing* and *being done* when possible.

Tantra and Eastern sexual arts have more to teach us than just new positions. *Fucking* (the phenomenon, not the word) is used to reach a higher religious plane by integrating sex and spirituality. The Eastern usage has nothing in common with vulgarity. Besides, vulgarity is in the eye of the beholder. As D. H. Lawrence wrote:

> What is pornography to one man is the laughter of genius to another. If a woman hasn't got a tiny streak of harlot in her, she's a dry stick as a rule. . . . And there are, of course, many people who are genuinely repelled by the simplest and most natural stirrings of sexual feelings. But these people are perverts who have fallen into hatred of their fellow man; thwarted, disappointed, unfulfilled people, of whom, alas, our civilization contains so many.

Fucking, Doing, and Being Done: Your Neighbor's Views

Fucking is a subjective quality accompanying some sexual acts, including intercourse. Fucking *without* intercourse is possible—it's the embodiment of "anatomy-independent" eroticism and part of your sexual potential. Being able to fuck only during intercourse is anatomy-dependent; still, that's further than many couples get. It doesn't make sense to think of fucking as synonymous with intercourse, because many who've done the latter have never experienced the former. Some people "make love" specifically to avoid it.

Fucking involves a unique tone of engagement and experience. People who know it know when they feel it—and with whom they feel it. To those who like it, it's often more important than orgasm itself. Fucking embodies a lusty, lascivious eagerness for pleasure . . . a delicious, desirous wantonness. It is the opposite of crudeness; it is sex embellished with erotic virtuosity. There is deliberate intent to arouse (and satisfy) passion. Fucking makes for intense sexual encounters.

Fucking involves *doing* and *being done*—as in doing your partner and being done by him or her. It's the doing and being done that some crave and others fear. It involves energy exchange through patterns of coordinated stimulation and role behaviors.

Doing, being done, and *fucking* build upon everything we've discussed about tools for connection. It involves kissing and eyes-open foreplay because that's when *fucking* often starts (Chapter 7). You have to "stand on your own two feet" with your partner—even while you're horizontal in bed—like couples learn to do through hugging till relaxed (Chapter 6). Doing, being done, and fucking are all about following the connection and *feeling* while touching; they often involve lots of eyes-open sex (Chapter 8). They embrace simultaneous sexual trance, partner engagement, and role play (Chapter 9) and entail massive amounts of sexual vibes (Chapter 8)—that's partly where the subjective nuance of fucking comes from. These vibes make up a large part of your sexual "intent."

Do you know what it feels like when somebody's *doing* you—not just bringing you to orgasm or having intercourse—but really doing you? Do you know what it feels like to *do* somebody else?

I've asked these questions to thousands of people at my professional workshops and public lectures in North America and abroad. Invariably, those whose answer is yes reveal themselves through an instantaneous though somewhat self-conscious smile. I sometimes jokingly suggest that people who don't have a clue should strike up conversation with someone who's smiling!

In some presentations I ask audience members to write brief descriptions of what *fucking, doing,* and *being done* mean to them. I ask them to explain it as if they were talking to someone who doesn't yet know about it. (Sexual possibilities beyond your personal experience may be hard to imagine—until you remember back to when you didn't know about orgasms.) This activity always produces confusion, smiles, and laughter in the audience—especially for those sitting beside their partners! It gets interesting when one knows about fucking and the other doesn't. Shocked looks that say *how do you know—and how come I didn't know you knew?!* are quickly exchanged. Not everyone knows this phenomenon firsthand. Many couples of thirty years are still "virgins."

Doing

If spontaneous distinctions people make are any indication, *doing* your partner has commonalties from bedroom to bedroom. *Doing* is consistently described as: (a) moving *into* your partner, (b) tasting his or her essence, (c) ravishing him/her with fervor and generosity, (d) sending him or her to the edge, and (e) experiencing your own eroticism in the process. *Doing* someone is pleasurable in itself, but your partner reciprocates by receiving.

One woman described *doing* this way: "There's a process I go through when I want to be generous in sex. Doing someone usually starts with my being aroused by some way my partner looks or something he's said; it could be an awareness that he's feeling depleted—or quite receptive.

For example, he might say, 'I'm a little tired.' I say, 'Do you mind if I just play with you? You can just relax and let it happen.' Then I let myself play with both of our sexual response—mostly his, but it turns me on, too. I sense his cues of what he wants—moans or body responses. I feel things happen in my own body—pictures enter my mind of what might be nice to do next, a new way to play, something to try. While I like some things over and over again, my body is never the same to me, so each time I want to see which ideas come to mind. I used to be quite inhibited about new ideas, but now I know there's always some way a little different to do my partner—a different way of giving delicious gifts. That's when I have my strongest orgasms."

Another person's notion of doing was a little wetter, but no less intense: "*Doing:* When I feel very sensual—cover my body in oil—slip and slide all over my partner—swim on him, massage him, put oil all over him and his genitals—make oral love—even use his come to slip and slide more, then mount him if he gets a second erection and have my own orgasm."

The most explicit, erotic, creative, and carnivorous responses seem to come from women: "*Doing:* actively, playfully, increasingly passionately exploring, stimulating all parts of your partner's body using any part of your body that enjoys this. Usually for me it includes lots of sucking . . . tongue, ear, penis and balls, nipples, and fingering his anus. Important to let yourself make any noises that want to come—grunts, moans, laughs. The partner takes a responsive receptive stance—enjoys being given to—the 'do-er' enjoys the giving. Intense feeling of body and mind connection."

Power describes the interpersonal flavor of *doing* as well as its subjective intensity. At another professional workshop a woman complained that a joke I told about "normal marital sadism" (something we'll discuss next chapter) was about "male domination of women." In the story, a prostitute is on her knees performing oral sex on a man. The audience member complained that the story depicted a woman in a subjugated position and the man in a position of power. I knew she was checking out where I stood on feminism, power issues, and political correctness—and indirectly, my level of differentiation. These are volatile and important issues—women's disempowerment is something I take seriously. Just then another woman spoke up. She said, "Well, I don't know about the rest of you women, but I say this for myself: when I'm on *my* knees giving a man oral sex—and I have his penis in my mouth with his balls in my hand—*who do you think has the control?* I have *power*!"

Another woman clearly understood the power of submission. She described doing her partner without touching him. She let him watch her touch herself: "Like a slave girl before a sultan—or a self-made professional woman who knows who she is. Unabashedly enjoying her personal power. Enjoying watching men realize they've met their sexual peer. Letting him watch me display my eroticism by masturbating myself. Watching him reveal himself in the way he watches. Using sex to 'show what I've got.' It took me a long time to stop taking it personally when men are threatened and pull back when I'm a woman!"

Being Done

Being done involves surrender, union, and the power of receiving. A woman wrote to me, describing her experience of being done by her partner:

"He set the environment. He picked the music and put on the stereo. He approached me. I could feel his presence close to me, but he didn't touch me right away. Abruptly but gently he took my face in his hands. Kissed me. Touched my face. My neck. Explored and played with my hair. The slowness was excruciating! I wanted him to touch me more. Slowly he moved his hands to my breasts . . . and then opened my blouse. I wore no bra. His fingers touched me but skirted my breasts and nipples. I began to ache. I moved to get his hands closer to my nipples. He teased me, moving around, not touching them. He stopped moving his hand altogether. I waited in anticipation. After what seemed like an eternity, he moved again. Touched my nipples. Squeezed them. Stopped. Caressed them again. He repeated this process many times as he proceeded to love and fuck my whole body."

Someone else explained the pleasure in being done: "To my surprise the total devotion of another to do me recreates me. Total absorption in long ecstatic experience. The 'do-er' never lets up or gives the 'do-ee' a chance to come down from pleasure. They 'know' one another. The do-er takes total pleasure in raising the do-ee to unbelievable heights. The do-er becomes aware of the maximum higher potential of sensuality or eroticism in herself, above and beyond control or orgasm—which triggers mental orgasms of self and body. Pleasure awareness! Passion over the top!"

A woman at one workshop proudly handed me a piece of paper, looking at me clear-eyed while I read it. She described the "tight grip on a loose rein" involved in "letting go": "The intensity of physical enjoyment is very high and it's not under my control. This is no loss of self or abdication of responsibility. 'Taking somebody' and 'being taken' involves no loss of self. There's freedom in saying, *'Take me!'* "

Fucking

Having outlined *doing* and *being done,* we now have the tools to explain *fucking:* fucking is the subjective experience of doing each other and being done simultaneously. Sound simple? It's not. In fact, it is difficult for people to really *fuck* their spouse (in the most wholesome, erotic sense of the word). If one is able to fuck, it is often done with someone *else's* wife or husband. Many people, male or female, have a hard time cranking loose their eroticism with the person they married.

Of the 150 therapists attending my presentation at the 1993 Networker Symposium (an annual conference on marriage and family therapy) less then a dozen (eight percent) acknowledged personal experience with *fucking* or *doing* and *being done.* At the Louisiana Association for Marriage and Family Therapy Annual Conference the figure was fifteen percent. I estimate that only ten to twenty percent of the general population know about *doing, being done,* and *fucking* (more women seem to know than men). As I said about eyes-open orgasm, if lots of people don't know about these styles of sex and can't/don't do them—including the "pros"—don't feel too bad if you don't either. With this in mind, let me share with you what people have to say about fucking.

To one person, fucking is "being taken to the limits of your own fear and ability to handle yourself and then taking it one step further." To another, "fucking is a natural high, feeling totally complete with yourself and your partner—a transforming experiences to a higher level of being." A third wrote that fucking is "using my and my partner's body to experience me and him in an alternatively fused and separate state. Absorbing and squeezing out like a sponge." And a fourth felt that fucking is "God/goddess union floating in an erotic aura. Trusting in myself to let my larger self 'take over.' "

More concretely, fucking is commonly described as: (a) two-way vs. one-way energy, (b) equally shared, (c) a profound energy link, (d) effortless flow, (e) aggressive "give it to me!" sex, (f) no secrets/self-revealing/nothing held back, (g) clearly *seeing* and accepting each other, (h) brain/body/soul connection, (i) going to the limit, (j) losing oneself (wild abandon, uninhibited), (k) finding oneself, (l) amazing, (m) timeless, and (n) transcendent. Paradoxical qualities of fucking are often noted: fullness—emptiness (spent, drained), high meaning—low meaning ("getting down and dirty"), and primitive—spiritual.

People have sent me word associations that include: intense, powerful, energetic, ecstatic, altered consciousness, cellular level, total body, freedom, exhaustion, abandon, and completion. My favorite response was from the person who wrote, "What's *fucking*? It's a figment of your imagination! (Just joking!)"

It is quite possible for couples to create the sensation of *doing* or *fucking* without any genital contact. As you saw in people's responses, intercourse is rarely mentioned. There seem to be two tough parts in accomplishing this: one is tolerating the *I-contact* involved. (I'll mention the other in a moment.) Many married people have reservations about fucking with their spouse in any way—except perhaps euphemistically. At best, they permit themselves to fuck during intercourse. Fucking outside the context of intercourse is often so intensely erotic and intimate that it exceeds people's ability to self-validate with their spouse.

You may be wondering why I'm discussing anatomy-independent fucking rather than fucking during intercourse, when most people don't even do it during intercourse. It's because intercourse is one of the hardest ways to learn to do it. Just as following the connection in simple behaviors can eventually lead to eyes-open orgasms, once you can access the "part" of you that can fuck, you can apply it to almost any behavior you like—including intercourse.

Phallicness and Muliebrity

This, however, is the second obstacle to *doing* and *being done*: developing and harnessing your sexual power and aggression in healthy, loving ways. I've found this process is intricately entwined with enhancing your differentiation (like so many other aspects of sexual potential). My work with hundreds of couples has shown me men *and* women greatly fear the power of their sexuality.

In *Iron John* Robert Bly addresses an aspect of men's ability to do their partner and allow themselves to be done: *phallicness*. Bly refers to this as the *deep male* or the *Hairy Man*. In workshops and with clients I refer to this as a man "screwing his penis on tighter"—it sounds a little crude but the image seems to help people organize the differentiation issues involved.

Male phallicness isn't confined to the bedroom—it's an integral part of a man that surfaces in every aspect of his life (when it's there). It (or lack of it) shows up in business negotiations, in family interactions (especially with parents and adolescent children), and in daily commerce with other men and women. Partly this surfaces as productivity, re-siliency, and a "go for it" attitude, but don't confuse this with bel-ligerency, volatility, destructiveness, or selfishness. *These* traits are the mark of someone who's poorly differentiated and whose penis isn't "well attached." Men who are secure in their potency tend to be gentle, nonreactive, and considerate; a really phallic man doesn't have to "wave his weenie" all the time. Potent isn't the same as destructive, although men back away from this part of themselves when they confuse the two.

If the plethora of men's support groups, sweat lodge retreats, and drumming workshops are any indication, untold numbers of men are searching for this part of themselves. And while the men's movement has much to offer, really accessing, validating, and using the part that *fucks* doesn't happen during male bonding weekends. It happens when a man is alone with his wife.

As a concept, male phallicness isn't hard to explain (Freud did so at length)—it's just harder for men to develop this side of themselves than many of us think. However, the analogous concept (*and* process) for women seems to be difficult to grasp: when discussing men's phallic-ness, women who've attended my workshops and Couples Retreats have searched for an analogous term for themselves. "Facho" (as in macho), "vaginality," "ovarious," and similar terms have been sug-gested. Each lacked the richness phallicness has for men. *Femininity* is often mistaken for fragility. *Seductress* acknowledges women's sexual power—but only in reference to men. *Phallic woman* (like *penis envy*) is phallocentric. *Butch* and *dyke* demonstrate how negatively we view women's potency.

It's not as though it's impossible to imagine female sexual power in its own right—except perhaps in Western culture. In *Constructing the Sexual Crucible* I noted that the desired conceptualization is readily available in Eastern traditions. *Lingam* is the spirit of phallicness; *Yoni* captures the similar creative power of women. In fact, a Hindu myth exists that the gods *Shiva* (male) and *Parvati* (female) competed to see who could create a better race of people without the participation of the other. The *Lingajas* turned out to be stupid, feeble, misshapen creatures, whereas the *Yonijas* were a well-shaped, well-mannered, attractive race that beat the *Lingajas* in battle.

A woman I know came across the term *muliebrity* in the book *Wom-anwords*. Muliebrity in women is similar to *virility* in men, except that many dictionaries define virility as "not weak or effeminate"—negat-ing the existence of female potency. Muliebrity refers to *womanliness*: the power and qualities that distinguish mature women from girls. It is the power patriarchal societies try to diminish by infantalizing women by calling them *doll, chick, babe,* and *girl* regardless of their age. Granted, *muliebrity* is awkward to pronounce, but the concept shines a light for women seeking to articulate their erotic essence in a single word.

Developing your phallicness/muliebrity requires the courage to accept what Bly refers to as the "nourishing dark side" of yourself. While this notion directs our attention to a part of us we hide, considering this our "dark side" implicitly casts this part in a negative light—something many people believe to begin with. The very fact that we see it as a "dark" side contributes to widespread difficulty *doing* someone we love. (Jesuit monk Sebastian Moore says that even the animalistic side of us is God-given and therefore not to be diminished. We'll discuss this in Chapter 14.)

The real issue here is *potency,* in this case manifested as *sexual intent.* Sexual intent is closely related to—and often confused with—aggression. Lexicographer Hugh Rawson notes the built-in aggression in common expressions: "Fuck it!" "Fuck you!" "I've been fucked!" (cheated or victimized), and "Go fuck yourself!" Fucking does involve some aggression and force. (Spouses point to this when they urge, "Put more into it!") The two important issues here are: how does aggression fit into sexual intent, and what kind of aggression is it?

Sexual intent is not simply aggression. When people encounter the issue of sexual aggression, they commit the error pointed out in Chapter 1: confusing a part for the whole. Aggression is one component of sexual intent—an important one, but not the only one. And just as similar part-whole mistakes have lead us to develop distorted views of intimacy and sexual desire, the same has happened around sexual intent.

There are many components to sexual intent. In marriage, sexual intent can involve love, care-taking, mutuality, and nurturance, among others. We so rarely address sexual intent that we never think of *fucking* as loving (in fact, many think of it as "debased sex" and the farthest thing from making love). We think love and caring lead to desire for tender sex, but we don't associate these with the carnivorous intent involved with *doing* your partner. The *only* part we think is involved in *fucking* is people's "dark" side.

This brings us to the other issue noted above: what "kind" of aggression is involved? Society may accept that anger can be healthy—but not when it's mixed with sex. Because sexualized aggression too often fuels degradation, abuse, and rape, all forms of it have been banished from the bed. The problem is that healthy aggression plays a role in healthy fucking.

Competition is often a problem between spouses because they deny it or act it out in destructively. Healthy competition, like the urge to dominate (or submit to) your spouse, can be sublimated in constructive ways through *doing, being done* and *fucking.* So can some tensions that arise between partners of opposite genders. I'm not suggesting spouses should screw because they are angry or frustrated with each other. I'm referring to harnessing the male and female "energy" in a couple's union—*Yin* and *Yang* in Eastern terms—forming the "energy loop" Tantric sex has focused on for centuries. Before this gets too esoteric, think of it as a productive way to use pent-up energy in the relationship. Having sex with as much energy as you expend at the gym is good for you physically and emotionally, and much better for your relationship. People don't have sex to the point of exhaustion the same way they do in their workouts, but it would probably help everything if they did.

"Growing the part of you that fucks" has everything to do with dealing with your anger and aggression toward your spouse. The part that needs to grow is the part that learns how to "digest" anger—metabolize it, break it down to fuel something useful and life-giving. (We'll discuss this in the next chapter when we consider *normal marital sadism.*) Growing that part involves further differentiation—learning about your aggression and anger toward your spouse, soothing yourself, mastering yourself, and recognizing your partner as a separate person. In other words, this is another "opportunity" to tolerate pain for growth.

To clarify this tricky issue about aggression, remember that we're really discussing the role of differentiation in fucking—and differentiation is about self-modulation. Anger and aggression can embody evil. But our attempts to recognize and metabolize them—rather than inflict them—makes them worthy of inclusion in our sexual intent and makes us capable of *fucking* our spouse.

To summarize, there seem to be several reasons why those who love to fuck are ashamed to do it with their spouse: they experience difficulty in (a) self-validating this sexual style in the context of their spouse, (b) dealing with aggression and anger towards their spouse, or recognizing these in themselves, and (c) tolerating being known. The ability to fuck is something that ripens in later life (if ever); it's not something you simply tap into at will. At one Couples Retreat a young man began confronting his inability to fuck his wife—who desperately wanted him to do just that. Across the room an older gentleman offered consolation. He said, "Don't feel bad. I'm fifty-eight and I'm just getting to the point where I can fuck my wife."

Given our suspicion of eroticism and our fear of sexual aggression, it's easy to make fucking look like the work of the devil. In his weekly audience of October 8, 1980, Pope John Paul II said, "Adultery in the heart is committed not only because a man looks in a certain way at a woman who is not his wife, but precisely because he is looking at a woman that way. Even if he were to look that way at a woman who is his wife, he would be committing the same adultery in the heart."

But the *"b-a-a-d"* side of sexual aggression fits nicely within long-term monogamy. It's the good part of digesting the part of you that's "bad." Being able to *use* someone and *be used—well!* Carnivorous intent. It's important and disquieting. It's the part many people want.

If fucking involves carnal knowledge beyond common propriety . . . what better place to explore *un*common impropriety than within the sanctity of your marriage?

Betty and George

Couples who seek my counsel have various difficulties with fucking. In some of these couples one partner knows about fucking and the other doesn't—or isn't interested. In other couples both partners know about fucking and shared it early in their relationship—but no longer. Sexual frequency in this group drops to nil by quasi-mutual consent. Both groups anticipate that treatment will be dull and slow. But getting things moving isn't difficult if you change the question from, "Why don't you have sex more often?" to *"Have the two of you ever fucked? And if you have, why did you stop?"* It's a tad more personal and to the point.

Betty and George, a couple who consulted me, represent still another group. The issue for them was style rather than frequency. They have been together twelve years and married for ten. George had been single for twelve years prior. He divorced his first wife of fifteen years when he realized she was having an affair. Betty had been widowed for two years before she met George. Her first husband, to whom she had been married for three decades, had been her high school sweetheart.

In our first session George looked like a man who owed his wife lots of sex to make up for lost time. He praised Betty for "standing by him." George could have good erections whenever Betty used her hands or mouth—in fact, he was having some of the best sex of his life. But during intercourse he'd often go soft. In our later sessions we learned this involved George's underlying fear of his own aggression. Erections weren't a problem when Betty did him manually or orally because the dynamics didn't trigger his conflicts. Sometimes he had no difficulty with intercourse when Betty was on top—because in George's mind, she was doing him. When he was supposed to do her, however, he'd pull back emotionally—and unwittingly sever their vibrational link.

George pulled back from doing Betty with his penis—actually he pulled back from doing her with his hands and tongue too, but these he could fake. Without a connection to follow, George was at a loss for exactly what to do—so he usually rubbed or thrust harder. Between the reduced sexual energy, his anxiety, and feeling inadequate, George often lost his erection. At the outset of treatment, however, he was oblivious to all of this.

"I never had this problem with my first wife."

"Did you ever have sex like this with your first wife?"

"No."

"I'm not casting aspersions on your first marriage. But if you never pressed this part of your development with her, it wouldn't have become an issue. Would you prefer to have sex like you had with your first wife so that the problem will 'disappear'?"

"No . . . I'm wondering if this is why she had an affair."

Things had been good for Betty and George since they got together. Before George, Betty could reach orgasm only during solitary masturbation—and *that* was only after her first husband died. At first she learned to have an orgasm with George present, using her vibrator on herself. Then she learned to reach orgasm when he used his hands or mouth. It wasn't reliable and "took a long time and a lot of effort" as far as she was concerned. But Betty liked her growing sense of prowess. For years she'd felt inadequate because she couldn't come—especially during intercourse.

Betty was acquiring a taste for what sex can be. "It seems just a little different every time we do it," she remarked in one session. When George lost his erection, he tried to bring Betty to orgasm some other way. The quality of their encounters varied. Some of their really good times became landmarks in their increasingly meaningful relationship.

One particular time stood out. It had occurred when George and Betty were deeply engrossed in one another. Betty referred to this experience in one of our sessions. She said, "I want to have what I once had a taste of. I now know it exists." She was referring to a curious phenomenon they'd experienced in profound sexual union: Betty's hips had moved automatically as she straddled George with his penis inside her. She wasn't cut off or "dissociated" from her body. Rather, she was intensely involved with George. Her pelvis did what was appropriate to the connection. Her groin stopped slapping woodenly against him.

She moved up and down with a delicious hip movement that said *I'm into this!* She came down with enough force to satisfy but not bruise.

"You were 'in the groove'! You let yourself move with the vibes and energy."

"Exactly!" Betty's smile said, "So you've been there, too!" She turned to George. "You should find this easy to do. You're into grooves!"

George blushed at the double entendre. "She means I'm a music buff. I collect old recordings."

"You collect old recordings instead of CDs?"

"I appreciate the recording itself."

"Do you take pride in your collection? Do you have some recordings most people have never heard of?"

"I have some very rare recordings. Why?"

"Do you play the same song all the time?"

"No."

"Why do you approach sex so differently?"

George and Betty had been trading noncoital orgasms for months—and loving it well enough. But George had not found a way to solve his intermittent difficulty with erections—or the issues that lay behind it. Betty wanted to have sex with George in ways that made it impossible for him to get around it. Sometimes she wanted him inside her, big and hard. She wanted to experience orgasm that way if she could. He could see the legitimacy of it—he just couldn't do it.

George was uncomfortable with his own phallicness. He had difficulty "putting it to" Betty—difficulty doing her in *any* way. Using his fingers or his mouth, he could rub enough for her to come. Rubbing didn't involve *doing* her. But in George's mind thrusting during intercourse was so closely related to aggression that he often lost his erection, especially if he was on top. As I understood it, (1) George was having a hard time fucking someone he cared about, (2) he had difficulty "keeping the lead in his pencil" in the face of Betty's ever-growing importance, and (3) he was afraid of his aggression, intensity, and potency. In sexual terms he was still trying to get his penis "firmly attached."

I asked Betty if she could *do* George and if she thought George could really let himself be done. Betty described "putting him into orbit" with her hand or mouth. An unmistakably wanton look appeared on her face that said, in essence, *I can really do this guy!* Pure carnal intent! I saw the look and pointed it out. Betty acknowledged it with a smile.

What stunned me was that George acknowledged seeing it, too! I wasn't sure he would. Now I had a tool to work with.

"*That's* what you're afraid to do with Betty!"

"I know!" George looked down. It confirmed what I'd suspected.

"You've known all along! You're afraid to *fuck* her and do it eye to eye!" George picked his chin up from his chest and looked at me in surprise.

George had previously told me that he had masturbated three or four times a week while he was single. He disposed of an extensive collection of girlie magazines when he became serious with Betty. I had guessed part of what George liked about his masturbation: he mentally fucked the women in the magazines. He thought he had fucked several women he'd dated—more accurately, though, they had done him and encouraged him to reciprocate.

"Maybe I have a Madonna/whore complex," George said.

"Maybe you have three ordinary developmental tasks: screwing your penis on tighter, validating your eroticism, and cranking it loose with someone you love. That doesn't make Betty a Madonna. Maybe it makes you one of many little boys. . . . You like to fuck, don't you?! Is that what this is about?"

George was shocked. He thought this was his dirty secret—the "dark" side of him. He was ashamed of this part, never imagining it was something to be shared with his loving wife. He had relegated his fucking to bad pornography, and associated it with "adult bookstores" (which he didn't frequent) and the seamy side of sex. But my straight talk now seemed to help him come to a decision. He realized it would be much harder to bring this topic up later if he passed up this opportunity.

"Yes, I do!"

"People don't fuck with their support systems—in all meanings of the word."

"Support system? I thought the problem was my fear of anger. My father was a mean drunk. He yelled and threatened all of us—me, my mother, my two sisters. I've seen what anger can do. I think I'm so afraid of being like him that I have a hard time getting aggressive." George, by the way, was one of the sweetest men I'd ever met. I could see why Betty loved him.

"So you know who you *don't* want to be. If you're not like your father, maybe you don't have to be afraid of healthy sexual aggression." George was not convinced. "So who does your penis belong to?"

"What do you mean, who does it belong to?"

"Does it belong to your father? Are you still so tied up with him that it's basically the same thing?"

"I don't think so."

"Then who does it belong to?"

"It belongs to . . ." George trailed off into silence.

"It belongs to *him*!" Betty was emphatic.

"That's interesting—you're telling George his penis belongs to him! If it does, why do *you* have to tell him?"

"Well, I don't want it belonging to *me*! I can't even make it hard!"

"I didn't say it belongs to you. It doesn't belong to you just because George isn't sure it belongs to him. Maybe this one doesn't belong to . . . anyone—yet!"

Betty and George laughed.

"Maybe the problem here is we have a penis in search of a home!"

Betty smiled to George. "Well, it's welcome to have a home inside me."

"I think that's the problem. That's what you two have tried. Maybe the only place this penis will be at home is attached to a *man*." George and I looked at each other.

Betty tried to be supportive. "Well, I'm just getting to the point where I'm at home inside myself, too. Sex never existed in my house growing up. Then everyone found out Mom was having an affair—and then we had two reasons sex wasn't talked about."

George cut in. "My dick belongs to *me*!"

These was a brief silence while all three of us adjusted to this bold pronouncement. George had been seriously thinking about the question while Betty was talking.

"I'm tired of feeling like a little boy! Apologizing because I like sex!" George took off another layer of protective vagueness. He turned to Betty. "It's so damn hard to fuck you with my dick! You never come that way!" It wasn't an accusation. George's frustration with himself filled the room.

"Then why don't you stop trying to make her come that way?"

"That's the way she wants me to do it!"

"As I understand Betty's position, having contact with you during intercourse is her first priority. Orgasm with you during intercourse is optional. You told me you like music. Do you ever play music when you're having sex?"

"No."

"I'm surprised. I thought you'd be listening to 'John Henry Was a Steel Driving Man'!" George and Betty laughed and the mood lightened.

"The trouble is nobody tells you whether John Henry was any good in bed. It's your dick, move it any way you like—or not. But there's a difference between 'pile-driving' someone and *doing* her. When you get in a panic 'banging' Betty, I think you both share a common problem: *humping without feeling*. You're thrusting faster and feeling less. That may be part of your difficulty with erections."

Betty recognized this. Sometimes he'd thrust vigorously—but it reeked of anxiety rather than eroticism. His moves were as devoid of life as Betty's used to be. She turned to him. "Don't get me wrong. I like the humping and bumping, too. But if you really want to 'bang' me, a little less force and more *feeling* might do it!"

"And consider changing the music in your head. Try the Pointer Sisters' song 'I'm So Excited.' Remember the line, 'If you move real *slow,* I'll let it go'?"

George smiled and nodded in comprehension. These were sober realizations for both partners. Betty's hunger for sexual connection was like a womb hungering for life. If George didn't confront himself, they would never meet on that level. And there was very little she could do about it.

It's Hard to Do Your Spouse

Some can't put their mouth where they put their genitals. Others can't put their genitals where they put their heart. For lots of us, loving someone is the kiss of death for sexual desire and passion.

It's hard for women *and* men to "run with the wolves." Hard enough, in fact, that some people become sexual vegetarians in marriage but carnivorous in extramarital affairs. In men it's called the Madonna/whore complex—but women have their version of this split, too. These people love a good fuck—but are "too ashamed" to share it with their spouse. "Madonna/whore" men *and* women try to keep fucking separate from loving. Many people have no idea about *doing* and *being done*—but some who do pretend they don't. It's difficult to prove. Even if you can, you still can't make your partner do you.

George's professed ignorance about fucking—and his hidden delight in it—was not mean-spirited. (In the next chapter we'll talk about when it is.) Betty's deprivation was unintended but inevitable, given his limitations. This fact actually fueled George's resolve to emancipate himself. Men like George—in a second marriage of later adulthood or in a thirty-year first one—often come to the long-overdue realization that they want to be their own man, and don't want to deprive their spouse of passionate connection any longer.

Many couples are not as generous or concerned about each other as

George and Betty. In some cases, both spouses lack the required maturity; they insist on blaming each other's shortcomings for their own unwillingness to grow up. In the converse situation of George and Betty's, the woman is still "deciding" while the man is raring to go.

It is commonly believed that women have no difficulty mixing sex and love—that, in fact, that's the only way they can have sex. But many women have the same difficulty as George: they can't put their heart where they put their genitals. It just looks different because they have different ways around it. Some women restrict their sexual activity to a style of partner engagement that, in essence, denies that genitals are even involved. Their goal isn't to look into their partner's eyes—it's to keep from looking down. Some are middle-aged little girls who blame everything on "the church." Some have overcome their religious prohibitions about intercourse but have not escaped Sister Catherine long enough for oral sex. (We seem to be very choosy about which religious prohibitions cripple us—they coincide with things we're squeamish about doing in the first place.)

Other women, like Betty, know what they like but don't have the courage to validate it in front of their spouse. Before they got married, they fucked "bad" guys—men bad for them but great in bed. Once married, they can't fuck their "good" husband. Some can't bear to "dirty" their clean Prince Charming with their juices, while others can't stand the thought of accidentally cleaning up the dirt. They *like* the sneaky, naughty, dirty part—they're often having an affair. It's not that hubby won't get down and dirty—he's not invited—it would spoil the thrill. The third of married women having affairs aren't doing so only because their husbands won't "communicate."

And then there's a wonderfully large group of women who aren't quite fire-breathing sexual animals yet—but they'd be willing to give it a try. They're "happily" married—and ready to be happier. They've tasted muliebrity. They're ready for *doing* and *being done.*

Women Are More into Doing and Being Done

Women seem to know more about doing and being done. They also seem to be more interested. Women stick around after workshops to learn more about fucking—more specifically, how to get their partners to do them. Explicit sexual issues appear more frequently in women's magazines than in men's, reflecting women's greater worries about sex appeal, greater interest in sex, and desperate hopes of improving it.

Twenty years ago I heard researchers at the Kinsey Institute report data suggesting that women are more erotically inclined then men. As a man it scared me—scared me just like the time I gave a woman a back-rub during a college party. She came while we watched TV with class-mates all around!

Although there are wide variations within genders, there does seem to be a trend: women may be choosier than men about their sex part-ners, but once they choose they are more interested in doing and being done. More men are looking to "just get laid" than there are women who want to be "scored." But lots of women want to "really get it on." Many of them are married. And they'd give their hearts (and respect) to their husband if he'd *do* her—and let himself be *done*.

Women don't want to be *used* poorly—but many love to be used *well*. They want to be the object of their partner's carnality—but they want it personal! They're dying to be "rode hard and put away wet." When May West said, "A hard man is good to find!" she wasn't refer-ring to body building.

Whether from child-care or self-care, women are more at home with bodily fluids and orifices than most men. Some men never fully accept that women like taking someone (or something) inside them. They never get beyond thinking of it as penetration—they can't get their head wrapped around the notion of being taken in. Tampons and men-struation remains a mystery—and an anxiety—for many men. For a few, this surfaces as difficulty with vaginal intercourse. For many more it comes up around anal stimulation. Some men will push for anal in-tercourse but refuse to accept that their partner *likes* it. If the man fi-nally relaxes while *he's* receiving anal stimulation, he's usually reached a developmental milestone.

In general, many men find it hard to allow themselves to be done be-cause it violates traditional gender roles in and out of bed. Women complain that it's not much fun to give oral sex to someone who can't receive—but they're hesitant to say this to their partner. One told me, "I want my partner shaky-legged and groaning. I want him thoroughly lost in the experience with me! I hate it when he pulls back!" I've heard the same complaint from men—they feel more entitled to complain if the woman keeps her arousal a secret.

Women readily admit to masking their own eroticism to stroke their partner's reflected sense of self. I think we underestimate how often this occurs and the negative impact it has. In *Sexual Personae* Camille Paglia argues that women have modulated their "earth mother" sexuality for centuries because it frightens men—frightens them enough, she con-tends, that men developed modern science to compensate!

Consider the case of a woman who learned about orgasms at age ten by putting a pillow between her legs and tensing. Raised as a strict Catholic, she was a virgin when she married her husband at age nineteen. But she had been mortified and guilt-ridden all through adolescence because she would reach orgasm when kissing and hugging with the boys. In their twenty years of marriage she and her husband had created a paradox I've seen many times: she was viewed as the sexual "dud." Her husband described her as "frigid," unimaginative, and unwilling to experiment. They had settled into rear entry intercourse as a reliable but boring way to bring her to orgasm. He thought it was the *only* way she could come. He considered himself the more sexual of the two. Eventually he started an affair with a woman he thought "really liked sex."

The wife had successfully hidden her eroticism for almost twenty years. She was afraid of her own responsivity and kept it under control. Her husband didn't know what she could be like—or that she was ready to break out of her self-imposed dud pattern. Eventually, with his encouragement, she began an affair. He literally couldn't imagine what she was doing with her new boyfriend—his girlfriend was tame by comparison! He never believed it—that would have required recalibrating his picture of his wife, himself, and their marriage. In some ways their relationship was a casualty of common denial of women's eroticism: they eventually divorced.

When women mask their eroticism in the name of "not hurting the man's ego," they paradoxically create what they fear. Loads of sexually frustrated women are angry and patronizing toward their "little-boy" husbands who shrink from female sexuality. (I've said people don't fuck with their support system. It holds for those who are doing the supporting, too.) There are many sexually frustrated husbands who ask themselves, *Is this all there is?!* Often "more" is no further than the other side of their bed.

My purpose is not to glorify women or threaten men. Certainly some men will protest that everything I've said should be stated in reverse. (I agree it can and should be.) They'd give anything to be married to the "dud" I just described. Unfortunately, some are.

"If You Move Real Slow, I'll Let It Go!"

These issues, though rarely easy to discuss, yield impressive gains when dealt with. George and Betty are a case in point; they were a little amazed by their own progress. Betty showed George some of the eroticism she'd been holding back. Increasingly, she gave off the glow of a sexually mature woman. On one occasion she invited him to enter her from behind. George was intimidated and verbally snapped at her. Betty confronted him gently that she had done nothing wrong. It was clear she was hurt. George realized that he'd "blown it"—he'd become reptilian and bitten her.

George went through a dark period struggling with his "dark side"— but that side turned out to be his inconsiderateness, not his sexuality. The realization that he hurt Betty when she was trying to be loving was intolerable to him. He spent weeks recalling experiences with his father and in struggling with himself in a way his father probably never did. George emerged as the man he wanted to be (and probably more man than his father ever was).

George stopped being afraid of his assertiveness and aggression. He finally let out his "killer instinct": he started winning racquetball games against people who had always beat him. There was a bounce to his step and more gleam in his eye when he came to therapy.

George began to make changes in his business, pursuing plans he'd been afraid to try. The first thing he did was fire his assistant. The man had been a "goof-off"—irresponsible in ways George recognized in himself. George wasn't giving anybody any "slack" anymore, including himself.

One particular night George initiated sex because *he* wanted to. Betty hadn't made any overtures or hints like she usually did. George made a straightforward approach, not the old hedging of "I want to if you do, too." This was, "I want to! And by the time I get done with you, you'll be glad you did!" He put himself "out there."

Betty reached out to George as he approached. He took her gently but firmly by her hips and turned her around. She was surprised and off-balance for a moment. She didn't understand what he was doing. George put his arms around her and ground his pelvis against her behind! Betty bent her knees slightly and "presented" herself. He kissed her neck. Her body melted into his like warm taffy. She thought, *This is interesting—we don't even have our clothes off yet!*

The heat rose between them. Five minutes later it was too much effort to stay balanced on their feet. They were both hot. Their buttons took forever to undo. They kissed in between.

George put Betty on her back with her knees up by her shoulders. He slid between her legs as he knelt over her. He put his hands on the mattress on either side of her shoulders and carried his weight on his straightened arms. Her legs came down to rest against his arms and they both relaxed.

"Hi!" Her eyes were glistening in the candlelight.

"Hi!" George smiled. He leaned forward to kiss her and she moved her head to meet him. He brushed his lips against hers and stopped to look at her. Then he kissed her deeply. Betty took his tongue in like a dear old friend. Breathing in her smell, George felt as if he were already inside her.

He raised his head to see her. "Are you ready for me?"

Betty nodded wickedly. She didn't take her eyes off him. She put a finger inside her vagina and rubbed her wetness on the head of his penis.

"Uh-huh! I'm *ready*!" She guided him towards her and prepared to feel him deep.

But it didn't happen.

George only put his penis in about an inch.

He's rubbing his penis against my lips! That's nice! Then Betty realized George had a rhythm going. *Wait! He's doing just my opening! We've never done it like this before! He's always either lost his erection or tried to hammer me into an orgasm!*

At first Betty couldn't figure out exactly how George was doing it. He had just the head of his penis inside her. He was moving, but just barely—just to the point where his penis began to slide inside her. Instead of friction-while-sliding, there was friction . . . but no slide. As George barely moved slowly back and forth, he was tugging her vagina and labia. Instead of thrusting into her, he gently took her with him as he moved.

The sound came from the back of her throat. "Mmmmmmmm!"

"I like that, too!" George took a breath. *Boy, this is peaceful! When we don't talk, it's dead silent! There's not a sound but us!* He felt present in a way he hadn't since their early days.

Infinitesimally small movements commanded both their attentions. They focused on the same spot at the same time at opposite sides of their skin. It brought them into contact. They watched each other feel it. And they let themselves be seen. There was silence for several minutes. Talking would have detracted from their intense contact.

"I want to eat you!" George's voice was deep. Not his usual tentative falsetto, "Do you want me to eat you?" Betty thought, *I like that husky tone. If George goes down on me, he usually does it before he enters.* She was glad to have him do it.

"Don't you want to come all the way inside me?"

"That's next. After I eat you. Show me your pussy!"

Betty smiled to herself. *This is new!* She had never had sex like this before. She felt very daring—and mature. She was on an adventure. They knew this was a stretch for both of them.

Betty brushed back her pubic hair and spread her labia. He usually tried to part her hair while he balanced himself on his elbows between her legs.

George looked down and thought her hands were like those of a ballerina. Long artistic fingers. He watched her touch her labia like she enjoyed it. Then he realized she *was* enjoying it! He realized she knew *exactly* how to touch herself the way she wanted—and she was! For the first time in a long while, he wanted to feel her like she could feel herself.

George looked up and realized Betty was watching him. She looked dreamy—as if half her attention was focused on her finger as it took moisture from inside her and slowly spread it on her labia. George smiled. Betty's eyes brightened and refocused; she smiled back. He wanted his penis inside her. But he was in no rush. He let his tongue travel.

While he was eating her, George felt like he had a second penis protruding from his forehead. He realized his tongue wasn't a replacement for his penis—his brain was! He focused his mind on doing Betty and channeled it through his mental "dick." This wasn't cognitive gymnastics, a fantasy, or imagining himself fucking her. It involved harnessing his intent and *doing* her. He could feel his penis bulging hard although she hadn't touched him there. He thought, *So this is what giving head is all about!*

George felt the energy diminish when Betty moved her hands to run her fingers through his hair. It felt great but he could feel it was "off."

"Come back here!" His tone was half-request and half-demand.

An electric jolt passed through Betty. She immediately recognized what George wanted. He was doing her. She moved her hands back and spread her labia, offering herself to him like a peeled fruit.

"Here, baby! Is this what you want? Am I pink?!"

That *did* George! *I can't believe we're doing this!! Me and my wife!! Whew! HOT!*

"You *were* pink! Now you're *purple!*"

Betty giggled. George put his tongue against one labia and slowly dragged it to the other—stopping in the middle to play with her clitoris. Betty's giggles turned to moans. She knew she was doing him by letting herself make more noise than usual. George knew he was letting himself be done. He figured one favor deserves another. George hardly lifted his tongue to speak.

"Aural oral sex!"

Betty obliged with giggles and moans.

As Betty lay there a fear crossed her mind. *What if he's doing this to get around having to do me with his penis?!* She looked at George. She realized it didn't fit with what was going on. *Right thought. Wrong time.* Betty moved her body so she could reach down and touch his groin. She ran a finger down his penis like a woman seeing her lover after a long separation.

George jumped. He loved seeing her long fingers on him. He suddenly wanted to be inside her. He brought himself closer and Betty guided him again. He felt he was implanting himself. *He* wanted it.

"Mmmmmmm!" Betty obviously wanted it too!

George started intermixing thrusts shallow and deep. Then he stopped thrusting and tightened up his rectum. He felt his penis jump inside her.

"Mmmm! Mmmm!"

She's purring like a cat! George's muscles were getting sore—but he liked it. He played with her. He kept his penis deep inside Betty, varying how hard he pushed himself into her. There was no "up stroke." It was a form of thrusting that involved almost no movement. Betty was ready for him and had no discomfort. He realized she was moving to meet him—instead of pulling back like she did when he went deep before she had relaxed around him. He relaxed. The bruise he sometimes got from "hammering" Betty was to become a thing of the past. He discovered a wonderful world of "pounding" available with a narrow range of force. He even experimented with a "circular thrust," rolling his hips and using the shaft of his penis to rub the sides of her vagina.

"Mmmmmm! Yeah! Do that! That's good!" Betty could feel his energy. She felt it wasn't fair to make George "do all the work." She asked, "Do you want me to get on top of you?"

George held her hips so he wouldn't come out and rolled over on his side. Betty held onto his shoulders and pulled herself up. She settled atop his penis and put her hands on his chest. She leaned forward slightly and worked her hips on him until she was wet with sweat.

George moved his arms behind her back with his hands on her shoulders. He pulled her down gently so he could kiss her. As their lips met he pulled down harder. Betty could tell he wasn't trying to pull her closer—he wanted the force and tension. She used her arms to brace a little against his pull. They were free to kiss and move their heads but there was pressure on their torsos. George felt them complete the connection. Betty felt it too—that's when she tightened her vagina.

"You feel that?!"

George's response was to rock her as they kissed, carrying most of her weight, *doing* her with his penis. She met him in that movement. George finally knew the difference between "pile driving" and "being in the groove." They were in synch!

They interspersed this pattern with periods of quiet. Betty lay on his chest, his arms around her and his penis inside. They did hugging till relaxed. George moved just enough to keep his penis hard. Then he'd start another cycle of forceful rocking/pumping. Eventually their breath and heat hung around them like a cloud. Betty was the one to break it off.

"Wait! I need air, but I don't want to lose this."

George's voice was warm and calm. "Don't worry!" He put his elbows on the mattress for leverage so he could comfortably raise Betty's hips with his hands. He lifted her an inch or two so she was suspended in the air, squatting slightly above him. Betty realized how he wanted her positioned. She put her feet flat on the bed and crouched, taking some of her weight on her legs. The only part touching between their waists and knees was George's penis going in and out of her vagina. He finally stopped being afraid of his own aggression.

"Uhh! Uhh! Uhh! Uhh!" Betty's noises were automatic, keeping pace with each thrust. For several minutes there was no silence in the room. George thought Betty was the nicest metronome he'd ever heard.

"Oh, you like that?! Here, baby! Here's some more!"

"Uhh!! Uhh!! Arrghh!!! Oh, God!!!"

George broke into laughter. Betty's face was mottled with her sex flush. "Your face is turning purple! First your labia and now your face!"

Betty was laughing, too. "I don't doubt it! Don't stop! I bet I can come this way if we do it more often!"

"Stop?! Are you kidding! This is the best sex of my life!"

"Oh, my legs! They're like Jell-O!"

"Good for you! You deserve it! Couldn't happen to a nicer person!"

Betty moved her legs. She leaned forward and gave him a long, slow kiss. It was as if they both exhaled and relaxed in unison. His eyes twinkled. The connection was still there. Betty started grinding her hips against George again. She looked him in the eye the entire time—until she burst into tears as she came. She had a look of wonder on her face as George flowed into her.

D*oing* your partner—and allowing yourself to be *done*—takes more than getting over hang-ups. It often takes developing what hasn't existed before: self-mastery *and* self-development. That's why clients feel more self-respect when we're through.

The Betty and George who showed up for their next appointment were like different people. The emotional atmosphere was calmer than ever before. They leaned into each other, enjoying the buttery "mush" between them, as they sat on my couch.

"He was an *animal!*"

George related a subsequent experience of "going out with the guys"—something he didn't usually do. He listened as the other men complained about feeling controlled by their wives—and laughed to himself. He and Betty were dealing with the other end of the spectrum: letting Betty tie him up!

The topic had come up as a joke in the midst of daily conversation. That evening, Betty went right to tying him to the headboard with scarves. She touched herself in front of him, sucked him, and mounted him. The really hard part for George was when she put her vibrator between his scrotum and rectum—and he liked it. This brought up disquiet about that part of his body and all its meanings.

In session we dealt with (a) his fears of homosexuality and emotional connection with other men (including me), (b) his right to use his body *his* way—including his anus, (c) his desire to no longer worry about life—or other people—"penetrating" him emotionally, and (d) his deciding, once and for all, that he wasn't an "asshole."

Surrendering is no simple matter. It's frightening to keep thinking, *I can't let go enough*, but it's also no fun to "lose yourself" unless you know you'll find your way back. When you feel as if you are turning yourself over to someone, you have to worry about what *they* will do. The process works differently when you realize the key is holding onto yourself.

Paradoxically, refusing to surrender is the key to sexual surrender. Refusing to surrender to your spouse, or to your fears, or to other people's standards. We tell each other, "Surrender to your sensations!" But real sexual surrender involves removing psychic armor—not your common sense. Doing your spouse (or allowing yourself to be done) involves "standing on your own two feet"—not forcing yourself on someone against his or her will.

"Letting go" requires a strong grip on yourself. It's about holding on. Self-control has *two* sides to it: one is about not suppressing your sexuality, and the other is about containing it. Personal development focuses sexual energy and consciousness into a tight, precise beam. Sexual gluttons use a "shotgun" approach; well-attuned partners use a laser.

The kind of sex George and Betty developed takes personal integrity, because it takes integrity to face the challenges and demands of exploring your sexual potential. Integrity is a fundamental ingredient of self-validated intimacy—and your ability to *do* and *be done* by your partner.

Observations
on
the Process

Chapter 11

Two-Choice Dilemmas and Normal Marital Sadism

Not a day goes by that a man doesn't have to choose.
Between what he wants and what he's afraid to lose.

—*Blues musician Robert Cray*
"Consequences"

If Audrey were a cat, she'd be hissing now. Her back would be arched and her hair would stand on end. She entered our first session on the defensive, and that's where she wanted to stay. "I can't be sexual when I'm feeling so much pressure! I don't want sex when I feel pressured to have it!"

I watched Audrey back her husband, Peter, into an emotional corner by accusing him of being "just like all men." Generally he dished out as good as he got, withholding from his wife in petty but meaningful ways. He had grown up as an invisible son, sandwiched between his athlete-of-the-year older brother and his perpetual baby sister. He was used to not getting what he wanted. He wanted someone "to have and to hold"—someone to belong to.

Audrey had grown up with a chronically depressed father and a mother whose "terminal forgetfulness" created havoc in Audrey's life. One crisis followed another—whether it was losing Audrey's report card when it needed to be signed and returned, or "not remembering" to pick up Audrey's prom dress on the afternoon before the prom. Audrey's anguish was labeled "whining and complaining"; her frustration as "disrespectful." Anger was interpreted as an accusation that Mom did these things deliberately.

At this moment in my office Audrey obviously felt she was on the defensive. But, in fact, she was very much on the attack.

"Sex isn't even very good when we have it!"

"Do you mean *he's* not very good?"

"I'm trying to be kind."

"Kind—or delivering the message without saying it straight?"

"If you think this is going to make me want sex, you're as crazy as Peter!"

In contemporary sex therapy there has been an implicit pressure on the partner with the low desire to learn to want sex more often. During the 1970s and '80s therapists saw this partner as the one with the problem. Today, some therapists know better—but the general public doesn't. Audrey anticipated that (a) I would see her as the bad/sick one, (b) I would accept Peter's greater sexual desire as the frequency she had to learn to meet, and (c) I would push her to do it.

"Maybe you think I automatically advocate 'more sex' because I'm a sex therapist. I always assume it makes sense when someone doesn't want sex. Sometimes I have to wonder about the partner who wants to keep going." (Now I had Peter's attention, too.) "I have also found— all things considered—that people want sex when sex is worth wanting, and they can afford to want it."

Audrey didn't know quite what to make of this.

"I already know there's no point in pressuring you. It hasn't worked when Peter's tried it—and he's in bed with you. I never have sex with my clients, so there's no point in my even trying. I never become a 'bigger hammer' for the partner who wants more sex. There's no reason why you have to have sex—or even like it."

This wasn't going the way Audrey planned. She looked both disoriented and relieved.

"I never sell out one spouse's options to the other—but not because I don't take sides. I take *both* people's sides. Peter is never going to get *wanted* if I push you into sex. You might do it, but you will never *want* it—or him. It's easy for me to take your side, too, because it happens to line up with his."

Audrey looked at me with curiosity and suspicion.

"Peter won't get what he wants if you don't hold onto yourself. I'm not going to encourage you to 'be more considerate' or 'do it just for him.' "

Now Peter had his hackles up! "Thanks a lot! You're telling her it's okay not to have sex with me!"

"I can't tell her if it's okay or not. I don't get a vote. But I understand you feel like I'm selling out your interests. Would you prefer that I tell your wife that she *has* to have sex with you whether she likes it or not?"

"... No."

"At the Couples Retreat we play Bonnie Raitt's song, 'I Can't Make You Love Me.' Ever heard it?"

Peter's eyes filled. "I know it. I can't listen to it without welling up. I know the helplessness she sings about."

"Then what do you have to lose by not forcing Audrey to have sexual desire?"

"I get afraid she'll never want sex if I don't push. I feel like she has no respect for me."

"Did it ever occur to you that *not* pushing her shows *self*-respect? I say that, fully understanding what *you* want. If you want more sex and you think pressuring Audrey will get it, then do what you think is best. I never sell out one partner's interests to the other—or to 'the relationship.' I have no difficulty advocating that you have the sex you want, in the same way I advocate Audrey shouldn't have sex she doesn't."

Peter started to calm down. He was genuinely surprised when, seconds later, Audrey erupted. He thought she'd like what I was saying. He could see the futility of pressuring his wife to have sex. He thought Audrey would be smugly triumphant.

"I don't want to be under any pressure to have sex!"

At first Peter thought Audrey was aligning with me to gang up on him—that she was reacting the way he anticipated and even taking it a step further. He thought she was laying down the law: progress was to occur on *her* terms at *her* preferred rate. Then Peter realized Audrey was fighting with me. He didn't know what to make of that. Things were happening fast.

What Peter didn't realize was that Audrey was getting nervous. It was dawning on her that my "support" for her position didn't include supporting her "against" him. I wasn't going to champion her issues, or "tone him down," or "soften him up" for her.

I responded to Audrey, "There are several ways we might remove the pressure. If you could have your preference, what would you choose? Would you like me to help you develop more sexual desire, or would you prefer that I help you kill your husband's desire? Either way you'd feel less pressure."

"I wouldn't care if we never had sex again. That would be fine with me. I wouldn't care if sex dropped off the face of the earth!"

"If I understand you, it's not just that you 'wouldn't care'—more like, this is what you'd prefer!"

"Right!"

"If you like, I could help you make that happen. Maybe you can find a way to kill Peter's desire for sex." (Peter had a faint look of panic.) "On the other hand, since I don't take sides, I'd *also* be willing to help Peter become more resilient to your efforts to make sex so bad he won't want it." (Peter looked relieved.)

"I mean it! You're not going to get anywhere with me if I feel pressured!"

"Meaning you weren't feeling pressured before you came here?"

"Meaning I don't want *you* pressuring me!"

Audrey obviously thought the best defense was a good offense—she was skilled at keeping people off-balance. I suddenly realized Audrey anticipated that I wouldn't like her—she was already responding to her anticipation. It wouldn't take much to trigger an emotional reaction we'd all regret.

I needed to do something to shift my alliance with Audrey. She clearly was more comfortable having me as an attacker than as an ally. It helped me appreciate the flavor and impact of her experiences growing up. Peter, on the other hand, was ready to have *anyone* on his side.

I thought of something humorous that might shatter our adversarial positions. The problem was, I could imagine Audrey using it to blow things up. Taken the wrong way it could sound sarcastic, patronizing, and authoritarian. Everything hinged on how differentiated Audrey and I could be at the moment. My intervention was part therapeutic, part diagnostic. Using all the irony I could muster, I said (tongue in cheek), "I'm sorry. I didn't make this clear earlier. You can't *pay* me enough to make me pressure you. Actually, the therapy where I pressure you is $1,000 an hour. I don't think you can afford that kind of therapy. And if you could, you couldn't afford the aftermath. In *this* therapy you have to pressure yourself! It still 'costs.' But it's probably within your means."

Audrey took ten seconds to sift through my response. Then she smiled—almost in spite of herself. She wasn't so far gone that she couldn't see the humor or my layers of meanings. She cued me that resources lay behind her snarl. She could reorganize quickly. That had come in handy dealing with her mother. Now it allowed her to move out of the emotional corner into which she was rapidly backing herself.

It's not my job as a therapist to make people choose. (Several clients have offered to pay extra if I would!) In truth they seek me out because I'm careful not to interfere with the choices built into their dilemmas.

"I can't promise you won't feel pressure if you come into therapy. But that's not the same thing as me—or therapy—pressuring you. I think the pressure you're feeling is inherent in your situation. In fact, it's a pretty good bet that you're going to feel pressure whether you consult me or not—it's guaranteed if you stay in treatment with me. You haven't been exactly anxiety-free while you've avoided things that pressured you. Now you're anxious that your relationship might end—or it might stay this way forever."

Audrey backed off a hair from "red alert."

"So what are you saying?"

"I won't pressure you to have sex—but you will probably have to choose what you want."

"Like what?" Her suspicion was back.

"You may have to choose between having sex and not being married."

"I'm sorry, but I'm just not going to accept either one!"

Audrey's implication was clear: Peter had to have less sexual appetite and indefinite "patience"—unless he wanted to save them both lots of trouble and just forget sex altogether. At another time in another context, Audrey's statement was the path of differentiation. Now it was the epitome of emotional fusion. I shared this with her in a subsequent session, once she had stopped seeing me as the enemy.

Audrey dropped her strident tone and sounded almost apologetic as she turned towards Peter. "I just don't have any feelings for you anymore."

Peter looked desperate and wounded. If he folded it might relieve Audrey, but it wouldn't help her resolve what was eating at her. I decided to stay in the fray.

"None at all?"

"Well, I still love Peter. Just . . . you know . . . sexual feelings."

"Where'd they go?"

"I don't know," said Audrey forlornly. Peter was looking worse by the second.

"Maybe you accidentally left them in your shirt pocket and they didn't come back from the cleaners?"

There was stunned silence. Then Peter broke out in laughter! Disparate desire is wonderful for the humorous dramas of differentiation—if you're intact enough to appreciate them. Audrey tried to regain control of the situation.

"Well, I *don't* have those feelings for you!"

It was clear Audrey had no intention of leaving. Instead, she wanted

Peter to accept marriage without sex if he "truly loved" her. After all, she was willing to do that for him! I turned to Peter.

"Audrey's lack of sexual feelings—has this been a bigger problem for you or for her?"

"It's been a bigger problem for me."

"Then why are you laughing?"

"I suddenly realized it's not just my problem. If I decide I want sex and I want Audrey, then her lack of desire for me is her problem."

I didn't believe for a moment that Peter could hold onto this stance for long. But at least he could think it and say it. Now I knew there was more to him than showed. I wasn't surprised. I always keep in mind that people pick equals for partners.

"You mean your wife's lack of desire for you is a bigger problem for her than for you?" I paused and then said, "Well, maybe finally things are as they should be. Everyone's entitled to feelings—or lack of them. But the person with those feelings is the one most entitled to pay attention to them."

Audrey was playing with Peter's reflected sense of self—the price he paid for his dependence on her validation. But Peter's laughter made their entire pattern shift. Audrey could feel it.

"You're making fun of my feelings," Audrey huffed. She was still trying to get our interaction back on familiar turf.

"Not at all. If your lack of sexual desire for Peter is a problem for you, I'll be glad to help you with that any way I can. Maybe now that your lack of desire for Peter is more a problem for you than for him, you'll be able to do something new about it. But it is interesting that not having 'those kinds of feelings' isn't much of a problem for you until it's less of a problem for him."

I looked directly into Peter's eyes. We continued to look at each other silently for a moment. I shifted my gaze and said quietly to both of them, "If you stop being so reactive, situations often move on in ways you don't anticipate."

The Two-Choice Dilemma

Many people have asked me, in one way or another, "How do you get people to do such daunting things? Why would people want to put themselves through the anxiety of risking rejection and exposing their innermost selves—especially when their marriage isn't very good? How do you motivate people to be so brave?"

Often I answer with a question: "Do you think the Pilgrims came to the New World because they were so brave—or because they couldn't stand things where they were?"

We have the fantasy that we have the choice between being anxious or not. Unfortunately, we don't. Our choice is between one anxiety or another. Do something scary—or face problems from not doing it. Make an error by commission—or omission. Face the anxiety that things will change—or stay the same. Do (sexual) things you've never done—or forfeit that taste of life. Face the anxiety of growing up—or the terror of facing life as a perpetual child. Confront the fear of differentiation or the dread of marital living death.

These are examples of the two-choice dilemmas inherent in emotionally committed relationships. Such dilemmas arise from our human nature: we are fundamentally separate life forms who value both *attachment* and *autonomy*. In Chapter 4 we unmasked the illusionary notion of "being in the same boat." Once you realize you and your partner are in two separate "boats," you understand the nature of your dilemma: you want to steer your own boat—and your partner's, too. We call this "togetherness"—as long as you are steering for both of you. When your partner does the same thing, however, it's called "control." If you want both *absolute* certainty of your partner's course and certainty that you're not controlling him or her—you've just run into a two-choice dilemma.

If you check your dictionary, you'll find the phrase "two-choice dilemma" is redundant—technically, a dilemma is a situation necessitating a choice between two or more unpleasant alternatives. However, many people think of a dilemma according to the dictionary's secondary definition: a perplexing or awkward situation. In my clinical work I use the term "two-choice dilemma" to highlight that (a) we often try to remain in our perplexing, awkward, and painful situations to keep everything in check, (b) a choice is often required to solve our situation, (c) we usually want two choices but we only get one, and (d) we try to avoid choosing (by remaining in difficult situations) to avoid losses inherent in giving up one option for another (i.e., a solution). While not linguistically correct in all cases, clients have found the term "two-choice dilemma" a powerful tool; I use it here for that reason.

You and your partner will face two-choice dilemmas specific to your relationship at some point (if you haven't already). They may surface as you try to use what you've learned in this book, but they will surface even if you don't do a thing. Dilemmas are part of the fabric of life— and thus part of your marriage. Disparate desire is just one of marriage's "natural" crucibles; two-choice dilemmas lie at the heart of sexual monogamy.

When relationships hit gridlock, everyone wants *two* choices. The problem is you only get one at a time. You make a choice and then your partner gets to make his (or vice versa). That's when you encourage your partner to be "reasonable"—so you don't really have to choose.

Expecting your partner to sacrifice for you in the name of love *kills* marriage, sex, intimacy, and love. What makes us feel loved—the illusion of fusion—destroys sexual desire and growth. That's why if you're "normal," your marriage is an accident looking for a place to happen. That "accident" is gridlock—which is no accident at all. Two-choice dilemmas are grindstones of differentiation. They are part of a system in which your partner's mere attempts to have a self puncture your narcissism.

No One Wants to Face Two-Choice Dilemmas

None of us *wants* to face our dilemma(s) and choose one option over the other. Manic attempts to "do it all" maintain our secret fantasy that we can have it all—and never have to face our anxiety. The 1960s free-love ethic that "it's unrealistic to expect one person to meet all your needs" subtly reassures us that we can have everything we want (all we have to do is spread our needs around several people). But decisions, commitments, friendship, and integrity only become meaningful in a world of finite options.

Pop psychology tells us what we want to hear: you should expect your partner to accept, understand, and validate your position even if he doesn't agree—he should even say you make sense! That strategy works as long as there's enough room for everyone to have his or her own feelings and *act* upon them. But many marital therapy approaches don't work in the bedroom because they try to avoid two-choice dilemmas. We can agree to disagree as long as we are focused on feelings and perceptions. When the issue is *behavior,* however, flexibility is reduced significantly. You can't agree to disagree about sex. When your spouse says he or she is never doing a particular sexual behavior—or never having sex again—you don't feel like saying, "Thanks for sharing!"

When we tell ourselves we have no choice in a situation, we act as if we can sit pat until we do. But "no choice" is a rationalization for the fuller truth: "There is no choice I *want!*" There is always a choice—but not often the one we want. We want the choice to (not) do what we (don't) want—and avoid the consequences (like not have sex with one's partner indefinitely and feel secure he'll stay). Or we want to exercise one option for ourselves—and prevent our partner from exercising his. (Many people think monogamy is a good thing—for their spouse.)

It makes sense that so many of us feel "stuck." Going forward means *choosing*. Maintaining the status quo offers the fantasy of never having to choose—or the illusion that if you stall long enough, the choice you want just may appear.

You *can't* choose not to choose—unless you stop your spouse from making choices that affect your life. That's hard—if not impossible—to do indefinitely. You have to make sure your partner doesn't change (grow up). You hope he stays intimidated, too frightened to make a move on his own. You hammer at him to keep him from taking his own shape. Or you make sure you don't take yours (at least openly).

When partners bend over backward to be accepting and considerate, more often than not, one or the other doesn't like having sex in that "position." We're afraid to stand up for what we want—so instead we try to dictate our partner's response. We don't want to speak up—but we do want things to change.

Spouses often try to avoid marriage's forced choices by usurping their partner's options. A clandestine affair can be understood as an attempt to steal a partner's choice for monogamy. The adulterer wants it both ways: to have sex with someone else and still be married to the spouse. It's like saying, "I want this other person *and* I want you. If I tell you about the affair, you might choose to leave. To hell with what you want—to be in a monogamous relationship. I get both choices and you get none. That's because I *love* you and don't want to give you up!" Granted, the other spouse might not want to have sex at all. But that doesn't remove the dilemma; it just means neither really wants to choose.

Facing any two-choice dilemma is so wounding to some people's narcissism that they just shut down—or won't shut up. They regress and the reptilian part of their brain takes over (Chapter 5). Some hold siege until their partner capitulates. Others verbally (or physically) bludgeon their spouse into surrendering all priorities so that their two-choice dilemma doesn't surface. Both types overlook the *internal* dilemma that their behavior creates: demanding they be "loved" by their partner, but acting in ways that are neither loving nor lovable. The way in which we deal with our two-choice dilemmas mirrors our level of integrity. Audrey's mother showed reptilian responses when Audrey reacted to her sadistic "forgetfulness." By mislabeling Audrey's distress as disrespect or accusation, her mother attempted to silence Audrey and remove any cause for self-confrontation.

(We could also examine this point by looking at the impact of Audrey's chronically depressed father. It's not hard to see that her "invisible" husband wasn't too different from her "invisible" father. I have focused on Audrey's mother because she was Audrey's primary association, and these issues lie more in the direction our discussion is headed. It only takes a minute to see how Audrey's father's depression, whether or not it had a medical basis, may have been *used* or inflicted on his wife and daughter.)

Our problem is not the two-choice dilemma itself but our refusal to face it, our unwillingness to meet life on its own terms. Difficulty with two-choice dilemmas commonly takes several forms:

- We can't remain calm in the face of our partner's agenda.
- We are so reactive and poorly defined that we can't change our position even when it's in our interest.
- We refuse to see our partner as a separate person.
- We are unwilling to tolerate the anxiety of personal growth.

You can *use* two-choice dilemmas or you can seek to avoid them. The latter is always an option but, as in any dilemma, there is a price: you can't avoid or minimize two-choice dilemmas without truncating your own and/or your partner's growth or happiness. When you choose the latter option, you usually intend that the unhappy truncated "someone" will be your spouse.

For example, Audrey faced more than one dilemma: she didn't want sex *and* she wanted to be married to someone who did. On another level, she didn't *want to want* Peter, but she *wanted to be wanted*. Audrey wanted to want Peter about as much as she wanted to want—or depend on—her mother. She could get around her dilemma with Peter as long as he was so insecure that he would take her on those terms. The two-choice dilemma of wanting to be wanted but not wanting to want was always there—Audrey came into the marriage with it. It fit well with Peter's lapdog willingness to belong to *any*one. But when Peter felt better about himself and expected more, problems surfaced.

Let's also think about how this works across generations. Think about Audrey's mother, whose behavior perfectly enacted her own dilemma of wanting to be wanted but not wanting to want. Her punitive "forgetfulness" kept Audrey wanting and needing her. If she had really wanted Audrey (i.e., was concerned for her), wouldn't she have addressed her "forgetfulness" rather than silence her daughter's reactions? Audrey's mother managed to get *wanted* without *wanting* and thereby dodged her dilemmas—but not without limiting and saddening her daughter's life.

It might seem that Audrey never established much of a bond with her erratic mother—but the reverse is true. Audrey was poorly differentiated from her mother because she never had a stable platform from which to "shove off." Worrying what Mom would forget next, what catastrophe would befall, trying not to anger her—all these made Audrey's life revolve around her mother even when they were apart. But perhaps the most powerful fusion is the hardest to see: the only way Audrey could connect with her mother was on the receiving end of Mom's sadism.

Masochism is an exceedingly powerful form of attachment. When it is the only synchrony parents offer, children take it. Masochist and sadist—victim and perpetrator—are powerful forms of emotional fusion. Children in Audrey's position approach future relationships from either side of this sadism-masochism coin. It makes little difference which side they're on, although it usually feels better to "dish it out." They acquire a taste for this and it becomes part of their erotic "map." Audrey had years of experience in a masochistic relationship, so she knew how to do it to Peter. From his own history, Peter was ready to play out Audrey's old role.

Peter was as involved in, and beset by, his own two-choice dilemmas as was Audrey. *Both* partners always face anxiety-provoking choices. It makes no difference whether the issue is sexual frequency, style, or particular behaviors.

Peter was under equal pressure, although Audrey was more the focus of our sessions. Audrey appeared to be under "pressure to change," but both spouses were equally confronted with the difficulty of holding onto himself/herself (differentiation). Peter faced losing his marriage if Audrey got upset enough about sex—whether or not he was pressuring her. He bought Audrey's threats that "she couldn't take it anymore." He was pressured to be "extra nice" to her, placate her in other ways, and keep her from becoming upset. He also faced the pressure that he might keep his wife but lose sex forever. Ultimately Peter was pushed against his childhood pattern of feeling invisible. In essence, the marital situation was asking him, "What do you think you're worth?"

All couples with disparate sexual desire (meaning everyone in a relationship) face difficult choices between alternative anxieties. Peter could be patient and understanding—maybe good things come to those who wait? Or was he believing in the tooth fairy—and would wind up without sex forever? Was he being understanding—or a dope?

The choice we finally make often reflects only which anxiety is the least tolerable and which options are the more expendable. We rarely accept we're choosing the anxiety we'll have to deal with. We want choices without prices and solutions without anxiety. (As one client said half in jest, "It's bad enough I have to pay for therapy! You mean I have to grow up too?!") Anxiety per se isn't the problem. Anxiety is inherent in growth (sexual and otherwise). It plays a productive and necessary role in sexual development and pleasure. Sexual novelty always involves anxiety and ambiguity. The real problem is our *intolerance* and *fear* of anxiety. The long-term solution (which doesn't kill sex) involves becoming more mature. That doesn't mean "keeping a stiff upper lip," but it does involve learning to self-soothe.

Audrey seemed to say that her lack of sexual desire stemmed from anxiety and pressure—anxiety about the future of her marriage and about doing something she didn't want to do. Audrey also felt that something else made her emotionally "uncomfortable" during sex. She wasn't sure what it was, but she didn't want to get into bed for a closer look. She wanted these anxieties and pressures *gone* before she had sex. On the surface that seems reasonable. We all want anxiety-free sex.

Unfortunately, the way we want it is not the way it is. Relief from pressure and anxiety may be the hallmark of a good marriage—but it is not the precursor. Audrey had spent three years in prior therapy searching for the elusive cause of her low desire. She had theories and insight but no improvement in sex. She did "accomplish" something, however: her therapist told Peter to put sex on ice while they searched for the discovery that would set Audrey free. Whether by ignorance or design, the therapist removed Audrey's dilemma. Without the pressure of her dilemma, Audrey had little motivation to face her anxiety. It wasn't surprising that Audrey stayed with this therapy even though it produced few tangible results—except a delay in the inevitable.

Going *through* the trauma of maturing—differentiating—opens up the possibility that we may yet become adults. Digesting and self-soothing marriage's restrictions ripen intimacy and eroticism. Choosing between gut-wrenching anxieties and options makes us more differentiated, more capable of truly loving.

In Chapter 10 I mentioned the possibility of metabolizing aggression into something useful (fuel for fucking). That "digestive" capacity comes from going through two-choice dilemmas. These are bitter pills to swallow—but swallowing and self-soothing increase what you can "digest" without indigestion. Shortly we'll discuss what happens when this process is avoided—and what happens when it is engaged.

Perhaps now you see other sides to my "egalitarian" (differentiated) stance: people shouldn't have sex they don't want, any more than those who want it should go without. I don't pressure my clients because I don't have to. Their relationship does that most effectively. Conflict of interest is part of marriage—and it can enhance differentiation and self-definition.

"You Never Give Me a Chance to Initiate!"

Several sessions later Audrey and Peter were still at it. It was as if we were slowly working through Audrey's repertoire of systemic conundrums. I was developing more respect for her—and what she'd been through. She had been worked over by a pro.

"It's Peter's fault I don't initiate! He never gives me chance!"

Peter rolled his eyes and shook his head in disbelief.

"It's true! You always beat me to the punch. You initiate all the time!"

"We'd never have sex if I didn't initiate! I don't believe you'd initiate if I didn't."

"Try me!"

They eventually agreed to this arrangement without encouragement from me. Audrey didn't initiate the first night. She felt she would be just doing it to do it. Peter didn't comment. The second night passed. And the third. A week later Peter finally exploded.

"You never initiated! Even though I never made a single move towards you!"

"Well, I still felt pressured! I knew you expected me to initiate, so I didn't! As time went by, I knew you expected me to do something. I'm just not going to have sex with you when I feel that kind of pressure! I'm not going to let you dictate when I'm supposed to initiate by when you *don't*!"

"I kept *my* part of our agreement!" Peter was beside himself with frustration and anger.

"I don't care! I'm not going to have sex when I feel pressured!"

Audrey was "using" the system within monogamous sex the same way her mother had used the dependency system in a parent-child relationship. Audrey seemed as heedless to Peter's plight as Mom had been to hers. The topic of both their childhoods had become a thread through our therapy sessions. Audrey's experiences of abuse had been labeled. It came as no surprise to either of them. Her prior treatment had focused on nothing but her abuse.

Audrey looked as unwilling to confront herself as her mother had probably been—but was this really as far as her potential extended? Or was she able and willing to digest the fact that she was acting out a dynamic that had been handed down through her family? I decided to find out.

"You're trapping yourself and pressuring yourself. There's very little Peter can do about it."

"There you go taking his side!"

"I'm taking *your* side. As I understand it, you want to stay married."

"How am *I* pressuring myself?" Audrey's question dripped with sarcasm.

"Your agreement that you would initiate sex if Peter didn't is a perfect demonstration. Yes, you feel 'pressured' to have sex. But the pressure is part of your choice. You agreed to monogamy—not celibacy. You're backing yourself into a corner every time you refuse to initiate. I'm not telling you to initiate. I'm just describing the dilemma you've created for yourself: the longer you wait, the more you know Peter wants to have sex—and the more pressure you feel. The only way he can take the pressure off of you is to promise never to want sex for the rest of his life. Or wait indefinitely for you to get in the mood."

"He would if he loved me!"

"If he promised to wait forever, he would be either a fool or a liar—because even if he gave you that guarantee, would you push yourself harder to work through your issues about sex?"

"Yes . . . well, probably not."

"And if he promised to wait forever, would you believe him?"

"No!"

"And if he were willing to give up sex for the rest of his life, would you really see him as sexually desirable?"

". . . I guess not."

"Then for Peter to abdicate interest in sex isn't really in anybody's interests. I'm not telling you to have sex; I'm just describing the way marriage works. What you do about it is up to you."

Audrey had backed Peter into a corner. She trapped him every time she backed herself into a corner through her own avoidance. Peter couldn't take the pressure off her without giving up his own preferences.

Audrey assumed he would back down as he had in the past. Just the passage of time increasingly pressured him to "give her more time"— meaning, give *himself* an out from having to face his growing belief that Audrey wasn't available for the relationship he wanted.

Audrey had a perfect right not to have sex when she didn't want it. But she also wanted Peter to accept this, remain married, and be loving and generous. Like all spouses, Audrey trapped Peter every time she dodged her two-choice dilemma. *We are often most sadistic when dodging our own development.*

"Why do you keep focusing on me?!"

"Because you keep drawing the focus—and control—back to you."

"Focus on Peter!"

"I'd like to. He's got his own issues in this. But if you're asking me, 'Why does Peter get to sit there like the good guy?' the answer is because you won't take the step in front of you. He gets to avoid his issues while you're avoiding yours."

"Why do I have to go first?"

"I don't make the rules. It's where you are positioned in this dilemma. Besides, you just saw what happened when Peter 'went first' by not initiating. If he goes first, you feel more pressure to respond. Eventually it comes back to you."

Audrey tried to diffuse her anxiety by shifting the focus to nonsexual aspects of their relationship. She seized upon problems outside the bedroom, insisting these had to be resolved for her to feel desirous. Sometimes she implied these problems *caused* her lack of desire. Other times she implied that they diminished her motivation to tackle her mysterious anxiety during sex. It was no different from Mom telling Audrey her disappointments were her own fault for not "reminding" her mother—and then punishing her for being "disrespectful" when Audrey did.

Some issues Audrey picked were difficult for Peter to acknowledge. Others had little to do with him. Many were things both she and Peter had let slide by unstated mutual avoidance. It wasn't that some of Audrey's points weren't "legitimate." It was the way she tried to use them: she tried to link their resolution to *her* resolution, buying time she seemed to have no intention of using.

Gradually, Peter became increasingly willing to let Audrey make it perfectly clear that she didn't want their sex life to improve. He would make his own choices based on that fact.

Audrey took countermeasures. She had to keep him *wanting* and hoping. On the surface, she was trying to "understand" why she didn't want to have sex with Peter—but "unfortunately" she remained "confused." However, her behavior said, *I'll get around to it when I feel like it. Until then, you can just wait. You be uncomfortable rather than me!* I thought what Audrey was doing to herself was more serious than anything she might be doing to Peter. Besides, he was increasingly able to handle himself. I was worried for Audrey.

"Peter doesn't believe that I'm doing as much as I can to improve our sex!"

This wasn't just Audrey's narcissism talking, it was her sadistic part—her accusation simply wasn't true.

"If you are interested in finally getting over your experiences of abuse, you might not want to take that position."

"Why not?"

"You are misrepresenting your own position. If you don't want sex, so be it. Have the guts to openly state what you want—or don't want—and what your intentions are. Don't hide behind 'If only I could.' "

"You're taking his side!"

"You wish! I'm saying this because I'm taking *yours*!"

"You're worried he won't get laid!"

"I'm worried that you are violating your own integrity! If he's not getting laid, that's his problem—and I'll be glad to help him with it. If you violate your integrity, I don't think you are going to want to lay him. And if you do, I don't think you're going to offer him much. . . . Besides, how did you like it when Mom said, 'If only I'd remembered!'? "

Audrey understood exactly what I meant. The association upset her. She didn't want to look like Mom. She turned to Peter.

"You know I would never deliberately do anything to hurt you, dear!"

Before Peter could say anything, I said, *"Then I think treatment may be over!"* Audrey looked shocked.

I went on, "I don't work with couples who won't acknowledge deliberately doing things to hurt each other. I'm not going to waste the next six months dancing around whether or not you folks hate each other or do things to hurt each other. You're both mad as hell at each other. From what I've heard, you do lots of things—or withhold doing things—to hurt each other. But from what I'm seeing, that's not the problem."

"What is?"

"The problem is, *you both deny doing them*. You can't tolerate seeing your partner or being seen accurately. We all do things deliberately to hurt each other. I'm not advocating it. It's simply part of the deal. If you can't stand that, it's going to be very hard to stop doing them. And you're going to have a hard time being married. You can't learn to control what you deny exists."

Peter and Audrey looked sheepishly at each other.

"Why should I have sex with him when he's holding out on me? There's lots of things I ask him to do that he 'forgets' or just won't do. He's just like my mother!"

"If Peter is like your mother, that's his problem. If you're like your mother, that's *yours*. I think you're holding out on yourself. You are using the flaws you perceive in him to rationalize what you withhold. You are willing to cut off your nose to spite his face."

Audrey looked smugly bemused. "How am I holding out on myself?"

"I apologize in advance if I'm wrong. As I understand it, you like sex. I mean *really* like sex. You like to *fuck,* don't you?"

Peter nearly fell out of his chair! He looked incredulously at Audrey but didn't say a word. Audrey looked at him. Then she looked away.

Peter had naively thought Audrey's anxiety was about doing things she'd never done before. Audrey couldn't look him in the eye because she'd encouraged Peter to believe his own distortion.

"What makes you think so?" There was less defiance in Audrey voice. She wanted to know how much I knew and how much I could prove.

"It was clear from our first session. You complained that the sex with Peter wasn't very good. That's not the talk of someone who always hates sex or never wants to have it. I started asking myself how you would know the difference. It occurred to me that you might indeed know the difference between hot and mediocre sex. Maybe better than Peter. I imagine you're furious about Peter's tentativeness in bed—but you insist on it at the same time. I have a hunch you're mad as hell about looking like you don't like sex."

Audrey didn't say anything—but she didn't object. That bespoke two things: my perception of her dilemma was accurate, and she was ready to deal with it.

Audrey was *fucking* "bad" guys before she married Peter—and after. She had two brief affairs early in their marriage. Eventually she revealed them to Peter. She felt "honest." Peter felt terrible. She told Peter she realized the affairs were a replay of her abuse with her mother—and the sex was lousy anyway. Audrey had made him promise not to reveal the affairs as her condition for participating in treatment.

It was true that Audrey didn't like the bad guys with whom she'd had the affairs. But their disrespect and anger toward women made them sexually aggressive and dominant in ways Audrey had enjoyed. In a funny way she felt safe fucking them: she thought of them as "low-life" guys. Peter was a "good" man and a far better choice for marriage—but she neither respected him nor found his passivity sexy. She correctly sensed he'd be threatened by her past experiences and sexual preferences. She had difficulty validating these for herself.

"Well, I never told him I was a virgin!"

"Nice try. You're overlooking your intent. Did you know he believed your problem was that you didn't like sex and were inhibited across the board?"

". . . Yes."

"Did you do anything to clarify his distortion when you realized it?"

". . . No."

"Did you do things deliberately to reinforce his misperception of you?"

". . . Yes."

This was a ray of hope—but as far as Audrey could see, it was another step towards Armageddon. But she took it. There would have been no way to resolve the situation unless the truth finally came out. Hearing her admissions brought Peter's anger to the surface again. That was *his* problem and I planned to help him with it. Audrey's problem was different: was she going to confront the reality of her marriage—and her life? Would she face the hostility and emptiness that pervaded her fusion with Peter—her hatred of him and of herself, and repeated violations of her own integrity?

I softened my voice to match Audrey's growing availability. "I'm saying this for *your* benefit, not Peter's. I'm not suggesting you should share this part of yourself with him. Your body and your eroticism belong to *you*. But if this has to do with prior victimization, I don't think you'll get over it by acting like you'll share your sexuality with him as soon as it arrives. If you're not going to share it with him, you might want to be open about it. It's about your own integrity—getting clear that you belong to *yourself*. And letting the past be the past."

"I was my mother's victim!"

"Now you're a perpetrator."

Normal Marital Sadism

I am *not* suggesting that all people who experience abuse (whether physical, sexual, or emotional) demonstrate Audrey's characteristics. And you don't have to be abused—or female—to do similar things: men do them, too, and it doesn't take "trauma" to make us that way. Audrey isn't very different from you and me. She may be a more extreme version for more extreme reasons. But untoward experiences don't just put things into us—they bring out what's already there.

We *all* have a nasty side. Not the "dirty sex" type of nasty (which so many cannot harness). Nasty, as in "You're not a very good person." There's a side to all of us that's *bad*—evil. All of us have a touch of it; some have more.

We all torment those we love while feigning unawareness. Marriage is perhaps the place we do it most frequently—and with impunity. We withhold the sweetness of sex and intimacy while acting like we want to please—and in the course of this deceit, we pervert our sexual potential. Early American philosopher Thomas Paine said that infidelity (as in "religious infidel") is not about what we do or don't believe—it's professing to believe what we do not.

Jokes about marriage and masochism abound, but we rarely acknowledge marital sadism. "Snorgasms" ("I've had my orgasm; good luck getting yours!") and lousy oral sex may originate in ignorance, but they are perfected within marriage. The long-term marital relationship is where you learn to screw your partner two ways at once—withholding the erotic gratification he craves while having sex with him. J. P. McEvoy said, "The Japanese have a word for it. It's *judo*—the art of conquering by yielding. The Western equivalent of judo is, 'Yes, dear.' "

The American Psychiatric Association glossary defines *sadism* as "pleasure derived from inflicting physical or psychological pain or abuse on others. The sexual significance of sadistic wishes or behavior may be conscious or unconscious. When necessary for sexual gratification, [it is] classifiable as a sexual deviation." The Association also considered (and then dropped) a diagnostic category of "sadistic personality disorder." The criteria included (a) humiliating and demeaning others, (b) lying to inflict pain, (c) restricting the autonomy of people in close relationships, and (d) getting others to comply through intimidation. Apparently, the psychiatrists favoring this diagnostic category considered marital sadism to be normal: *the diagnosis wasn't applicable if sadistic behavior was directed toward one person, such as your spouse.*

If given the chance, spouses (hesitantly) acknowledge hating their partner. They seem relieved to admit it—as long as they're not sitting next to their spouse when they do. But exactly this kind of difficult face-to-face acknowledgment enhances differentiation and reduces normal marital sadism. Author Stella Gibbons has written, "There must be a dumb, dark, dull, bitter belly-tension between a man and a woman. How else could this be achieved save in the long monotony of marriage?"

In my workshops and public lectures I discuss marital hatred. Audience members laugh nervously, realizing they are in a sea of nervous smiles. Most of us feel it's okay to be angry, angry, angry at our partner—as long as we don't *hate* him or her. Labeling what we feel as hatred can seem like crossing a line beyond which love cannot exist. Hating is to anger as fucking is to sex. It makes us nervous to do either one. Lots of people act like they're ignorant of both. More of us know more about hating than fucking.

Sometimes we hate our spouses *because* we love them. Our love makes us vulnerable to what they can do to us, what they can do to themselves, and what can befall them (and, indirectly, us). We deny our hatred because it hurts our narcissism and makes us feel unlovable (but it's apparently okay as long we're "blind"—that's *normal* marital sadism). Why do we attempt to deny when we feel hatred? The superficial reason is that most of us are taught that it's bad, bad, bad to hate. But there's something deeper: children (and immature adults) can't tolerate the powerful tension of ambivalence towards those they love. Many people believe, "You can't love and hate the same person at the same time." They believe:

- "If you love me, you can't hate me."
- "If you hate me, you can't love me."
- "If I hate you, I must not love you."
- "If I love you, then I can't hate you."

The fact is, people who cannot acknowledge their hatred are most pernicious to those they "love." One cannot control what one won't acknowledge exists.

Mature adults have the strength to recognize and own their ambivalent feelings towards their partner. They self-soothe the tension of loving and hating the same person at the same time—and the fact that their partner feels similarly. Marriage invites the necessary differentiation: it's hard tolerating hatred when your marriage is rancorous. But it's tougher seeing it when everything is going fine. It makes you respect couples who are friends.

Marriage helps you realize you're living with an out-and-out sadist! And then there's your partner to deal with . . .

Normal sadism is observable in every family. At some point every parent, for one reason or another, withholds the emotional gratification his or her child wants. And at some point, spouses are bound to use torture to achieve their ends. (One husband tortured his family by making them all whine about his procrastination; then he wouldn't fulfill his commitments because they had complained.)

Emotional fusion fuels and shapes normal marital sadism. You see it when a spouse attacks the partner's reflected sense of self. Statements like, "If you were good enough, I'd have orgasms . . . or no sexual difficulties . . . or desire for you" are invitations for the partner to feel bad. Or when women fake orgasms and then have contempt for their partner, who feels proud. One variant involves faking *not* having an orgasm! Women who practice this kind of sadism want the pleasure but don't want their partner feeling good about it, so when they reach orgasm they hide it. Some husbands do it by blatantly ogling younger women, or sending sexual vibes to their wife's best friend.

Disparate sexual desire is inevitable, but emotional Siamese twins interpret any disparity as sexual incompatibility. It's better to think of sexual compatibility as having the willingness to *use* divergent preferences. Properly managed, you picked the *right* partner. As commonly managed, disparate desire is a playground for normal marital sadism.

Monogamy operates differently at different levels of differentiation. I didn't know this until I saw it with my clients. We think of monogamy as an ironclad agreement containing no ifs, ands, or buts. But it is really a complex system with rules and dynamics of its own. Differentiation changes monogamy by returning genital ownership to each partner. Emotional Siamese twins act as if their partner's genitals are communal property.

Monogamy is a prison when it's based on emotional fusion, for fusion shackles desire and prompts withholding as a means of reaffirming emotional boundaries (Chapter 5). But monogamy per se is not the problem. The problem arises when *we lack the differentiation necessary for the kind of monogamy we want.* Monogamy between undifferentiated partners creates a sexual monopoly: the partner with the lower desire controls the supply and the price of sex. Deprivation and extortion flourish at low levels of differentiation in ways that dating and open marriage "free markets" won't allow.

Poorly differentiated couples approach monogamy as a promise *to each other*—and later blame their spouse for their mutual deprivation pact. Some inflict the effects of personal (sexual) difficulties on their spouse. They justify this by citing their partner's shortcomings or saying, "Look, it's happening to me, too!" They get so good at inflicting their problems on their partner that they overlook the fact that they *enjoy* the act of inflicting per se.

Some spouses wield monogamy like a bludgeon, battering their partner with their commitment in ways never intended by marriage vows. They say, "You promised to love me for better and for worse—and that includes my (sexual) limitations!" Yes, we all marry "for better and for worse," but the assumption is that spouses will do everything possible to overcome their limitations—not simply demand their partner put up with them!

Although many of us lack sufficient differentiation for the kind of monogamy we *want,* the monogamy we *have* often provides the crucible in which we can develop it. Like a pressure cooker, monogamy harnesses pressures and tensions that produce differentiation. Absence of other sex partners, along with disparate sexual desire and styles, drives spouses toward gridlock. This forces the two-choice dilemma of self-confrontation/self-validation vs. normal marital sadism. This is the process Audrey and Peter were going through—although they hardly appreciated the elegance of it at the time.

Monogamy operates differently in highly differentiated couples: it stops being a ponderous commitment to one's partner (or "the relationship") and becomes a commitment to *oneself.* The relationship is driven more by personal integrity and mutual respect than by reciprocal deprivation or bludgeoning. It's no longer your partner's fault you don't have sex with other people; it's part of your decision to be monogamous. And the pressures of disparate sexual desire come with your decision, too. Having an affair becomes more a self-betrayal than a betrayal of your partner (since you promised yourself and not him). That same integrity supports the self-validated intimacy necessary to keep your sexual relationship alive and growing. You feel less controlled by your spouse, and less motivated to have an affair. That's fortunate, because it's also not safe to have affairs or withold from a partner whose integrity runs his monogamy: if he won't tolerate adultery or sexual laziness from himself, he's not likely to tolerate either one from you. There is less room to offer *mercy fucks*—and no reason to believe they'd be accepted.

I first learned the term *mercy fuck* from a client. Couples intuitively recognize that it refers to, "I'll do you a BIG favor. I really don't want sex or *you*. But if you insist, I'll accommodate you. You can use my body—and you'd better appreciate it!"

Normal marital sadism surfaces in gifts given or received that are never quite right. Mercy fucking withholds the sweetness of sex, breaks your partner's heart (if he or she catches on), and leaves little recourse. You let your partner climb on top of you to get him off your back. The goal isn't *doing* your partner—it's *getting done with it* so you don't have to do it tomorrow.

People who accept mercy fucks can rationalize that it's better than no sex at all, but is it really? If you accept mercy fucks "until the good stuff comes along," it never does and it never will. Your partner knows you'll settle for lousy sex, so there's no reason to deal with the problems blocking better sex.

People who give mercy fucks often get angry when their partners *accept* it, accusing them of just wanting their body—and they've got the proof: they know that's all they offered! Well-differentiated people can have sex when they aren't really in the mood, but it's not mercy fucking. It's another form of mutuality, and it doesn't have the withholding, sadistic quality of a mercy fuck because there is no sense of loss of self in responding to the partner's preference.

But watch what happens when mercy fucks are *refused!* The marriage becomes unstable: if there is to be no sex without real connection, then there may be no sex at all—at which point, *anything* can happen. It also means partners have to *want* each other for sex to take place. The partner offering mercy fucks gets furious! (Mercy fuckers may want to avoid sex, but they want to avoid wanting their partner even more.) If this sounds familiar, you understand why I refer to marital sexual sadism as *normal*.

Overt pressure from your partner to have sex can be hard to tolerate—but it can be even harder when it's gone. Anxiety and pressure increase when your partner stops pressuring you and, at the same time, refuses to give up what he or she wants. You *both* have to face the anxiety of choosing and wanting, and that pressures *both* of you. When either spouse refuses to continue mercy fucking, it changes the marriage—one way or another.

Peter and Audrey had gone through this dynamic. Eventually, Peter found her less appealing and decreased his focus on her. One might think Audrey would have liked this—but that's not what happens when you want to be wanted but you don't want to want. Audrey didn't want sex when she thought Peter expected it, but she was threatened by Peter's disinterest—it hinted that he might just manage to differentiate. At first Peter didn't tell her for fear of her reaction, but Audrey sensed it nonetheless. Peter's admission that he found her less appealing had triggered their request for treatment.

Couples who don't play with each other's genitals often play with each other's minds instead. *Mind-fucking* is a popular marital pastime. It's more like "getting it in the ear" than a full-body contact sport. Mind-fucking is an attempt to cover your tracks while you're busy dodging two-choice dilemmas and avoiding yourself.

You can't *make* your partner put his mind (and heart) into sex—the lousy sex you're having may be what he has in mind. And it's impossible to get your spouse to "understand" what he may already know: he's withholding *fucking*. Some folks really don't know about fucking, but others, who feign naiveté or stupidity, are really cunning, passive-aggressive, and gut-level shrewd. They torture their partner by acting ignorant (and disgusted).

The million-dollar guessing game is, "Does my partner really know how to *fuck*? Is he withholding—and mind-fucking me?" A clue to the answer is his curiosity and eagerness to find out about *fucking*. Realizing your partner knows what's going on (a) is particularly upsetting, (b) changes your picture of reality, and (c) creates the opportunity for self-validated intimacy when openly confronted.

You can "tell your partner what you want," as pop psychology books on sex often advise, but you're not going to get it until he's good and ready to give it to you. The bad news is that your partner often knows what you want. The fact that he's not doing it is his way of saying, "Over my dead body!"

Peter Makes His Move

What do you think it's like to tell a "victim" like Audrey that she is also a perpetrator? Many therapists wouldn't—not that they wouldn't like to. Audrey is the kind of client who scares and intimidates therapists. She had me scared, too.

It wasn't her challenges to my competency, or her emotional volatility, or her seeming irrationality. Each of these made sense to me. I've experienced these tactics many times with other clients. What scared me was the possibility that Audrey might not confront *herself.* She was a bright woman going to waste. When she tormented Peter, she was also tormenting herself. She wasn't so far gone that it didn't hurt her, too. Audrey hated herself. The thought that she could live differently made me hang in there, trying to find something solid inside her. I saw hints of that solid core, but the longer it didn't surface, the more concerned I grew.

When I challenged Audrey with the statement "now you're a perpetrator," I spoke to a part of her that had stopped listening to the world. I was appealing to what was good and solid in her rather than the weak "wounded" parts. Audrey was sure I wanted to find the part of her that was "damaged." She kept showing me the part she thought needed fixing; I kept talking to the intact part. I kept reaching for the part of her that could fix herself. My goal was to motivate that part of her to "stand up."

My statement didn't land Audrey in her crucible. The unfolding of her life did that; she was already "in it." My job was to help her use her situation to see herself—and help her become who she wanted to be. The same statement at another time or place—or a different preceding process in treatment—would not have had the same impact. The groundwork had already been laid when our fateful confrontation occurred. Audrey's sadism and experiences growing up had become a framework that defined and gave meaning to the *self*-confrontation my comment provoked. However, my comment wasn't nearly as difficult for Audrey as when Peter finally made his move during the next session.

"I think it's time to shit or get off the pot."

Peter sounded quiet and determined—which really scared Audrey. It wasn't an epithet said in the heat of the moment. It was an act of self-definition—Peter was saying it as much to himself as to Audrey.

Peter looked her in the eye and said, "I'm fed up with myself. I hate the way I let you work me over. I feel like I have no balls! The fact that I do it to you too is no longer an acceptable trade-off."

I didn't say anything for several moments. The silence underscored the enormity of what was happening. Then I said, "Are you saying 'shit or get off the pot' now because you think Audrey is still reeling from what I said to her last session?"

Peter seriously examined his motivation for a minute. It didn't seem like he was jumping on Audrey "while she was down." He'd been moving towards this position for some time. But challenging whether Peter was "tailgating" on my intervention was as much for him as it was for Audrey. I wanted it clear I wasn't "supporting" his move—they both needed to know this for different reasons. Peter had everything to gain by struggling with my question.

Peter's quiet voice was filled with emotion. "I don't think so." Audrey was gearing up to defend herself. "I don't really see Audrey as falling apart. She was pretty quiet after last session, but she wasn't hysterical or weepy like she often gets after we fight. I actually think Audrey handled herself pretty well under the circumstances. I was surprised. It made me respect her—I even feel sad for her." Audrey was taken aback and settled down.

Peter slowly shook his head from side to side. He seemed to be talking to himself. "No more. . . . I can't take this anymore. No more begging for sex. No more shouting matches." Then he looked at Audrey. "I'm not going to punish you anymore because you won't have sex— that just makes me feel like I don't deserve it. Decide what you really want. I'll do the same."

Audrey stopped preparing her rebuttal. She just sagged. She looked down and stared at the floor, saying nothing. It was clear she wasn't falling apart—she was falling *together.* Instead of immediately deflecting Peter's words, she took them in. She was letting herself realize the magnitude of what was happening: Peter was starting to differentiate.

Crucibles are always interlocking. When one partner goes into his crucible, the other partner goes into hers—or gets out of the marriage.

Audrey responded in ways I've seen innumerable times. It's still awesome when it happens. In the face of direct confrontation she functioned *better.* The defensive maneuvers ceased. Audrey was clearly upset but in a way appropriate to the self-confrontation at hand.

In the past Peter had tried confronting Audrey. Her usual response was to put him on the defensive. But when that didn't work, she had another way out: Audrey would "fall apart." Faced with her own sadism, and unable to acknowledge her personal imperfections, she would retreat into tears and demand that Peter reassure her she was lovable.

Actually, Audrey's prior behavior was another form of mind-fucking. She would frighten Peter into thinking she was "cracking up" and he would dutifully back off and once again "support her." She wasn't "falling apart" because she was under "too much pressure"; she was trying to stave off the real pressure in her situation: acknowledging her own sadism and facing her two-choice dilemma about having sex or getting divorced.

Audrey was neither empty nor fragile—she wouldn't have survived her past if she were. She was full of anxiety, anger, narcissism, and discontent. The empathy she demanded for her "childhood wounds" only reinforced their impasse and postponed her confrontation with her own issues of self-responsibility.

Now, with Peter's decisive move, there was no room to demand "safety and security." All that mattered was what she was going to do.

This time, instead of running away by falling apart, Audrey "took the hit." She finally confronted that it was okay with her if Peter suffered due to her inactivity. From there, it was a short step to see herself being sadistic to Peter, just as her mother had been to her. Audrey went into crisis—she was still in it a week later at our next session.

"I *am* just like my mother."

"In what way?"

"I let Peter suffer because I didn't do what I needed to do, just like she did with me!"

"Are you sure you're like your mother?"

"What do you mean?"

"Would your mother be upset about this like you are?"

Audrey was momentarily lost in her anger. *"My mother would never let herself be confronted with what she was doing!"* Then Audrey realized that this was my point. What happened next surprised Audrey *and* Peter, but it occurs repeatedly when people "stand on their own two feet."

Audrey *relaxed*. When she did, the reality of her life hit her in a way it couldn't when she kept trying to defend against it. Audrey *grieved* in a way not possible before—down to her core. She tasted her hatred toward her mother and Peter, the resentment and aggression permeating their interactions, and choked on her vindictiveness. She was filled with pain the likes of which she never expected—nor thought she could handle. To her amazement, she wasn't depressed and she stopped being ashamed of herself. This was her first of many experiences with *clean pain*. (We'll discuss clean pain in the next chapter.)

Like many people, Audrey thought the process worked by "getting things out of her system." Now she had gotten far enough to take the experience *in,* to digest it, and to change it. She was ready to regain a part of herself instead of getting rid of her past. Growth is not about purging ("expressing") your emotions—it's about taking more in.

This process of digesting her own aggression and anger is what we talked about last chapter as the fuel to *fuck*. It turns vitriol into lubrication.

Although Audrey and Peter got angry at their parents, our focus stayed on their replay of family dynamics in the present rather than on exploring the past. They knew enough to see multiple levels of meaning in their daily interactions. We focused on what they were *doing*—not just on "understanding"—to avoid interpretations and theories. Peter and Audrey talked about their feelings when they wanted to understand *themselves* better—not to get validation and understanding from each other. In the process they learned about each other, but that wasn't our primary focus. It did, however, create a new basis for self-validated intimacy: when you know yourself—when who you are doesn't hinge on what your partner feels—you have something to disclose to your partner and the self-support to listen to his disclosures. Peter and Audrey became less overreactive to each other's anxieties.

What's important in this approach is not the fact that Audrey and Peter had "childhood wounds" but *how they resolved them.* We made no attempt to explain away Audrey's mother's behavior by hypothesizing that she too had been wounded by her parents. The lack of accountability this theorizing encourages is antithetical to what the solution required. What was important was whether or not Audrey was going to stand up, unilaterally confront herself and her life, and become the person she wanted to be.

This has interesting implications for forgiveness. When we stand up and confront ourselves in ways our parents have not, a desire for justice makes it harder to forgive them in some ways. However, the increased differentiation this endeavor provides allows one to better self-soothe, to validate one's own experience, thereby unhooking the need for confession from one's parent. At this point, forgiveness becomes an act of self-caring and a deliberate decision to get on with one's life.

There was an intricate interweaving of "moves" by Peter and Audrey that occurred as they confronted themselves. During one session Audrey told Peter she didn't have much sexual desire because she didn't respect him. It was a statement about herself rather than an accusation. She felt defective for *not* respecting him and was appropriately cautious about hurting him. But she was also stating her preferences. She knew what she found appealing in a man, and she wasn't apologizing for that anymore.

Peter was hurt and started to regress. *"So you respected those beach bums you fucked?!"*

I helped him pull himself together by pointing out several things: Audrey *said* she was having difficulty respecting him, rather than acting out her disrespect. Paradoxically, she was finally treating him respectfully by telling him of her disrespect. She was treating him as if he could take it and conduct himself as a man—a man who didn't need to be propped up, a man who could confront the truth without falling apart. Audrey was actually treating *both* of them respectfully for the first time in years. She wasn't demeaning herself or him.

The question on the table was: would Peter regress and punish her for telling the truth? Or would he face the truth as he knew it and do what he thought was right? Peter later said that he'd come too far to throw away his hard-earned progress. He swallowed hard and pulled himself together.

"I guess I don't blame you. I don't have much respect for myself."

This stark admission sent a jolt through all three of us. Peter wasn't dodging self-confrontation, or raging, or apologizing. His voice was steady and accepting. In this self-revelation Peter was the epitome of self-respect. He didn't blow up and he didn't cave in. He just settled down. All three of us were a little amazed by how quickly he did it.

This session had quite an impact on Audrey. She *fucked* Peter that night. Audrey's step forward had given Peter moments of anxiety, disequilibrium, and further growth. His own step forward had done the same for Audrey.

Peter thought he would never get over the pain of Audrey's affairs— or of being mind-fucked about her eroticism. But confronting himself healed him in a way he couldn't have foreseen. Even the process was different from what he had imagined. Only in retrospect did he realize he had gotten over his sense of betrayal. It happened as he learned to take care of himself. As he stopped taking other people's behavior as a reflection upon himself, his self-respect grew. He was on his way to resolution before Audrey expressed remorse for her affairs.

In one of our next sessions Audrey spoke of this to Peter.

"I *am* sorry."

"Thank you."

After they exchanged soothing words, I spoke to Audrey. "I'm sure you are sorry. That has to do with you. But if your statement has anything to do with Peter, the issue becomes *remorse*. True remorse involves more than a verbal acknowledgment; it also requires an immediate change in behavior."

"Meaning I have to have sex with him if he wants it but I don't."

"Meaning you are straight about when you want it and when you don't. If you don't want it, say so in ways that make *you* vulnerable rather than him."

"What if I don't know if I want sex before we start?"

"Then *you* struggle with it. It's your lack of clarity. Make it your problem instead of his."

"I want to see more of the Audrey I saw in bed last night."

Peter and Audrey returned to the next session amazed it didn't take years for her to get over her "mysterious" difficulty during sex—or her crisis of being like her mother. In explaining the rapid change, Audrey said, "I have more important things to do with my time."

"You mean you're not willing to kill the good times now by being angry about the past? What's the matter with you? Don't you listen to your parents?"

Audrey smiled with pride. "I guess not. You just can't count on children these days!"

I smiled back.

Peter was glowing about their encounter—but it also worried him. "What if *that* Audrey doesn't show up again?"

"Well, you can either demand it or be the Peter to whom she's attracted—the man you're attracted to also. You can decide which is more likely to bring her around."

"I'd rather be the Peter *I'm* attracted to."

"Don't let me stand in your way."

Peter and I looked at each other with appreciation. After a respectful pause Audrey spoke up.

"You believed in me, didn't you?"

"Yes, I did."

"I didn't see that at the time. Now I believe in myself. Maybe part of it is that you believed in me. I think a lot of it comes from confronting myself. When you didn't budge, I hated you—but somehow it also made you trustworthy. I really thought terrible things about you for the longest time."

"It's part of the deal."

Enjoying Your "B-a-a-d, Nasty" Side

Recognizing hatred in your spouse (particularly a beloved one) is hard. Acknowledging the hateful, malicious, and vindictive in yourself isn't much easier. It requires integrity and the ability to self-soothe.

Denial has its price. Your ability to really *do* your spouse comes from the same place within as your urge to "screw him over." Confronting normal marital sadism has its positive side: it's the path to accepting that you can love and hate the same person at the same time. And to being really *b-a-a-d.* That low, drawn-out exclamation, "Oooh, you are so *nasty!*" Getting so you can *enjoy* your nasty side and put it to good use is a real accomplishment.

As stated last chapter, hatred and aggression—and carnivorous sexual intent—aren't our "dark" side. Our dark side is the side that denies its own existence. That's what normal marital sadism does. When we deny the hateful side of ourselves, we wreak havoc on others in the name of love. Acknowledging normal marital sadism makes it possible to stop the cycle of sadism and denial. Self-confrontation and self-soothing make it a reality. That reality includes our ability to *fuck* our spouse.

Many people like "naughtiness" in their sex, but being "naughty" with your spouse takes a level of development few of us reach. Have you any idea how long it takes to get really *good* at being *b-a-a-d?* Many of us die never having really explored our sexual potential. A dose of *b-a-a-dness* makes engaging your partner during sex more likely—and more interesting. It's the part of eroticism we usually hide and it opens options for diverse styles of sex. The bawdy-house songs that accompanied the birth of jazz celebrated it. Just listen to Bessy Smith's "Copulatin' Blues" talkin' 'bout "*B-a-a-d* Momma and her sweet 'jelly role'!"

Chapter 12

Hold onto Yourself: Your Crucible Survival Guide

> If only we arrange our life according to that principle which
> counsels us that we must always hold to the difficult, then that
> which now still seems to us the most alien will become what we
> most trust and find most faithful.
>
> —*Rainer Maria Rilke*

A couple once entered their therapy session offering me a gift. It was a framed cartoon strip from the syndicated "Hagar the Horrible" series. In it, Hagar and his friend struggle up a high mountaintop to ask the Great Guru the secret of true happiness. There the Guru informs them the path to happiness is deprivation, abstinence, poverty, and celibacy. Hagar's response is to ask, "Is there someone else up here I can talk to?"

This simple cartoon carries many meanings. The surface message is clear: we all want a way around our problems. Couples don't run to therapy at the first sign of trouble. Researchers estimate it often takes five to seven years for some to seek help. Like prisoners exploring every nook of our cell, we search for some way out, avoiding the open door that would lead us through our gridlock. When desperate that an escape hatch might not exist, we finally seek a therapist. We may doubt our own abilities at this point—but we never doubt that therapists have clever tricks to get us around our problems without going through them.

Few of us enter therapy to change ourselves—we are usually seeking ways to change our situation or our spouse, while we remain the same. We seek out simple tips, techniques, and benedictions that tell us how to communicate and be compassionate (read: easy ways to feel understood and receive compassion). The underlying message of any ther-

322

apeutic technique is, "Apply this properly and your problem will dissolve." But techniques can't dissolve interpersonal problems—only changes in us can do that.

I'm not suggesting that you should be eager to change. None of us is. Changing yourself is hard. Many people want to be grown up (the end result), but few want the struggle of growing up (going through the process). But the system of marriage seems to be constructed to take this into account: there is no way around your marital gridlock—you've already tried that in your prior attempts, to no avail—but there is a way through it.

This is another meaning in the Hagar the Horrible cartoon: our tendency to look to someone else for the answer. In the psychotherapy setting, it is the therapist who becomes the Great Guru. My clients' gift symbolized deeper truths they had learned in therapy with me. The Guru's advice to Hagar the Horrible about happiness required self-mastery and self-control. Hagar's journey to pose the question about happiness to the Guru contained the answer he sought—and the process he wanted to avoid: self-mastery to get to the top of the mountain, enduring hardship, braving danger, self-soothing with well-needed rest, and pushing oneself forward when necessary. This is what my clients had learned: that the "trip up the mountain" embedded in their own marriage was the path to their happiness, to the capacity to love on life's terms.

Holding onto Yourself

Going through gridlock in your marriage is much like climbing a mountain: if you feel in control of yourself, rather than trying to control the terrain and weather, you can relax and enjoy the climb. When you're tense and feeling out of control, the climb seems far more difficult. It helps if you keep in mind that you never really master the mountain—you master yourself in the process of climbing the mountain. The mountain remains the same; it is you who changes. And, remember, you have to climb several mountains before you feel confident of yourself—but you can't wait until you feel safe and secure before you venture out for your first climb.

My clients and workshop participants use one guideline that sums up the process of self-mastery and self-control: "Hold onto yourself!" They use it as a mantra to center and refocus whenever events or interactions threaten to swamp them.

"Hold onto yourself" is a simple idea with many meanings. Self-mastery and self-control involve learning about yourself, confronting yourself and shifting to self-validated intimacy, and taking care of yourself (self-soothing). Learning to hold onto yourself nudges your personal development and your marriage forward, and fundamentally changes how you and your partner interact. Holding onto yourself is a shorthand way of talking about differentiation. It involves several activities and processes:

- *Maintaining a clear sense of who you are* as you become increasingly intimate with a partner who is increasingly more important to you; knowing what you value and believe, and not defending a false or inaccurate self-picture.
- *Maintaining a sense of perspective* about your anxieties, limitations, and shortcomings so that they neither drive nor immobilize you.
- *The willingness to engage in self-confrontation* necessary for your growth. This includes standing up to your fears—taking the hits about yourself, your family of origin, your marriage, and your life; confronting your own selfishness, hatred, manipulation of others, sadism, withholding, and self-denigrations; and resisting your attempts to avoid yourself.
- *Acknowledging your projections and distortions* and admitting when you are wrong—whether or not your partner does likewise.
- *Tolerating the pain involved in growing;* mobilizing yourself toward the growth you value and aspire to; soothing your own hurts when necessary, without excessive self-indulgence; supporting rather than berating yourself.

Holding onto yourself—maintaining a relationship with yourself—is not easy. However, the benefits to you and your marriage are incalculable. Your ability to hold onto yourself allows you to pull out of negative interactions and conduct yourself in ways that lead to positive ones. It lets you break the "set" of your communications—habitual topics, patterns, intensity, and tone. Instead of *matching* your partner's feelings and emotional tone when you're locked in protracted arguments, bad feelings, or flaring tempers, holding onto yourself allows you to break free of this form of emotional gridlock called "negative affect reciprocity."

Holding onto yourself means you don't "go down" with your partner when he or she becomes depressed, despondent, and hopeless. Often this is interpreted as a lack of caring or empathy. ("If you understood or cared about me, you'd feel as bad as I do!") But not getting upset whenever your partner is distraught stabilizes your relationship. Poorly differentiated people can only contain their reactivity by becoming indifferent. The ability to hold onto yourself permits deep connection with your partner's feelings without breaking contact or becoming reactive.

When you have a firm hold on yourself, you can allow yourself to be influenced by your spouse (and others)—while, at the same time, remaining resilient to pressure to conform when it's against your better judgment or feelings. Having a solid but permeable self allows you to take others into account; there is room for your spouse's reality without losing your own. You can be interested in his position during arguments rather than trying to dispute it.

Holding onto yourself permits true *mutuality*. Facilitating your partner's goals at the expense of your own involves going with your deepest values rather immediate personal gratification. The personal "expense" doesn't stem from losing yourself; it's part of the two-choice dilemmas inherent in marriage: often you have to sacrifice your own prerogative to further your partner's agenda. This can be extremely gratifying—but you have to be able to self-soothe the resulting inner tension and losses that result.

Holding onto yourself is a key ingredient in intimacy and sex. Intimacy involves self-confrontation and self-disclosure in the presence of your partner. When you don't hold onto yourself, intimacy always suffers. And holding onto yourself is vital if you want more sexual passion, novelty, and desire in your marriage.

One particular form of holding onto yourself—self-confrontation—is so fundamental to going through marital gridlock, and so radically changes the pattern in your marriage, that we will consider it in depth.

Self-Control Lets You Stop Controlling Your Partner

Your marriage is a complex system geared around self-mastery. Emotionally committed relationships respond better when each partner controls, confronts, soothes, and mobilizes himself/herself—and that's exactly what dynamics in your relationship will push you to do. This involves pushing your differentiation forward by addressing developmental tasks that lie before you.

When you can control yourself, you have less need to control your partner. Mastering yourself through marriage's two-choice dilemmas and interlocking effects creates a more stable and enjoyable relationship. Avoiding self-mastery makes you and your spouse like the prisoners mentioned earlier. Emotional Siamese twins are like prisoners on a chain gang shackled together, constantly irritating each other, needing to control their partner so they can move. Self-mastery, in contrast, is the basis of cooperation. Even well-differentiated couples face the reciprocal impacts inherent in marriage—the difference is how they respond. And even well-differentiated couples don't always respond ideally.

Ruth and I have taken many trips up the mountain, both metaphorical and actual. And I've seen Hagar the Horrible in myself more times than I care to recall. During the course of our marriage we've both had more opportunities than we wanted for self-confrontation and self-soothing, pushing our own limits, daring to be what we aspire, and going forward in the face of doubt, adversity, and hardship. Along the way we've learned that confronting ourselves (instead of each other) holds many rewards.

Ruth and I are avid backpackers and we've worked on our marital issues on many mountain trips (and from opposite ends of a canoe). My interest in rugged hiking exceeds hers and precedes her; it's something I did long before we met. Ruth took it up and it's something we now share. Because my legs are longer I often walk ahead of her, stopping at intervals for rest, company, and safety. We see this as the "differentiated" way to hike. Sometimes we walk at our different natural paces, enjoying the silence and freedom of interest and attention. I usually scout out good places to stop, help Ruth with her pack when she arrives, and offer her refreshments I've arranged, since I've had time to revive. Sometimes we walk together, sharing the moment or traversing difficult terrain. Overall our pleasure conjointly and separately is enhanced.

My physical size makes rugged trips easier for me. When Ruth tries hard I cut her lots of slack: I give her lots of latitude and consideration for her effort. But cutting Ruth slack doesn't mean I expect less from her. I still expect her to take care of herself, carry her own load, and function to her capacity. When I see her really trying, I relax. I'm agreeable to her suggestions and thoughtful of her needs. I don't feel I'm dragging her up the mountain or making her do it. I'm quick to help her with a blister or muscle cramp and give her time to recover. I know we'll get to our destination as quickly *and enjoyably* as possible if I let her set her own pace. Ruth isn't at her best if I monitor her progress. That makes her nervous and she feels pressured and controlled by me.

Does this start to sound condescending towards Ruth? That's probably because everything here is from my perspective—something that's easy for me to lose track of when I'm focusing on how magnanimous I am. What I haven't said—and sometimes overlook—is that all this occurs because Ruth is willing to accept my pacing, she is considerate of our differences, and she's willing to go into the boonies with me in the first place. She's not the "passive" or "lesser" partner she might appear from my description. It's easy for me to lose sight of how I subtly establish my pace as the correct pace—and when I do, I'm one step closer to making us both miserable. When I confront myself on my egocentrism, I'm less self-righteous and more considerate.

The same is generally true in marriage. The entire system operates differently—more effectively—when partners push themselves to address their own issues involved in their gridlocked situation. I become considerate if Ruth says this is truly an inopportune time for her. Some issues, like some difficult mountain climbs, are foolhardy to take on when you're not up to it. When I ask Ruth with concern and caring on the trail, "Are you really up to this? You weren't feeling good this morning. Maybe should we take it easy today?" she is more likely to say, "No. I'm just a bit off. Come on, let's go. We'll be glad we did this."

This holds true as long as I see some effort from Ruth in the immediate future. It's easy to be considerate of each other when you have faith your partner wants to go up the mountain with you, whether it's your marriage or Mount Rainier. I am much more tolerant of Ruth's physical limitations (from my perspective) when I see she is trying to do something about them. And conversely, she is more tolerant of my ungracious attitudes when she sees I'm confronting *myself* about them.

In part, this has been our lesson that relationships go well when both partners self-confront and drive themselves forward. In part, it also demonstrates how easy it is to claim the pivotal position around which your spouse is supposed to revolve. Both have been important for us to remember.

When you don't see your partner self-confronting and self-managing as best she can—especially when she is—the walk up the mountain (and your marriage) is entirely different. I'm not as considerate when I feel I'm driving the whole process forward single-handedly. My voice has been known to take on a guilt-producing accusatory or angry tone. As Ruth arrives at our rest stop, I mention how long I've been waiting in a humorless way. I complain she's moving slowly, especially if she's stopped to rest before catching up with me. (I then put more distance between rest stops to make up for "lost time.") I act superior and demean how far she's come. I fear compliments and consideration will encourage her to walk slower. I act as if she'll walk faster if she knows I'm unhappy. I talk about the importance of making our intended campsite rather than enjoying the moment—or her company. I walk ahead while Ruth stops to catch her breath; she takes her rest stop alone and without peace. Ruth becomes more resistant and participates begrudgingly (which I use to prove my suspicions). My behavior pushes Ruth to give up the rest she needs. We shift from being teammates: I become the slave driver, and Ruth becomes the slave.

The good news for us is that this happens infrequently—I've improved a lot as I've gotten older. If this were a common occurrence, Ruth wouldn't even accompany me to the trail head. The bad news is that it can still happen. In part, that's because becoming more differentiated hasn't made me perfect (although that's no excuse). In part, it happens because self-mobilization (or lack thereof)—self-confrontation and self-soothing—inherently affects emotionally committed relationships. It's part of a system that exists independent of specific issues at hand.

At this point (when it happens) I have my own two-choice dilemma: I can give up my mental time schedule—which has become *the* schedule—calm myself down, relax, and enjoy the trip. Or, I can keep the fantasy in my head of how things are supposed to be—and rush Ruth, go slower, and lose our enjoyment. I'm clear about which choice I really want: I want Ruth to walk faster, eagerly, so we can stay on (my) schedule so we can "both" be happy. (I know I'd be happy—if Ruth just did it happily and fit into my plans. That's my notion of "both be happy" in this idealization.) Unfortunately, I don't have this choice when I want it the most—and that frustrates me. (More accurately, I frustrate myself.) But "taking your own shape" (differentiation) is about recognizing that your plan is just your plan, and not somebody else's.

When I have myself under control, I relax and we have a good time. When I've lost my grip on myself and can't self-soothe, I take my frustrations out on both of us and make things worse. More than once we've faced a two-choice dilemma on the trail: give up being together when we couldn't agree or get along, or adapt in some way and maintain positive frequent contact. Walking separately when this happens is entirely different from walking separately with a positive connection between us. Backpacking, like sex, always has a "tone."

On the trail and at home, most times Ruth and I operate in a positive system of mutual good will (therapists call this "positive affect override"): we give each other the benefit of the doubt when things are unclear or uncertain. And we remember enough positive interactions between us to plow through potentially difficult situations and turn them into positive experiences. It gives us more incentive and ability to tackle the issues that would become negative if we got bogged down in the middle of them. But this mutuality hasn't come from mutual stroking—it's evolved from shared adventures, hardships, and conflicts that build mutual respect and admiration. We've witnessed each other's willingness to self-confront, to each do our best, and to operate with integrity. But not always—and we pay dearly when it's not the case.

Are You the High Desire or Low Desire Partner This Time?

Both aspects of holding onto yourself—*self-confrontation* and *self-soothing*—fundamentally change the basis of your relationship and your patterns of interaction. When these aspects are absent in one partner but present in the other—or it looks that way to you—the impact is dramatic. For example, when you see your partner stonewalling on gridlock issues, or demanding reassurances and promises before he takes a step, or complaining every step of the way, you're much less likely to be patient and understanding. It begins to seem as if talking about his fears is really code for "I don't want to change and I'm not going to."

There is a high-desire and a low-desire partner on almost every marital issue—and these positions often reverse across the many issues married couples face. In my marriage, for example, I am the high-desire partner when it comes to having sex—but I was the low-desire partner when it came to having a baby. The effect that mobilizing yourself or not has on your marriage depends on whether you're the high- or low-desire partner: when I bought lingerie for Ruth, it had one meaning. When she showed up in bed with something she had purchased on her own, it had another. The difference in meanings to each of us changed the nature of the sex and connection we shared. The tone and pattern of our interactions were fundamentally different, as was the way we affected each other. So were the times I said something positive about having children, as opposed to when Ruth did.

Who schedules the vacations? Who puts the kids to bed early? Who closes the bedroom door? Who scouts out the next car or house to buy? The impact of each action depends on who did it: the high-desire or low-desire partner. The issue isn't the behavior but the meaning of the behavior in the context of partners' positions in the marriage.

Are you the high-desire or low-desire partner on a particular issue? It makes no difference if it's sex, intimacy, spending money, visiting in-laws, or disciplining your kids when they need it. If you're the low-desire partner, confronting and mobilizing yourself settles your marital system down. If you're the high-desire partner, mobilizing yourself heats things up when your spouse refuses to do likewise—which is why the high-desire partner often stops self-mobilizing and the tyranny of the lowest common denominator surfaces. (Or, the high-desire partner tries to bludgeon the low-desire partner into mobilizing in the same direction.) If the high-desire partner perseveres while the low-desire partner remains inactive, both spouses eventually confront the two-choice dilemma: give up one's goals and values or possibly give up one's spouse.

This can be the low-desire partner deciding he/she really doesn't want what the spouse does (e.g., more sex, more discipline for the kids, or having a child). Other times this occurs by the low-desire partner dragging his or her heels on the gridlocked issue—refusing to self-confront and self-soothe—and expecting the high-desire partner to slow down.

Paradoxically, when you stop expecting your partner to put up with your limitations, he or she becomes more willing to do just that, which creates a dynamic push for growth. When partners won't confront themselves they start confronting each other instead, attempting to control their partner to keep from feeling pressured by the marital system. (We saw this last chapter, when Audrey felt pressured to have sex simply because Peter didn't want to give up his right to have it.) Partners who hold onto themselves don't have the same need to control each other; they can encounter their partner's influence without feeling engulfed.

The impact of self-soothing on the development of mutuality is similar to that of self-confrontation. Placing the burden of controlling your anxiety on your relationship makes it rigid and inflexible. Partners' willingness and ability to self-soothe impact how they affect and try to control each other. When you are the low-desire partner and you're willing to self-soothe, your partner is more likely to be patient, more willing to soothe you, too. Self-soothing on the high-desire partner's part also quiets down the system. And as with Peter, the high-desire partner must soothe the fear that self-soothing is a dodge from recognizing that his partner isn't going to "walk up the mountain"—at least on this particular issue. (We'll talk more about self-soothing after we discuss confronting your personal crucible in your marital gridlock.)

Holding onto Yourself Doesn't Have to Be Adversarial

Holding onto yourself isn't the same thing as an adversarial stance against your partner. If you're being adversarial, you're not really self-validating. The outcome of self-confrontation around conflicts of interest is usually the exact opposite; it diminishes hostility and manipulation. Holding onto yourself actually promotes good will, although it doesn't look that way to your partner when he or she is "losing it." I know this from personal experience.

Twelve years ago, on one particularly difficult stretch of a long mountain ascent, Ruth didn't show up when I stopped to wait for her. I began to worry as time went on, but I also wasn't eager to retrace my hard-earned progress. Another two-choice dilemma. Eventually I found Ruth several miles back, sitting on the trail; she was overjoyed to see me. I responded angrily, relieved but frustrated that she was in none of the dangers I had imagined.

Ruth had wandered off the trail where it was poorly marked and found her way back—but she wasn't sure how to proceed, and getting lost would put her, and our trip, in jeopardy. She decided on the prudent course of action: she sat down where she knew I'd find her when I came to look for her. There was nothing adversarial about the way Ruth had held onto herself. This wasn't just common sense (which many novice hikers lack); it involved her differentiation—she could have given into her anxieties and wandered off in search of me. She was scared (as I was) about hunters in the area (whom we had previously run into and knew had been drinking). She was also worried about my worrying about her. (In retrospect, we realized we should have walked this stretch together.)

I, however, could not contain my frustration. I was exhausted, cold, and hungry, and I "lost it." My physical and emotional resources were spent; I just couldn't soothe myself. I dimly realized Ruth was trying to be thoughtful and responsible. But I had spent the intervening time alternating between worrying about her and assassinating her character—working myself up instead of soothing myself down. I accused her of slacking off, giving up too easily, giving into her anxiety, expecting me to come to her, making me do all the work. Imagine an alligator in hiking boots! That characterizes my level of functioning—socially and brain-wise—at that moment on the mountain.

Ruth had done nothing wrong. She then held onto herself for a second time that afternoon: she didn't get defensive about my tirade, which allowed me to get a hold of myself. This wasn't my usual style of relating to Ruth, and this unfortunate incident helped it become even less so. I confronted a pattern I perceived in myself that I intensely disliked: not appreciating what people did for me, imagining the worst in them, and holding them accountable for my happiness. This was emotional fusion, expecting them to read my mind or do as I would have done. Self-confrontation and self-soothing turned me from reptile to mammal and eventually back to a human: I apologized to Ruth and acknowledged I was wrong. (I'm not proud of this incident, but the use I derived from it then, and the insight you may gain from it now, gives it some redeeming value.)

Holding onto yourself isn't about fighting off your partner's influence or control. Sometimes holding onto yourself is about holding to a particular perception of reality or exercising a particular option. The crucible in any relationship becomes apparent the moment one partner defines a self that reduces the other's options: when one partner starts to control himself/herself, the other partner feels controlled. Even in highly differentiated relationships, one partner's redefinition reduces the options of the other, because the options in a marital *system* are finite in many respects.

Holding onto yourself doesn't have to be adversarial, but it often feels and looks that way at first. (There are predictable times when the process becomes adversarial. We'll talk more about when and why this occurs in the next chapter.) People who feel they have "lost themselves" in their marriage tend to be adamant and reactive when they first start to hold on—like adolescents, who view their parents as the enemy holding them captive. When we give ourselves up, we blame our partner for "taking us over" and demand our "space" back.

At our Couples Retreats there is often an ongoing chorus of laments and complaints: "I've lost myself—I don't even know who I am anymore!" "I've humiliated myself!" "I've sold out my integrity!" When people feel like they're desperately holding onto their tenuous sense of self, they don't tend to be gentle or refined. Sometimes they take stands they feel are necessary but which create irreconcilable differences. Having proven to *themselves* that they won't sell out to their own anxiety, however, they often become more flexible.

Couples who go through their crucible are less adversarial and more respectful of their partners' separateness. They realize they didn't get themselves back from their partner—*they stopped letting go of themselves.* Sometimes holding on involves maintaining their position in the face of pressure to conform—but not the way couples first envision the process. They stop trying to disprove their partner's arguments or perceptions and start confronting themselves instead.

Holding onto Yourself Requires an Accurate Picture

Though pursuing marital happiness is never easy, it's often harder than it needs to be. Scaling marriage's heights is more difficult when your "trail map" is inaccurate. Couples think they are "off the path" when they encounter gridlock—when often that means they're "on." Their assumption that gridlock shouldn't be happening sends them looking for a detour around their "road block" instead of going through it. But the marital trek is further complicated by an inaccurate picture of who's going on the journey.

We all have distorted views of our own lives—it's part of being human. We develop ways of stringing together events that are plausible and give them particular meaning. Sometimes we create overly bland pictures of our childhoods; other times we may overemphasize some points and ignore others. Overall, the interpretation and emotional impact of things remembered—not just things forgotten—are blunted. The truth is often hidden—right out in the open—camouflaged as something else. People make a lot more sense (and seem less crazy) when their picture is accurately focused; until then the hazy image can be interpreted in ways that they prefer.

We've encountered many examples previously. Audrey (last chapter) wanted to picture herself as a victim instead of a perpetrator. Bill (Chapters 3 and 4) wanted to see himself as "easygoing" and his family as "close-knit" so he could avoid confronting his feelings of being exploited; he didn't appreciate it when Joan pointed out another view of their weekly family dinners. Warren (Chapters 5 and 6) tried to act like his childhood with his alcoholic mother was no big deal so he wouldn't have to confront its impact. His wife, Carol, tried to convince herself that her low sexual desire stemmed from one incident when her grandfather was sexually inappropriate, thereby ignoring years of subtle abuse from her parents.

Invariably, poorly differentiated people hold onto the part of themselves that constructed the distorted self-portrait. They demand that their partner understand them, in part, because they don't really understand themselves. They feel understood, accepted, and validated when their partner sees them the way they picture themselves. Their partner's refusal to see them the way they want to be seen is upsetting. But the problem isn't a failure to communicate: their spouse *can't* understand them the way they demand, because they view their own behavior and the details of their life differently than their partner does. This discrepancy challenges their inaccurate picture of themselves— which they have difficulty maintaining to begin with.

You may think it's a problem when your partner won't "accept you the way you are," but consider what happens when you demand that he validate the distorted lens you use to look at yourself, your life, and your marriage. The problem in many marriages is not that spouses won't validate each other, it's that *what gets validated is an inaccurate self-portrait.* Distortions and projections keep us from seeing our partners and ourselves. That's important to remember next time you feel like demanding that your partner "understand" you the way you understand yourself.

When your efforts to improve yourself or your marriage seem to be going nowhere—with or without a therapist's assistance—it often stems from using an inaccurate self-picture. The resulting failures make you think your problems are more severe or ingrained than you feared. More strenuous effort doesn't help, as long as your picture remains inaccurate. Once you've allowed an accurate picture to form, it's easier to hold onto yourself—although it still isn't easy (particularly, at first).

Constructing Your Crucible

If you construct your crucible of self-confrontation, as I'm about to outline, you can do for yourself what I help my clients do: you can get a more accurate self-picture, increase your ability to hold onto yourself (raise your level of differentiation), and change the dynamics in your relationship. You can discover how personal development and relationship development can occur in mutually facilitating ways—and replot your trail map of how marriage works. But knowing what to do is not the same as doing it. If you're not able to apply these suggestions to yourself, a therapist can help. (See referral information at the end of this book.)

Basically, constructing your crucible involves extracting your unresolved personal issues embedded in your gridlocked situation and confronting them as an act of integrity. You do this unilaterally, without counting on your partner to do likewise, and without getting lost in what he is or isn't doing. Sometimes this involves owning your projections, even when your partner doesn't reciprocate. You focus on yourself instead of "working on your relationship" or trying to change your partner. You stop trying to make your partner listen, validate, or accept you; you listen to yourself. It's not easy, but this act of integrity is possible when you let the best in you run the show.

Ruth presented me with a chance to practice what I preach. As we discussed in the last chapter, the system of marriage is such that when one partner goes into the crucible, it impacts both partners. Both high-desire and low-desire partners on any issue face—or dodge—self-confrontation. My wife created a growth opportunity for me I didn't welcome: after a difficult period of self-confrontation, Ruth stopped taking birth control pills because she wanted to have a child. She was open about this and gave me the option of using condoms. Contraception became my responsibility since I wasn't quite ready to have a child.

I wish I had been differentiated enough to have recognized the legitimacy of Ruth's position and acted accordingly. But I had to push it, mounting arguments and statistics to change her mind: condoms reduced my pleasure; birth control pills offered greater reliability, etc. In all honesty, I wanted to see if Ruth would back down and indulge me. She didn't.

When we had first discussed the possibility of marriage, I outlined my stance to her: I hoped I would eventually decide to have kids, but if I remained unsure, I planned to regret not having kids rather than have them and resent them.

Ruth had thought long and hard about her position regarding birth control. She was ready to have a child. She wasn't trying to force me to have one—she just couldn't participate any longer in ways antithetical to her own desires. It was as much about birthing herself as it was about conceiving a child. It wasn't that having a baby (whose father didn't want it) would make Ruth more of a person; she was calling the issue to a head in a way I could not ignore. Ruth was daring to live what we offer our clients and she knew I wasn't going to applaud. Ruth held onto herself. She was well-positioned in our conflict of interest and stood her ground. I admired her decision. She really pissed me off.

My decision about children heated up. No amount of oral sex could avoid the birth control issue or the differentiation taking place. And, ironically, the more I respected how Ruth handled herself, the less daunting my fears of having a child seemed. Gradually two things happened: I got fed up using condoms. And having a child seemed more like what I wanted to do. Then I found myself in another crucible: was I just giving in because that was easier, or was I really ready to be a father? Was I making my own decision or deferring responsibility to Ruth? I knew I preferred regretting never having a child over having one I resented. But why did I have to approach the situation as if I was going to make a mistake I'd regret? Maybe I could go after what I wanted rather than striving to protect myself, as I had been doing. What did I really want?

I had empathy for Ruth's situation—and that increased my dilemma. I felt selfish being preoccupied with "protecting myself" knowing that Ruth was clear she wanted children. Understanding each other's feelings didn't solve the problem—we both felt worse.

I went through a difficult time for which I'm thankful—after the fact. This crucible helped me see that I really wanted a child, too. Our wonderful daughter and our marriage are the result. If you're interested in going through a similar process—without a guarantee of similar results (I didn't get one either)—here's how to build your crucible:

•*Look within your gridlocked issue or situation and extract your own unresolved developmental tasks.* In other words, approach your gridlock as a personal dilemma to be solved, rather than as a situational problem or your partner's problem. You'll lose your puffed-up sense of righteous indignation and you won't feel like a victim. Think of someone who would respond to the situation quite differently from the way you do, and you'll realize that your reaction is not inherent in the situation; it has something to do with you.

Focus on your own issues to identify ways in which you are contributing to your own unhappiness. How is this current situation personally relevant to you? How have you construed or constructed similar situations with other people? How will *going through* your current situation help you develop enough to resolve this pattern in a more permanent way?

Looking into my difficulty deciding whether or not I really wanted a child, for example, I found: (a) fear of resenting my child because I'd regret my decision, (b) fear of being stuck in my marriage by my responsibility as a father, (c) doubts about my parenting abilities, and (d) fear of competing with my child for Ruth's attention. I could see lots of positives in having a child, but these other issues were tying me up in knots.

•*Confront yourself for the sake of your own integrity and personal development.* Self-confrontation may be good for the soul—and your relationship—but that doesn't make it easy. Holding onto yourself requires giving up your favorite ways to dodge self-confrontation. It also involves lots of self-soothing for what you see when you stop slip-sliding away. That was certainly true in my own case: previously, I would have picked on Ruth, found fault with our relationship, or hid behind my work. I might have accused her of manipulating me, or used her stopping birth control as proof that what I wanted didn't matter to her. But the way she held onto herself made me look into myself. I didn't like what I saw. A dear friend asked me if there was room in my life for a child. At first I said that wasn't the issue. Then I realized I didn't want it to be the case—but it was. I ran into my selfishness and self-centeredness.

I also recognized my fears of replicating my own childhood—or at least my vision of it at the time. I had yet to realize how good my childhood was, and how fortunate I am to have the parents I do. I was still resolving my emotional fusion with my mother: I was not yet able to accept imperfection in her, I was still vulnerable to her anxieties, and I did not hold onto myself when I experienced her as intrusive. I was also not over my fears of women, still unable to own my overreactions, projections, and distortions.

One key to holding onto yourself is to stop disproving that there is "something wrong with you" or claiming that you're good enough the way you are. Stop inviting your partner to "prove" you need to change. People don't change when they feel under attack—and defending yourself invites attack. The issue isn't whether you're good enough the way you are. It's a question of who you want to be.

•*If you're having difficulty identifying your own issues, look at both sides of your two-choice dilemma.* How are the style and content of your dilemma characteristic of your life or particularly relevant for you? When have you faced something similar before—and dodged it? Here's another hint: think about what your partner frequently says about you that you vehemently dispute. Find ways that what your partner says is true. Your partner will probably be more than happy to "help." The task of marriage seems to be finding out who you really are—while fending off someone who's all too ready to tell you! (Social commentator H. L. Menckin said someone may be a fool and not know it—but not if he or she is married.)

•*Stop taking your partner's reaction personally.* If you can't get any mileage out of my last suggestion, try it the other way around. Ask yourself, *Why am I taking my partner's reaction personally and getting defensive?* Pull out the elements of your two-choice dilemma: (a) If you think you should take it personally, what is it you've been doing (or not doing) that leads you to assume your partner's reaction has anything to do with you? In other words, what culpability are you dodging that makes you reactive to what you claim is your partner's distortion? (b) If you're not culpable, why are you taking your partner's reaction personally? The answer to this question can't be found in blaming others in your past. It's about why you continue to react as you do and what you plan to do about it. The answer has to do with your inability to hold onto yourself in relation to your partner and your dependence on a reflected sense of self.

Notice that, either way, there is no need for defensiveness. Owning either answer leads you to develop more of a relationship with yourself, maintain your integrity, and reduce your reactivity (i.e., increase your differentiation).

•*Don't count on your partner to confront himself/herself in return.* You can't move forward by agreeing to acknowledge your issues as long as your partner does likewise. Breaking through gridlock requires the same solution as the fabled Gordian Knot. You don't "untie" it—you cut through it by unhooking from your partner and confronting yourself. If you demand reciprocity, your partner can control you and your marriage by simply refusing to confront himself/herself.

•*Forget about "working on your relationship" or the idea that "the relationship is the problem."* This usually doesn't work—and it's what couples try first. "There's something wrong with our relationship" usually means you want to work on your partner's half of it. When people say, "I'm not getting what I want out of our relationship," often the real issue is that they are not getting what they want out of themselves in their marriage. When they get what they want from themselves, they generally like their relationship more—or do something constructive about it. When you work on yourself you're working on your marriage—because when you change, your relationship changes.

•*Stop focusing on what your partner is (or isn't) doing. Focus on yourself.* Some therapists suggest that examining one's part in an interpersonal conflict takes the pressure off the partner and demonstrates courage, fairness, and goodwill that the partner will hopefully emulate. I believe this small truth masks a bigger one: focusing on yourself increases the pressure on your partner to change. Contrary to what you might fear, it doesn't give your partner permission to goof off. Being happy with yourself doesn't guarantee you'll be happy with your partner (although it's more likely). People who like themselves are discerning about who they spend time with. Goodwill may facilitate change, but poorly differentiated people are more likely to move when their two-choice dilemma hits "critical mass" (more about critical mass in Chapter 13).

•*Stop trying to change your partner. Pressuring your partner actually reduces the pressure on both of you for change.* When you stop avoiding your own two-choice dilemmas, you'll also stop cajoling your partner in any particular direction. You'll simply want him to stand up and define himself, too. You'll stop disputing his position and pay attention to his point of view so *you* can make intelligent decisions. If your partner thinks you're trying to drag him forward into your version of happiness and a better life, you make it safe for him to "dig in his heels" and remain complacent or resistant. When you stop pressuring your partner to change, it pushes you to clarify what you want and what you're willing to do to get it. When you're going to make decisions about the rest of your life, the safest thing your partner can do is make sure he is the person he wants to be.

•*For solutions, look in different directions from where you've looked in the past. Reconsider options you've previously rejected.* Gridlock narrows your perspectives and options. Reconsider issues, options, and solutions you've rejected as "unthinkable," "undoable," and "unacceptable"— especially the latter. Ask yourself, "What about me would have to change—or what would I have to accept or give up—for this to become a real option? Would I like myself more if I could do this?" Don't mistake this for the road to compromise. Sometimes you will realize that some things are truly non-negotiable. But more things become negotiable when you're not negotiating a reflected sense of self.

•*Stop trying to make your partner listen, accept, and validate you. Listen to yourself.* Wise sages from every age have noted that we see the world not as it is, but as we are. Insights are always true about the perceiver but not necessarily about what's perceived. Ask yourself, "What is it in me that predisposes me to see my partner this way?" Even when observations about our partner are accurate, arriving at this realization may mean that this particular truth is most relevant and timely to our own development.

•*Keep your mouth shut about your partner's issues—particularly concerning things you're certain are true.* "Sharing" your insights about your partner—especially when it repeatedly angers him—is more often an expression of your own need for validation. The more patently obvious the issues are to you (while remaining utterly mysterious to your spouse), the more crucial (and difficult) it is to remain quiet. Consider the wisdom of silence: don't let your partner fight with you instead of himself. Shift your efforts to being an expert on yourself. Prior generations recognized that marriage is often improved by the two or three things not said each day.

•*Don't identify with your feelings.* The issue isn't whether you're entitled to your feelings. If you're entitled to them, keep them. The problem is, the feelings we defend usually aren't the ones we want. If you want them to pass, stop making them an issue of your personal validity. Emotional Siamese twins can't change their feelings because those feelings are so integral to how they see themselves. They have no consistent sense of identity when their mood, behavior, or situation changes.

•*Pay attention to your tone.* There is a tone to what you say and do.

Your attitude while going through your crucible is just as important as when using the tools for connection: your emotional stance determines what you get out of the process. There are countless variations of tonality; "going through the motions," "cautiously curious," "militant," and "quietly determined," are just a few. "Quietly determined" happens to be the hallmark of people who have reached critical mass (discussed next chapter). But if you can't hold onto yourself and modulate your tone, then use it a different way: your tone can teach you a lot about yourself.

•*Own your projections as an act of integrity.* Recognizing your distortions and expectations from the past—disentangling inner and outer "realities"—is important and difficult work. It both requires and yields a kind of moral integrity that's severely limited in some people. Openly acknowledging your projections, especially when your partner is ready to blame everything on you, requires a deep breath and a leap of faith— not faith he won't try to use it against you some time (he probably will), but faith you will hold onto yourself when he does. Also remember, it isn't the end of the world when your self-disclosures are used against you. Relax. Hold onto yourself: stop being outraged or "wounded." It will raise your differentiation. Your partner is likely to stop abusing your self-revelations when he sees it doesn't work to his advantage anymore. If you won't disclose your distortions because you're anticipating your partner's response, you are still dependent on a reflected sense of self. Acknowledging your projections embodies tolerating pain for growth and maintaining a clear sense of self in close proximity to your partner.

•*Acting differentiated interferes with being differentiated.* Participants at the Couples Retreat often joke about not wanting to say or do anything that looks undifferentiated. Then they realize the paradox: trying to *act* differentiated is undifferentiated! Well-differentiated people don't worry about how they look or seek validation for being differentiated. Stop focusing on acting more differentiated (holier) than your spouse. Pay attention to who you are and who you want to be.

•*Let the best in you do the thinking and talking.* There is a place within each of us that recognizes the truth when we're confronted with it. That moment of recognition comes from the part that knows right from wrong and values justice. Let what's good in you, the part that can do something new, do the listening. Nothing's going wrong when you find yourself confronted with difficult two-choice dilemmas about what you hold dear. It's part of living. I have found that speaking to the best part of people evokes the best in them; spouses become less adversarial and more preoccupied with confronting the reality of their own lives.

Carl Jung said, "To become acquainted with oneself is a terrible shock." It's hard admitting that our lives are full of error and self-deception. But this very admission, though painful, makes possible its opposite—a differentiated life, lived with integrity. Tears of recognition and relief often flow with the dawn of self-awareness. But while the truth will set you free, remember psychologist Erich Fromm's observation of humankind's attempt to escape from such freedom. The truth is liberating—but only when you have the courage to live it.

"Taking the Hit" and Soothing Yourself

Now I want to focus on another aspect of holding onto yourself: modulating your own anxiety and not taking on your partner's.

It's often hard to "take the hit" of going through your crucible and moving on. That's why many of us have yet to "get a life." (We get a support group instead.) "Taking the hit" refers to the subjective experience of challenging your identity, your world view, and your relationship. Self-soothing decreases marital mayhem by reducing your reactivity and the chance of emotional or physical violence. "Taking the hit" develops your ability to modulate your own anxiety and tolerate the pain of growth (differentiation). It means going through—not around—your two-choice dilemmas without reflexively stopping the process because it hurts or makes you nervous.

Becoming more differentiated is gut-wrenchingly difficult work. Usually, only extreme circumstances are sufficient to provoke the personal metamorphosis that is part and parcel of differentiation. Within the context of marriage these circumstances often involve the violation of your mutual validation pact and a shift to self-validated intimacy by one partner. Though circumstances and issues differ for each couple, they are uniformly disruptive, alienating, and upsetting—yet paradoxically lead to a more solid sense of self and greater depth of connection, when responded to in a conscious way.

Oysters don't produce pearls because they want to make something beautiful—pearls are the byproduct of an attempt to reduce their irritation (a grain of sand). Like the action of the oyster in response to the sand, self-soothing turns marriage's irritants into useful and productive relationship gems. Earlier we discussed how marriage is a system that is affected by spouses' self-confrontation. Self-soothing has a similar impact. The more partners can regulate their own anxiety (hold onto themselves), the more stable their relationship becomes and the less need they have to control each other. Hugging till relaxed illustrates how holding onto yourself makes you better equipped to hold your partner without needing to lean on or cling to him/her.

When we expect our partner to shield and protect us from anxiety and insecurity, we are placing undue demand on the marital system. (Likewise for expecting empathy and validation.) We are more likely to exhaust the system: whenever anything goes wrong, we expect our partner to fix it. When angry, we take it out on our partner; when unhappy and scared, we demand reassurance. Eventually we drain our partner, especially when he has issues of his own to self-soothe. When we've finally exhausted our partner's resources—including his patience and his ability to self-soothe—he stops soothing us. The slave driver appears—and it could be either one of us.

As noted previously, it is possible to reduce your anxiety through your relationship. But depending on your partner for this assurance, rather than developing your own ability to self-soothe, saps the flexibility from your marriage. You make your partner and yourself more vulnerable to stress. Its resources depleted, your marriage is less adaptable in times of pervasive or protracted stress. This is why prolonged life-threatening illness, a child dealing drugs, or home remodeling often sends couples right to the brink of divorce—or over it.

Self-soothing bolsters the stability of your relationship by allowing you to maintain yourself and your connection with your partner in troubled times. (It actually makes other-validation and other-soothing more likely.) But it's not as simple as expecting to soothe yourself rather than demanding it from your partner. There are times when you can't self-soothe enough to handle what's happening in your relationship. At those times, couples tend to fight. Partners start demanding accommodation from each other to reduce their own anxiety, blaming each other for their unrelenting stress, and attacking each other out of frustration. (This is the "reptilian" brain regression we discussed in Chapter 5.)

This pattern holds true for all marriages when anxiety becomes sufficiently extreme or chronic. It just depends on how well you can rise to the occasion. And all couples go through periods when they don't respond as well as they'd like. Your level of differentiation determines when and how often this happens.

All couples go through times when they can't self-soothe sufficiently to cope with their circumstances and hurtful interactions ensue. My personal experience illustrates this point beautifully—and painfully. Ruth and I had worked hard through many difficult issues over the years to finally develop a relationship we treasured. Then, about two years ago, we embarked on our greatest mountain adventure, literally and figuratively, in ways we'd never imagined.

In 1995 we both gave up almost twenty years of clinical practice, friends, and stability in New Orleans, Louisiana, and moved to Evergreen, Colorado. We dared to climb the heights life and marriage had to offer by pursuing our goals and dreams.

Lots of self-confrontation preceded this life-changing move. We were drawn to the mountains and repulsed by the crime and violence of New Orleans. We valued the lifestyle and family life that Evergreen offered. I felt it would have been a violation of integrity to stay in New Orleans purely for the economic advantages. It meant ending the work with my beloved clients, who were in the midst of their own process. We went into the crucible of decision and emerged with our new clinical offices overlooking 1,500 acres of dedicated elk preserve.

The enormity of relocation took us almost to the breaking point. We had pulled out the scaffolding from our relationship, intentionally letting our lives "unravel," so that we could reorganize ourselves in another location, lifestyle, and reality. Unfortunately, once in the actual situation, we were stressed and stretched beyond our limits and started to unravel in ways we hadn't planned. It wasn't pretty.

Each of us was called upon to do things our new situation demanded that we'd never done before. We both had to do tasks we disliked or weren't good at. We had to depend on each other to a greater degree than our life in New Orleans required. Differences in personality that our prior lifestyle had allowed us to buffer now hit us in ways we couldn't avoid.

I thought Ruth wasn't carrying her weight. It seemed to me she wasn't trying hard enough. I occasionally used the metaphor that she wasn't moving fast enough while we traversed dangerous ground. Ruth complained that I complained about her all the time. I felt my sins were excusable because I was shouldering the majority of the load and responsibility. We had anxieties about money. Our daughter took the loss of her babysitter hard. We knew two people in our town. We had no prestige or professional recognition, and no referral base for clients.

Our functioning began to deteriorate further under the massive stress. When people regress, they return to former dysfunctional patterns. Just as in our hiking experience twelve years ago, my tendency was to judge that Ruth wasn't trying hard enough. I remember one point where I yelled at Ruth that she needed to self-soothe and get a grip! It didn't help that I was losing myself at that very moment. By her own admission, Ruth screwed up on several occasions that had dire consequences for our business and family. I made it worse by making these issues in our marriage. I could understand how screw-ups could occur, given the pressure she was under (which I contributed to). I just couldn't tolerate the impact on us—or me. I blamed *my* screw-ups on the "fact" that Ruth's screw-ups had exhausted my ability to self-soothe.

We were both losing our grip in the face of our new circumstances. Our fights became more frequent, longer, and less productive. Eventually we were at each other's throats all the time. Never did we imagine we'd become Rocky Mountain reptiles once we left New Orleans.

Ruth and I became living experiments on the importance of self-soothing in stabilizing a marriage in times of stress. After all our time together I thought I had an almost unshakable grip on myself. I was wrong. So was Ruth. We scrambled to grow what we lacked. In the process, we achieved things—sexual, intimate, and otherwise—I'd given up on having. Our respective individual development—our ability to hold onto ourselves, and especially our ability to self-soothe—increased markedly.

Our experience illustrates how the ability to self-soothe in times of stress is crucial. We all regress when our anxiety gets high and our reptilian brain takes over. Reptiles don't fight fair, they go for the kill. At that point fairness becomes a moot point—you have to handle whatever comes up.

We turned out far better than we ever were. At different times Ruth and I individually held onto ourselves and pulled out of the cycles of negative reactions and failed attempts to repair our relationship. One of us usually managed to say or do something that emphasized our overriding caring and investment in each other, our marriage, and our daughter. Or, talk about the excitement and joy of being in Colorado and starting a new phase of life. Or, offer a heartfelt apology for the latest transgression or reaction. Our ability to self-soothe, to put ourselves back together, and to make renewed efforts to repair the damage kept us going.

Except, there came a brief period of time when it didn't. Even after all we'd been through between us, and all I'd witnessed with my clients, there came a point where I lost hope. Neither one of us could pull out of our fights. I honestly thought we were so far gone we could not recoup. I was fairly certain we were headed for a divorce. (Ruth started calling me "Mr. Differentiation.")

It was during this time I recognized my subjective experience that coincides with my losing myself and becoming reptilian: I think I have perfect clarity about the situation, every one of Ruth's faults, and how the two go together. I feel I am magnificently maintaining myself against Ruth's attempt to "get me." It took three weeks for me to realize I had totally lost myself.

Until that point I considered Ruth and me to be moderately differentiated people. Unfortunately, we were overwhelmed with more anxiety than we could digest. Just as any physiological immune system can be overwhelmed, our emotional immunity to anxiety (our differentiation) was exceeded. There are limits to what anyone can handle at his or her level of development. It took getting to this crisis point to make us grow and rise to the occasion.

Ultimately, we held on. Seeing aspects of each other that we still respected helped us turn things around. We are now contenders for the self-soothing Olympics. Something will probably happen in the future to challenge our equilibrium, and we'll be better equipped to handle it when it does. But you're never invulnerable and the unexpected can surface out of nowhere. It's one more reason why pursuing your differentiation is so important to you and your marriage.

Ruth and I thought a lot about disclosing this about ourselves. We are very private people. Even in therapy I disclose little personal history, partly for this very reason and partly because it detracts from clients' struggles to become themselves. Ruth and I decided to include this after recent experiences at our Couples Retreats: our story had a powerful impact on participants, who told us it made us seem more real. They said it soothed and challenged them that even we couldn't avoid the issues and processes they struggled with, the same ones all married couples face. That we had difficult times—times we lost our tempers, times we were overwhelmed, times we did unkind things, times we were reptilian. They stopped being ashamed of bad times in their own relationship and feeling bad about themselves. Some who thought their marriage was irreparable decided to hunker down and see if they could turn things around.

To my surprise I found it beneficial, too: I stopped feeling the obligation to look like I—and we—always have (and had) ourselves together. In earlier retreats, participants said they liked watching Ruth and me interact—that we seem to "walk the walk, and not just talk the talk." In part, that's because the terrible encounters described above are rare for us. Their feedback was gratifying, but there's a limit to how much of us they get to see while we're working.

I've always feared someone might think less of the sexual crucible approach if they saw flaws in us—or me. Because what you've read in *Passionate Marriage* differs so radically from what many people think, I felt a responsiblity to not make it easily dismissable because of my personal shortcomings. Knowing this, you may appreciate how I felt when I thought we were headed for divorce. And you can understand the enormity sharing this vignette holds for us.

If I limited my disclosure to old incidents like clinicians often do (e.g., my reptilian backpacking episode from twelve years ago), I could imply that Ruth and I are beyond this kind of difficulty because we learned this approach. Participants at the Couples Retreats specifically mentioned that our disclosing recent history made all the difference— acknowledging that we too are still a work in progress. (Believe me, self-validating a recent personal vignette is much harder.)

But how can I work with my clients if I act as if Ruth and I are no longer subject to the same issues and processes they face? In theory and practice I maintain that becoming more differentiated is an ongoing life-long process, rather than something you do once and then you're done. And throughout this book I've said many marital difficulties are inherent to the natural system within emotionally committed relationships. The challenges stay the same as you become more differentiated; it's your ability to handle them that becomes infinitely better.

Our move to Colorado was a time when we were overwhelmed, we regressed, and we put ourselves back together—stronger and better, in fact, than we've ever been. We haven't finished our differentiation— it's a long-term process with no single step to completion. But it does take a lot more to shake us, and we quiet down much more quickly than previously. The tone in our home is peaceful; our ability to pull out of squabbles is a blessing. We don't "have it all together," but we have more of what my mother means when she says, "I only wish for you and Ruth the love and happiness your father and I have."

But Ruth and I thought long and hard about the possibility that some readers might misinterpret our story and ask themselves, "Why should I bother with this book if it doesn't even help them?" The point is this approach has helped us—and many people—tremendously. Actually, sometimes it has been the other way around. This approach hasn't just developed from my experiences with Ruth, which I have then applied to my clients. Ruth and I have also applied what we've learned from working with clients.

I say this because we also considered the other side of the coin: we were concerned some readers might conclude that this entire book (and the sexual crucible approach) is merely projection of our personal experiences, generalized to everyone. True, things discussed in prior chapters apply to us, but they are not allegorical. We worried our disclosure might be misperceived as suggesting that all couples are like us, or that others should take us as models. (This is why I self-disclose relatively little in therapy.)

We also worried some readers might be uncomfortable with such personal disclosure, feeling we've crossed over the line into what should remain private. Maybe this kind of disclosure is okay at the Couples Retreat but too sensational in print. Would some perceive our story as self-aggrandizing ("Look at what we went through!") or feel inadequate in comparison? Was there some way I could write this so Ruth wouldn't look like the "weak" partner or relieve readers who wonder if her version was different? (After all, this is written from my perspective.) We went through the crucible one more time.

In the end, integrity demanded we include our personal story. We were confronted with the question of whether or not we had anything to be ashamed of because we went right to the edge of divorce. We decided we didn't—and if we did, I'd have difficulty discussing *critical mass* as a part of differentiation in marriage (next chapter) without sounding condescending or being hypocritical.

You might want to decide for yourself: should you be ashamed because you have, or have had, or will have rocky times in your marriage?

Getting Used to Being Out of Synch

How can people be expected to self-soothe in the face of life's traumas and the frustration, pain, and fear that inevitably accompany them? I believe two answers apply: first, consider what one woman at the Couples Retreat said, "We go through our crucibles because the price of *not* doing it is so high." Second, it's in our nature.

After Ruth and I were again basking in the warmth of our marriage, I came upon some remarkable research about infants, which explained how a marriage could be stretched to the breaking point and yet survive—and even flourish.

Research reveals that infants possess remarkable ability to self-soothe. Mothers and infants are constantly going in and out of synchrony. *Normal healthy infants and mothers are in synch during only one-third of their interactions; they are out of synch but "get back together" in another third; in the remaining third, healthy infants and mothers are out of synch and stay that way.* How do babies handle the out-of-synch times? By age three months they are able to regulate their emotional response in two ways: they soothe themselves when mismatches with their caretaker occur and try to reestablish connection; and they break contact when they are overstimulated by a good connection and then restart it. This process is so well-established that by six months of age infants demonstrate stability in their characteristic style of self-soothing.

When people understand the magnitude of infants' self-repair processes, their entire picture of human nature and their expectations for marriage often shift. I hope widespread awareness of these facts hastens the departure of the "trauma model" of life and therapy that currently dominates contemporary society. We have reduced adults to infants and reduced infants to a distortion of themselves. This research emphasizes crucial—and long overlooked—aspects of human nature.

•*We are not as fragile as we think.* But we create ourselves in our own image by seeing ourselves that way and acting accordingly. Expecting ourselves to freak out in the face of marriage's realities keeps us and our relationship infantile—in the worst sense. In Chapters 1 and 4 we noted that society has looked at only one type of intimacy—other-validated—thereby excluding the self-validated variety and hampering many marriages. I propose a similar omission is present in our understanding of human nature: we have ignored our basic capacity to self-soothe and stabilize ourselves. Instead we have emphasized infants' drive for attachment (social connection). The result has distorted our picture of infancy, adulthood, and marriage. Relationship involves both self-soothing and other-soothing. Overemphasizing attachments suggests that soothing must come from our significant other. Differentiation, however, involves balancing our two basic drives (our drive for attachment *and* our strivings for autonomy and self-regulation), and allows soothing and relationship repair to start with ourselves.

•*Resilience is built into our nature.* Self-repair is innate to humans. Healthy infants regulate their emotions and physiology in the 60–70 percent of their interactions when they are out of synch with mother (in half of which they never achieve synchrony).

The drive for emotional connection is powerful in humans—but not as strong as the need for emotional self-regulation and self-preservation. Babies eventually break contact with their mother to reorganize themselves when the interaction is not going well—and even when it is! The need to self-regulate is so strong that infants will do it at the expense of connection. Humans are not organized to seek connection or solace from others at all costs—that's emotional fusion. Reducing ourselves in our minds to needy children, dependent on a reflected sense of self from others, fuels our narcissism and "fears of abandonment." This distortion, enshrined by therapies that emphasize mirroring, empathy, and validation, stimulates our loneliness anxiety (discussed in Chapter 14). The image of the hungry infant, eager to suck up every morsel of mother's attention, is as erroneous as that of the ever-hovering mother. This kind of mother does exist—but it's not a healthy situation. The view that we are "wounded" during childhood in lasting ways whenever our caretakers are not vigilant responders is true only in the extreme and not credible in normal situations.

•*Being out of synch is normal.* Being out of synch with your partner and maintaining yourself is just as normal as synchrony. *Both* are necessary for healthy interaction. Knowing this often changes your feelings about gridlock, being out of phase with your partner, time apart, and having to self-soothe.

You can expect to be on a different wavelength from your spouse frequently, and to get back in synch about half the time. Though we don't know exactly how much infants and adults differ in this respect, a rough generalization is a reasonable place to start. It's likely that long-term partners can be in synch more often than infants and mothers. But this doesn't mean low levels of togetherness are pathological or problematic. Do something about it if it's not to your liking, but don't automatically expect more. Just because you don't have what you want doesn't mean that something is wrong.

Stop thinking of yourself as an infant with an infant's supposed mentality (e.g., "fears of abandonment"). Think of yourself as a adult with an infant's resilience harnessed to your increased abilities to survive and cope. It is reasonable and necessary to expect adults to self-soothe and self-regulate better than infants.

•*Time out of synch with your partner is neither traumatic nor wasted—unless you insist on it.* Time out of synch is not only *not* negative, it's positive; it's a functional, purposeful, part of the process: it helps infants and spouses reorganize themselves so they can sustain the overall interaction. It also provides the same challenge of differentiation that infants require as well. Like the shift from other-validated to self-validated intimacy, self-soothing and repairing mismatches with your partner yield positive experiences that facilitate a positive core sense of self. They expand your coping capacities, enhance your sense of mastery and effectiveness, and generalize into social competency with other partners and situations.

Self-Soothing Strategies

Are you curious about how babies self-soothe and buffer their relationships? Their styles have been classified into distinct categories, which, in adults, would correspond to different levels of differentiation. The adult correlates of these patterns are listed below (beginning with the most differentiated):

- You are able to self-soothe while concurrently trying to repair mismatches in the connection with your partner.
- You break contact with your partner for brief periods of self-soothing, focusing on other interests to replenish yourself, and then renew your efforts to regain connection with your partner.
- Your attempts to reestablish connection become less frequent, as you increasingly withdraw into yourself and focus on other interests to compensate for needs not met in your relationship.
- Attempts to regain connection with your partner cease, and your emotional and physical activities focus around minimizing negative interactions.
- You actively avoid your partner, sometimes for protracted periods, and you resist any attempts your partner makes to repair the connection with you.
- Your functioning is now severely affected by the disruption in connection with your partner. You are neither able to reestablish connection nor successful at involving yourself in other interests that replenish you.

The first strategy is the most differentiated: maintaining yourself (self-regulation) in close proximity to your partner (attachment) and trying to get back in synch. The other strategies are attempts to regulate your equilibrium by decreasing contact with your partner. Like an infant, your style of self-soothing both reflects and shapes your temperament, influencing how you handle yourself in relationships and how others respond to you.

These natural ways of coping can also become problematic defense mechanisms if you use them chronically and reflexively (particularly ones lower on the list). When infants habitually make self-soothing responses that discourage approach responses from their caretakers, the result is ongoing cycles of being out of synch. The same happens for adults. When gridlocked spouses can't self-soothe and can't adapt to their partner, they usually make maladaptive attempts at self-repair. That's the behavior you just hate in your partner, which he continues to do no matter how often you ask him not to, and which you assume means that he doesn't love you anymore. No doubt you can easily identify this behavior in your partner. It's an act of differentiation to see it in yourself.

Every client asks, "How can I do a better job of soothing myself?" You have to hang in with yourself, just as you would with any friend going through a difficult time. Here are some specific suggestions:

•*Don't take your partner's behavior (or lack of change) personally.* If you're going to try to get back in synch without a period of time apart, you have to keep your neocortex in gear. Focus on your breathing: stop talking, catch your breath, and slow your heart rate. Lower your volume and unclench your teeth. Use each of these as another "opportunity" to let go of a reflected sense of self.

•*Give your dilemma purpose and meaning* by recognizing how issues and tasks in your current situation are likely to confront you in the future. This perspective makes your dilemma important to confront and master now. In searching for personal coping resources, look at your past history and recall similar challenges that you faced successfully.

•*If you can't regulate your emotions, control your behavior.* Don't make things harder than they need to be. Try to keep some perspective—reactions and situations don't last forever. Remember, reptiles can't tell time and have no sense of the future. Handle yourself in some small way you respect if that's all you can manage. When you start saying, "Maybe I shouldn't say this, but . . ." take your own advice.

•*Stop your negative mental tapes.* Stop "awfulizing" the situation or telling yourself, "I can't believe this!" Accept your present reality and settle down. Quiet yourself instead of exacerbating your state and holding your partner accountable. Cage your reptilian brain.

•*Self-soothing may require breaking contact with your partner.* You may have to break off contact to self-repair when arguments get too far out of shape and you find yourself becoming a reptile. The duration and degree of physical separation required are determined by your level of differentiation: how badly are you losing your grip on yourself and how quickly can you recover? Make it clear that this "time out" is for self-repair and not withdrawal. You can also offer to schedule time to reconnect—not to placate your partner's anger or "fears of abandonment"—but to demonstrate your good intent. It's best you show up on time.

• *Use your time out of synch effectively.* The quality of time apart is vitally important. More is involved than marking time until you get back together. Take care and replenish yourself: exercise, read something you like, do something productive. Friends, hobbies, and outside interests can soothe and refuel you, depending on how you use them. One person's hobby is another's way of dodging intimacy. "Hiding out" is part of the pattern of emotional fusion and doesn't offer the same inner repair and replenishment. Spending all your time commiserating about marital problems with friends isn't really time apart from your spouse.

• *Self-soothing does not involve self-indulgence, emotional regression, or food or substance bingeing.* Self-soothing does involve taking care of yourself while you're not getting along with your partner. Self-soothing permits you to quiet and comfort yourself as well as to self-confront. It's self-care but not self-indulgence. The purpose of self-soothing is to promote your resilience and to continue striving toward your goal.

• *Promote yourself.* Move up the list of self-soothing responses a step toward greater differentiation. If you have yourself pretty well under control, use a coping style that involves less physical distancing and facilitates contact with your partner while you maintain your emotional equilibrium. Hugging till relaxed can be helpful in many ways.

Self-soothing is critical to developing a more accurate picture of yourself and your situation. You need to self-soothe the embarrassment that commonly accompanies a more accurate picture (once you have it); the obviousness of it, in retrospect, makes you wonder how you managed to delude yourself so long. Typically, some chagrin accompanies every growth spurt.

Conversely, the accuracy of your picture affects your ability to self-soothe, because that accuracy determines whether you feel clean pain or dirty pain. *Clean pain* comes from moving forward from an accurate self-picture, accepting what has been, is, and will be. That's not easy to do or often done, which is why most of us know a lot more about dirty pain. *Dirty pain* comes from defending, denying, or deflecting, to keep from seeing or doing something. The dirty feeling comes from dodging yourself. Dirty pain is what you feel before you "take the hit." It is the pain of repeated mistakes promoted through self-imposed blindness and offers no healing.

Clean pain is different: there's no shame and less anxiety in the hurting. You stop struggling and relax. It is the healing pain of accepting the reality of your life and embarking on effective assessment, planning, and implementation. It's hard to soothe clean pain. It's almost impossible to soothe dirty pain.

If you're having difficulty self-soothing, reconsider what you're trying to soothe yourself about. At times I've been amazed how well I can handle clean pain—how much I could hurt and still keep going. I could function well—actually, increasingly better—while my chest physically ached. It's not the same, however, if it's dirty pain. You can't really soothe yourself while you're dodging part of the truth. Deciding whether you're trying to soothe clean pain or dirty pain is part of the two-choice dilemma in learning to trust yourself.

If people's reactions at a recent Couples Retreat are any indication, it's not too hard to tell the difference. After nine days of laughter, tears, self-confrontation, and self-soothing—and couples having more sex and intimacy than they'd had in years—they composed a song for our final night's celebration (sung to the tune of "The Banana Boat Song" Day-oh! chorus):

> *I'm glad to say I'm on my way,*
> *to loving myself in every way.*
> *It's not too late to differentiate.*
> *I don't need you to validate!*

Chapter 13

Couples in the Crucible: Reaching Critical Mass

Do not confuse your vested interests with ethics. Do not identify the enemies of your privilege with the enemies of humanity.

—Max Lerner

In the last chapter we joined two hikers, walking through their marriage as individuals but affecting each other through their relationship. We watched what happens when one feels like he's dragging the other up the mountain. In this chapter we'll shift our vantage point from ground level to a bird's-eye view to gain more perspective on the process. We'll consider marriage as an entity, two people functioning as a single unit, and ponder what happens when one wants to move on and the other refuses to budge.

Marriages, like people, go through cycles of growth and disruption mixed with periods of comfort and stability. Sometimes partners are in different cycles. What happens if one partner is ready to change and the other isn't? What if you want to expand and deepen your relationship and your partner doesn't? What do you do when gridlock intensifies to the point that you are faced with the dilemma of "take it or leave it"?

Answers to such troubling times involve last chapter's discussion of self-mastery, particularly two components of holding onto yourself: self-confrontation and self-soothing. Let's put these into a mental "map" that will pull together everything we've discussed throughout *Passionate Marriage*.

Marriage Is a System of Balancing Growth and Stability

Imagine two concentric circles depicting two cycles: a growth cycle (the outer circle) and a comfort cycle (the inner circle). Then look at Figure 3.

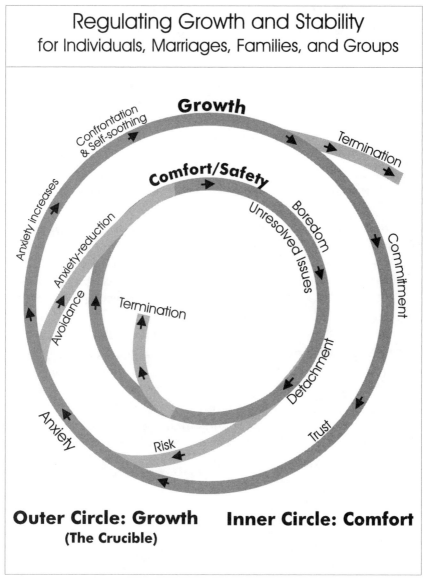

Regulating Growth and Stability
for Individuals, Marriages, Families, and Groups

Growth

Confrontation & Self-soothing

Termination

Comfort/Safety

Anxiety increases

Anxiety-reduction

Avoidance

Unresolved Issues

Boredom

Commitment

Termination

Detachment

Anxiety

Risk

Trust

Outer Circle: Growth
(The Crucible)

Inner Circle: Comfort

Figure 3

At first we might think of self-confrontation as the growth cycle and self-soothing as the comfort cycle. But then we'd be minimizing the importance of self-soothing while we're in the growth cycle. Instead, think of the comfort cycle (inner circle) as a place where your need to self-soothe is low; anxiety, challenge, and change are minimal; and relationships are as womb-like as you get as an adult. Peace, tranquillity, stability.

If you think of the growth cycle (outer circle) as the place where self-soothing comes in handy, you'll understand how it differs from the comfort cycle (inner circle). It's the crucible: self-confrontation and self-soothing in the face of challenge; holding onto yourself. It's where your integrity is on the line.

Think of how growth and comfort cycles apply to you as an individual. Effectively managing your personal development involves steering yourself back and forth between the inner and outer circles—times when you push yourself to grow, and times when you prudently rest and consolidate your gains. Sometimes you may not push yourself enough to leave the comfort cycle when necessary. Then you gradually become bored, your life seems meaningless, and your problems fester. If you don't make some efforts towards change, eventually you feel physically alive but not living, and you are at risk for substance abuse or suicide. However, if you venture into the growth cycle, you have to hold onto yourself through the anxiety of change. If your self-confrontation and self-soothing continue, eventually you grow. You develop faith in your abilities and enjoy a more exciting and productive life.

The same holds true for relationships. Both growth and comfort cycles are necessary in marriage. Unfortunately, couples often try to keep their relationship in a permanently comfortable cycle. Previously we discussed how often we demand stability in our marriage and then complain of sexual boredom (Chapter 5). The inner circle of Figure 3 depicts this dynamic: avoiding anxiety and emphasizing comfort and safety leads to low sexual desire, lack of intimacy, and withdrawal from your partner. Unresolved issues you repeatedly dodge fester, quietly but steadily eroding your marriage.

On the other hand, you may be willing to lead your relationship into the growth cycle. That's when you address unresolved issues within your marital gridlock, confronting who you are and the true nature of your connection. You explore new sexual behaviors, styles, and meanings. Maybe you try having your first eyes-open orgasm. (Hugging till relaxed can be useful in both the inner and outer circles. It can profoundly deepen your level of connection when times are good, and it can stabilize your marriage and help you work on your issues when you're in the crucible.) In the process, your self-validation and your tolerance for intimacy are challenged and your level of differentiation increases. Your marriage becomes more stable during stressful times, making the prospect of future growth cycles less frightening. These shared growth experiences lead to renewed interest and commitment to your marriage, while building trust and positive feelings. True interdependence becomes possible.

In other words, the growth cycle is not simply about destabilizing your marriage and the comfort cycle is not just about stabilizing it. The growth cycle also promotes long-term relationship stability, and the comfort cycle often does the opposite.

Venturing into the Outer Circle

Like many aspects of marriage, the comfort and growth cycles operate differently for well differentiated and poorly differentiated couples. First we'll consider these differences and then examine what happens when one partner wants to enter the growth cycle and the other doesn't.

The comfort cycle of poorly differentiated couples emphasizes reciprocity, soothing each other's fears, and overriding concern for moment-to-moment security. Partners' dependence on other-validated intimacy and borrowed functioning (reflected sense of self) hastens lack of intimacy, sexual boredom, and gridlock. Emotional fusion dominates this environment, causing partners to feel easily threatened and more likely to dodge anxiety at any cost. All these factors eventually increase the pressure to shift to self-validated intimacy to solve the problems.

But poorly differentiated couples don't see this build-up of pressure as an opportunity. They try to define their relationship in terms of the comfort cycle alone and experience the anxiety of the growth cycle as evidence that their marriage is falling apart. Their preoccupation with safety and security makes the growth cycle seem terrifying. It is as if their map of marriage doesn't exist beyond the inner circle—and they fear their marriage will be destroyed by the monsters lurking outside. But like Christopher Columbus leaving Barcelona, you can't get to the New World without leaving the safety of the harbor. Excitement, exploration, and adventure lie outside the comfort cycle.

How do you find the trust to go "exploring" with your spouse? Many couples think it's based on safety and security, which means staying in the comfort cycle. Trust can be based on a pact you'll never leave the inner circle, or developed from a trip through the growth cycle. But the trust that results is totally different: before you've ventured into the outer circle, trust is based on blind faith. It lacks the safety and security of knowing how you'll do when "what if" happens; it is an uneasy trust, an untested trust. What's actually required is the leap of faith, because *real* safety follows rather than precedes your first trip through the growth cycle. Trust based on shared mutual experience and hardship— watching what your partner and you do under pressure and adversity— is solid and resilient.

When we think of people giving up on their marriage, divorce usually comes to mind. But many people who give up on their marriage (or themselves or their partner) don't leave; they stay in the comfort cycle— until their marriage presents the inevitable dilemma: venture into the growth cycle or face divorce, loss of integrity, or living death. Validating and soothing each other has its place in marriage—but not when you're dependent on it. You get stuck in the comfort cycle because neither of you has the strength or motivation to break out. That's when the other side of the process comes in: holding onto yourself (self-confrontation and self-soothing).

I don't want to draw too extreme a picture of less differentiated people. Not all poorly differentiated couples are suffering; therapists are more likely to see the ones who are. Some happy couples do everything together, never fight, and never change; they have stable marriages as long as circumstances make this pattern of adaptation possible and sufficient.

Well-differentiated couples escape the seductive pull of the comfort cycle and periodically venture into the outer circle. For them, the comfort cycle plays an entirely different role: they re-enter the comfort cycle to digest and integrate the changes and gains of the growth cycle. The safe harbor of the comfort circle makes the growth cycle seem like a quest rather than survival training. The challenge of the growth cycle makes the comfort cycle seem like rest and relaxation rather than hiding out. Other-validation and other-soothing occur, but spouses are less dependent on it. A memorable night of profoundly intimate sex, lying quietly in bed with less anxiety and more connection than either partner had ever thought possible, is a powerful lesson in how the growth cycle fuels the comfort cycle rather than replaces it.

No couple can maintain a marriage solely in the growth cycle—those who try burn out quickly. True, highly differentiated people don't see the outer circle as being terrifying, as do emotionally fused couples, and they enter it more readily. But even they need time for reflection and grounding. Relationships that are constant adventures into the unknown or perpetually involved in conflict resolution don't thrive or develop depth—nor do their participants. You can't be "working on your relationship" every moment. There must also be positive interactions around familiar shared daily events and tasks of living, and catching up on the latest news in the world. The growth cycle produces positive shared experiences, the shared joy of resolving difficult issues, and the excitement of expanding intimacy and eroticism—but we also need the familiar and routine.

Well-differentiated couples soothe themselves—and each other—during the growth cycle. But, again, the soothing is entirely different from that exchanged in emotionally fused couples. In the outer circle well-differentiated partners soothe themselves and each other to settle down anxiety in the relationship. This keeps the relationship relatively calm and stable while one or both spouses push toward growth. This soothing takes the threatening edge off difficult issues while couples are in the thick of it.

Spouses are more likely to divorce when they constantly criticize each other. Happy, successful long-term couples make more positive statements than negative ones about each other by a ratio of five to one. But the solution to marital discord is not as simple as making more positive comments about your partner's personal attractiveness or ability, or trading several compliments a day. There is often a more complex process involved.

This doesn't mean you *shouldn't* compliment your spouse. Positive comments build goodwill and the range of compliments can expand. The problem is that poorly differentiated couples with troubled marriages don't continue giving compliments after an initial "focus" period, particularly if they don't receive them in kind. Couples need shared meaningful experiences that provide motivation and substance to their positive statements, if their positive exchange is to be resilient. Such experiences in the growth cycle also increase differentiation, making couples better able to maintain positive sentiments when one partner doesn't reciprocate. Compliments about personal attractiveness ("You look great!") and ability ("What a wonderful cook you are!") are important, but they can wear thin and provoke anger: people dependent on a reflected sense of self can take them as messages that their value to others is the service they provide (e.g., their looks or doing housework).

The most important positive reinforcements are those often-difficult life experiences that bond people together, events only the participants share in common. War buddies and survivors of catastrophes often have an unshakable link—but catastrophe can also blow marriages and families apart. (For example, the death of a child leads to lots of divorces.) The better differentiated you are, the more likely your marriage will survive unfortunate but common marital crises. It all depends on how well you can rise to the occasion, and *that* has everything to do with differentiation and why the growth cycle is so important.

There is nothing "wrong" with conflict-avoidant marriages in which partners try to keep anxiety low at all costs; the price, however, is they are often unable to deal with the catastrophes of life. As long as both partners agree to never change or grow, and circumstantial challenges remain low, they can have what they consider a good or happy marriage. But as I'll explain in a moment, if one partner starts to differentiate, they both experience an intense anxiety that they are ill-prepared to handle. They are likely to consider (and create) their subsequent divorce to be a catastrophe.

When the growth cycle involves a conflict of interest, well-differentiated couples don't sound like therapists conducting empathy and listening skills exercises. They push their own point—but they use humor and positive feelings to diffuse the adversarial quality and reduce the likelihood of evoking defensive reactions. They laugh through tense times, and when humor isn't appropriate, they still ease the situation to avoid escalations. There are enough statements of caring and motivation to maintain the marriage *and* support meaningful discussion about conflicts without dodging their seriousness. Confrontations that could be taken as personal criticisms are approached more neutrally.

This is where poorly differentiated couples suffer greatly and increase their likelihood of divorce. Their interactions are more brittle because they can't modulate the hard edge of confrontation with humor. Their issues are more likely to become battlefields of self-interest, and they become entrenched in their personal agendas. They have few shared accomplishments to draw upon, they don't offer each other positive sentiments, and they are merely placating each other when they do. Emotionally fused couples have difficulty entering the growth cycle to resolve their issues and do so only begrudgingly. They don't soothe themselves and they certainly don't soothe their partner: they have no soothing to spare and usually blame their spouse for this unwanted journey.

Now we can understand what happens in different relationships when one partner wants to enter the growth cycle and the other doesn't: it is easier for well-differentiated couples to handle this situation. Both partners enter the growth cycle more readily and they are more capable of sustaining themselves individually. Couples steer their relationship into the unknown through their individual self-confrontations—or lack of it. Venturing into the growth cycle is done unilaterally, even if both partners do it simultaneously. Emotionally fused couples have much greater difficulty dealing with this process. If you think of emotional Siamese twins, it's easy to visualize one pulling and tugging to make the other go along—independent action is literally impossible.

In the last chapter we discussed holding onto yourself through self-confrontation and self-soothing, which changes the dynamics in your marriage in positive ways. We said that as partners become better able to self-confront and self-soothe, they have less need to control each other. They can maintain their own emotional stability and worry less about what their partner is doing. They stop expecting their partner to understand them and focus more on understanding themselves, which, in turn, reduces defensiveness and combativeness, and encourages good will and growth rather than resistance and stagnation.

All this holds true—except in emotionally fused couples, because when one emotional Siamese twin begins to hold onto himself/herself, the other automatically feels controlled.

Here's where the tyranny of the lowest common denominator resurfaces. The irony is that the partner who wants to enter the growth cycle always has more control of the process, because of how he or she is positioned in the system: either spouse can unilaterally drive the marriage into the growth cycle, but the relationship remains in the comfort cycle only by consensus. The partner who doesn't want to grow attempts to freeze everything in place by embroiling the other in conflict or undermining all forward-moving efforts. This consensus-by-stalemate renders the comfort cycle the avoidance cycle, and while it's not anxiety-free, it's still not the anxiety of growth.

Remember we said spouses would rather fight with their partner than fight with themselves? In this case, one spouse is fighting to keep the fusion intact and his personal picture out of focus. Let's say you are the partner initiating the growth. When you start confronting yourself, your partner "tailgates" on your disclosures, trying to humiliate you with them or prove that you're responsible for everything bad in the relationship. "I'm glad you finally see the light" is really an attempt to divert your attention from confronting yourself—or your partner. Once you rebel and fight back, it's like punching the proverbial "tar baby" used to trap Brer Rabbit in the Uncle Remus story.

An adversarial quality surrounding gridlocked issues is inevitable in highly fused couples. Their conflict is both actual and symbolic: one partner is holding onto herself as if facing the mythical dragon; the other is fighting desperately to avoid the outer circle where his monsters dwell. When the venturesome partner starts to hold onto herself, gridlock intensifies. Poorly differentiated couples often take their marriage right to the edge of divorce. They don't change except under great duress. I deliberately selected such couples as examples in this book so that you could see what it's like going through the crucible at high levels of intensity. But that doesn't mean that's where you have to be headed.

Couples who are moderately differentiated don't have to "hunker down" and bottom out before things move. They are more willing to go through their dilemmas. They are more willing to self-confront and self-soothe while what's good in them takes over. Poorly differentiated people don't do that until they realize their partner won't accommodate or help them avoid self-confrontation. It takes their partner's growing differentiation to push them to confront themselves. Their only options are further attempts to subdue their partner and undermine her growth (keep her in the inner circle), withdraw from the relationship, or hold onto themselves and grow, too.

Which Couple Are You?

Three couples I've treated illustrate the differences in the amount of conflict and pressure required to trigger fundamental change in the partners and their marriage. The first couple's presenting problem was the husband's apparent lack of sexual desire. Although Bud claimed to like sex with Claire, they had it only once every other month and only at her initiation. Bud acknowledged Claire's distress and frustration but steadfastly maintained he liked having sex with her. When pressed in therapy, he was unable to explain his lack of initiation and apparent acceptance of their low sexual frequency. At first Bud thought I was challenging his professed interest in sex, but when I encouraged him to hold onto his perception—and look further—that's when Bud's self-confrontations started.

Bud was honestly shocked when his passive-aggressive pattern of withholding from Claire was exposed. He had never seen this part of himself—but he acknowledged it when confronted. He was perplexed, his picture of himself shattered, and Bud entered into an intense showdown with himself. He realized that he had overlooked his own passive-aggressiveness just as he had overlooked the same quality in his parents and grandparents. He saw it in everyday events too, like the unfairness of how he wouldn't walk their dog when it scratched at the door—and then punished it for urinating on the carpet. Shortly thereafter he apologized to Claire and frequently initiated passionate sex. Impressed by her husband's integrity, Claire acknowledged her own sexual withholding. They went on to develop their sex and intimacy in ways they both had resisted in previous years.

In this case, Bud's crucible arose from his willingness to confront himself, which led to corresponding growth in his spouse. This is the prototype we discussed last chapter. Self-confrontation greeted by positive response from the partner is characteristic of moderately differentiated couples. The part of us that always knows the truth takes the hit and goes forward.

Sometimes, however, even moderately differentiated couples have to hunker down with each other and take strident positions to create sufficient pressure for change. Marge and Fred, our second case, had made great strides in treatment. They stopped their habitual bickering and experienced passionate renewal in their marriage. But one area was still unresolved: Marge repeatedly asked Fred to play out sexual fantasies with her, but he couldn't bring himself to do so. Her favorite fantasy included Fred wearing a sequin jockstrap and whisking her away to a mysterious place for wild, passionate sex. (Marge liked to "dress up" for sex and frequently did, much to Fred's delight.)

Marge and Fred left therapy full of hope and good intent. Their relationship improved drastically in most respects, but the dress-up and the abduction never happened. They had sex more frequently and with more variety, but nothing on this order of explicit eroticism or phallicness emerged from Fred. He acknowledged not fulfilling Marge's request and admitted he wasn't pushing himself to work through his inhibitions.

Eventually, Marge decided she wasn't waiting anymore. Instead of nagging Fred, she put herself on the line saying, "I'm going to do my piece. Whether you do yours is up to you. I'm not going to keep waiting and hoping. You can either do it or not. I need to do what I say I want and see what happens. I'm going to the bar. You best be there. No telling who I might go home with." Marge's last statement was said with a seductive smile, not delivered as a hostile threat. Fred never seriously thought Marge would have sex with someone else that night, but he recognized sex between them was about to change irrevocably—for better or worse. Marge wasn't nagging—the whole point was she wasn't willing to nag anymore. Fred was pushed to take a stand: do it or not.

At their table in the bar, Fred jokingly pointed to the napkin in his lap. When Marge looked over, he lifted its edge to reveal his open fly. Sequins glistened. Afterwards he blindfolded her and drove her to a lovely hotel specializing in "fantasy rooms." As Fred led her blindfolded through the hotel lobby, several patrons standing nearby applauded. Marge spent the night in "Hawaii" on a bed canopied with palm fronds next to a hot tub with a waterfall.

Marge delighted in her experience with Fred in large part because she felt great about what *she* had done: she had entered the growth cycle alone, fearing Fred would not go, too. She went after what she wanted, exposing herself to the risk he might not show up. Fred realized Marge was serious and time had run out. When she took herself on, Fred took himself on, too.

In our first case, when the low-desire partner self-confronted, the high-desire partner readily did the same. In Fred and Marge's case, the low-desire partner moved forward when the high-desire spouse self-confronted. Claire did have to confront Fred, but the adversarial quality was overshadowed by their positive emotional flow, and blunted by self-confrontation and a touch of humor. They didn't require the same level of pressure and anxiety to create change that our third couple did.

Our third couple, Joe and Fay, never imagined themselves to be emotionally fused—although they were classic emotional Siamese twins. Their presenting problem was Fay's lack of sexual desire and Joe's pervasive jealousy. In their marriage Joe played the role of the manipulative, controlling, and suspicious spouse. He often "wondered" about Fay on her numerous business trips. Fay's role was that of the overly sensitive and "weak" spouse. She refused to have sex with Joe because she felt pressured, and she demanded his "recommitment" to stay in the marriage.

As discussed last chapter, it's hard for emotionally fused couples to develop an accurate picture of what's going on. The real problem wasn't Joe's manipulativeness and Fay's oversensitivity. It was his insecurity and her manipulativeness. Both were insensitive to each other's plight.

Joe's behavior was admittedly manipulative, and while he didn't exactly like the label, he did enjoy looking shrewd and powerful. More accurately, Joe was terribly insecure. He had grown up in a family where lying, stealing, and cheating were common. He had capitalized on his experiences by becoming an aggressive businessman. But labeling Joe manipulative masked his insecurities and stroked his narcissism.

Fay came from a family where no one disagreed with Dad. If you didn't agree with him, you were against him—and that was not tolerated. Mislabeling disagreement as disrespect, her father snuffed out challenges to his judgment and everyone's development. Although later in life Fay looked too fragile to tolerate disagreement, she actually annihilated her opposition. She accused anyone who disagreed with her of invalidating her feelings. Cloaked in the guise of weakness, she wielded her claim of invalidation like a club, pressuring the people around her to give up their opinions and preferences for fear of injuring her. Fay had even kept her prior therapists from disagreeing with her by accusing them of not caring about her, or acting like she would "fall apart."

Fay felt pressured whenever Joe had any desire for sex. She was pushing him to have no expectations at all, a common pattern in many cases of disparate levels of desire. In Fay's case, however, her refusal had another personal relevance: it was her way of annihilating opposition, just as her father had done in the family. I pointed this out to Fay, emphasizing this was characteristic of emotionally fused families and couples. The notion of emotional Siamese twins helped her see a process in her marriage that went beyond her feelings or Joe's.

This insight gave Fay cause for pause—but soon she was back claiming the entire matter boiled down to her feeling pressured by Joe's jealousy and demands for sex. She tried to use Joe's limitations to mask her own. She kept trying to keep the focus on his traits. At this point, I shifted the focus to Joe because it was in both their interests.

I asked Joe why he was willing and eager to have sex with someone who didn't want to have sex with him. The question led him to confront his underlying insecurity and lack of self-worth. He couldn't believe that anyone would really want him—particularly a "good person" with the moral values and integrity so absent in his childhood family. He was struck by the insight that his sneaky, devious ways of checking on his wife actually made him think less of himself, reinforced his anticipation that Fay would find him undesirable, and stimulated his own jealousy. He detested the idea that he was acting just like his parents. Joe went deep into his personal crucible and his jealous snooping stopped. And the scaffolding in his marriage collapsed.

Rather than feeling relieved by Joe's behavioral changes, Fay felt more pressure to be better in bed to keep him in the marriage. She was up against the two-choice dilemma her father had skirted by bludgeoning his family to give up their choices: ultimately, Fay wanted to have herself *and* her marriage, but keeping both would require differentiation, going through her crucible, which she didn't want to do.

Fay resented that Joe wouldn't stay with her if he was unhappy—and that therefore she would have to have sex with him. For Fay this was tantamount to "giving into him" and "being blackmailed"; she refused to acknowledge that her husband's desire for sex, and his unhappiness when it was withheld, brought forth a dynamic inherent in any marriage. She wasn't differentiated enough to see her own selfishness and Joe's right to his feelings, until *he* went into crisis. Confronting herself and her two-choice dilemma was the last thing she wanted to do—and she only did it begrudgingly.

Only when it became clear that the problem wasn't just Joe's did Fay enter her crucible. She could no longer push Joe to accommodate by confronting him, because he was confronting himself and holding onto himself. With only herself to hold onto, she sagged briefly and then moved forward. Gridlock had to reach an intense and seemingly adversarial level before real change took place.

In this case, the low-desire partner wasn't willing to enter the growth cycle until the high-desire partner took a steadfast position. This is the same pattern we saw with Marge and Fred, except that Joe and Fay were more poorly differentiated. They had to reach a more intense critical point in order to create change. Both people hunkered down and scared themselves. Poorly differentiated couples seem to need to play "chicken" with each other, where the possibility of divorce is high. In fact, testing the waters of divorce seems to bring them to their senses—if they don't become totally reptilian and bolt from the marriage.

Reaching Critical Mass

Having the kind of marriage you want often involves a personal metamorphosis. Every individual and every relationship has a point at which fundamental reorganization takes place. New behaviors and solutions appear because the system itself is changing. The required conditions can occur when your marriage hits critical mass, a term from physics that means "the amount of energy necessary to create a self-sustaining reaction."

In gridlocked relationships critical mass is the amount of pressure and anxiety necessary to trigger differentiation. The intensity of pressure required to reach critical mass differs depending on partners' levels of differentiation. For well-differentiated people, critical mass requires no more than a disappointing realization that changing their plans best serves their interests. (This can be realizing your partner isn't interested in sex tonight like you hoped, or your child isn't going into the profession you hoped or isn't going to college at all.) Less differentiated people require greater pressure: it may take an explosion to get their attention, to dislodge them from the comfort cycle, and hurtle them into the outer circle.

There are many reasons why poorly differentiated relationships require high levels of pressure and anxiety to reach critical mass. For one, emotionally fused partners have a high tolerance for pain and a low tolerance for anxiety and novelty. For another, when one partner starts to self-confront and enter the growth cycle, the implications of these startling changes are not immediately clear to the other partner, who is still entrenched in the old pattern. He may mistakenly assume that (a) his wife's self-confrontation is indirect admission she was wrong, (b) her role in the relationship is to de-escalate tension, which he thinks she's doing by acknowledging her shortcomings (i.e., business as usual), and (c) he knows she's sold out before and figures she's not serious and will back down again. It takes further probing for the entrenched partner to realize that none of these is true. In the process, pressure in the relationship intensifies to unaccustomed levels.

Reaching critical mass involves a rather delicate ballet, but there's nothing delicate about the way it feels. When you hit critical mass for the first time, it feels like you're slamming into a wall.

Gridlock and critical mass are universal experiences. Even being sex and marital therapists didn't help Ruth and me avoid numerous encounters with critical mass in our relationship. We handle it more effectively, no longer get overly upset by it, and use it to fuel our relationship. And critical mass now occurs at much lower intensity.

The concept of critical mass can be enormously helpful. Participants at our Couples Retreats and my psychotherapy clients are heartened to realize that their marriages follow fairly predictable patterns of conflict and growth. Those who have reached critical mass but had no name for it, and no perspective on it, are relieved to realize that it does not reflect personal shortcomings or a bad relationship. Typically, people feel embarrassed or even ashamed that they let their relationship "get that bad." When they shift to self-validated intimacy and break gridlock—not knowing that that's what they're doing—they feel guilty for potentially breaking up their marriage.

Most couples reach critical mass at one point or another, with or without this knowledge. When couples realize they've been going through the natural people-growing process of marriage, they stop feeling defective and become more respectful of themselves and their relationship. It helps them go through succeeding episodes of critical mass more easily and productively. What many couples take as an indication of a bad relationship is actually the potential hallmark of a good one.

We've seen repeatedly in this book that healthy relationships are anything but smooth. If anything should be regarded as aberrant, it's the expectation that a good marriage is a serene one.

We move forward when our discomfort with the present outweighs our fear of growth. It takes a lot to counterbalance our avoidance of change. Many people find they are able to move forward through gridlock only when they feel their integrity—their selfhood—is on the line.

Hallmarks of Critical Mass

Critical mass is experienced differently by people at different levels of differentiation. The lower your level of differentiation, the more likely you find it frightening. But even poorly differentiated spouses experience critical mass differently, depending on how they approach it: if you're willing to enter the growth cycle (like Joe), you feel unsettled and unsure but composed. You're nervous but not overwhelmed with anxiety. You're resolved and determined to maintain yourself but not militant and inflexible (except maybe at first). If (like Fay) you're dodging self-confrontation and your two-choice dilemma, you're usually frantic and agitated, until you settle down and "take the hit." At that point, you feel more like Joe did.

When both partners hold onto themselves as critical mass arrives, hostility markedly disappears. They are often surprised, confused, and don't know what to do next. Here are some tips on how to recognize critical mass when it occurs and how to conduct yourself while you're there:

•*One partner can sense that the other is changing . . . differentiating.* Many of us know critical mass by feel even if we've never labeled it—it's what we keep trying to avoid. One partner may be shifting to self-validated intimacy, no longer taking the state of the marriage solely as a personal failure, and no longer needing or seeking the other's validation.

•*Partners settle down.* If you envision people "freaking out" at critical mass, you'll be surprised to learn that isn't what typically happens. People settle down when pressure in their marriage reaches critical mass because they realize that they are playing with their future. (In one couple, the husband was plagued with severe stuttering since childhood. Much to everyone's amazement, his stuttering completely ceased when he and his wife reached critical mass during one session.) Those who explode or fall apart may do so to keep the situation from closing in on them—their reactions are actually defenses against critical mass. These are the people we discussed in the last chapter who can't or won't tolerate the anxiety and discomfort of growth. They often have messy divorces because they are still emotionally fused with their spouse.

• *The tone becomes quiet.* The stony silence of gridlocked emotional Siamese twins is replaced with a calm, sober, reflective, and respectful tone. The change in tone reflects the underlying shifts in differentiation. It's not simply a matter of not shouting, although people do stop yelling. Some couples misinterpret critical mass as a "quiet fight" the first time it occurs; it's part of the "business as usual" misperception I mentioned earlier. When one partner can't hook the other into an escalating argument—and silence becomes pregnant rather than stony or empty—both spouses suddenly realize "something is really happening!"

• *Distancer-pursuer oscillations stop.* At critical mass the common chase between the pursuing partner and the distancing partner stops. The pursuer stops criticizing and nagging as a way to engage the distancer and maintains his/her own position. The distancer stops withdrawing or stonewalling because these only work as long as the partner is pursuing or willing to wait. Reaching critical mass stops the repetition and erosion in the relationship. Often the pursuing partner, who previously looked highly dependent, now acts autonomously, and the distancing partner, who seemed so independent, becomes highly emotional.

• *The full picture emerges.* Mounting pressure within the marital system puts all the pieces of the puzzle on the table. The traits and limitations of each partner are fleshed out to reveal the underside of what appeared on the surface. A "flighty" partner may actually be quite serious and intelligent but afraid to harness her energies and face new responsibilities, expectations, and competition. A highly "successful" partner may reveal that he is driven by fears that he won't produce if he feels good about himself. "Insensitive" and "unfeeling" partners often turn out to be highly sensitive—they just can't tolerate what their sensitivity lets them feel. One wife was advised by their prior marital therapist that her husband was incapable of "accessing his emotions." I perceived the husband quite differently, as did the wife. Only when confronted with her intent to leave the marriage did he reveal the depth of his emotionality—barely in the nick of time.

• *People stand up and take action.* Reaching critical mass involves recognizing the seriousness of the situation. There is no more "business as usual." Tactical arguments, posturing, or denial don't work any longer. Raising your level of differentiation requires that you *do* something. Partners redefine themselves and then stand up for what they believe or hold dear.

Don't confuse actions taken from a position of increasing differentiation with those of poorly differentiated couples, who suddenly make compromises and promises they don't keep once their anxiety goes down. This is the point at which the pursuing partner is able to drag the distancing partner into marital counseling. The distancing spouse is often making a desperate attempt to stop the differentiation process (rather than go through it) and maintain the status quo, but that isn't the same as trying to save the marriage. The distancer isn't serious about participating in treatment unless and until it becomes clear that the pursuer won't be placated or bought off. At this point the distancer, whose reaction often determines the future course of the marriage, enters therapy in earnest or drops out all together.

•*Partners talk straight.* The "leap of faith" to self-validated intimacy occurs. Partners express themselves from a position of quiet conviction. They make their point, but don't push their partner to agree or give up his agenda. They talk about their dissatisfactions with themselves, their partner, and the status quo, often making breathtaking self-disclosures. Partners state their own views without antagonism. Couples report that this exchange makes them feel more heard, understood, and seen by each other, even when hearing negative things.

When couples realize their future is at stake, they are very attentive, and their nods, vocalizations, and facial expressions show a high level of engagement. They "share the floor" as appropriate to each other's needs and the topic at hand. They are flexible about minor issues and acknowledge positive points in their partner's assertions. When information is unclear, they request and receive clarification.

•*Blaming and criticism stop.* When you stop seeing your partner as the problem, you stop blaming and criticizing—which decreases your partner's defensiveness. Couples at critical mass drop the laundry list of complaints and settle down to the issues of contention that are crucial to survival of their marriage. Blaming and criticism stop because it is no longer safe to do so: one or both partners will not take it any longer. There is less impulse—and less tolerance—for taking out frustrations on one another.

•*Anger doesn't escalate.* Anger may flair, but it doesn't escalate into repeated belligerent exchanges. It's just a quick burst that one or both partners quickly harness. No one wants to upset the precarious balance of the relationship and the special quality that critical mass lends to the moment. They know how bad the relationship can get and don't want to give up what they are starting to experience. Anger is often replaced by sadness as both partners confront their own crucibles and realize their partner is in one, too. The lack of anger, criticism, and blame conveys both partners' overriding goal of maintaining the relationship.

• *Ultimatums are rare.* People avoiding self-confrontation push their marriages into crises all the time. Yelling and screaming to intimidate others is one way to hide fear of losing control of the situation. There is no need to issue threats and ultimatums if you are serious—and it's a foolish strategy if you're not: ultimatums are only binding on the person who issues them. If you don't follow through on your ultimatum when your partner doesn't comply, you violate your integrity—and your partner knows you're not serious. People who issue frequent ultimatums have little integrity. Those who want to keep their integrity and their marriage intact settle down when they arrive at critical mass.

• *Respect and empathy increase.* We often feel afraid to say things that might affect our marriage, and in our fear we withhold information. Then we look with disrespect upon our partner, who we assume couldn't handle what we fear to say! The best sex and intimacy in marriage often come out of mutual respect. Respect is a bond of the highest order.

Empathy for your partner means giving him something solid to confront—a clear picture of yourself—so that he can make informed choices. This is particularly true at critical mass. Empathy is no excuse for withholding necessary information or for excoriating your partner with the truth. Real empathy and compassion lie in what you *do,* not in how either of you *feels* at the moment. Ironically, when your partner feels you "show up," it often relieves him even if he doesn't like what you're saying.

At the point of critical mass, when you think your marriage may be over, you are finally more likely to speak your personal truth. Paradoxically, once you're willing to say the important things you thought would ruin your marriage, it often saves it. At critical mass partners treat each other (and themselves) respectfully, conveying the belief that they are both resilient enough to handle the truth. Signs of contempt—such as insults, facial expressions of disinterest and dismissal, and eye-rolling—all stop.

The problem is not the loss of respect per se; it's that we don't say it. When you won't say "I don't respect you," there is a further loss of respect for yourself and your partner. At critical mass partners stop defending and strive for a more truthful and complete picture of themselves and their situation. They speak to the best in each other, even as they reveal hard truths. The hallmark statement of critical mass in emotionally fused relationships is, "I don't respect you and I no longer respect myself."

No one wants to hear this, but it's often a relief if you've known it on some level. Some readers will recognize this statement as the harbinger of their previous divorce. It can be that if it is said as a final statement of rejection, or the listener can't self-soothe enough to contain his reaction. Unfortunately, many people bolt from their relationship upon hearing these dreaded words—just when things are starting to get interesting . . . which brings us to the next tip:

•*Don't lose hold of yourself and overreact when discussions of respect surface in your relationship.* This may be the beginning of the end of your marriage, but it can also be your new beginning—if you soothe yourself enough to stay with the process. It's time for you and your partner to hold onto yourselves during this unraveling, so that you can reorganize on a fundamentally new basis. At this point you either embark on the growth cycle or call your attorney.

The Specter of Divorce

The qualities of critical mass differ markedly from those that reliably predict divorce: criticalness, defensiveness, contempt, invalidation, withdrawal-avoidance-stonewalling, and escalation of negative responses. These traits characterize many clients when they first come to see me, not when they are at critical mass.

What behaviors are predictive of divorce when couples reach critical mass? One partner tries to stop the process rather than going through it: he refuses to grow and tries to undermine the other's differentiation via argument, abuse, withdrawal, or "falling apart." Basically, he is trying to overpower the process of differentiation inherent in the system of marriage. His strategy of "I'm not growing and neither are you" is inherently doomed.

Although the possibility of divorce is omnipresent at times of critical mass, it is not what people who stay together focus on. They turn all their attention to their personal dilemmas, aware of the possibilities but not haunted by them. They don't want to give up themselves *or* their marriage. New solutions often exist at the higher level of differentiation created by self-confrontation; partners no longer have to choose between "self" and "spouse." People get divorced when they feel they can't stay and keep their integrity intact. More accurately, that's when they leave—the emotional divorce usually occurred long before. Others divorce rather than go through the growth cycle because they are afraid to test themselves.

Many couples hit critical mass spontaneously and get divorced unnecessarily. Even couples who declare divorce "not an option" go through crucibles driven by their integrity, and their marriage changes fundamentally in one way or another. The fact that our integrity gets put to the test is not the big problem. It's that we don't expect this inevitability in marriage and think something's wrong when it happens. When we dodge the test time after time, divorce becomes likely. When we embrace it in the midst of marriage—while we're still deeply invested—it works to strengthen the relationship. The test to our integrity is greater at this point because we face the loss of two things we still hold dear (ourselves and our marriage), rather than throwing away a relationship and a partner we no longer value.

Critical mass marks the turning point in your connection with your spouse. It either shifts you from emotional fusion to greater differentiation, or from marriage to divorce. When couples use critical mass wisely, there is an intense sense of intimacy, yet the future remains uncertain. You realize you are two separate people in two separate "boats." You hope you'll continue sailing in the same direction, but you can also end up going different ways. It's in your interest to give your partner signals that make your friendly intentions clear. Given the intensity of issues and time spent self-soothing at critical mass, that's not easy to do. However, showing yourself to be a peaceful vessel rather than a man-of-war can be an act of integrity too.

Now let's discuss some *do's* and *don'ts* that can help you through critical mass.

• *Repair the positive connection with your partner.* Send some positive signals to your partner. Infants smile and coo. Most couples have their own code. Neutral or negative signals (e.g., expecting your partner to make an approach; fussing) only increase the likelihood that he or she will break contact with you to self-soothe or actively start an argument.

• *Pay attention to your partner's attempts at repair and don't take them for granted.* Poorly differentiated people take their sweet time to get back together and feel entitled to keep their partner in pursuit mode. If you're not ready for sexual contact with your partner, then you're not ready—but let him know. If you're not sure, handle it in a way that spares your partner unnecessary vulnerability. Encouraging your spouse to wait until you're more responsive is empathic when done in good faith.

•*Be willing to make the first move.* Research documents that babies lead their mothers through the cooing dance. As an adult you can make the first move—if you can self-soothe and self-validate. Two types of "first moves" are important: pulling out of a discussion that is going nowhere, and then making overtures to get back together. Doing both has an entirely different impact than one without the other.

•*Pace yourself so you don't "burn out" quickly.* It takes lots of unrequited overtures to turn things around. If you made all or most of the approaches early in your marriage, you may already be burnt out and bitter, waiting for your partner to reciprocate. Going forward at critical mass involves self-soothing about the past and answering a question: "Is making an approach now in my best interest?" This doesn't mean you must make all future initiations. If you're too afraid you'll fall into that pattern—or afraid your partner will expect you to—then you're still emotionally fused. If you've become more differentiated, making an approach now may feel quite different. If it doesn't, then it's your "opportunity" to do something about that. You can always decide you're going too far and stop.

•*Don't make deals or commitments on your way into critical mass.* If you want security you can count on, don't ask your spouse for commitments. You won't be disappointed and you'll be less vulnerable. "No exit" contracts and "commitments to the marriage" are not enforceable and the security they offer is illusionary. Verbal commitments are unnecessary if people follow through on their intent and worthless if they don't. Instead, watch what your partner does. There are two commitments you can count on: the one your partner makes to himself that he won't violate, and the similar one you make to yourself. We've already noted how monogamy shifts as your differentiation increases from being a promise you make to your partner to one you make to yourself. The fact that we want our partner to make a commitment to us—to give us something to hold onto—underscores our underlying attempt at borrowed functioning.

•*Don't expect your partner to "be there" for you.* The irony of this common expectation is that poorly differentiated people are *most* likely to demand their partner "be there" for them and *least* able to count on it or reciprocate. When partners can't regulate their own anxiety, they are too dependent on soothing their anxiety through the relationship to put their partner first in times of discord. The character of happy, stable marriages is not quid pro quo; this characterizes the most rigid, unstable, unhappy ones.

When you reach critical mass and your former quid pro quo is no longer viable, your partner may check to see how serious you are: he may stop doing things for you to see if you really can take care of yourself. (Remember, normal marital sadism can always occur, but it's not safe to inflict it as freely at critical mass.) Be prepared to take care of yourself the same way you would if you were single—cook, clean, and do your own laundry.

Differentiation takes resilience and motivation. Don't expect your partner to support and encourage you onward. Your partner will always "be there" for you, but not the way you anticipate. He will be stimulating your development—but you'll probably wish he wasn't. Murray Bowen noted that the differentiating spouse is probably not getting anywhere unless the partner is saying, "you're ruining everything":

> When someone attempts to be more of a self in a relationship system, the absolutely predictable response from important others is, "You are wrong; change back; if you don't, these are the consequences!" In fact, if such responses do not occur, one's efforts to define more of a self are probably inconsequential.

Another reason you can count on your partner "being there" for you (in ways you don't like) involves the fact that you often confront the same unresolved issues with different people in close succession or simultaneously. You can't get support from your spouse while you deal with your parents (or vice versa) because you probably have the same core issues with both. Recognizing the same issues with different people often creates critical mass for change. Ironically, when you stop counting on people being there for you and stand on your own, that makes you more capable of truly being there for them.

Taking care of yourself at critical mass is important for you and a kindness to your partner. Poorly differentiated people do hurtful things when their anxiety goes up. Don't let your partner hurt you—for his sake as well as your own. Your partner's reflected sense of self is going to be bruised if you get "wounded." Expecting your partner to take care of you in times of crisis further drains his or her ability to cope and increases the likelihood of destructive cycles. You help your partner by taking care of yourself. "Being there" for your partner in the positive sense is great if you can do it. It's the essence of true mutuality. But don't expect it in return.

•*Holding onto yourself doesn't mean you're right.* Holding onto yourself doesn't just mean you won't settle for less from your partner; it means you won't settle for less from *yourself*. You're hoping and pushing for more from both of you. The emphasis is positive, turning toward your partner rather than away, seeking to share more together rather than less. Speaking to the best in yourself involves expecting the best from yourself and not letting your fears and negative self-portrait control you.

But holding onto yourself isn't an exercise in self-righteousness: you can differentiate around an issue about which you are wrong. You get the benefit of differentiation but pay the price for your decision.

I can offer my clients no safeguards that their decisions will be wise and appropriate. Critical mass is a time of "trust yourself" trials. Trusting yourself doesn't necessarily mean that your perceptions and feelings about circumstances or your partner are accurate. It means accepting that this is how you see things at this particular point in time. (Notice that people who scream "I'm entitled to my feelings" want everyone else to operate as if their feelings are accurate, while others' feelings aren't.)

You can't correct an error in judgment unless you recognize your mistakes. If you're wrong, you'll eventually discover your self-deceptions—and in the process you'll learn about yourself. One client said, "I have a great self-image but a lousy relationship with myself. My self-image isn't connected to anything—I keep telling myself I'm better than what I see myself do. But I don't really trust myself."

There are many paths to differentiation, but there is only one path for each person. That path is shaped by choices we make in response to our opportunities and misfortunes. Our mistakes and regrets are not barriers to becoming who we can be; they are a necessary ingredient. There would be no differentiation if not for these hurdles and detours. But rather than glibly reassuring ourselves that everything always turns out for the best, we must recognize that our choices irrevocably shape our life for better and worse. None of us is privy to knowing what we're supposed to do. How we shape our lives brings risk and responsibility. We may well give thanks in years to come for today's mistake, but we can't know that at the time.

For example, how do you know when you've "tried hard enough" and it's time to get out of your marriage? What about the kids? At what point have you fulfilled your responsibilities to yourself, your partner, and your family? Is there ever a good reason to leave? When have you actually been *too* patient? The best answer I can offer has four parts. First, if you haven't tried working with a *good* therapist, I recommend you do. A well-differentiated therapist can sometimes move things forward even when spouses are sure everything's hopeless. (Therapy works best when it's not a last-ditch effort, so don't wait until this point.) But when I say there are limits to what a therapist can do, I mean it in a different way than you might think; this is the second part of the answer.

No therapist can tell you when it's time to leave your marriage. Therapy is not a safe route to paradise. Understanding this provides a way to select a therapist: ask what the therapist does when he or she knows a couple should divorce. If the therapist offers *any* plan of action—implicitly presupposing to know when a couple *should* divorce—quickly find another therapist. Therapists do not know when someone should leave a marriage.

Thirdly, the preceding answer assumes physical or psychological abuse (beyond normal marital sadism) is not an issue. Domestic violence is a legal issue first and a psychotherapy issue second. I never encourage people to place themselves in physical danger, in part because nobody thinks straight when acutely anxious—or angry. If a therapist is involved, often he or she will confront the battering spouse, but the partner still has to self-confront, self-soothe, and mobilize herself out of her situation in a way that ultimately involves differentiation. Emotional fusion can keep battered spouses oscillating in and out of their homes like yo-yos. People dependent on a reflected sense of self have difficulty letting themselves *see* their spouse, and acting on it when they do (especially if they have a strong masochistic streak). They "dodge the hit" and take a beating instead; as I've said, they have low tolerance for anxiety and high tolerance for pain. Sometimes I confront clients about why they aren't taking their own perceptions (of their spouse) seriously—this, too, is part of trusting and holding onto yourself.

"Working on yourself" isn't a way to avoid dealing with your partner (more accurately, confronting yourself about your partner). If this avoidance involves further violation of your integrity, it makes you a sitting duck for more abuse. Self-soothing isn't about modulating your anxiety while your partner repeatedly batters you physically or emotionally. Eventually something must be done; differentiation is insight put into action. Holding onto yourself with a partner who's pummeling you to conform doesn't mean you have to stay there indefinitely. In this case, maintaining your own shape can involve taking yourself elsewhere.

Partners can be equally undifferentiated, but in very different ways. One may be a relatively naive woman, totally dependent on a reflected sense of self and eager to please; the other is a smart sociopath who manipulates others like puppets to fulfill his needs (i.e., vampire-like borrowed functioning discussed in Chapter 5). When the wife finally "wakes up" (self-confronts and mobilizes herself), in many instances she will leave; the same is true for men who realize they've married a venom-spitting cobra.

Every spouse must decide if and when things have gone too far; this can be difficult in less extreme cases. After serious self-confrontation and effort to repair your relationship have failed, it can be an act of differentiation, integrity, and *sanity* to divorce. When my own marriage seemed at this point after our move to Colorado, however, this is when everything turned around. Either way, your efforts to increase your differentiation still benefit you—the same development that makes it easier to stay in your marriage also makes it easier to leave. You have more choice.

Some people who've gone through a prior divorce realize that their fear of looking like a "loser" is the same reflected sense of self that got them divorced. Others self-confront whether or not their prior divorce was "necessary." If either of these sounds familiar, realize you could have stayed married, raised your differentiation, and come to the same conclusion to leave (for the same or possibly a different reason).

Which brings us to the fourth and final part of the answer to, "When is enough, enough?" The decision to divorce is another aspect of your crucible: making that decision further increases your differentiation. Carl Jung observed that these complications and personal entanglements are part of an uncanny crystallization process (he called it "individuation"). The challenges and choices force us to make "leaps of faith"—holding onto ourselves and moving forward one way or another. But holding onto yourself doesn't mean ignoring your partner. Differentiation is the ability to appreciate the impact of your actions and inactions on others and factor this into your assessment of what's right and necessary. This leads to mutuality rather than an attitude of every-person-for-himself. Self-repair, self-validation, and self-mastery allow—and require—you to recognize that you are dealing with another human being.

Going through the Looking Glass

Even when people have all this information about critical mass, they come out of it amazed with themselves and the process. Critical mass is unbelievable when you go through it the first time.

My clients refer to this experience as "going through the looking glass." In many ways they feel like Alice in Wonderland. They come out more solid, quietly centered, and more respectful of themselves and their partner. There's more empathy, other-validation, and generosity in their growth and comfort cycles. New solutions surface because there's less defensiveness and fewer personal issues contributing to gridlock. Kindness flows from strength rather than weakness or anxiety. When a gift is given, there is no doubt it is given freely.

"Going through the looking glass" is an apt description. Critical mass often feels like you and your partner are stuck forever—and then there's movement! The shift seemingly appears out of nowhere, although in retrospect it always makes remarkable sense. And just when you're congratulating yourselves on making it through, something else surfaces and you're back in the crucible again. There are usually more cycles in the chute. "Going through the looking glass" is not a one-time trip, but it's easier to get back to "wonderland" as you are better able to hold onto yourself.

The first time couples reach critical mass they think it's the end of their relationship, but it's really a milestone in developing the strength to love. Critical mass is an opportunity to turn toward your partner rather than away. But it's a time-limited opportunity when you're on the brink of divorce.

You learn a lot about togetherness and separateness by going through critical mass. We all go through our crucible alone, though partners' crucibles are always interlocking. And, ultimately, going through your crucible alone helps you experience your interconnectedness with everyone and everything. (We'll discuss this in the next chapter.)

Critical mass seems to function like surgery for emotional Siamese twins. As couples move through their immediate crisis, they feel more intensely intimate *and* separate, rather than isolated and drifting apart. They are more interested in improving their connection than in ragging about each other's inadequacies. Fights about "what really happened" evaporate. Partners become tolerant and more satisfied with themselves, their relationship, and each other. That's when they face yet another two-choice dilemma: relinquish the growing benefits of increased differentiation or give up fantasies of fusion forever.

Life presents us with the choice of getting what we want, but not the way we might want it. It's disquieting when long-sought improvements occur in ways we don't anticipate. We are challenged to give up cherished notions that keep us stuck. Facing that dilemma is part of becoming an adult.

Giving up fusion fantasies isn't easy. We tell ourselves, "We are two because we don't get along, but we'll be one when we resolve our differences." Learning that we must still maintain ourselves when things get better comes as an utter shock and complete disappointment—a reality avoided as long as we remain combative. Our desire to merge and relinquish personal responsibility dies a slow and painful death, but there's no peace until it does. Recognizing our immutable separateness makes intimacy meaningful, but this recognition is intolerable as long as we cling to fusion fantasies.

The Other Side of the Looking Glass

There are two paths to we-ness: one through change and the other through sameness. The we-ness that comes from hiding out in the comfort cycle is threatened by any growth in yourself or your spouse. The we-ness gained from experiences in the growth cycle, examining yourself and your marriage, fosters further growth. The most lasting we-ness often follows rather than precedes critical mass, because monogamy operates differently as your level of differentiation increases: it ceases to be a mutual deprivation. It feels like an ongoing commitment rather than a prior vow that constrains you.

As couples go through the crucible repeatedly, the benefits become obvious. Couples schedule time together because they *want* to be together, and they protect this time from invasion by other demands and activities. They address issues as they arise rather than waiting until things feel intolerable. There is a stability that transcends day-to-day ups and downs.

That doesn't mean that struggles and conflicts disappear, however. The difference is that couples accept certain limitations as part of making room for one's partner. And they stop fighting their partner's influence because the final determination on many issues remains internal. Differentiation yields a solid but permeable self. Allowing your partner to influence you creates new options and de-escalates fights. Feeling you have influence in your relationship reduces the urge to criticize or withdraw. When partners try to influence each other on issues about which they disagree, they do so in a straightforward manner that is softened with playful persuasion.

People relax. Their facial features soften and their body tension melts. They touch more frequently and more easily, leaning into each other for contact when sitting close. Sensuality and intimacy are no longer restricted to the bedroom. They no longer fear that straight talk will become adversarial. They have the comfort that comes in knowing both of them can stand on their own two feet.

But this doesn't mean partners receive "unconditional positive regard"—forget that! They get respect, sometimes begrudgingly. Respect develops from watching their partner master himself or herself and maintain integrity during critical mass. It is a respect that includes rueful admiration that partners won't knuckle under to each other or their own anxieties. Respect makes partners willing to give each other the benefit of the doubt in times of misunderstanding.

We need a long-term view of happiness that includes the ups and downs. Experiencing profoundly deep connection makes the daily wear and tear worthwhile. The meaningfulness and peace are often more important than the thrills and sensations. It makes partners so dear to each other that just the smell of their hair is comforting.

And yet the process of getting there is nerve-racking. The intimacy can be profound but uncomfortable, because the most intense intimacies often don't make us feel warm, safe, and secure. But these form the foundation from which soothing intimacies flow long-term. Perhaps every couple getting married today should add two lines to their wedding vows: "I'll hold onto myself. And though I expect blisters, I intend to hold out for bliss."

Chapter 14

Sex, Love, and Death

The philosophy of one century is the common sense of the next.

—*Chinese fortune cookie*

Differentiation is both beautiful and hard. There is a spiritual grace to the process but it's not always graceful. I have been blessed with the opportunity to watch many wonderful people go through their crucibles. What I have witnessed has changed my life and my practice. We have changed each other. *Passionate Marriage* chronicles many of these experiences with my clients, as well as my gratitude and respect for them.

Four elements of differentiation leap out at me: heroism, generosity, spirituality, and lack of shame. These are central in my mind because they repeatedly surface in my work with clients. I have spent a great deal of time questioning why these qualities seem to emerge of their own accord. If you think back to many of the couples we've met throughout *Passionate Marriage,* you'll see these traits in retrospect.

These characteristics don't just appear in the privacy of my office. As I write this chapter, I'm still savoring a poignant example that occurred at one of our Couples Retreats—the kind of thing that happens fairly often:

Ruth and I are standing at the front of a quiet room filled with a dozen other couples. Two couples sit at each round table. This is the eighth day of the nine-day retreat. Many of the people have turned around to give their attention to someone sitting in the back of the room.

Charlie is in tears. Spittle hangs from one corner of his mouth. He has been quiet for most of the retreat. Occasionally he has offered thoughtful comments befitting the school teacher he is. But now, on the morning of the last day, he has erupted in a torrent of epithets like those he had faced as a frail young boy. "Fuckin' dickhead! I'll kick your ass! Asshole!" Charlie has spent his life trying to escape his childhood in Hell's Kitchen in New York. Today he has decided to hold onto himself for his own emancipation.

"I can be a man! And I don't have to be like the idiots I grew up with! I've been afraid of anger all my life! Afraid of getting the shit beat out of me! And afraid I'd be like them! I'm tired of being afraid of my own aggression! I feel like a wimp! I know exactly why Laurie is fed up with me!" Respectful silence fills the room. Charlie seems to have surprised himself as much as everyone else.

Laurie, his wife of twenty-five years, puts her hand on his shoulder. She is supportive but unconcerned by his uncharacteristic outburst. She hates Charlie's passivity in and out of bed. She might have felt amazed or vindicated by his admission had it come before the retreat. But Laurie went through something similar several days earlier: she stopped bitching about what Charlie wasn't doing long enough to consider what she wasn't doing for herself. The last two days of self-confrontation have been difficult but productive for her. She recognizes the pattern: Charlie is falling together rather than falling apart.

Bud and Angel are sitting at the same table with Charlie and Laurie. Bud is the kind of gorgeous, "dangerous" man women love to screw but usually don't want to marry. He has been divorced four times. Married to Angel for two years, he doesn't want to blow this one. By his own account Bud "eats people alive" when he feels frightened, angry, or trapped in a relationship. He also displays the gentleness of someone horrified by his own capacity for violence. He's recently retired after twenty years in army intelligence and special forces.

Bud has subjected himself to eight days of excruciating self-examination in his process of self-redemption. He often participates in group discussions, making gut-wrenching disclosures that conclude with self-deprecating humor. He can't let himself accept the respect he's earned from everyone. Now, triggered by Charlie's outburst, he is staring down into the abyss of his life. He seems to see in himself the thugs who terrorized Charlie. Bud's eyes fill with tears as he speaks to him: "I think you're more of a man than I am. I destroy. You create. You teach children."

Bud's comment catches Charlie by surprise as he wipes his mouth with the back of his hand. "Thanks," he says flatly, and then adds with a laugh, "I can't believe I did that! I've never said anything about this in my life! . . . I'm open with my students, but I never show myself to other adults." Charlie seems to be talking more to himself than to the people in the room. As if suddenly aware of Bud, he says, " Really . . . thanks! I appreciate what you just said. You are exactly the kind of guy I was intimidated by. I never would have imagined you have this gentle side." Bud nods his head up and down with his eyes closed to keep his tears inside. He stretches his neck forward to swallow, as if his Adam's apple has swollen with emotion.

Charlie has deeply touched many of the other couples attending the retreat. Suzanne and Ronald are sitting at the next table, and Suzanne is visibly moved. She is a marketing executive in a large computer equipment firm; he is an accountant in a small solo practice. Four days ago Suzanne revealed that her boss, a senior corporate officer, has been sexually harassing her. He looks at her in ways that make her skin crawl. He has yet to do something overt enough for Suzanne to feel comfortable filing a sexual harassment suit. In the three years she's worked for him, there have been subtle innuendoes she might rise faster in the corporation if she were "more collaborative and easier to get along with." Suzanne was clear this meant being sexually available but couldn't prove it.

It was a big thing for Suzanne to let other people know this. When she discussed this with Ronald two years ago, he used it to bolster his assertions that Suzanne was a "ball-buster." He told her at the time, "Don't get fired because we need your income. I keep telling you you're too pushy. Don't make this guy angry!" Suzanne was devastated by Ronald's attitude; similar things had happened for years. This incidence was common knowledge, too: two days ago Ronald revealed it as part of his own self-confrontation. He finally acknowledged he was embarrassed that Suzanne made more money than he did, and that he felt intimidated by and jealous of her straightforward intelligent style. They hadn't had sex in over a year, but his disclosure helped to warm things between them.

At this moment, Charlie's remarkable self-validation has launched Suzanne into more thoughts about setting boundaries with her boss. "I admire what you just did, Charlie, and you've helped me make a decision. I've spent a long time being afraid of my anger because some men might be threatened or intimidated. I've always been told I'm too much to handle." It was clear Suzanne was referring to Robert as well as her boss. "I no longer want my boss's confession or apology. But I am determined his sexual harassment crap will stop!" Ronald nods his head in agreement; a number of other people are nodding and smiling too.

Ronald says to Suzanne and Charlie, "I take my hat off to both of you. I admire your willingness to finally stand up for yourselves. I wish I had more of that." Suzanne turns to look him in the eye to see if he is serious. There's another day in the retreat yet to go.

Lynn and Jonathan are next to speak. They have sat in the back of the room every single day. Jonathan is short and slight of build. Lynn is slightly taller and outweighs him by at least fifty pounds. "I'm like you, Charlie," he says, "I never speak up in groups. And I know what it's like to feel disgusted about never standing up for who you are. I've been apologizing for myself all my life. I've had intermittent difficulty keeping an erection for as long as Lynn and I have been together."

Jonathan pauses to reflect on what he's just said. The tone in the room is relaxed. Other people seem impressed but not shocked by his disclosure; they've witnessed similar wonders for the last eight days.

"Eighteen years is a long time to feel sexually inadequate . . . but I guess I started feeling inadequate a lot earlier than that. Lynn has always intimidated me. I was afraid whenever she got angry at me—hell, I was afraid whenever she wanted sex. We've been gridlocked for years. I'd tell her I can't fuck a timebomb that might explode, and she'd say any woman would be rageful if her partner went soft half the time they had sex. I guess I've known that I've been withholding from Lynn in lots of ways. I denied it when she accused me of it—I felt like she made me inadequate. Now I'm realizing that Lynn may get angry, but I'm scaring myself and making myself feel inadequate—and sneaky."

Lynn looks over at Jonathan with more respect than previously. She gives his hand a squeeze. Jonathan searches her face for the derogatory smirk he usually expects to see. Not finding it, he returns his gaze to Charlie. "I don't know if it's going to last, but since I've confronted how I've been holding out on Lynn—and myself—I haven't had difficulty with erections! I guess a little integrity and self-respect go a long way." Charlie and Jonathan nod to each other in mutual respect and recognition.

Looking on from across the room, Paul and June reach out to hold hands. Paul is an ex-priest and everyone takes June to be an ex-nun, although she isn't. They exchange a warm smile and Paul speaks to the entire group. "It was my turn to be in the crucible two days ago. That's when I finally had the courage to stop trying to please June sexually and let her do me. I used to think I was close to God when I wore my collar. Last night I felt close to God when June wore her sexy outfit. We had sex in ways I've never given myself permission to do. I finally feel communion with all you other couples as a peer! I believe I am experiencing the true nature of Spirit in this room. I'm more certain than ever my difficult decision to leave the priesthood was the right move."

June adds, "On the opening night of this retreat, I amazed myself by announcing I was good at doing myself during masturbation. I said I wanted to share that depth of responsiveness with Paul. I want you all to know my prayers have been answered—and then some!" Laughter and applause ripple through the room.

Someone at the adjoining table is trying to cut through the noise. Ted is speaking earnestly. "I don't want the seriousness of Charlie's struggle to get lost! That takes a lot of guts! Yesterday was the best day of sex in my life, too! But I don't think it is anything to applaud."

"I do!" It's his wife, Didi, speaking up. Someone on the other side of the room is laughing and crying at the same time. As usual, Didi has the group in stitches.

Ted obviously has something serious to say and the group quiets down. "I'm the doctor who insulates himself from his wife and kids through his job and investments—a rich man who hasn't believed he had a right to take up space on the face of the earth . . . everyone's savior who couldn't save himself. Doing hugging till relaxed—slowing myself down enough to make contact with Didi—scared me! Charlie, I know what you just did is important. Yesterday I kissed Didi in front of the window in our hotel room. A little thing like that finally made me feel like a man—like my money is as good as anyone's, and I have a right to do what I want in my room with my wife. That may not sound like much, but it meant everything to me."

Didi chimes in again. "To me, too! I knew it as soon as I saw Ted standing in front of the window in his underwear without first closing the blinds. Ted is so painfully modest and deferential, he worries someone might be staring at the building with binoculars and see him. He worries about offending waiters and parking attendants when we go to a restaurant." Ted nods towards Charlie as he laughs at himself, "It's true!"

"Thanks for recognizing it," says Charlie. "It did take a lot. Maybe if I keep doing this I'll start to believe in myself. Normally, the fact that you thought it was important would be what counted to me. What other people think of me has always carried more weight than what I think of myself. I've wasted a good part of my life worrying about what other people thought—even when I thought they were jerks!"

"That's emotional fusion! I know all about that!" Phyllis is speaking up. She is married to Eric, a chronic philanderer. "I think Eric and I have been fused since our first date. I used to take his affairs as negative messages about myself. I did the same thing when he wouldn't have sex with me. I used to wonder what was so awful about me that my husband kept having affairs. I was ashamed to be seen in public. But now I don't take his behavior personally. It's taken a giant leap of faith to believe I'm not somehow defective." Phyllis and Charlie share a smile.

"You're not the defective one. . . . I am!" Eric, who hasn't spoken during the entire retreat, is ready to talk. Everyone gives him the floor. Eric continues to stare at Phyllis until she realizes he is talking to her. Then he turns towards Charlie and continues. "Someday I'd like to be as much a man as you are. I've acted tough and I've screwed a lot of women, but it hasn't made me more of a man. I've made a mess of my life and brought lots of heartache to others. I've apologized to Phyllis in private, but I think I need to do it in public, too. . . ." Eric pauses until Phyllis looks him in the eye again.

"As an attorney I was paid to convince everyone that I was right even when I knew I was wrong. Whenever you suspected I was having an affair, I would try to make you feel stupid and crazy. When it comes to normal marital sadism, I'm a master. Whenever you caught me in a lie, I claimed you were trying to control me. I criticized you for everything because I was afraid if you felt good about yourself, you'd leave me."

"I still may, Eric."

Eric looks like he's just had the air knocked out of him. The man of words is momentarily at a loss for something to say. "I understand that," he continues slowly. "At the moment I wouldn't pick myself either. That's the issue, isn't it? That's why I can't seem to break off my current affair. I haven't been able to choose between you and her because the choice isn't about which woman. It's about picking a man. Myself. And why should I? I've repeatedly violated my own integrity and lied to everyone—including myself."

No one in the group rushes to offer support or comfort. No one wants to interfere with Eric's process. Phyllis gives no immediate reaction. Several people nod towards Eric in begrudging respect. Paul, the ex-priest, smiles at me, making me think back to his statement about Spirit being present in the room. Although it's premature to know if Eric's declaration will turn into something substantive, it feels like our "congregation" of couples has witnessed another small miracle.

Our Urge to Differentiate

Each day, couples attending the retreat have become awesome displays of self-confrontation, creativity, humor, and pathos—people holding onto the best in themselves and rising to their potential. In many ways, this process involves more than just self-confrontation and self-disclosure (i.e., intimacy). These are demonstrations of personal faith—faith in themselves and their potential to function at a higher level than they've previously attained. They manifest the qualities I mentioned earlier: heroism, generosity, and spirituality.

Mind you, all this occurs with no promise of confidentiality because there is no way it can be guaranteed. You can get a great deal out of the retreat without ever saying a word publicly—but no one ever remains silent the entire time. People who never talk in groups make amazing self-disclosures. These demonstrations of self-validated intimacy are all the more remarkable because they are characterized by a distinct absence of personal shame. People maintain themselves when facing their partner and other participants as well.

Many times throughout this book I've referred to poorly differentiated couples as "emotional Siamese twins" to keep their characteristics vividly in mind. They are the antithesis of what I'm describing: emotionally fused couples are often controlled by their shame and give no evidence of heroism or generosity. While some are active in organized religion, their daily existence seems devoid of spirituality. The couples I've just described looked this way at the outset of the retreat. I am often surprised when emotional Siamese-twins like Eric and Phyllis start the process—until I remember the power of our urge to differentiate.

Some time ago I ran across a book on the lives of real Siamese twins—physically fused identical twins. I was deeply moved by what I learned: within their life histories I found the same powerful drive to differentiate that I see in my office and at the Couples Retreats. I also recognized the same characteristics: heroism, generosity, and lack of shame about themselves. While I couldn't be sure about their own sense of spirituality, I found that's what their stories stirred in me. I felt I had found another piece of the puzzle about differentiation. Let me introduce you to one such couple.

Chang and Eng were born in 1811 in Meklong Siam (Thailand). They were the famous conjoined twins whose country became synonymous with the syndrome. They were completely formed except for a protrusion as thick as a wrist several inches in length that joined them at the center of their chests. As adolescents, they were brought to the

United States as curiosities. They had taught themselves English by the time they arrived (eventually they became literate, articulate, and developed a love of poetry). Although Chang and Eng were foreigners in a strange country, they were quick to take offense at insults. They broke away from P. T. Barnum, who displayed them as freaks. They set up their own around-the-world tours and entertained—and were entertained by—Europe's royalty. At the age of twenty-eight they chose a new lifestyle and became successful farmers in North Carolina. They learned to leverage their physical fusion to advantage: they developed a double-wide plow they could work behind, and devised a way of chopping wood by alternating swings of their axes. Neighbors said the two could do the work of four.

The congregation of the church Chang and Eng attended built a special double-wide seat for them in the front row. The brothers eventually courted the local pastor's two daughters, Adelaide and Sarah, despite community outrage. The two couples persevered and eventually married. Each brother maintained his own home and family. Chang and Eng built one of these homes, a large two-story dwelling, working in unison on tall ladders. Chang's marriage produced three sons and seven daughters; Eng had six boys and five girls. Sexual etiquette between Chang and Eng and their wives is unknown, but other details of their marriages exist.

When Chang and Eng were in each other's house, the visiting brother totally deferred to the will of the other. In his own home, each was free to go and do as he wished. The visiting twin remained quiet when decisions were made, allowing the other to be an effective father in his own way. Every three days the brothers went to the other's family and dominance reversed. Except during their subsequent world tours, Chang and Eng adhered to this routine without failure until the end of their lives.

Chang eventually suffered a stroke, which paralyzed his right arm and leg. For the next three years, Eng physically supported his disabled brother. The brothers continued their three-day rotation schedule, regardless of illness, family crisis, or inconvenience. Their scrupulousness lead to their death in 1874 at age sixty-three. Although Chang was ill, the twins made the scheduled shift by open wagon in the midst of a storm. Chang eventually died from complications. Eng died two hours later. One can only imagine the time in between.

Close friends said Chang and Eng differed in personality, interests, and temperament as much as any two brothers. Although they were generally hospitable, Chang was more irritable and hot-tempered. Occasional disagreements arose between them, and on one occasion they physically fought with each other. Generally, however, their relationship was the essence of mutuality and self-management—except for one incredible detail: Chang was a severe alcoholic; Eng was a teetotaler! How did they keep this from poisoning their relationship the way it might have been for emotional Siamese twins like Eric and Phyllis? In contrast to emotionally fused couples, these physically fused twins were the epitome of emotional differentiation.

Consider this: normal identical twins and physically conjoined twins both have identical genetics (from a single fertilized egg). Identical twins reared apart display striking similarities, but physically conjoined twins are just the opposite: despite similar environments—or perhaps because of constant contact—conjoined twins have distinct personalities and preferences. J. David Smith researched conjoined twins and found they prefer different foods, beverages, and reading materials. They tend to have different sleep patterns, pulse rates, hand dominance, spending habits, hobbies, and interests. They often differ in intelligence, scholastic achievement, aggressiveness, talkativeness, nervousness, irritability, attention to detail, emotional maturity, physical vigor, and preoccupation with health concerns.

Physically fused twins accommodate personal differences and collaborate to unimaginable extents. Some have become adept at acrobatics, golf, and playing musical instruments. They also accomplish something many married couples don't: they speak for themselves as separate individuals rather than as "we." Recently these patterns have been observed in Abby and Brittany Hensel, age six, physically conjoined twins, who appear to share a single body from the neck down. They have learned to run, swim, and ride a bicycle. Their courage, generosity, and lack of shame are an inspiration to others.

How can twins with identical genetics and environment become so different and tolerate these differences so well? J. David Smith suggests that conjoined twins demonstrate an important aspect of human differentiation: intentionality. He notes that the role of self-determination has been lost in the "nature-nurture" debate about whether heredity or environment rules our lives. These two perspectives may appear to be complete opposites, but they share a common deterministic outlook. Even a compromise position still ignores how self-direction shapes our destinies. When we ignore the role of free will and active participation in our own lives, we damage and discourage ourselves.

Physically fused twins can teach emotionally fused couples many lessons about freedom within human relationships. Freedom doesn't come from getting away from your partner—it comes from mastering yourself enough so there's room for two people in your relationship. You stop trying to control or limit your partner to make sure there's enough space for you. It is not the freedom to do whatever you wish, because the quality of intentionality is not about being stubborn, selfish, or inconsiderate. Intentionality brings freedom from tyranny of the lowest common denominator. Without freedom, commitment and marriage lose their meaning. And without differentiation there is no freedom. It is the path of personal liberation.

The live-changing acts of self-definition I've described in my office and at the Couples Retreat enrich my soul. They illustrate what happens when what's good and solid in us gets shaken, when we refuse to denigrate ourselves any longer or tolerate our own self-deceptions: we hold onto ourselves, face our long-avoided development, and rid ourselves of our overriding sense of shame. To me, these are triumphs of human spirit. I felt the same when I learned about how infants are able to self-soothe. These intimate acts of heroism always filled me with a sense of spirituality that was often beyond my grasp to explain. Throughout *Passionate Marriage* I've referred to the sociobiological foundations of differentiation, but that view, by itself, misses unique aspects of the process.

Spirituality in Everyday Life

My connection to my own spirituality has surfaced and grown from doing this work. I am not alone in this regard. When I help people become more differentiated—especially helping them reach their sexual potential—they often bring up the topic of spirituality spontaneously. At first I was surprised because I never talked about spirituality—and still don't, unless clients raise the topic. The couples were also surprised, since many did not consider themselves to be "spiritual people." Others had a strong dislike of organized religion. At times I joked, "Whom do you think you're going to meet if you pursue your sexuality to its limits—the devil?" But I couldn't explain to them or myself why this was happening.

As I began to recognize the spirituality of everyday events in marriage, I started including segments on sex and spirituality in my workshops and lectures. More people were hungry for this than I ever imagined. It was even well received in Australia, a country where organized religions don't enjoy wide support. Eventually I made presentations to U.S. Army chaplains and in churches and synagogues. But I still couldn't explain the linkage in a way that satisfied my scientific interest.

Why was it that helping people differentiate—balancing our two basic urges for self-direction and communion—seemed to trigger their spiritual yearnings? My problem was that, like most people, the very notion of science turned my mind away from thinking about differentiation in terms of spirituality. I'd fallen into the common tendency to divorce science from Spirit. In retrospect, my splitting these two was similar to how the scientific-sounding notion that "sex is a natural function" led us to split sexual function from creativity and eroticism. I thought about differentiation in terms of sociobiology and as a process of personal growth. But I hadn't seriously considered how spirituality might be another dimension to differentiation. Then I came across Ken Wilber's most recent work.

In *Sex, Ecology, and Spirituality: The Spirit of Evolution,* Wilber asks: is the shape of our existence the result of a cosmic "oops"? This seems to be the best answer Western science has offered to date. But the rest of world seems to think that behind the daily happenstance is a deeper or higher order. Wilbur notes that, although the varieties of Deeper Order (variously known as the Tao, God, Geist, Maat, Archetypal Forms, Reason, Li, Mahamaya, Brahman, and Rigpa) disagree with each other at many points, they all agree that the universe is not as disorganized or as random as it might appear.

Wilber brilliantly synthesizes every niche of science to show how, sociobiologically, we seem to be moving towards an "emergent" human(ity) of greater spirituality. Drawing together voluminous research and diverse philosophers, he suggests that humans (and all of creation) are expanding in four dimensions like a "Big Bang" radiating outward: self-preservation, self-adaptation, self-transcendence, and self-dissolution. (I have drawn this according to Wilber's verbal description in his book.) (See Figure 4.)

Look at both sides of the horizontal axis in Wilber's framework. You will find that it represents what we've discussed about differentiation: the ability to maintain your "self" in the face of pressure from significant people to conform (self-preservation) and the ability to sacrifice one's goals in the service of others (self-adaptation). Wilber would describe this as our ability to function as a whole (individual) and also as part of a larger whole. This is the balance between self-direction and mutuality; it is how increased capacity for self-soothing coincides with greater capacity for communion.

Current notions of "consciousness-raising" lie along the horizontal

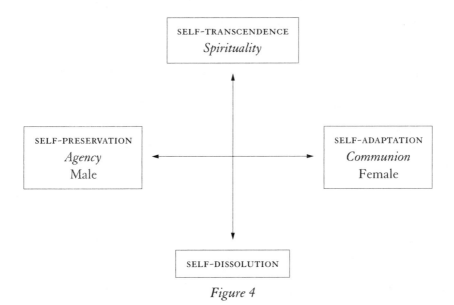

Figure 4

axis, with little consideration of qualities along the vertical axis. Yet, as I discovered with my clients, the tug of war that goes on along the horizontal axis leads to the emergent interest in spirituality surfacing today. Expanding our self-preservation and self-adaptation abilities allows us to transcend our former selves in ways that amplify our spiritual capacity and mindfulness as individuals, as a society, and (over generations) as a species. This also involves leaving behind the "self" we used to be (i.e., self-dissolution, which we'll discuss shortly).

Wilber's words might seem somewhat mystical and certainly unscientific. That's because, he suggests, as a species we are still developing a complete understanding of the relationship between nature and Spirit. We have passed through the primitive stages of equating nature with Spirit ("magical indissociation") and divorcing nature and Spirit ("mythic dissociation"). The widespread popularity of Joseph Campbell's work on mythic dissociation reflects our emerging third stage: understanding nature as the expression of Spirit. This differs from nature worship or sentimentalism by its emphasis on understanding the union of human moral endeavors with nature. Wilber sees the growing trend to recognize ourselves as members of a global community and links in a planetary ecology as a manifestation of this union. He writes:

> And *that* realization—a profound fruition of the decentering thrust of evolution—is the only source of true compassion, a compassion that

does not put self first (egocentric) or a particular society first (socio-centric) or humans first (anthropocentric), nor does it try merely in thought to act as if we are all united (worldcentric), but directly and immediately breathes the common air and beats the common blood of a Heart and Body that is one in all beings.

The "decentering thrust of evolution" Wilber places at the center of this growth is differentiation, the same force that makes marriage a people-growing machine (when we have the wisdom and faith to use it that way). In previous chapters I've tried to show how common events in marriage are part of this process: how our lack of differentiation makes us dependent on other-validation and reflected sense of self, which in turn induces us to marry and operate in ways that create grid-lock, low sexual desire, and lack of intimacy—and how all this creates the stimulus and opportunity for the leap of faith to self-validation and greater differentiation.

Just as we saw how sexuality played an integral sociobiological part in the emergence of our neocortex, Wilber looks at the historical emer-gence of mind and consciousness and sees the link between sex, spiri-tuality, ecology, and evolution:

> Whatever else we might say, the world does hang together, and evo-lution does have a direction: Eros as Spirit-in-action. Thus, both [philosophers] Shelling and Hegel would maintain that evolution is not simply the drive toward Spirit; it is the drive of Spirit toward Spirit, manifested in a series of increasing wholes and integrations (holons) that express increasing degrees of Spirit's own self-realization or self-actualization. Eros is fully present at each and every stage of the process, as the very process itself.

Understanding Wilber's ideas helped me explain the decidedly spir-itual quality to my clients' attempts to become more differentiated and explore their sexual potential. Men tend to become more the men they want to be—at the same time they become more like women. They're more capable of, and interested in, emotional connection. And, like Charlie, whom we met at outset of this chapter, they stop emasculating themselves because they fear their anger and aggression. Likewise, women reach a deeper appreciation of their femaleness. And, like Suzanne, who decided to set limits with her boss and her husband, they stop hiding their eroticism and power. They stop constantly throttling themselves down in fear of intimidating men.

Decades ago, psychiatrist Carl Jung observed this same process. As people became more differentiated (he used the term individuated) their female (anima) and male (animus) aspects became more balanced and enhanced. And they had greater appreciation of, and need for, spirituality. He noted that this coincided with an increase in spirituality. Jung thought of this natural, spontaneous, and inherent development as a manifestation of the Divine through expansion of the human soul.

Desire out of Fullness

What makes us seek greater self-direction, mutuality, and spirituality? Ken Wilber suggests it is Spirit seeking itself. I would say it is Spirit surfacing as our urge to differentiate, which we experience as our intentionality, our own desire. Like many people, I thought that absence of desire was the hallmark of spiritual enlightenment. I never suspected that desire can fuel spiritual and emotional development. That's why other aspects of working with my clients continued to confuse me.

As I developed the sexual crucible approach, the pattern of my work with clients began to change. They wanted more treatment as time went on, not less. In most conventional approaches people receive frequent sessions up front when they "can't cope" and taper off as they become more competent to handle their own lives. I was seeing the opposite pattern. As people became more competent and happy, they wanted more therapy!

At first I feared this reflected unhealthy "transference" or emotional dependence, but my clients were functioning more autonomously and better than ever. They weren't initiating more therapy out of feelings of inadequacy. Clients stopped trying to enter and leave my office without being seen, as they typically did at the start of therapy. They were no longer embarrassed; they were proud and glad. They entered their sessions "jet propelled" in pursuit of their own potential, rather than reluctant to find out what was wrong. They were curious about what they could accomplish, not overcome or avoid. It became commonplace for couples to tell grown children or close friends of their experience.

Once again, I found myself profoundly moved by my clients' behavior, their growing faith in themselves, and their loss of shame. The more they believed in their own goodness, the more they hungered for their own development. It made sense to me intuitively, but I couldn't pull it together in a way that explained what seemed to be a spiritual side to all this. (I had yet to encounter Wilber's idea of Spirit seeking its own fulfillment.)

Then a client suggested I read the writings of a modern-day Jesuit monk, Sebastian Moore, who talks about desire out of fullness. Since the early days of Western civilization, sex and spirit have been kept at a "safe" distance at best—and at worst, pitted irreconcilably against each other. Where Christian theology's view of spiritual desire is devoid of sensuality, Moore's is unabashedly erotic. His view is more in keeping with the spiritual "passion" of saints.

Spiritual awakening is often assumed to involve transcending all desire—but some desires set us free: desire for wisdom, compassion, justice, honesty, generosity, for greater capacity to love and understand life. Our desire for these qualities drives us to expand our capacities for both the self-direction and communion that ultimately leads to self-transcendence and spirituality. This is why Moore argues that spiritual enlightenment is marked by the ability to desire more fully rather than by the absence of desire.

Just as sex, love, and intimacy involve a myriad of developmental tasks, so, too, does spirituality. And just as society has limited its view to other-validated intimacy and other-soothing—thereby blocking awareness of self-validated intimacy and self-soothing—we've done the same with spirituality and desire. Moore distinguishes two levels of spirituality, which occur at different levels of personal development and differ in their quality of desire: level-1 spirituality is desire out of emptiness; level-2 involves desire out of fullness. Moore's two levels parallel our distinction between other-validated intimacy and sexual desire out of deprivation versus self-validated intimacy and wanting your partner. Spirituality can stem from high or low levels of differentiation. As with sex and intimacy, we can turn to spirituality out of strength or weakness, self-negation or self-affirmation.

We begin life knowing only level-1 spirituality: desire out of emptiness and deprivation. Moore refers to this level as the "magnet model" of desire that permeates romantic notions of being drawn to someone by his or her allure. At this stage we experience our desire and desirability indirectly by desiring someone else or realizing he or she desires us. It's what I've referred to as our "normal neurosis"—the quest for a reflected sense of self and validation from others. You attribute your desire and desirability to this "other"—be it your partner or God. Many people never get beyond seeking spirituality (and partners) out of a sense of deprivation. Moore suggests that as long as we depend on others for our sense of self, we never glimpse the joy in being wholly ourselves, which gives rise to an entirely different kind of love and desire.

Growing into Moore's level-2 spirituality and desire out of fullness is similar to enhancing sex and intimacy with your partner: the growth is seeded when you first draw upon your belief in yourself rather than continuing to rely on a reflected sense of self-worth. The transition itself is a developmental task that often surfaces in marriage. Sebastian Moore describes it as the leap of faith to self-validated intimacy we've discussed throughout this book:

> This new moment, of self-acceptance in a love relationship, is the crucial moment. It is the watershed of all human relations. It is what most of us most of the time stop short of. For this is the vital point at which our belief in our goodness is not strong enough to carry us forward. It is always some, often subtle, self-rejection that hinders us from believing in another's finding us attractive and from seeing that the other does so when this happens. . . . And thus our weak sense of our goodness holds us short of interdependent relationships, and keeps us in dependent relationships. We are willing slaves to beauty rather than sharers in beauty.

This isn't very different from my earlier statement about the spiritual aspects of marriage. For example, I've seen a number of women whose feelings of guilt about sex and embarrassment about their bodies drive them into their closet when undressing. These women often received strict religious indoctrination as children. I use their belief in God to help them make the transition to level-2 spirituality. Our dialogue in therapy goes something like this. I start out by asking:

"Can God see everywhere?"

"Yes."

"Even in your closet?"

"Yes!"

"Even in the moment when your underwear comes off and the granny nightgown goes on?"

Silent confusion and conflict. I plunge in:

"Medieval moralists would say He doesn't see you. They believed God absents Himself when married couples have sex. They also believed that God dwells in heaven but not on earth. What kind of God do you believe in?"

"I believe in a perfect God who is everywhere."

"You mean He's perfect—except He screwed up when he made you?"

Beliefs in a perfect deity and self-perceived defects coexist only as long as you keep sex and spirituality compartmentalized. Once clients try to integrate these sides of themselves they're in the crucible.

When people face the two-choice dilemma of giving up either their belief in a perfect deity or their belief that their sexuality is bad or flawed, they usually choose the latter. As my appreciation of this link has deepened, I've helped people align sex with spirituality as a way of working through their sexual and marital difficulties. When you consider it, these problems always involve a test of faith: believing in yourself and holding onto yourself—or pathologizing yourself, diminishing your self-worth, and running scared.

My clients display changes in the source, quality, and intensity of their desires as they progress, consistent with Sebastian Moore's description of desire out of fullness: their desire now stems from feeling good about themselves rather than feeling dependent or inadequate. Their desirability comes from an internal source: their sense of selfhood. They are more capable of sexual passion, of deeply wanting their partner.

Like the desire for knowledge, desire out of fullness for your partner involves wanting to want. Intentionality and free will are central ingredients when your desire is consciously undertaken and freely chosen. Like the desire for wisdom, this desire for your partner doesn't disappear once you've been satiated. It grows with time. This was the kind of desire for therapy, like the desire for sex and for their partner, that I saw in my clients. I think this is the kind of desire most couples seek.

Many clients became wonderfully creative, but not in hope of feeling more worthwhile. They produced as an expression of who they already were. I'm amazed to realize how many people only work hard when they are driven by feeling inadequate (desire out of emptiness). When you dare yourself to enjoy your talents, rather than believing you are a failure who's fooled everyone again, you make the leap of faith to level-2 spirituality.

I've also observed clients shift from giving up as little as possible (a "least lost" life strategy) to going after what they want. They give something up in the process, but that's the point: two-choice dilemmas become an acceptable fact of life. They go beyond realizing that you can't have it all. They grasp that happiness lies in not needing it all. Loss is inherent in getting what you want—unless you want everything, which guarantees you'll be unhappy.

This is important if you want your marriage to feel like an invigorating investment in your personal goals, rather than a stultifying commitment that now constrains and deprives you. Constraints can bring temporary stability to a troubled marriage—but they also create contention, sexual withholding, low sexual desire, and normal marital sadism. Even couples who originally agreed to monogamy as a mutual deprivation pact discover that, as they go through the process of differentiation, their commitment becomes a promise to themselves. They don't spend much time monitoring the alternatives, and they accept the path their life has taken and will take. They stop seeing attractive people they meet as "someone I could have/should have married." It's easier to soothe the loss of paths not taken, and people not tasted, when you and your spouse are exploring your sexual potential.

Self-Transcendence and Self-Dissolution

Earlier I mentioned that Ken Wilber views what I call differentiation as movement in four directions—but so far we've only discussed three: self-preservation (self-direction), self-adaptation (communion), and self-transcendence (spirituality). Now we can consider the fourth dimension: self-dissolution. Dissolution of marriage and personal identity as we've known them go hand in hand with growth and self-transcendence. Actually, we reached this same point in the last chapter when we saw how one path on the growth cycle leads to "termination" (the concentric cycles of comfort and growth in Figure 3, p. 355).

Sebastian Moore says that desire out of fullness is, in essence, a "death wish": life crises like falling in love, undergoing conversion, or suffering bereavement present the painful and bewildering demand that the "you" whose desire brought this about must die. Boundary experiences arise from confronting the limits of what you can attain as the person you are currently. To fulfill your desires, you have to change in ways that make that fulfillment possible. This means that the smaller "you" dies as a fuller "you," a more unique "you," is born. We desire our self to death in the most positive sense.

We can consider this paradox from another perspective: throughout this book (and especially Chapter 12) we have explored the need to hold onto yourself. But holding onto yourself and becoming more differentiated eventually leads to the loss of the self you've been holding onto. My clients begin to mourn their "old self" dying in the process of a new self being born. (It's no different from their fear/realization that their growth will lead to the end of therapy.) It's the death that gives life, but they're often wistful about it. They talk of not knowing who they are, but more accurately they mean who they are becoming. Ironically, they've never been more clear about who they are.

This process of your "old" self dying as your "new, larger" self is born is how self-transcendence and self-dissolution go hand in hand. Eric Jantsch recognized the implications of this on a global scale. In *The Self-Organizing Universe,* he proposed that evolution is self-realization through self-transcendence. Ken Wilber underscored the spirituality in this when he said, "Spirit does not build up nature around us, but puts forth nature through us." Self-dissolution is as much a part of this process as is self-transcendence.

Herein lies an important point that is sometimes hard to grasp: many people who seek self-transcendence don't want to give anything up, and they want the path safe and clearly mapped. However, our unwillingness to give up what no longer fits (i.e., self-dissolution) blocks us from self-transcendence. And once you recognize yourself, as Wilber does, as the manifestation of Spirit seeking its own fulfillment, then your refusal to grow is not just a personal shortcoming but also a thwarting of Spirit. This is where sin fits in, according to Sebastian Moore.

Sin isn't about unconfined desire—it's our refusal to desire and grow, our refusal to believe in ourselves, and our willingness to live below our potential. Sin is our "not wanting to want." Moore suggests that the answer to sin is not self-denial but allowing ourselves to desire more fully.

This may sound outrageous at first because many people associate religion with denial or rejection of the pleasurable parts of life. But as Lama Yeshe, Tibetan master of Buddhist Tantra points out, religion often becomes a form of suppression instead of a method for transcending our limitations. Instead of viewing pleasure and desire as something to be avoided at all costs, Tantra recognizes the energy aroused by our desires to be an indispensable resource for spiritual enlightenment. This same view is expressed in the Talmud in the words of third-century Rabbi Arika, who said that we will have to account to God for all the good things our eyes beheld but which we refused to enjoy.

It's not hard to understand why we sin in this way (not pursuing our own potentials): self-transcendence is fraught with discontinuities—and self-dissolution. Wilber notes that nature progresses by sudden leaps and deep transformations, rather than through piecemeal adjustments. He cites evidence from many fields of science to illustrate that dynamic systems do not evolve smoothly and continuously over time, but, rather, in comparatively sudden leaps and bursts.

Becoming is never safe or secure, especially if we're dependent on a reflected sense of self. We don't get to stop when we're scared or uncomfortable, because we grow by going into the unknown, including the Great Unknown.

The Limits of Self-Transcendence

Honoring the achievement of long-term marriage requires a balanced perspective. No matter how successful our self-transcendence, there are things we will probably never transcend in our lifetimes. One is our existential separateness from those we love. Another is the death of our partner. (Differentiation is still crucial for coping, however.)

In his Pulitzer prize-winning book *Denial of Death,* published more than twenty years ago, Ernest Becker wrote poignantly about the limits of human nature and self-transcendence. He was critical of "psychotherapeutic religionists" who claim

> . . . that the life force can miraculously emerge from nature, can transcend the body it uses as a vehicle, and can break the bounds of human character. They claim that man as he now is can be merely a vehicle for the emergence of something totally new, a vehicle that can be transcended by a new form of human life. Many of the leading figures in modern thought slip into some such mystique, some eschatology of immanence in which the insides of nature will erupt into a new being.

Becker said that we keep trying to make the world other than it is by legislating the grotesque out of it and inaugurating a "proper" human condition. The problem, he suggested, was that we don't take life seriously enough. He wrote:

> I think that taking life seriously means something such as this: that whatever man does on this planet has to be done in the lived truth of the terror of creation, of the grotesque, of the rumble of panic underneath everything. Otherwise it is false. Whatever is achieved must be achieved from within the subjective energies of creatures, without deadening, with the full exercise of passion, of vision, of pain, of fear, and of sorrow. . . . And we know that in some very important way, [ignoring] this falsifies our struggle by emptying us, by preventing us from incorporating the maximum of experience . . .

Becker understood how heroism moves something deep in our souls. When we deny the realities of life, we cheapen and trivialize the heroism and unheralded triumphs of couples such as we've encountered throughout this book. Idealizing human nature strips meaning from our struggles of self-development. But so do the trauma model of life and "wounded child" view of adults that currently pervade society.

Maintaining a balanced perspective is like walking a razor's edge. From the island of my personal reality, I can look out upon the panoramic interconnectedness of nature. I feel our lives to be part of a larger process, vital links in our planetary ecosystem and human evolution. I watch us take our place in the intergenerational flow of life, joining countless lovers who've brought forth our species' capacity for intimacy and desire out of fullness.

I recognize my life is peripheral yet integral to a much greater reality. Like M. C. Escher's drawing of two hands drawing each other, we create our reality, which creates us. I am part of the world trying to figure itself out. As I accept the existential fact that we all live in different realities, I become one with everyone who lives a similar fate. I am no longer alone in my aloneness. I am one with Existence, expressed through my own existence.

But walking the razor's edge is painful and difficult. Wilber says that we eventually transcend our existential loneliness. Ernest Becker and psychologist Clark Moustakas say we never do. At this point in my own development, I find both positions speak the truth: eventually, we must grapple with the immutable separateness of being human. Loneliness is a basic condition of our existence. It's part of understanding and appreciating intimacy and, when correctly handled, deepens and extends our humanity. Moustakas writes:

> To love is to be lonely. Every love is broken by illness, separation, or death. The exquisite nature of love, the unique quality or dimension in its highest peak, is threatened by change and termination, and by the fact that the loved one does not always feel or know or understand. In the absence of the loved one, in solitude and loneliness, a new self emerges, in solitary thought. The loneliness quickens love and brings to it new perceptions and sensitivities, and new experiences of mutual depth and beauty.

Moustakas says that we confuse existential loneliness and loneliness anxiety. Loneliness anxiety is our common but unnecessary fear of being alone, our normal neurosis, our alienation from ourselves. It surfaces in the pervasive "never be lonely" themes in modern society and what we now call "fears of abandonment." Existential loneliness is an inevitable part of being human. We can erase loneliness anxiety and ease existential loneliness by becoming more differentiated, but the fundamental loneliness of being human isn't something you transcend entirely (unless you achieve a profound level of enlightenment). We don't "defeat" existential separateness—we simply see it rightfully as part of a larger whole.

What Ernest Becker labeled heroism Moustakas calls courage and hope:

> It is not loneliness that separates the person from others but the terror of loneliness and the constant efforts to escape it. We must learn to care for our own loneliness and suffering and the loneliness and suffering of others, for within pain and isolation and loneliness one can find courage and hope and what is brave and lovely and true in life. Serving loneliness is a way to self-identity and to love and faith in the wonder of living.

Both acceptance and denial of our separateness can motivate us to seek others—but only acceptance enhances marriage. Seeking love and intimacy to deny reality inevitably ends in disappointment. When psychologist Erich Fromm said that intimacy is the way we escape from "the prison of our separateness," he presumed an acceptance of existential loneliness rather than denial of it.

Loving Is Not for the Faint of Heart

I hope one day to grow beyond my current observations, but at this point it seems to me that no amount of self-transcendence transcends death.

Loving your spouse, like desire out of fullness, is an act of integrity. Like all acts of integrity it involves liability: in this case, what if you succeed? You just might get the wonderful marriage you thought you wanted and felt deprived and guilty for not having. As the ancient Chinese curse warns, be careful what you pray for. Often we're not ready to pay the price of success.

Happiness in marriage takes courage, flexibility, and faith. We often think it's easier to be happy than unhappy, but if that's the case—given our tendency to take the easy way out—don't you think more people would be doing it? Happiness doesn't fill the void when you finally remove your hang-ups and resolve your disagreements. That's only half the process. You still have to hold onto yourself. You have to maintain yourself through life's tragedies and not internalize them. A wonderful marriage doesn't make life easy or painless. It just makes the work sweeter and the pain more meaningful.

Wonderful relationships are an inevitable source of pain. Playwright Oscar Wilde said life has two tragedies: one is not getting your heart's desire and the other is getting it. Wilde thought the latter was worse because it's always a disappointment. A fantastic marriage kills the fantasy of "having it all." Even a beloved, considerate partner will profoundly disappoint you at times. But there's a larger issue: deeper pain lies ahead if your partner doesn't disappoint you. It's not the utilitarian or "bad" marriages that are so hard to bear, it's the really good ones that break your heart. Having a profoundly good marriage means the vulnerability of having more to lose.

The end result of loving a cherished long-term partner is grief few of us are prepared to handle. One of you will bury a beloved, irreplaceable friend. Many of us would rather have a partner who's "a pain in the ass" than risk pain in our heart. A "pain in the ass" is easier to love less, so the loss won't be too great when he or she dies.

The biggest trust issue in marriage isn't about trusting your partner. It's about whether or not you can really trust yourself. The better your partner, the better your ability to soothe and console yourself needs to be. It's not safe to love your partner more than you can self-soothe, especially if you always need him or her to "be there for you." Your partner won't be there to hold your hand and comfort you through his or her death. You'll go through that alone. The increasing vulnerability that arises from your partner becoming more important to you makes a passionate marriage daunting. Many of us know we can't trust ourselves with this enormous risk.

Loving is not for the weak, nor for those who have to be carefully kept, nor for the faint of heart. That's why there's so little of it in the world. Love requires being steadfast through many difficulties. If our society ever tolerates a realistic view of marriage, we will be less cavalier about encouraging people to love and want each other.

In my workshops I often discuss how many spouses hope to beat the system: they hope they'll die first. This isn't necessarily normal marital sadism, it's what I noted earlier: they simply seek to dodge a grief few are prepared to handle. Lack of differentiation forces us to take a stance often antithetical to our intent: in essence, we wish the one we love more suffering. Our unwitting attitude is, "You take the hit. Better you then me."

Who among us has the strength to love on life's terms? How many of us can say to our partner, "You go first. I don't want you to die, but you're entitled to your own life and your own death. Go easily. Don't worry. I'll take care of myself somehow. Holding onto myself with you has made me strong enough to do that." I'm not suggesting we choose our death like deciding who jumps off the diving board first; rather, this attitude underlies many marital interactions, and surfaces during times of illness and the golden years of life.

My point is one we began this book with: nobody's ready for marriage; being married makes you ready for marriage. Marriage is where you build the strength to love and soothe yourself through the loss of an irreplaceable life mate. The same personal development required to keep sex and intimacy alive in marriage allows you to soothe your heart enough to truly love your partner. In other words, the differentiation necessary to *do* your spouse also gives you the strength to bury him or her.

As Ruth and I were making our final decision to move to Colorado, on the day before the New Year's weekend, I suddenly faced the possibility that I might have to practice what I preach—in a big way. Ruth was informed she had a "suspicious lump" in her breast. We spent four long days wondering if she had cancer. Her mother had died from this terrible disease. Did I really have the strength to tell Ruth, "You go first"?

At one point in our soul searching we wondered if we had the inner resources to cope with this crisis. Life was shaking our denial and ruining our plans. Should we cancel our ski trip scheduled for two weeks later? Should we cancel our move to Evergreen altogether? The huge sums in hotel and travel deposits we would lose now meant nothing. What a powerful lesson! But were we up to learning it once and for all? If the lump was benign (which, fortunately, it was), would we promptly forget that our time together was finite?

That weekend we lay in bed talking long into the nights, looking into each other. We had some of the most tender and passionate sex of our marriage. We reviewed how our sex and our love for each other had matured over the years. Our eyes became windows into our souls. I looked at Ruth and we saw each other. She said, "Everyone who thinks your eyes are intense should see you now. They're so soft and deep." Hers were bright blue and the tears that filled them from time to time were like pools of grief and solace for me. Moments like these bring painful awareness of our separateness from those we love.

About this time, several clients encouraged me to see the movie *Shadowlands,* the true story of author C. S. Lewis. I cried when I saw it for more reasons than Lewis finding his humanity by losing his wife to cancer. I realized my clients were directing my attention to lines of dialogue in the movie similar to what I'd said to them: "The pain of your partner's future death is part of the pleasure now." "That's the deal." And "we love—and read—to find out we are not alone."

The message of the movie was also heartbreaking because I was about to tell my clients about my intended move to Evergreen—another type of profound loss for everyone. In the midst of my own grieving I worried: had I helped them enough so that they could say, "You go first"?

In the midst of one session with Michelle, a woman who had made tremendous progress in therapy, I reflected on the significance of what had transpired between us. Several times we said nothing, sitting there for long pauses, quietly looking at each other. Michelle said, "You look both happy and sad." I sat there slightly stunned. She was absolutely right! She had seen me and let me know it.

After a moment's reflection, I said, "You're absolutely right," and made no attempt to hide it. "You have truly come along way; I'm impressed by your perceptiveness." It took several more seconds for me to decide what else to say, knowing this was an important moment between us. "What you see is true. I'm happy and sad for several reasons. I have to deal with sadness in my own life, like you have in yours, like everyone else. I'm also sitting here incredibly proud and admiring of you and what you have accomplished. This makes me very happy in the same instant I'm acutely aware that one day I will not be privileged to watch you grow. That makes me sad."

Having said that, I felt something pass silently between us. Our eyes promptly filled in equal measure of joy and pain.

Michelle said, "I know in my heart you wouldn't have answered me as openly about your sadness a year ago. You would have asked me why I wanted to know. I can tell from your response, you think I've come along way." I just nodded silently as I choked on the bittersweetness of the moment.

"Do you love me?"

Michelle's question fueled my joy and pain. I genuinely wished Michelle well and took pleasure in her happiness—even as I was sad for myself. Yes, I loved her.

But I don't tell my clients I love them. And I've stopped asking stupidly, "Why do you want to know?" I gave Michelle a more respectful and difficult answer:

"You tell me."

Hopefully her answer would be one of her final acts of self-validation with me.

"How should I know?! Why won't you tell me?"

"Because your question is too important to ruin by answering it."

Much to my disappointment, Michelle dropped the issue. I went home thinking we both might miss her being certain of my feelings for her.

Shortly thereafter I received a between-session phone call from Michelle. It was noteworthy because I rarely receive calls from my clients, and I couldn't remember any previous one from her.

"I just want you to know that while I was driving my car, it suddenly dawned on me. I know it in my guts. YOU LOVE ME!" My heart leapt and I felt like laughing and crying.

"Well, I'm glad to hear I do!"

"You're not going to screw this up by telling me, now that I've said this, are you?!"

"Nope!"

Michelle laughed. "Well, I want you to know, I love you, too." And with that we hung up.

My clients don't "taper off" their sessions as they approach termination. As I mentioned earlier in this chapter, the frequency often increases—treatment isn't designed to prop them up and they can digest more as they get further along. When they leave, they're giving up something and someone that's still important to them. We stop altogether when they're ready to "take the hit" of termination.

Michelle and I were lucky. We went through termination at her own pace before I left New Orleans. Other clients and I were not so fortunate. Saying goodbye is often hard, but this was harder than I'd ever experienced. In the end, I was saying goodbye to eight clients a day who wanted to continue.

During all this upheaval, I also had a full schedule of workshops to conduct. At one presentation, Julia, a young woman in her early thirties, asked me to lunch. She wanted to tell me how my work had affected her life. I will never forget that meal, though I hardly ate a bite.

In the previous year Julia had suffered a severe inner ear infection that left her bedridden with vertigo for several days. To fill the time, a friend gave her recordings of several of my lectures. In one of these I discussed the issues of having the strength to love.

For two days Julia lay in bed questioning if she could say to her beloved husband, "You go first." She emerged from her crucible having decided she could. Julia and Morgan had one of the most important conversations of their lives.

Morgan died two days later of a sudden heart attack. He, too, was in his thirties and in apparent perfect health.

At the time Julia told me her story, she was in the painful process of getting on with her life. As I sat and listened to her, I was speechless most of the time. My thoughts flashed to Ruth and myself, to Michelle, and to my other clients. I looked around at all the people in the restaurant, busily eating and chattering away. I wondered how many realized that at some point, we all face Julia's fate. The final sentence of *Constructing the Sexual Crucible* kept coming to mind like a silent prayer:

May we all develop the strength to love well.

Referral Information

Although the process described in this book occurs in every marriage, you may want or need a therapist to help you effectively harness it. A therapist can do a lot more than empathize or teach communication skills. He or she can monitor important topics to keep you on track, help you observe the process, and assist in modulating and containing anxiety in your marital system to increase your differentiation. The less differentiated the couple, the more likely they will need the assistance of a therapist—and the more differentiated the therapist needs to be.

You may have to try several therapists before you find one who can really help. I believe a therapist can't bring someone to a higher level of differentiation than the therapist has achieved—when anxiety and pressure in your marriage exceed the therapist's differentiation, he or she gets "infected," too, and treatment effectiveness declines. But there is nothing in most therapists' training or licensing requirements that ensures they are more differentiated, or know more about sex and intimacy, or have better marriages than the average individual. Unfortunately, you will have to assess their differentiation for yourself. Fortunately, this isn't too difficult—if you throw away conventional guidelines for picking a therapist: don't pick someone you are totally comfortable with. That's usually someone whom you're sure won't confront you. Find someone with whom you feel *productively* uncomfortable. A good match is not the same as your therapist "understanding" and "accepting" you the way you want to be seen; it's one in which you self-confront, self-soothe, and mobilize yourself to do what you need to do. On the other hand, therapists can be wrong—working with a therapist to get farther than you can on your own is not the same as turning yourself over to him or her.

The Marriage and Family Health Center (MFHC) conducts training for health-care professionals in the sexual crucible approach and maintains a database of therapists who have attended one or more programs. MFHC will be happy to inform you of such therapists in your area and the training they received. If a therapist presents himself/herself as using this approach, be aware that advertising guidelines have been developed and workshop participants have voluntarily agreed to follow them. This involves listing specific details of their training (for example, "a two-day introductory workshop," or "a six-day workshop treating sexual desire problems using the sexual crucible approach," or "a weeklong clinical practicum"). Vague statements such as "studied with Dr. Schnarch" are misleading and potential misrepresentation. MFHC does not "certify" therapists' ability and cannot be responsible for the actions of a particular clinician. Audio, video, and printed materials are also available from MFHC.

Several professional organizations are also available to help you. The American Association of Sex Educators, Counselors, and Therapists (AASECT) can refer to you a certified sex therapist (who may or may not be familiar with the sexual crucible approach). Likewise, the American Association for Marriage and Family Therapy can refer you to a marriage and family therapist whose training and preparation meet established criteria for clinical membership. Ideally I recommend finding a therapist who has both credentials, although they are relatively rare. For sexual health-care information relevant to marriage and family life, contact the Sex Education and Information Council of the United States (SEICUS) or your local Planned Parenthood affiliate.

Marriage & Family Health Center
2922 Evergreen Parkway, Suite 310
P.O. Box 3789
Evergreen, CO 80437-3789
(303) 670-2630; fax (303) 670-2392
http://www.passionatemarriage.com

AASECT
P.O. Box 238
Mount Vernon, IA 52314-0238
(319) 895-8407

AAMFT
1717 K Street, Suite 407
Washington, DC 20006
(202) 452-0109

SIECUS
130 West 42nd Street, Suite 2500
New York, NY 10036
(212) 819-9770

Notes

Chapter 1: Nobody's Ready for Marriage—Marriage Makes You Ready for Marriage

37   When Karen untied me: A complete discussion of *doing* someone and *being done* appears in Chapter 12.

38   A sociologist once observed: Keifer, C. (1977). New depths in intimacy. In R. W. Libby and R. N. Whitehurst (Eds.), *Marriage and Alternatives: Exploring Intimate Relationships*. Glenview, Illinois: Scott Foresman & Co.

39   It is this "other: James Thurber & E. B. White, *Is Sex Necessary?* 1929, p. 161.

39   Using the same rationale: See Helen Singer Kaplan's *Disorders of Sexual Desire* (Brunner/Mazel, 1979).

40   It's hard for couples: known as *DSM-IV & ICDM*.

42   Pulitzer Prize winner Ernest Becker: In *The Denial of Death*, Becker suggested that every society is a living myth of the significance and design of human life. In effect, each society is a "religion" with its believers. This concerned him, as it did philosophers William James and Paul Tillich, because beliefs about people, human nature, and what we may yet become affect our actions.

42   In *Care of the Soul*: p. 203.

43   However, radically new information: Psychologist Ed Tronick has researched how infants' self-directed behaviors (e.g., looking away, thumb sucking) and other directed behaviors (e.g., making eye contact, smiling, fussing) are part of a complex pattern of mutual regulation between infants and their caretakers. He emphasizes that while infants' capacities are limited in many ways and require the assistance of their caretaker, they are neither solely dependent on the caretaker nor passive recipients in the interactions. Infants actively regulate their own emotions directly, as well as indirectly by attempting to regulate the

behavior of their caretakers. See E. Z. Tronick, "Emotions and Emotional Communication in Infants" *American Psychologist,* Feb. 1989, p. 112–119. Also: A. Gianino & E. Z. Tronick (1988) "The mutual regulation model: The infant's self and interactive regulation coping and defense." In T. Field, P. McCabe, & N. Schneiderman (Eds.), *Stress and Coping.* Erlbaum (pp. 47–68).

47 Barbra Streisand once asked: p. 324. Cited in L. J. Peter (1980). *Peter's Quotations: Ideas for Our Time.* New York: Bantam Books.

51 The solutions we seek: People who've gotten divorced five or six times are often attempting to beat the system by bailing out when the process begins to close in on them. We'll discuss this in chapter 10.

51 Only if we are: Prather & Prather (1990) *Notes to Each Other.* Bantam Books (p. 10).

Chapter 2: Differentiation: Developing a Self-in-Relation

58 In lots of cases: Differentiation-based therapists Michael Kerr and Murray Bowen said it best in *Family Evaluation* (Norton, 1988): "A common assumption about people with emotional problems is that they did not receive enough 'love' and support from their families. Many people have an attitude that if only they could get more 'love' and attention, they would feel and function better. The concept of differentiation places this assumption in a broader context, namely, that the most needy people have achieved the least emotional separation from their families. The broader context can provide a guiding principle for an approach to human problems that runs counter to the feeling and subjective process. An approach based on the feeling process is one that says, 'People who feel unloved need more love.' An approach based on a systems principle is one that says, 'People who feel unloved are [overly dependent on] love.' An intense and nonthreatening relationship may relieve the person's symptoms, but it does so by replicating what once existed in the early parent-child relationship (in reality or fantasy), not by supplying a need that was never met.

"Many dedicated mental health professionals have tried to give patients the 'love' and 'caring' both the professional and the patient are sure the patient never had. Many therapists have then found themselves in a hopelessly ensnared transference in which the patient perceived the therapist to be as 'ungiving' as the mother. When a therapist's remarks to a patient are guided by the assumption that people who feel rejected and unloved are the product of an intense emotional attachment to their families, the remarks may not 'sound' or 'feel' right to the patient or the therapist. Regardless of how they feel, the remarks usually open up communication and reduce tension in the therapist-patient relationship. The constructiveness of the remarks appears to be based on a 'collision' of different ways of thinking, different basic assumptions." (p. 109)

59 Because our identity depends: If you're following the nuances of our discussion, it may seem as if I'm saying two different things. On the one hand, poorly differentiated people demand their partner adapt and accommodate. On the other, they demand their partner not change. Both are true, which is an example of how low differentiation contributes to inherent paradoxes and conflicting demands in relationships.

60 "People whose identity is: Much of Western psychology following Freud embraced the "self out of relationship" idea of development. This says we develop

our sense of identity and worth by extricating ourselves from entanglements with our caregivers—especially mothers. Feminist psychotherapists rightly pointed out this may fit a stereotype of how boys develop, but girls develop by remaining in relationship with their significant others. Unfortunately, they didn't go far enough: boys and men, like girls and women, develop *in* relationships, although in different patterns.

However, this is not the same as getting your sense of self from your relationship, which some therapists encourage as the path to mutuality. Ironically "self in relationship" (identity from the relationship) doesn't lead to mutuality—just the opposite. You can gain self-worth by facilitating the goals of others, but you're also likely to manipulate and control those around you if your identity and value are dependent on relating to them in particular ways.

62 According to Bill's father: This common confusion of business and family dynamics in emotionally fused family-owned businesses contributes to their high rate of failure.

62 The greater the differentiation: Other species show corresponding aspects of differentiation: bees and ants distinguish between different castes (for example, queens from workers), and vertebrate animals recognize infants, juveniles, and adults of their own kind. Animals' territoriality and people's sense of "personal space" are examples of the "me versus not me" responses inherent in differentiation; so is your autoimmune system's response to foreign substances, including organ transplants from other people.

63 Differentiation allows each person: see Kerr & Bowen, *Family Evaluation.*

65 The husband expressed a desire: November 19, 1993 Associated Press article "Castration won't spoil celebration," in *Times Pycaune* (p. A-B). Thirty-five-year-old Aurelia Macias, and thirty-nine-year-old Jack Macias.

65 "These people are usually: November 15, 1993 Associated Press article "Woman run over by boyfriend asks judge to drop case" in *Times Pycaune*. Darlene Kincer, age thirty-two, and William Powell, age thirty-five.

66 The difference is that: "While pseudo-self is always vulnerable to being molded and changed by others, it is most vulnerable in emotionally intense relationships. That is where people have the most difficulty permitting each other to be what they are. Each reacts to the beliefs, attitudes, values and way of being of the other and tries to reshape them. If one person gets the upper hand, that person's beliefs, attitudes, and values become dominant in the relationship. The dominant one gains strength and confidence in what he thinks and feels. He is sure his compass (what he believes, values, and thinks) is pointing in the 'right direction.' Meanwhile, his partner loses confidence in her compass. One becomes the 'strong' self (really pseudo-self) and the other the 'weak' self. Solid self is not negotiable in any relationship system and little 'borrowing' and 'trading' of 'self' occurs in well differentiated relationships." (Kerr & Bowen, 1988, p. 104)

73 Someone once said that: R.M. Rilke. In John J. L. Mood (1975). *Rilke on Love and Other Difficulties.* New York: Norton.

74 It's what Gloria Steinem: *Outrageous Acts and Everyday Rebellions,* NAL-Dutton, 1986.

Chapter 3: Your Sexual Potential: Electric Sex!

78 If we want kids: Parents and educators interested in an intimacy-based approach to sex education may want to listen to *I'm Finally Normal . . . and It's*

Been Downhill Ever Since!, the keynote address I gave at the 1995 Planned Parenthood of America Annual Meeting. The recording is available from The Marriage & Family Health Center, Suite 310, 2922 Evergreen Parkway, P.O. Box 3789, Evergreen, Colorado, 80437-3789.

79 Although we love parables: Margery Williams, *The Velveteen Rabbit* (Avon Books, 1975).

79 Isadora Duncan had it right: in Chapter One of her memoirs, *My Life* (1924). (Republished 1995, Norton)

80 Some therapists taught that: Helen Singer Kaplan, *The New Sex Therapy* (Brunner/Mazel, 1974).

80 As a result, horizontal: I refer here to popular application of Masters and Johnson's work, and not how they themselves used this approach.

81 Let's approach sexual potential: A more complete discussion of the dynamics of this model is described in *Constructing the Sexual Crucible: An Integration of Sexual and Marital Therapy* (Norton, 1991).

82 Humans became capable of talking: This actually occurred from a major leap in human evolution of which our neocortex was a part. Humans became fully bipedal around this time, making us capable of face-to-face intercourse. Our neocortex is the result of the remarkable sociobiological recursion that anthropologist Helen Fisher documents in *The Sex Contract* (Quill, 1982). Humberto Maturana and Francisco Varela explain sociobiology and human evolution of understanding in *The Tree of Knowledge* (Shambhala, 1987).

85 Sensations have to be organized: Many women report that their initial experiences having intercourse were not really pleasurable—not because they had discomfort but because it felt "odd." They hadn't yet learned how to organize their physical sensations into a sexually stimulating whole.

87 A man may lose: Note that I'm referring to a lack of lubrication because the woman's excitement is below her arousal threshold. Lack of arousal needn't be the reason with menopausal women and others who simply don't lubricate a lot, no matter how aroused they are. For these women, commercial lubricants can help—and no woman need participate in intercourse when it hurts for *any* reason. But continually overcoming a lack of arousal with these products is antithetical to pursuing your sexual potential.

88 We compensate for something: The therapeutic technique of "bypassing" (Kaplan, 1974) exploited this to avoid dealing with underlying problems in marriages.

88 Women with this ability: B. Whipple, G. Ogden, & B. R. Komisaruk, Physiological correlates of imagery induced orgasm in women. *Archives of Sexual Behavior.*

89 Masters and Johnson did: R. C. Kolodny, W. H. Masters, V. E. Johnson (1979). *Textbook of Sexual Medicine.* Little, Brown.

93 This pattern of progress: So is learning to use any position in different ways for either partner's preference.

97 In more rare and esoteric: In *The Future of the Body* Esalen Institute founder Michael Murphy thoroughly documents esoteric phenomena that people experience during transcendent experiences. Murphy noted similar transformations are found in the regenerative, incarnational power of love apparent in religious passion. He cites the Indian saint, Sri Ramakrishna, as saying, "In the course of spiritual discipline ... one gets a 'love body' endowed with 'love eyes'

and 'love ears.' One sees God with those love eyes. One hears the voice of God with those love ears. One even gets a sexual organ made of love . . . and with this love body the soul communes with God."

Throughout recorded history in every sacred tradition, men and women of profound faith have transformed their bodies and the atmosphere around them. Religious mystics and saints have been said to exhibit striking physical radiance and energy. People in their presence felt touched by forces that had immediate physical effects. Lights, a liberating power, and a palpable spiritual atmosphere have been reported to surround them in the same way that people having profound sexual experiences describe their lovers.

98 Some people enjoy their: *Constructing the Sexual Crucible,* pp. 82–3.

Chapter 4: Intimacy Is Not for the Faint of Heart

112 I realize I'm disagreeing: In 1995 I participated in a two-hour panel discussion on "Empathy and Differentiation" with Drs. Harville Hendrix (founder of Imago Therapy) and Ellen Bader in which core issues and fundamental differences were explained. An audiotape is available from the Marriage and Family Health Center.

113 Long-term intimacy within: Michael Kerr and Murray Bowen observe how empathy-based therapies can make poorly differentiated people feel better temporarily, even when the approach is seriously flawed: "Lacking beliefs and convictions of their own, [poorly differentiated people] adapt quickly to the prevailing ideology. . . . Conviction is so fused with feeling that it becomes a cause. When comprised of beliefs and opinions that are comforting or provide direction, pseudo-self can reduce anxiety and enhance emotional and physical functioning. This can be so even if the beliefs conflict with facts."(Kerr & Bowen, 1988, pp. 102–103)

114 Functionally, therapies that emphasize: Some therapists argue that strategies based on other-validation might be useful for couples who aren't capable of becoming more differentiated—as if this can be determined at the outset. Although there may be merit to this idea, the approach is never presented to the public as such. It is promoted as the solution to most couples' problems, with the implicit or explicit notion that it can take a couple as far as a couple might ever want to go.

119 If you're strong enough: When we are unsuccessful at self-validated intimacy, we experience *shame.*

120 Perhaps this differentiation stuff: What if, for example, you feel you didn't get your needs met as a child? You can't "take care of your wounded child" to the point your wounds are no longer problematic—that only perpetuates the problem. Many childhood issues are *not* resolvable in adulthood through styles of intimacy appropriate for an earlier age. Giving up the fantasy of compensation for your childhood and taking care of yourself as an adult (i.e., self-validated intimacy) often provide the sought-after relief. The struggle to maintain yourself unilaterally in an emotionally committed relationship often provides the final resolution of childhood.

Giving up dependency on other-validated intimacy is an initial step that some people find hard to take. But for these people and others, the task is still self-validated intimacy—something that's not as impossible as our theories and frustrated expectations suggest. The task remains taking the "leap of faith." I say this not because I lack compassion for those with unhappy childhoods but because I care deeply that their adult lives should be different.

120   This is where the leap: Let me clarify: I'm not saying that other-validation is "bad." Indeed, it is the basis by which we form a sense of self in childhood. In adult relationships, however, dependence on other-validated intimacy predictably leads to gridlock.

Chapter 5: Sexual Desire: Who Wants to Want?

127   For most of Western history: How big a problem is low sexual desire? Research suggests low desire is the most common sexual complaint, plaguing 30–50 percent of all people seeking sex therapy. Among couples attending our Couple's Retreats, low sexual desire and discrepant desire are the most common complaints. Sometimes the issue is frequency, but as one wife put it: "My issue with our relationship is not enough playfulness, and wanting more spontaneity and passion." In recent years many causes of low desire have been recognized: physical illnesses, medications, situational factors like trauma or grief, secondary reactions to sexual dysfunctions, and emotional problems such as depression and chronic anger.

127   Society's view of sexual: There is no way this chapter could fully cover the nuances of human sexual desire. It takes a weeklong workshop just to teach experienced therapists basic ways to treat sexual desire problems using the sexual crucible approach. For a more thorough discussion of the intricacies of sexual desire, see Chapters 9 and 10 of *Constructing the Sexual Crucible*.

133   All is smoothed out: "Is Sex Necessary?" (p. 63)

134   In fact, modern research: Oxytocin and other pituitary hormones seem to *follow* rather than just precede sexual behavior. See M. S. Carmichael et al. (1987). Oxytocin increase in human sexual response. *Journal of Clinical Endocrinology and Metabolism, 64,* 27–31.

135   Basically the brain: This description is called the "triune brain," developed by Paul MacLean. The triune braine model fit well with Murry Bowen's view that many human emotions are outside conscious awareness or control (i.e., limbic rather than neocortical in nature), and greatly influenced the development of differentiation theory. See: MacLean, P. D. (1982). On the origin and progressive evolution of the triune brain. In E. Armstrong & D. Falk (Eds.), *Primate Brain Evolution: Methods and Concepts* (pp. 291–316). New York: Plenum.

135   Human sexual desire has: Several popular therapy approaches also mention the triune brain, leading many people to mistakenly assume, "They're all saying the same thing." Usage here differs from these others because they (a) emphasize the mammalian part of your brain, (b) focus on inability to keep from regressing when anxious, and (c) stress the need for safety from— and security provided by—your partner. The differentiation-based model you're learning here focuses on your neocortex, your ability to keep your neocortex in gear, and your ability to self-soothe when frightened, threatened, or pressured.

139   Couples allude to this: The distinction between individual characteristics and properties of the relationship "system" is somewhat artificial, since these two continually interact and shape each other. It is useful, however, because it

makes us look beyond our own neuroses (individual characteristics) to understand sexual desire within marriage.

140   Think of marriage as: James Maddock, Ph.D., first pointed out this handy frame of reference to me.

140   Every little part (species: Ken Wilber coined the term *holon* to underscore the part-whole nature of all existence. His book *Sex, Ecology, and Spirituality* explains why *everything* is a holon.

142   Carol had less "status": Buddhist teachings help us see that *status* is another form of what we are terming *reflected sense of self*—but the notion of status is so socially accepted, we often don't recognize it for what it is.

142   Warren escalated by alternately: Researchers, investigating what we can call "the executive's fantasy of control," have produced stomach ulcers in monkeys by repeatedly shocking them with electricity. Monkeys who think they have some control over the situation (by moving a lever) are the ones who end up with the ulcers. Monkeys who think the situation is beyond their control actually get less upset. See: D. A. Washburn, W. D. Hopkins, & D. Rumbaugh (1991). Perceived control in rhesus monkeys (Nacaca Mulatta): Enhanced video-task performance. *Journal of Experimental Psychology Animal Behavior Processes*.

144   Neither of you can: I've seen Carol and Warren's pattern in every possible combination of men and women—heterosexual and homosexual, with either gender playing either role. Change their situation to any combination—including your own—and it will still probably ring true.

Chapter 6: Hugging till Relaxed

159   When pubic hair starts: Of course, there are unfortunate exceptions. If as a boy or girl, you got an "icky" feeling from a parent's hug, it may be that you were being embraced by a seductive mother or father. Even if you couldn't explain it, you backed away because you could *feel* something was "off." You could feel the vibe going back and forth. When Carol said "nothing really happened" between her and her grandfather (Chapter 5), she was wrong in the sense that she probably *felt* him. Hugging children in ways they can *feel* are sexually inappropriate happens when spouses fail to hammer out the issues described in this book. Beyond lousy sex and/or intimacy and limited differentiation between spouses, there's a lack of differentiation between parents and children.

161   Rather than rush in: T. Berry Brazelton (1992). *Touchpoints: Your Child's Emotional and Behavioral Development*. Addison-Wesley.

163   They are part of: Some couples go through contortions to lean on each other in the *differentiation stance* and still keep from depending on their partner. The physical patterns they create are living pictures of the emotional dynamics in their relationship: they extend their arms (away from their sides) to keep from leaning, but never in equal amounts.

165   This is what true: Actually, this is inaccurate when you become highly differentiated, because your partner's goals become part of your own. It's more like putting one of your goals (your partner's goals) ahead of another of your goals (your individual agenda). This kind of prioritizing requires a person who can handle conflict internally rather than having to fight out the tension with his or her partner.

168   We all carry a base: In Chapter 3 (page 87) I mentioned a kind of anxiety that negatively impacted on sexual satisfaction but didn't create symptoms like sexual dysfunction. I said many are not aware of their baseline level of tension until they experience sex without it for the first time. I promised to explain this further in Chapter 6. This is that discussion.

168   Calming down enough so: Incidentally, there are two types of people who experience sex as relaxing: those who are fairly well personally developed, and those who are sexual slobs. The latter are the kind of people who could care less about their partner—they simply use their partner's genitals as their playground, and the bedroom as a stage for their ego games. They can totally tune out their partner and enjoy sex, period. (They often have a partner who is furious at them, and usually withholds.)

169   They feel the discomfort: Profound relaxation and involvement in an alternative sexual reality require terminating what Harry Stack Sullivan referred to as "security operations": subtle but constant monitoring of the world for potential signs of threat. Alfred Adler noted that many people maintain a low-level tension like it is emotional body armor, a state of alertness offering the fantasy of self-protection from sudden threats and disappointments. People find it difficult to let go of this low-level anxiety and become *quiet*—this is what Warren "heard" when he finally *relaxed*. See: H. S. Sullivan (1953). *Interpersonal Theory of Psychiatry*. New York: Norton. Also: A. Adler (1951/1983). *The Practice and Theory of Individual Psychology*. Totowa, NJ: Rowman & Allenheld.

171   I don't think I'll: Sarah now talks freely about self-soothing. Sometimes she approaches Ruth or me saying "I want you to *'self-soothe'* me—I can't this time." (She thinks it's one word.) Unlike many adults, she is learning as a child to soothe herself. She knows the difference between my taking care of her and my teaching her to take care of herself. The latter is part of the former. We hope it helps.

184   "The air in my office": "Clean" and "dirty" pain are discussed in Chapter 12.

186   But from time immemorial: S. Moore, *Let This Mind Be in You: The Quest for Identity from Oedipus to Christ*. Harper & Row, 1985 (p. 65).

Chapter 7: Love and Foreplay Aren't Blind, Unless You Insist on It

187   "Though I know he: "The kiss," *Helen of Troy (1911)* in *International Thesaurus of Quotations*, p. 336.

187   Several years ago *USA Today:* "A better sex life in five months" by Karen Peterson, *USA Today,* March 5, 1992. Reprinted in *Complete Woman* magazine, October 1993.

Chapter 8: Eyes-Open Orgasm: Making Contact during Sex

212   Sexual vibes are an: Biologist E. O. Wilson and therapists Michael Kerr and Murray Bowen hypothesize that humans share an interpersonal "emotional" network, as do ants, bees, dolphins, and whales, which have sophisticated communication systems (e.g., for locating food or danger, and mobilizing others); bees do it so well that they can trigger a gender transformation in a male when the queen dies. See: E. O. Wilson (1975). *Sociobiology: The New Synthesis.* Cam-

bridge, MA: The Belknap Press/Harvard University Press. Also see: Michael Kerr and Murray Bowen's *Family Evaluation.*

212 Researchers have documented: In the 1960s a German ethologist, Irenaus Eibl-Eibesfeldt, identified a pattern of female flirting that appeared so constantly across different cultures he believed it to be innate in humans. In this pattern, the woman smiles, lifts her eyebrows, and opens her eyes wide to gaze at her partner, then drops her eyelids, tilts her head down and to the side, and looks away. Helen Fisher suggests that the "copulatory" gaze preceding mating is probably the most striking human courting ploy and probably well engrained through evolution; similar patterns are common to many other animals. She notes that smiling, sequential flirting, coy looks, head tilting, chest thrusting, and eye gazing are all standard parts of the human repertoire for attracting a mate. Studying people in single bars, anthropologist David Givens and biologist Timothy Perper noted these (and other) behaviors occur in reliable patterns of courting cues. See: Helen Fisher's *Anatomy of Love* (Norton, 1992).

218 Reactions are visceral: Kinesthetic "sensory" memory is powerful in humans. Olympic athletes use it to rehearse their performances.

219 (This is one reason: What I'm describing here is the undifferentiated emotional systems which occur naturally in all families with young children. Thus far you may have thought of differentiation as an abstract concept, but here I mean it literally—like a bunch of interlocking nerve cells or nervous systems that collectively make up a complex "nerve bundle."

227 Eye contact has also: See Dixon, A. F. (1990). Neuroendocrine regulation in primates. In J. Bancroft, C. M. Davis, & D. Weinstein (Eds.), *Annual Review of Sex research: An Integrative and Interdisciplinary Review* (vol. 1). Eye contact is the third aspect of eroticism encountered thus far that highlights the role of sociobiology in human evolution; the evolution of non-cyclical sexual interest and pair-bonding, and emergence of the neocortex and the capacity for intimacy (Chapter 4) are the other two.

227 Eye contact (flirting): Charles Darwin was the first to consider the genetic encoding of human facial expressions and body postures; he eventually wrote *The Expression of Emotions in Man and Animals* in 1872. More recently psychologist Paul Ekman has confirmed that the same basic facial postures are used to express emotions by people around the world. See his book, *The Face of Man* (Garland STPM Press, 1980) and his 1969 *Science* article, "Pan-cultural elements in facial displays of emotion" (#168, pp. 86-88).

227 A seventeenth-century painting: N. Douglas & P. Slinger (1979). *Sexual Secrets: The Alchemy of Ecstasy,* p. 236. Rochester, VT: Destiny Books.

Chapter 9: *Where's Your Head during Sex? Mental Dimensions of Sexual Experience*

244 For example, the *Kama Sutra*: The *Kama Sutra* is the earliest surviving Hindu love manual, written around the second century A.D. by Vatsayana and translated in 1883 by Sir Richard Burton.

244 Taoist texts consider "nine: Douglas and Slinger quote from the *Kama Sutra*: "When a man bites a woman, she should do the same with double force. Thus, a *Point* should be returned with a *Rosary of Points*, and a *Rosary of Points* with a *Broken Cloud,* and if she feels chaffed, she should immediately begin a love

quarrel with him. At such times she should take hold of her lover by the hair, bend his head down, kiss his lower lip, and then, in the intoxication of her love, she should shut her eyes, and bite him in various places" (p. 246 in Douglas & Slinger, *Sexual Secrets*).

244 (Psychologist/sex researcher Donald Mosher: "Three psychological dimensions of depth of involvement in human sexual response" (1980) in the *Journal of Sex Research*, 16(1), 1–42.

Chapter 10: Fucking, Doing, and Being Done

261 Lexicographer Hugh Rawson notes: In *Wicked Words,* word specialist Hugh Rawson defines *fuck* this way: "Fuck. To copulate, and the act of so doing, with many extended nonsexual meanings. The once awesome power of this term has declined in the past several decades, but it continues to find many uses, primarily as an adjective, epithet, exclamation, and intensifier. It is the prototypical example of the close, not to say intimate, connection between sex and violence in our culture, and it also provides a litmus test of society's controls over sexual expression." (Crown, 1989, p. 157)

In ten pages, Rawson gives you enough information about the word to kill it's shock value. *Fuck,* he suggests, actually derives from standard English. It's oldest example in the *Oxford English Dictionary* occurs in Scottish poetry by William Dunbar, composed sometime before 1503. *Fuck* did not always have its current negative stigma either. It was included in Nathaniel Bailey's *Universal Etymological English Dictionary* (1721) and John Ash's *New and Complete Dictionary of the English Language* (1775). Samuel Johnson omitted it from his *Dictionary of the English Language* (1755), and his decision influenced most lexicographers for the next two hundred years, including Noah Webster and Sir James Murray, editor of the OED. Passage of the English Obscene Publications Act of 1857 and the American Comstock Act of 1873 made use of the word dangerous, and it disappeared from official public life. In 1933 the *Ulysses* Supreme Court case, and likewise *Lady Chatterley's Lover* in 1959, were turning points. The word reappeared in *The Penguin Dictionary* (1965) and *The American Heritage Dictionary* (1969). In actuality, we use the word most often in derivatives of its sexual sense (e.g., *fuck up, fuck off, fucking off,* and *not giving a fuck*).

Libido, noted grammatologist J. E. Schmidt's sexual dictionary (Charles Thomas Publishers, 1960), lists 73 *fuck*-related entries. Rather than merely reflecting crudeness, the term refers to lascivious, lusty, wanton sex embellished with refined erotic virtuosity. It often refers to particularly intense sexual encounters, and may appear as part of passionate verbal exchanges (e.g., "Fuck me!"). I use the term *fuck* in this book in this subjective (and stylistic) sense.

Eminent sexologist John Money writes, "To copulate and to fuck are the only one-word verbs for mutual genital intercourse. The former is too stilted for vernacular use. The latter, being tabooed as dirty, is often replaced by euphemisms like to screw and to ball." He notes someting my English teacher never mentioned: fuck can be a noun or verb. (*Lovemaps*, p. 284)

In a *Playboy* interview, Paul Newman shared his own lexicon for different kinds of fucking: *Sport* fuck, *hate* fuck, *prestige* fuck, and "feel better now, sweetie?" *medicinal* fuck. He also included the *mercy* fuck, which he reserved for spinsters and librarians. I've found it also applies to spouses.

262 They found that their: John Brophy & Erick Partridge (1930), *Songs and Slang of the British Soldier: 1914-1918*. London: Scholartis Press

263 But these people are: D. H. Lawrence contribution to *This Quarter,* Paris, 1929. Quoted in p. 237 of G. Seldes (1985). *The Great Thoughts*. New York: Ballantine Books.

268 In *Iron John* Robert Bly: (Addison-Wesley, 1990).

269 The *Lingajas* turned out: Walker, B. G. (1983). *The Woman's Encyclopedia of Myths and Secrets*. San Francisco: Harper & Row.

269 A woman I know: Jane Mills (1989). *Womanwords: A Dictionary of Words about Women*. New York: Free Press.

277 It's hard for women: Clarissa Pinkola Estes. *Women Who Run with the Wolves: Myths and Stories of the Wild Woman Archetype* (Ballantine Books, 1992).

279 In *Sexual Personae* Camille: Camille Paglia, *Sexual Personae* (Yale University Press, 1990). Previous discussions of the sociobiological evolution of women's eroticism and emergence of the neocortex provide a biological understanding of why women are more erotically inclined than men. Put this together with what I said earlier about fucking being particularly taboo for women and you'll realize we've created another paradox: women's erotic development is both more restricted than men's by contemporary society and more evolved by sociobiology. This is essentially Paglia's thesis.

282 Instead of thrusting into: For some women, this form of stimulation is an orgasmic trigger. Some couples play with progressively withdrawing the penis in the minutes preceding orgasm. In some cases the women report enjoying bearing down (as they do during childbirth) to "expel" the penis at the moment of orgasm. One couple developed an elaborate verbal banter around this: "Push it out, baby! You like me just barely inside you, don't you! Come on!! Push!!" The appeal of this method is no surprise, since it is the outer third of the vagina that is the most sensitive. Aside from being interesting in itself, this fact suggests a need to reconsider our preoccupation with penis size and deep penetration.

Chapter 11: Two-Choice Dilemmas and Normal Marital Sadism

308 Now you're a perpetrator: In contrast to the good/bad dichotomization and polarization of *victim* and *perpetrator* that helps neither party, James Maddock and Noel Larson recently published what they call the "victim-perpetrator dialectic" (*Incestuous Families: An Ecological Approach to Understanding and Treatment,* Norton, 1995). Their approach pegs everyone on a continuum that highlights the victim and perpetrator traits in all of us. Don't confuse my work with Audrey with the "victim to victimizer" notion currently popular among some abuse counselors. This latter approach whitewashes responsibility of victims who perpetrate (many do) and overlooks their sadism.

309 Early American philosopher Thomas: Quoted in *The Concise Oxford Dictionary of Quotations* (Oxford University Press, 1981), p. 179.

309 It's *judo*—the art: Quoted in Peter, L. J. (Bantam Books, 1980). *Peter's Quotations: Ideas for Our Time.*

309 When necessary for sexual: Page 120 of American Psychiatric Association (1984). *A Psychiatric Glossary: The Meaning of Terms Frequently Used in Psychiatry*. Washington, DC: American Psychiatric Association.

309 Apparently, the psychiatrists favoring: "Sadistic personality disorder" appeared in the *DSM-III-R* (1987) as a proposed diagnostic category needing further study. It was subsequently eliminated from the *DSM-IV* (1994).

310 Author Stella Gibbons has: *Cold Comfort Farm,* 1932, ch. 20. New York: Penguin.

Chapter 12: Hold onto Yourself: Your Crucible Survival Guide

322 Rainer Maria Rilke: J. L. Mood (Ed.) (1975). Rainer Maria Rilke on *Love and Other Difficulties.* Norton.

324 "negative affect reciprocity": J. M. Gottman (1994). *What Predicts Divorce: The Relationship between Marital Process and Marital Outcomes.* Lawrence Erlbaum.

340 Carl Jung said, "To: Jung's *The Visions Seminars*, page 206. (Spring Publications, 1976).

341 But while the truth: Fromm, E. (1941). *Escape from Freedom.* New York: Holt, Rinehart & Winston.

341 Though circumstances and issues: Self-soothing plays a critical role in your ability to change and grow. Psychiatrist Murray Bowen, prime architect of differentiation theory, thought some people are so unable or unwilling to "take the hit" that they are incapable of improving their lives. They are so driven by their anxiety that they cannot increase their differentiation. They are doomed to spend their lives avoiding what makes them nervous rather than going after what they want. (What they really want is never to be discomforted.) Everything revolves around how they feel at any particular moment. These are the most poorly differentiated people.

Bowen thought another group of poorly differentiated people look exactly like this first "stuck" group. The difference is this second group is capable of becoming more differentiated. What distinguishes this group isn't that they have few personal problems or less difficult situations. It's their willingness to self-soothe: to hang on and go through their process, doing what needs to be done until it's no longer required. (The remainder of society is differentiated enough to grow from their difficulties, with varying degrees of ease.)

I'm more optimistic than Bowen was about people's ability to raise their differentiation. I've seen people accomplish it by going through the crucibles of sex and intimacy in marriage, which Bowen never harnessed in his therapy. One wife attending a Couples Retreat concluded, "The reason you go through your sexual crucible is because the price of not doing it is so high." When you realize this, breaking gridlock and facing two-choice dilemmas isn't as impossible or overwhelming as might first appear.

347 (After all, this is written: You may want to know that Ruth agrees with this depiction of our/her experience.

347 *Normal healthy infants and:* E. Z. Tronick & A. Gianino (Feb. 1986). Interactive mismatch and repair: Challenges to the coping infant. *Zero to Three: Bulletin for the National Center for Clinical Infant Programs, 6*(3) pp. 1–6. Another study produced results that might seem to contradict other common expectations: Mother-son pairs were found to spend more time in coordinated states than mother-daughter pairs. See: E. Z. Tronick & J. F. Cohn (1989). Infant-mother face-to-face interaction: Age and gender differences in coordination and the occurrence of miscoordination. *Child Development, 60*(1), 85–92.

349 Time out of synch: According to psychologist Edward Tronick, time out of synch is actually when infants "refuel" themselves. It's what gives them (and you) the energy to stabilize and mount the next effort to get back in synch.

350 The adult correlates of: Based on the behavior coding scale reported in Tronick & Gianino, ibid.

351 *Give your dilemma purpose*: Here's an example parents can apply with children: (1) Don't lock into kids when they have a tantrum—that when kids get stuck overreacting to parents who are overreacting. (2) Help the child self-soothe by getting physically close to him/her (without interfering with the child's attempts to stabilize his/her body). Focus his/her attention on breathing slower and quieting himself/herself down. (3) Approach the event as an opportunity to help the child develop self-management. Consider this the equivalent of treating your partner with respect and talking to the best in him/her: Suppose your child came home from school saying, "Nobody likes me. They hate me!" If you don't automatically say, "That isn't true!" you can engage the child in constructive inquiry and pursue it any way the child wants to go: "What is it they are doing? Why do you think they are doing that? What do you think this says about you? Do you think this is really true or not? If you think it's true, what do you want to do about this? If this isn't really true about you, what do you think you should do?" (4) Treat him/her as if it's going to pass. This is not the same as negating feelings; don't minimize the importance to him/her or offer glib reassurances s/he will get over it. State your recognition that this is hard for the child, together with your believe s/he has the capacity to experience this and go on to better things and happier times.

When attendees at our Couples Retreats finally get themselves and their marriage under control by self-soothing and self-confrontation, they often recognize how they have been interfering with their children's functioning and necessary struggles.

353 After nine days of: "I'm on my way," written by Michelle Honig. Copyright 1996.

Chapter 13: Couples in the Crucible: Reaching Critical Mass

355 Then look at Figure 3: Don and Barbara Fairfield, leader couple for the Association for Couples in Marital Enrichment, originally developed this diagram to apply the sexual crucible approach to marital enrichment groups. They used it to illustrate how a group eventually disbands if it doesn't deal with anxiety-provoking but necessary topics, and how it becomes more close-knit and motivated if it does. This diagram is a dynamic model of how individuals, small groups, and businesses (especially family-owned enterprises) operate.

356 If you don't make: How "termination" applies to individuals in the growth cycle may not be immediately obvious. In the next chapter we will discuss this as death of the familiar self (i.e., self-transcendence).

357 But like Christopher Columbus: I recommend the audiotape of Bowenian therapist/Rabbi Edward Friedman's presentation "Anxiety and the Spirit of Adventure," in which he uses maps of Columbus' day to outline the act of differentiation involved in the search for the New World. Recording is available from the American Association for Marriage and Family Therapy c/o The Resource Link, Suite 310, 3139 Campus Drive, Norcross, Georgia, 30071-1402.

359 Happy, successful long-term: Gottman, ibid.
366 The required conditions can: Nobel Prize winner Ilya Prigogine describes how all systems have a point at which they shift from simple solutions to new, complex, and increasingly sophisticated operation. Likewise, John von Neumann says that individuals, groups, and even computers have what he calls a *critical complexity barrier*. In our increasingly computerized society, this notion of critical mass is of interest to those who speculate about computers building themselves better than humans can (i.e., when computers develop self-awareness and the ability to " think"). See: von Neumann, J. (1966). *Theory of self-reproducing automata*. Arthur W. Burks (Ed.). Urbana: University of Illinois Press.
372 The qualities of critical: Gottman, ibid. Also see: H. Markman, S. Stanley & S. L. Blumberg (1994) *Fighting for Your Marriage: Positive Steps for Presenting Divorce and Preserving a Lasting Love*. Jossey-Bass.
372 People get divorced when: This is the process behind "termination" on the comfort cycle (inner circle) in Figure 4. People terminate their relationship, or terminate their integrity by staying. In the following chapter we'll discuss "termination" on the growth cycle (outer circle): the end of the "self" you've been when you become the "self" you want to be (i.e., self-transcendence and self-dissolution).
374 Research documents that babies: B. M. Lester, J. Hoffman & T. B. Brazelton (1985). The rhythmic structure of mother-infant interaction in term and preterm infants. *Child Development, 56,* 15–27.
375 In fact, if such responses: Kerr & Bowen (1988), *Family Evaluation,* p. 100.
375 You help your partner: In the same way, differentiation offers adaptive advantages to an entire family. The requirement of taking care of someone who can't take care of himself places a drain on the family as a whole, and on other members' individual functioning. This thinking isn't antithetical to mutuality; taking care of yourself (especially in ways you'd like to avoid) is the essence of mutuality. When everyone takes care of himself/herself in difficult times, the entire family's anxiety is reduced, adaptively is increased, and generosity and help become more meaningful.
378 Carl Jung observed that: "Psychology and Alchemy," in *The Collected Works 1953–1979*, vol. 12. (Princeton University Press).

Chapter 14: Sex, Love, and Death

388 Some time ago I: J. David Smith's *Psychological Profiles of Conjoined Twins: Heredity, Environment, and Identity* (Praeger, 1988).
389 Sexual etiquette between Chang: The sexual behavior of physically conjoined twins has always attracted great public interest and scorn. A number have married despite public outrage. They have had to differentiate from their culture as much as from each other in order to accommodate their interests in sex and intimacy. In 1969 another conjoined pair, Violet and Daisey Hilton, explained how they managed romantic activities. Violet said they learned to "get rid of each other" using mental techniques Harry Houdini had taught them. She reported that she didn't pay attention when Daisey had a date and didn't know what went on. Sometimes she read and sometimes took a nap. "Even before that, we had leaned how not to know what the other was doing unless it

was our business to know it." Violet's application for a wedding license was rejected in twenty-one states. Two years after Violet finally married, Daisey eventually found a husband of her own. They were both soon divorced. (*Violet and Daisey Hilton*, 1969, p. 47).

389   One can only imagine: Sarah lived another eighteen years; Adelaide, for another forty-three. Irving and Amy Wallace traced the lives of Chang and Eng's children in the book, *The Two*. One grandson became president of the Union Pacific Railroad, another became aide to President Woodrow Wilson and an Air Force general, and another, a state legislator.

390   Identical twins reared apart: S. L. Farber, *Identical Twins Reared Apart: A Reanalysis*. New York: Basic, 1981.

390   J. David Smith researched: Ibid.

390   Recently these patterns have: Actually, Abby and Brittany share a single body from the waist down. Each possesses a single arm, but their chest contains two sets of internal organs. *Life Magazine*, April 1996, pp. 46–56.

392   (I have drawn this: Wilber devotes seven pages (pp. 40–46) to describing these four qualities (self-preservation, self-adaptation, self-transcendence, and self-dissolution), together with explicit details of how he visualizes them organized as the "cross" depicted in Figure 5. I have taken the liberty of drawing the mental diagram Wilber creates for his readers in words.

    In Chapter 2 we used a simple drawing to illustrate how differentiation isn't the opposite of emotional connection, but rather, the ability to balance individuality and connection. If you flip back to page 57, you'll see that it is basically the same as the poles of the horizontal axis of Wilber's diagram. Wilber, K. (1995). *Sex, Ecology, and Spirituality: The Spirit of Evolution*. Shambala.

393   And *that* realization—: Ibid., p. 291.

394   Whatever else we might: Ibid., p. 487.

394   They stop constantly throttling: In his scathing satire *Dead White Males,* Australian playwright David Williamson borrows from Shakespeare's *Taming of the Shrew* to suggest that women really want a politically correct Petrukio. Today's liberated woman may want a "New Age" sensitive man, but she wants him to be phallic, too. It's no different from men wanting a wife who's "a lady in the living room and a whore in the bedroom." Do you know anyone who doesn't want it both ways? This is one case, however, where you can have your cake and eat it too—if you're willing to do the personal development.

395   Like many people, I: Many of us are familiar with Buddha's warning that human desire is the source of suffering. Jesuit priest Anthony De Mello clarifies that desire that creates suffering is the desire for *things*. De Mello calls this "attachment desire" because we set our sights on someone, something, or some event, and convince ourselves we cannot be happy unless we get what we want. In emotionally fused relationships, your partner is a thing rather than another person. That's when desire for your partner creates the suffering associated with desiring *things*.

397   We are willing slaves: Ibid., p. 27.

400   In *The Self-Organizing Universe*: E. Jantsch (1980). *The Self-Organizing Universe*. Pergamon.

400   But as Lama Yeshe: Lama Thubten Yeshe (Jonathan Landaw, Ed.). *Introduction to Tantra: A Vision of Totality* (1987). Boston: Wisdom Publications.

400   Nature progresses by sudden: Ibid. p. 43.

401 Many of the leading figures: Ernest Becker (1973). *The Denial of Death.* (pp. 196–7). New York: Free Press/Macmillan. Becker included C. G. Jung and Erich Fromm among these "leading figures."

402 The loneliness quickens love: Moustakas' *Loneliness,* p. 101 (Prentice-Hall, 1961).

403 Serving loneliness is a way: Ibid., p. 103.

403 When psychologist Erich Fromm, ibid.

Index